The Bible Speaks Today

Series Editors: J. A. Motyer (OT)
John R. W. Stott (NT)

The Message of John

Here is your King!

Titles in this series

The Message of John

Here is your King!

Bruce Milne

With Study Guide

Inter-Varsity Press
Leicester, England
Downers Grove, Illinois, U.S.A.

InterVarsity Press
P.O. Box 1400, Downers Grove, IL 60515, USA
38 De Montfort Street, Leicester LE1 7GP, England

InterVarsity Press®, USA, is the book-publishing division of InterVarsity Christian Fellowship®, a student movement active on campus at hundreds of universities, colleges and schools of nursing in the United States of America, and a member movement of the International Fellowship of Evangelical Students. For information about local and regional activities, write Public Relations Dept., InterVarsity Christian Fellowship, 6400 Schroeder Rd., P.O. Box 7895, Madison, WI 53707-7895.

Inter-Varsity Press, England, is the book-publishing division of the Universities and Colleges Christian Fellowship (formerly the Inter-Varsity Fellowship), a student movement linking Christian Unions in universities and colleges throughout the United Kingdom and the Republic of Ireland, and a member movement of the International Fellowship of Evangelical Students. For information about local and national activities write to UCCF, 38 De Montfort Street, Leicester LE1 7GP.

All Scripture quotations, unless otherwise indicated, are from the British edition of the HOLY BIBLE, NEW INTERNATIONAL VERSION®. NIV®. Copyright ©1973, 1978, 1984 by International Bible Society and published in Great Britain by Hodder and Stoughton Ltd. Distributed in North America with permission from Zondervan Publishing House. All rights reserved.

The verse from David Mansell's song "Jesus Is Lord!" on page 40 is © *Springtide/Word Music (UK). Administered by CopyCare Ltd, 8 Marshfoot Lane, Hailsham, East Sussex BN27 2RA, UK. Used by permission.*

The poem "Judas, Peter," on page 208 is reprinted from The Sighting, *copyright* ©*1981 by Luci Shaw. Used by permission of Harold Shaw Publishers, Wheaton, Ill., USA.*

The extract from "Seven Stanzas at Easter" on pages 293-94 is taken from Telephone Poles and Other Poems, *by John Updike, copyright* ©*1961 by John Updike. Reprinted by permission of Alfred A. Knopf, Inc. and Penguin Books Ltd.*

The poem "Opening" on page 296 is used by permission of its author, copyright ©*1984, 1993 Elizabeth Rooney.*

Quotations on pages 226 and 280-81 are taken from Toward Jerusalem *by Amy Carmichael, and are reproduced by kind permission of SPCK, London.*

USA ISBN 0-8308-1233-4

UK ISBN 0-85110-971-1

Printed in the United States of America ∞

Library of Congress Cataloging-in-Publication Data

Milne, Bruce.
The message of John: here is your king!/Bruce Milne.
p. cm.—(The Bible speaks today)
Includes bibliographical references.
ISBN 0-85110-971-3.—ISBN 0-8308-1233-4 (U.S.)
1. Bible. N.T. John—Commentaries. I. Title. II. Series.
BS2615.3.M55 1993
226.5'07—dc20 93-8158
CIP

British Library Cataloguing in Publication Data

A catalogue record for this book is available from the British Library.

17	16	15	14	13	12	11	10	9	8	7	6	5
07	06	05	04	03	02	01	00					

General preface

The Bible Speaks Today describes a series of both Old Testament and New Testament expositions, which are characterized by a threefold ideal: to expound the biblical text with accuracy, to relate it to contemporary life and to be readable.

These books are, therefore, not 'commentaries', for the commentary seeks rather to elucidate the text than to apply it, and tends to be a work rather of reference than of literature. Nor, on the other hand, do they contain the kind of 'sermons' which attempt to be contemporary and readable without taking Scripture seriously enough.

The contributors to this series are all united in their convictions that God still speaks through what he has spoken, and that nothing is more necessary for the life, health and growth of Christians than that they should hear what the Spirit is saying to them through his ancient – yet ever modern – Word.

J. A. MOTYER
J. R. W. STOTT
Series Editors

Contents

Author's preface

Anyone attempting an exposition of John's gospel, however modest, faces a daunting challenge. Apart from the formidable demands of the text itself, the voluminous secondary literature poses a prodigious obstacle. The pages which follow make no claim to establish new critical landmarks; the New Testament specialist, should he or she chance to open these pages, will not discover any blazing new insights on the celebrated textual and theological problems which surround this gospel. As far as the latter are concerned I have been content to stand on the shoulders of others (though hopefully without surrendering an independent judgment). My particular debts in that regard will be evident from the footnotes.

In keeping with the goals of *The Bible Speaks Today* series, this volume is written for the thoughtful lay person (rather than the specialist) who seeks a deeper appreciation of the text of the gospel, and wishes for help in relating its message to the world of today. In particular I have tried to heed the plea of the General Editor, John Stott, that I have in special view 'the hard-pressed preacher', whether lay or clerical. Belonging to that company of preachers on a daily basis made my pursuit of that goal a little easier!

The gospel of John, as my former teacher George Beasley-Murray points out, is 'the preacher's gospel *par excellence*' (*John*, p. x). More than thirty years ago, I stood for the very first time in a Christian pulpit of a tiny windswept church in the remoter reaches of the Shetland Islands before a handful of long-suffering fisherfolk. Then I chose my text from John 6:35, 'I am the bread of life', neither the first nor last preacher to begin a pulpit career from this great gospel.

The fascination of John continues undiminished, its challenge unending. If these pages make even the slightest contribution to that renewal of expository preaching which, in this writer's judgment, remains the single most urgent need of the modern church, the author will be more than compensated for any effort expended in their production.

My most sincere thanks are due to the Council and members of the very special church I am privileged to serve, First Baptist, Vancouver, for three months' leave during the summer of 1991 to tackle this project. In particular I am indebted to Edith Paul, widow of one of my distinguished predecessors at First Baptist, for a peaceful hideaway in her home to install my computer, as well as the inspiration of her exquisite garden, and to Stephen Morton, another 'gift' from the congregation, whose contribution to the technical production of the manuscript is impossible to quantify. My thanks are also due to Herb Adams, who took time off from writing mathematics textbooks to correct the proofs.

My dear wife Valerie, as well as offering many editorial suggestions for improving the text, was an inspiration throughout.

The impact on the history of the world of John's twenty-one brief chapters is in the end incalculable. For all the controversy which continues to surround them they comprise a moral and spiritual potency which over the centuries has transformed communities, toppled kingdoms, liberated multitudes, and remade human character on a scale without parallel in the accumulated literature of the ages. That power remains present in this gospel, and the reader, whether Christian or non-Christian, can discover it today. Simply put, in the paragraphs of John's gospel the living Lord Jesus Christ is met in his glory and grace, his majesty and tenderness, and his presence can be experienced as a perceptible reality in your life. 'These are written . . . that by believing you may have life in his name' (20:31). May I challenge you to test that claim – and make the incomparable discovery that it happens to be true!

Vancouver   *Bruce Milne*
September 1992

10

Bibliography

Barclay, W., *The Gospel of John* (Saint Andrew Press, 1955), 2 vols.

Barrett, C. K., *The Gospel According to John* (Westminster, 1978).

Beasley-Murray, G. R., *John* (Word, 1987).

Bernard, J. H., *The Gospel According to John* (T. and T. Clark, 1928), 2 vols.

Brown, R., *The Gospel According to John* (Doubleday, 1966), 2 vols.

Bruce, F. F., *The Gospel of John* (Pickering and Inglis, 1983).

Bultmann, R., *The Gospel of John: A Commentary*, tr. G. R. Beasley-Murray, R. W. N. Hare, J. K. Riches (Blackwell, 1971).

Calvin, J., *The Gospel According to John* (St Andrew, 1959), 2 vols.

Carson, D. A., *The Farewell Discourse and Final Prayer of Jesus* (Baker, 1980), = *Jesus and his Friends* (Inter-Varsity Press, 1986).

Carson, D. A., *The Gospel According to John* (Inter-Varsity Press, 1991).

Dodd, C. H., *The Historical Tradition in the Fourth Gospel* (Cambridge University Press, 1965).

Dodd, C. H., *The Interpretation of the Fourth Gospel* (Cambridge University Press, 1953).

France, R. T., *Jesus the Radical* (Inter-Varsity Press, 1989).

Fredrikson, R., *John* (Word, 1985).

Godet, F. L., *Commentary on the Gospel of John* (T. and T. Clark, 1987).

Guthrie, D., *New Testament Introduction* (Inter-Varsity Press, 1970).

Haenchen, E., *A Commentary on the Gospel of John*, tr. R. W. Funk (Fortress, 1984).

Hendriksen, W., *A Commentary on the Gospel of John* (Banner of Truth, 1959).

Hoskyns, E. C., *The Fourth Gospel* (Faber, 1947).

Maclaren, A., *The Gospel According to John* (Hodder and Stoughton, 1907), 3 vols.

Marsh, J., *The Gospel of St John* (Penguin, 1968).

Michaels, J. R., *John* (Harper and Row, 1983).

11

BIBLIOGRAPHY

Morris, L., *The Gospel According to John* (Marshall, Morgan and Scott, 1972).

Morris, L., *Reflections on the Gospel of John* (Baker, 1986), 3 vols.

Newbigin, L., *The Light has Come* (Eerdmans, 1982).

Robinson, J. A. T., *Twelve New Testament Stories* (SCM, 1962).

Ryle, J. C., *John* (Marshall Pickering, 1990).

Schnackenburg, R., *The Gospel According to John*, tr. K. Smyth, C. Hastings, *et al.* (Burns and Oates, 1968–82), 3 vols.

Tasker, R. V. G., *The Gospel According to John* (Tyndale, 1960).

Temple, W., *Readings in John's Gospel* (Macmillan, 1961).

Westcott, E. F., *The Gospel According to John* (James Clarke, 1958)

Abbreviations

AV	The Authorized (King James') Version of the Bible (1611).
Gk.	Greek
JBP	*The New Testament in Modern English* by J. B. Phillips (Collins, 1958).
LXX	The Old Testament in Greek according to the Septuagint, 3rd century BC.
NASB	The New American Standard Bible, 1963.
NIV	The New International Version of the Bible (1973, 1978, 1984).
RSV	The Revised Standard Version of the Bible (NT 1946, 2nd edition 1971; OT 1952).
TDNT	*Theological Dictionary of the New Testament*, ed. G. Kittel and G. Friedrich, translated into English by G. W. Bromily, 10 vols. (Eerdmans, 1964–1976).

Introduction

1. Authorship

Most books published today begin with a title page identifying the author. When 'John's gospel' was first published, however, that initial authorial identification was omitted, and readers have to wait until near the end of the book before finding out who the writer is. Even then we are not entirely out of the dark, for he is identified simply as 'the disciple whom Jesus loved' (21:20) who 'is the disciple who testifies to these things and who wrote them down'.[1]

From one point of view the relative anonymity of the human author is not of ultimate importance since the true author is the divine Holy Spirit, whose superintendency of the human witness is attested at several points in the gospel.[2] Elsewhere, the book of Hebrews, for example, contains a writing which is anonymous and yet whose inspiration and canonicity are hardly in question. While that point is conceded, however, it is not unimportant for purposes of interpretation to try to clarify the human process by which a book came to be written. Furthermore, in the case of a gospel which is a record of events, the historical reliability and eye-witness credentials of the author are necessarily important considerations.

Traditionally the fourth gospel has been attributed to John, son of Zebedee, one of the 'inner circle' of Jesus' twelve disciples, and subsequently a leading apostle in the emergent church.[3] The grounds for this attribution are strong ones. We can distinguish between *internal grounds* (evidence within the gospel itself), and *external grounds* (evidence from other early writers).

The *internal* evidence for Johannine authorship was classically

[1] Jn. 21:24; *cf.* 19:35.   [2] *Cf.* 14:25–26; 16:12–15.
[3] Mk. 1:19–20; 9:2; Acts 4:1f.; 8:14f.

assembled by Westcott,[4] who argued that there were indications within the gospel that the author was (a) a Jew, (b) a Jew of Palestine, (c) an eyewitness of what he describes, (d) an apostle and (e) the apostle John. While each of these points has been questioned at one time or another, Westcott's case has never been completely demolished.

The author's Jewishness appears beyond serious question from the multiple allusions to Jewish customs, topography and history scattered throughout the gospel. It is also reflected in the style of Jesus' teaching. This last point, touching the literary provenance of the gospel, is a fruit of the discovery of the Dead Sea Scrolls at Qumran in 1947, which uncovered a parallel, first-century, Palestinian thought-world.[5] The authentic Jewish orientation of the gospel is also indicated by the absence of echoes of the controversies which were current in the non-Jewish churches around the time the gospel was written.

The eyewitness aspect is explicitly claimed at several points in the text.[6] It appears reflected in the many vivid touches throughout the gospel;[7] the realistic character portrayals of people like the woman of Samaria in chapter 4, or the man born blind in chapter 9; the writer's intimate knowledge of the reactions of the disciples[8] and of Jesus himself;[9] and the details such as a knowledge of the names of characters who are anonymous in the parallel accounts in the synoptic gospels.[10]

That the author is one of the twelve is indicated by his having been present in a place of some significance at the last supper (13:1ff., 23). Mark 14:17 indicates that only the twelve participated at that event.

The greatest controversy has gathered around the claim that 'the disciple whom Jesus loved', the author according to 21:24, is in fact John, son of Zebedee. The title appears only towards the end of the gospel.[11] Some have even questioned whether this 'disciple' is a real person at all since, it is argued, no-one would claim such a title for themselves, nor would anyone readily call someone else by it. This last allegation appears somewhat gratuitous. We cannot at this remove from the events dogmatize about how people are

[4] E. F. Westcott, pp. vi–xxvii.

[5] L. Morris, *John*; J. A. T. Robinson, *Twelve New Testament Studies* (SCM, 1962); R. A. Brown, article in K. Stendahl (editor), *The Scrolls and the New Testament* (Harper, 1957).

[6] *Cf.* 1:14; 19:35; 21:24; see also 1 Jn. 1:3–5.

[7] *Cf.* 6:9, 19; 12:3; 13:24; 19:39; 21:11.

[8] 2:11f.; 4:27; 6:19; 12:16; 13:22f.   [9] 2:11,24; 6:15, 61; 13:1.

[10] 6:7f.; 12:3; 18:10.   [11] 13:23; 19:26f.; 20:2–10.

perceived by others. While the title is certainly unusual it appears congruent with a fairly obvious desire for anonymity on the author's part. It may simply reflect his sense of wonder at the electing grace of God in his experience, or perhaps more plausibly be a nickname which arose from the individual's repeated reference to the amazing way Christ had loved him. An explicit equation of this disciple with John is not made within the gospel (though it is amply confirmed by external sources, as we will shortly observe). It is supported, however, by the otherwise astonishing omission of John, the son of Zebedee, from the gospel at any other point (except 21:2) when other 'lesser' disciple figures are quite regularly recognized.[12] There is also the notably close association in this gospel of the 'disciple whom Jesus loved' with Peter,[13] echoing the close association of John and Peter in Acts.[14] We note too the maturity of reflection expressed in this gospel, along with the evidence of John having lived to a considerable age, and also the many parallels in thought and expression with the three letters of John in the New Testament, letters written by one who had 'seen with our eyes, . . . looked at and our hands have touched . . . concerning the Word of life' (1 Jn. 1:1). If the writer is not John the Son of Zebedee, we are left asking who this disciple could have been who was clearly most closely associated with Jesus, attained such an intimate understanding of his heart and mind, composed this remarkable gospel, and yet disappeared from the scene without any trace beyond his enigmatic title, 'the disciple whom Jesus loved.'

The *external* evidence for the authorship of John is extensive. As with the other New Testament books, there is a body of literary traditions dating from the early centuries which comments on the authorship. While they cannot be followed slavishly, their witness certainly needs to be weighed, since these witnesses are patently much closer to the original composition of the documents than any scholar can be today.

The first major witness is Irenaeus, bishop of Lyons in the latter part of the second century, who reports that John, the Lord's disciple, wrote the gospel and published it at Ephesus, and that he lived on until the time of the Emperor Trajan (AD 98). Eusebius reports that Irenaeus' authority for this information was the aged presbyter Polycarp, who had been a confidant of the apostles themselves, and had conversed with John in person. Irenaeus' testimony is the more impressive when we recall that he was in close contact with the major church in Rome during his ministry in Lyons, and

---

[12] 1:40, 43, 45; 6:5, 8; 11:16; 12:21; 14:5, 8, 22.   [13] 20:2–10; 21:20–24.
[14] 3:1–11; 4:1–23; 8:14–25.

hence that it is highly likely from the breadth of his contacts that Polycarp was not the only source of his conviction about the authorship of the gospel.

This view of the authorship of John was accepted without question by other major second-century figures like Tertullian, Clement and Origen, who was himself the author of a major early commentary on this gospel. *The Muratorian Canon*, published in Irenaeus' time, also attributes the gospel to John, adding that he wrote it following a vision given to Andrew.

The fact that the gospel attained fullest acceptance in the churches from the second century onwards is the more striking when one weighs the fact that it had two major problems associated with it. One was that the gospel was quoted and used polemically by the heretical Gnostic teachers during the first half of the second century. Claiming to impart a secret knowledge of God (Gk. *gnōsis*, knowledge) they used its high Christological statements to support their denials of the true humanity of Jesus. (What they failed to see, and what orthodox apologists were to point out to them, was that this very gospel is also a clear witness to Jesus' true humanity).[15] The other difficulty with this gospel was its apparent distinctiveness of style and content when compared with the other three gospels. We will address that issue below, but it should not be imagined that this is a modern problem. The fact that despite these handicaps this gospel was afforded universal acceptance is simply inexplicable unless the original author was a distinguished figure of known apostolic credentials. Further, it is surely unthinkable that these early Christian leaders, many of them people of considerable culture and intelligence, could have embraced the Christian faith and faced the prospect of persecution, and even horrible martyrdom, without having enquired into the origins and authenticity of the documents upon which their faith rested.

In other words, it is difficult to believe that Luke was alone in his desire to have 'carefully investigated everything from the beginning, . . . so that you may know the certainty of the things you have been taught' (Lk. 1:3–4). It is the more impressive accordingly that in such a context John's authorship of the fourth gospel appears to have been universally affirmed.

In the light of these facts it might be thought that to question John's authorship is 'a rather desperate expedient that stands against

---

[15] Lesslie Newbigin interestingly reports a similar response to the gospel of John among Hindus, 'I have found that Hindus who begin by welcoming the Fourth Gospel as the one that uses their language and speaks to their hearts end by being horrified when they understand what it is really saying.' *Foolishness to the Greeks* (Eerdmans, 1986), p. 6.

the force of the cumulative internal evidence and the substantial external evidence'.[16] Scholarly opinion, however, is far from united on this issue. On internal grounds 'the disciple whom Jesus loved' continues to trouble interpreters, and externally much has been made of a citation by Eusebius, quoting Papias, another early sub-apostolic figure, which appears to distinguish between John the apostle and 'John the Elder'. This latter John, it is argued, was a disciple of John the apostle, and was the author of the gospel, but became confused with John the apostle to whom the gospel was mistakenly attributed. The Eusebius passage, however, is somewhat ambiguous as far as the alleged distinction between the two Johns is concerned, and there is no hint there of John the Elder, even if he existed, being the writer of the gospel.

Those wishing to pursue this issue should consult the major commentaries or introductions to the New Testament. Sufficient to say, the traditional view, that John the son of Zebedee was the author, certainly continues to be defensible. While no limits should be set to the activity of the sovereign Spirit of God, he commonly works through appropriate human vehicles, and it is reassuring to be able to affirm that in the composition of this great gospel he used one who stood in the closest historical relationship to the events described.

2. John and the synoptics

Even a cursory reading of the New Testament gospels indicates a difference in style and content between John's and the other three. These differences raise serious questions: are the gospels reliable accounts of what happened in the time of Jesus? More specifically, since on most points it is John who appears out of step with the others, is *his* gospel reliable?

Before identifying and commenting on the differences, it is helpful to first stake out the area of common ground between all four gospels. All four feature the witness of John the Baptist as the historical prelude to Jesus' ministry, the call and instruction of the disciples, the miraculous feeding of the 5,000, Jesus' voyage with his disciples on the sea of Galilee, Peter's confession of faith, the triumphal entry into Jerusalem, Jesus' remarkable claims and his acts of power, the developing opposition and hostility of the Jewish religious leaders, the cleansing of the temple, Jesus' final meal with his disciples, his arrest in Gethsemane, his trial, condemnation and

---

[16] D. A. Carson, *John*, p. 72. Carson presents a full and persuasive case for Johannine authorship, taking account of the most recent interpretations of the gospel.

crucifixion, his resurrection from the dead on the third day, his resurrection appearances and his commissioning of his disciples. In addition there are numerous specific sayings which are common or appear in parallel form in all four gospels. This is a not inconsiderable list.

The differences may be summarized under five headings:

a. Material which appears only in the other three gospels

Some of this covers incidents or teaching which occur in only one, or at most two, of the other gospels (e.g. the parables of the Good Samaritan and the Prodigal Son which are in Luke only; the raising of Jairus' daughter which is in Matthew and Mark only). So, despite their apparent appeal, John's omitting them is of no greater significance than their omission by one or more of the other evangelists.

More difficult to account for is John's omission of the transfiguration, the parables in their synoptic form, healings of demoniacs, the Lord's Supper, and the agony in Gethsemane, all of which appear in the three other gospels. The difficulty, however, is greatly reduced if John sees his task as complementing the other writers rather than as replacing them, or writing a full, comprehensive account of Jesus' ministry.

That John knew of the other gospels before writing his own is at least arguable. Scholars have claimed to find evidence in John's text of knowledge of Mark, and possibly Luke. If Luke was aware of 'many' other accounts when he came to write (Lk. 1:1), it is difficult to believe that John, writing as is generally believed some years after the others, could have been in total ignorance of the efforts of his fellow evangelists. The truth is that each evangelist is selective; John himself tells us that the available traditions about Jesus would exhaust any known library (20:30; 21:25). That 'Jesus did many other miraculous signs . . . which are not recorded in this book' could be uttered as truly by Matthew, Mark and Luke as by John. Each evangelist chose from within the mass of available material those elements which would serve his own particular purpose in writing. John has already given ample stress to the revealing of Jesus' glory so that the transfiguration is not essential to his account, particularly as his presentation identifies the cross as the supreme moment of the glorification of the Son. John has his own selection of Jesus' parables and vivid figures of speech, though they are cast in a different style. His account of Jesus' healing ministry is *very* selective and happens not to include the curing of a demoniac (nor other categories of needy folk, such as deaf mutes or 'lepers'). His cataloguing of the work of the devil, however, is clear enough. The agony in Gethsemane is foreshadowed in

12:27–28; and the last supper is given rich and compatible context by the footwashing. Furthermore, if John was able to assume that at least one or two of the other gospels were already in circulation, his omissions are the more comprehensible.

b. Material which appears only in John

This encompasses large sections of John's earlier chapters, *e.g.* the wedding at Cana, and the conversations with Nicodemus and the Samaritan woman. It also includes the raising of Lazarus, the discussions with the Jews, and the farewell discourses and foot-washing. A significant reason for the differences, however, arises from the fact that John concentrates almost entirely on the ministry of Jesus in and around Jerusalem during the temple feasts. The synoptic writers by contrast concentrate to a great extent on ministry in the north, around Galilee. We should bear in mind again the necessary selectivity of all four evangelists. If a 'gospel' is by definition an attempt to compile a biography, in our modern sense, of the entire life and teaching of Jesus, then not John alone, but all the evangelists fall short of the requirement. To assume this as the evangelists' aim is, however, at clear variance with their stated intentions.[17] A 'gospel' is rather the telling of the story of Jesus in such a way that the unique significance of his person and work impacts the reader, enabling him or her to meet Jesus for themselves and be guided in following him. Patently we are not dealing here with the usual genre of literary biography.

At this point it is worth stressing the many points at which John complements the synoptic account by answering questions which the synoptics leave unanswered. To cite just two examples, why did the first disciples suddenly leave everything to follow Jesus? Perhaps it was the sheer impact of his person, but John gives us a clearer answer. They had already met Jesus (1:35–50), and so the decision to follow him was the culmination of a growing acquaintance. Or again, the citation from Jesus' teaching made by the witnesses at his trial before the Sanhedrin (Mk. 14:58), otherwise obscure in the synoptics, is recorded in John 2:19.

c. Difference in presentation

There are more extended discourses in John, and less straightforward narrative, than in the other gospels. More specifically, the Jesus we meet in the fourth gospel employs rabbinical methods of argument and regularly utters unvarnished theological principles.

---

[17] *Cf.* Lk. 1:1–4; Jn. 20:30–31.

The synoptic Jesus is more anecdotal, and commonly employs a popular style in his preaching, using stories (parables) to make his theological points.

The difference, however, upon examination, is less significant than appears on the surface. The key is the difference of audience. As with all good teachers (and Jesus was arguably the greatest of teachers) the form was dictated by the hearers. The synoptic writers in their record of Jesus' teaching concentrate on his ministry in the north, in the Galilean region of his upbringing. John's primary focus, as we have already noted, was the more sophisticated, theologically aware milieu of Jerusalem. In addition, the methods and forms of the Johannine discourses have been shown to be congruent with those of synagogue teaching, which could involve dialogue with the audience, and the Scrolls at Qumran have uncovered a first-century thought-world in the southern Palestinian region which is wholly compatible.[18] In our examination of these discourses we shall see again and again how perfectly they 'fit' with their claimed setting and with the attitudes and beliefs of the hearers. Besides which, Matthew includes a passage which would be entirely at home in the middle of any of Jesus' discourses in John (Matthew 11:25–30). John *does* have his equivalent to the parables, though the form is less of a story. Who would dare assert, however, that the same creative mind was not capable of both forms? If a C. S. Lewis was capable of producing sophisticated literary criticism, celebrated children's fiction, poetry, Christian apologetics, science fiction and autobiography, then we need to take the greatest care before dogmatizing about what the only one sinless and divine teacher in history is or is not capable of producing.

d. Differences in historical detail and chronology

There are four particular problems: the cleansing of the temple (John sets it at the beginning of the ministry, the synoptics set it at the end), the duration of the ministry, the date of the last supper and the disciples' understanding of Jesus.

On the first of these there is no inherent impossibility about there having been two such incidents during Jesus' ministry. As we shall note in the exposition, there are good psychological reasons for this action as the ministry was launched and also as it drew to its conclusion.

The issue of duration is not an acute one once it is recognized that the synoptic writers often leave chronology and duration fairly vague. John sets Jesus in relation to three Passovers and so requires

---

[18] *Cf.* fn. 5 above.

a duration of two to three years. Nothing in the synoptics makes that impossible.

The question of different chronologies for the last supper arises because John in a number of texts appears to set the supper meal before the Passover began (*i.e.* on the Wednesday evening of Holy Week) with the crucifixion taking place the following day, the Thursday, coinciding with the slaughter of the Passover lambs in the temple. This is seen as a Johannine historical inaccuracy in order to make a valid theological point, *viz.* Jesus is the true Passover Lamb (just as he is the true Temple, the true Vine, *etc.*). That John sees Jesus as the fulfilment of the Passover sacrifices appears correct (*cf.* 19:36), but whether he alters the date of the crucifixion to make the point more forcibly is certainly not proved. The texts which are alleged to support a revision of date will be commented on below[19] but in no case appear to 'prove' a contradiction. Another approach suggests that John and the synoptic writers may have been operating with different calendars.[20] Whatever the solution there do not appear conclusive grounds to set the evangelists in opposition.

e. The appreciation of the person of Jesus

This provides a final point of apparent contrast. In the synoptics the disciples' understanding grows slowly and comes to mature expression only after the resurrection, although there are important points of realization along the way, notably at Caesarea Philippi (Mt. 16:16). In John the higher categories appear present much earlier (*cf.* 1:41, 49).

Again the distinctions are more apparent than real. It is to be doubted that the disciples in John's gospel have any genuine appreciation of who Jesus is in the early period of their association with him. Their limited understanding is evident at numerous points; and indeed as late as the last supper they are apparently still confused about Jesus' relationship to the Father (*cf.* 14:9f.), the very heart of his teaching as John records it. Then, no less than today, the real test of understanding is not an ability to use theological ideas and titles but action based upon the truths professed. By that standard all four gospels speak with the same voice. In John, as clearly as in the synoptics, when the disciples' faith is put to the test in the Garden of Gethsemane they forsake Jesus and flee.

[19] *Cf.* 13:1, 27; 18:28; 19:14, 31.
[20] *Cf.* D. Guthrie, pp. 296–298; R. T. France, *Jesus the Radical* (IVP, 1989), pp. 161–162.

Thus the distinctions, even where real, need not diminish our appreciation of the historical trustworthiness of John's account. In the presence of the Word made flesh no single approach can ever be sufficient, nor any four for that matter. But God has purposed in his gracious providence the existence of the four gospels, each special and each important. Each is a witness to Jesus in a way which truly enables us to meet with Christ and set our lives under his leadership. Within that chosen team of witnesses John and his 'spiritual gospel' take an honoured place.[21]

3. Purpose and date

A wide variety of purposes have been alleged for the gospel. These include the supplementing of the synoptic gospels, the correcting of the synoptic gospels, the combating of gnosticism, the combating of docetism (the early heretical view which denied the true humanity of Christ), the arraigning of unbelieving Jews, the opposing of the continuing followers of John the Baptist and the opposing of sacramentalism in the early church. In fact John tells us himself why he wrote: '. . . these are written that you may believe that Jesus is the Christ, the Son of God, and that by believing you may have life in his name' (20:31). There appears no reason to disallow this statement. John writes to bring his readers to faith in Jesus Christ.

It needs to be added, however, that there is a possible alternative reading in the Greek for 'believe' in this verse. The reading followed in the NIV reflects an aorist tense expressing a decisive act of believing: 'that you may (come to) believe (Gk. *pisteusēte*)'. By this reading John's purpose is evangelistic; he writes to produce decisive commitment to Christ. The alternative reading is a present tense (Gk. *pisteuēte*), and would give a meaning like 'these are written so that those who believe may go on believing', *i.e.* may hold on to their faith and grow in it, a discipling purpose. On balance the textual support for the former appears stronger. Certainly there can be no doubt as to John's intention to confront his readers with the claims of Christ and to challenge them to respond. The proven evangelistic power of this gospel needs no documentation. While acknowledging this to be the *primary* purpose, however, it is not

[21] This echoes Clement of Alexandria's second-century characterization of the distinctive witness of the fourth gospel. His full statement runs as follows: 'John, last of all, conscious that the outward facts had been set forth in the Gospels, was urged by his disciples, and, divinely moved by the Spirit, composed a spiritual Gospel.' In Eusebius, *Ecclesiastical History*, VI, XIV. 7.

impossible to affirm a number of secondary aims as well. There can be little doubt that John is conscious of addressing Christians as well as non-Christians through his gospel, and hence of encouraging Christians to continue and grow in their faith. The 'upper room' discourses in particular are replete with teaching for the disciple of Christ. It is also likely that John is not unaware of the docetic tendencies in the Graeco-Roman culture within which he wrote, so the clear stress which John places on the true humanity of Jesus may well have had that heretical tendency in view. Above all, however, John is an evangelist in the classical sense; he writes to win lost people for Christ. At a time when world evangelization is again on the church's agenda John's presentation of his Master is truly a 'tract for the times'.

The precise dating of John is not easy to determine. Once it is seen to contain its own relatively independent witness to Jesus, the gospel could conceivably have been written at any point in John's maturer years. One striking event which must be weighed in dating all of the New Testament writings is the destruction of Jerusalem by the Romans in AD 70. This massive upheaval of Jewish life and thought is not reflected in any way in the gospel. This would probably imply a date either some years after, by which time the dust would have had time to settle from the calamity, or the period before. In 5:2 John refers to the Pool of Bethesda by 'there is', not 'there was'. While too much ought not to be placed on this, it equally should not be dismissed. If the Pool was still identifiable when John wrote we are looking at a date in the late 60s, certainly prior to AD 70. A date around this time might also explain John's relative lack of contact with the other gospels. The traditions which surround the composition of the gospel in the early church would appear to support a somewhat later dating, perhaps sometime in the early 80s, though of course within John's lifetime. Final certainty is not possible, but we have clearly travelled a long way from the days when John's gospel was cavalierly discounted as an authentic first-century witness to Jesus Christ and dated well into the second century.

4. John and Jesus

John is the most explicitly theological of the four gospels and contributes important insights on all the primary loci of Christian doctrine. The nature and attributes of God;[22] humanity, fallen and

[22] *E.g.* 1:1–2, 14–18; 3:16; 4:24; 5:19–23; 6:45–46; 8:16–19; 10:27–30, 34–38; 12:27–28, 49–50; 13:3; 14:6–10; 16:5–15, 27–28; 17:11; 20:20–22.

redeemed;[23] the person of Christ (see below); the work of Christ;[24] the person and work of the Holy Spirit;[25] the church and its mission;[26] and the life of the new world.[27] The reader is referred to the relevant sections of this book and to the major commentaries for detailed theological exposition.

The supreme doctrinal focus of this gospel is, however, the person of Christ (although never in separation from his work). As far as the deity of Christ is concerned, John affords possibly the clearest witness in the New Testament.[28] The deity, however, is never separable from the true humanity of Christ.[29] He is simultaneously divine and human; not one at one point and the other at another point, but both together at every point.

When the church attempted to clarify its understanding of the person of Jesus Christ at Nicea in 325, and again at Chalcedon in 451, this gospel was of particular help in undergirding the confession of One who is both true God and true man. John makes no attempt to dilute the full reality of both the deity *and* humanity of Christ and so helped the church to confess Jesus Christ as one person in two natures. It is important to recognize that the framers of the early Creeds never imagined that they were providing an exhaustive explanation of who Christ was; that is a mystery forever beyond our grasp. What they saw themselves doing was simply (!) erecting, in the light of the witness of Scripture, certain boundary walls within which the person of the God-man was to be authentically encountered. Outside these limits lay heresy; within these limits lay truth.

Similarly, today, we are invited to approach reverently within the walls of the Word of God, to gaze wonderingly and adoringly upon the glory of the everlasting Son made flesh, and then go forth

---

[23] *E.g.* 2:24–25; 3:3–8, 19–21, 36; 5:40; 6:35, 53–57; 7:37–39; 8:12, 31–47; 10:27–29; 11:25–26; 14:17; 15:1–8, 18–25; 16:3, 8; 17:2–3, 6–9; 20:22, 31.

[24] *E.g.* 1:29, 51; 2:19; 3:14, 34; 4:22, 42; 5:25, 28f.; 6:33, 40, 44, 51, 53, 62; 10:9f., 11, 15; 12:24, 32; 13:8; 14:3, 18f.; 16:33; 17:2; 18:14, 36; 20:1 – 21:14.

[25] *E.g.* 1:13, 32f.; 3:5; 4:24; 6:63; 7:39; 14:16f., 26; 15:26; 16:7–15; 19:34; 20:22.

[26] *E.g.* 4:35f.; 13:31 – 16:33; 17:20–23; 20:19–23; 21:1–14, 15–25.

[27] *E.g.* 3:15f., 36; 4:14; 5:24f.; 6:27, 37, 39f., 47, 51, 58; 8:24, 51; 10:28; 11:25f.; 12:25; 14:2f.

[28] *Cf.* 1:1f., 14, 18, 49; 2:11, 19; 3:13, 18, 31, 34f.; 5:17f., 22f., 26f., 28; 6:20, 27, 33, 35, 38, 45f., 54f., 69; 7:28f.; 8:12, 16, 23, 28f., 42, 55, 58; 9:5; 10:7, 11, 14, 18, 30f., 38; 11:4, 25, 27, 44; 12:41, 44; 13:3, 19, 31f.; 14:1, 6, 9f., 14; 16:7, 15, 23, 28; 17:5f., 10, 24, 26; 18:5; 20:1–21, 25; 20:28.

[29] *Cf.* 1:14; 4:6; 6:42; 8:6; 11:33, 35, 38; 12:27; 19:5, 30, 31–42.

to live for him amid the realities of our everyday world. John's gospel helps us to do that. But who the Son is in himself remains a mystery beyond our comprehension.

It is this mystery which lies behind the revelation in this gospel, as in all the gospels. It is also the explanation of the effect of a study of John's gospel, for while by the end of it we sense we know Christ better, at the same moment we find ourselves having to acknowledge that he is even further beyond our grasp. This should not surprise us. If the ancient theological maxim is valid, *Deus comprehensus non est Deus* (a God who is comprehended fully is not God), then it is equally true to assert, *Christus comprehensus non est Deus* (a Christ who is comprehended fully is not divine).

The mystery of Jesus Christ is the theme of this gospel; always beyond us, yet always summoning us to explore it more fully. The exploration and service of the Godhead will be our endless, though blissful, task in the world to come; but we can begin it now, and there can be no better place to launch out into the depths of it than to study, and expound, this great gospel by John.

The Gospel of John

John's concern is to tell us about Jesus Christ; his book is a 'gospel', a proclamation of the good news (20:31). Arguably, he knows about several of the other gospels – he may well have studied Mark and has some acquaintance with Luke. John is probably aware therefore that the others have prefaced their accounts of Jesus' ministry by referring to his promised forerunner, John the Baptist.[1] Matthew and Luke go still further back to the birth of Jesus,[2] and also provide genealogical tables linking Jesus to Abraham[3] and Adam.[4]

John is especially conscious of the 'big picture'; Jesus' life and mission represent the critical central moment of all existence and all history, so he begins his account by setting Jesus against the widest possible horizon; he relates him to God and his eternal purposes, and to the entire life of the universe. 'The other gospels begin with Bethlehem; John begins with the bosom of the Father. Luke dates his narrative by Roman emperors and Jewish High Priests; John dates his "In the beginning". Matthew and Luke take us to the cradle and the manger, Mark to the prophecies of old, but John takes us back into the mists of eternity.'[5]

John attempts this specifically in his 'prologue' consisting of the first 18 verses. This opening paragraph achieves several things. It sets the scene for the events to be described later, introduces John the forerunner, and affords a 'prevision' of the gospel as a whole. Numerous commentators see it functioning rather as an overture to an opera. It tells of the deeds and significance of Jesus Christ up to the point of his entry upon the human story as a participant. In support of this way of understanding the prologue we can note

[1] Mt. 3:1–12; Mk. 1:2–8; Lk. 3:1–20.   [2] Mt. 1:18–25; Lk. 1:5 – 2:40.
[3] Mt. 1:1; cf. Jn. 1:1–12.   [4] Lk. 3:38; cf. Jn. 1:23–38.
[5] A. Maclaren, 1, p. 1.

that 1:1–18 is full of verbs rather than nouns and adjectives (there are no fewer than 44 verbs in the 18 verses); *i.e.* it is primarily about the *deeds* of Jesus rather than his nature or being. The prologue recounts the first part of his 'ministry'. This may seem too prosaic a view of a passage which has at times been interpreted as 'poetic', but it does not restrict the soaring heights of truth in these verses. It does help ensure, however, that we are captivated by the person and activity of Christ himself rather than by any alleged artistry on the part of the evangelist.

Chapters 20 and 21 similarly give an account of the deeds and significance of Jesus Christ after the conclusion of his earthly ministry. This allows us to attempt a division of the gospel. In dividing the gospel for purposes of exposition a commitment to a particular perspective is necessary. Recognizing that no single category can even begin to encompass the breadth and richness of John's portrait of Jesus, we take our cue from the dominance of the passion story in the gospel. In his presentation of the passion, John's preferred category, as we shall see when examining the text, is that of kingship. Jesus is the 'crucified king' – 'Here is your King!' (19:14). One way of dividing the gospel is therefore as follows:

A.   The ministry of the pre-incarnate king (1:1–18)
B.   The ministry of the incarnate king (1:19 – 19:42)
C.   The ministry of the risen king (20:1 – 21:25)

A. The ministry of the pre-incarnate king
John 1:1–18

1:1–2

1. Jesus Christ and the eternal God

John uses a special category: Jesus Christ is the Word of God. The Greek term is *logos*.[1] This word had a wide usage in the first-century world, touching a range of cultural and philosophical contexts. In using it John would have made chords resonate in the minds of a wide variety of his readers. Scholars have found it a particularly fruitful theme for investigation to establish possible sources for the *logos* concept, and to decide which one was especially determinative for this gospel.

The primary point of reference is almost certainly the Old Testament and Jewish religion. As we shall recognize again and again, John assumes a working knowledge of the Old Testament on the part of his readers. The opening phrase *In the beginning* ... links directly to Genesis 1:1: 'In the beginning God created ...'. This allusion is the more likely bearing in mind that Jewish readers referred to the Bible books by their opening words. Thus *In the beginning* is shorthand for Genesis. 'The Word of God' appears in Genesis chapter 1 as the means whereby God accomplishes his acts of creation, 'God said, "Let there be light" ' (so also 6, 9, 11, 14, 20, 24, 26). The Word of God is God himself in his creative action.

More generally in the Old Testament the Word of God is God in his powerful and effective action in creation (Ps. 33:6), deliverance (Ps. 107:20), and judgment (Ps. 29:3f.; Is. 55:11). It is the 'Word of God' who gives understanding to the prophets concerning the mind and will of God (*cf.* Is. 38:4; Je. 1:4; Ezk. 1:3). This thought of God's illumination is developed and personified in the

---

[1] For fuller discussion of this important category, see D. A. Carson, *John*, pp. 114–116; L. Morris, *John*, pp. 115–126; G. R. Beasley-Murray, pp. 6–10; also L. Morris, *Reflections*, 1, pp. 1–9.

concept of 'wisdom', particularly in the book of Proverbs; *cf.* 'The Lord brought me forth as the first of his works, . . . I was appointed from eternity, from the beginning, before the world began. . . . I was there when he set the heavens in place, . . . I was the craftsman at his side. . . . rejoicing in his whole world and delighting in mankind' (Pr. 8:22–23, 27, 30, 31).

'The Word of God' also served as a common replacement for the divine name when the Greek Old Testament was read in the synagogue, and the speaker required an alternative to express the unmentionable Name of the Lord. Generally in the Old Testament 'Word of God', *logos*, refers to an action rather than an idea.

While primarily rooted in this Hebrew background, *logos* would also speak to John's Greek readership. *Logos* had a long history in Greek philosophy going back at least to Heraclitus (around 500 BC), for whom *logos* was the shaping, ordering and directing principle in the universe. In the first century, Philo, the renowned Jewish teacher in North Africa, who had imbibed much of the Greek philosophical outlook, referred regularly to the *logos* under a wide variety of images, many of which personalized the action of the *logos* (*cf.* 'the *Logos* is the captain and pilot of the universe'; 'the Father's elder son'; and the like). While some points of contact with Greek usage can be established, John's understanding departs from it at one crucial point. For Greek thought in general the *logos*, as a participant in the divine order, was by that very fact distinct from the material and historical world. By contrast, for John, the Word is revealed precisely in its 'becoming flesh'; *cf.* 'That Jesus once spoke is more fundamental for its understanding than is the history of Greek philosophy or the story of the westward progress of oriental mysticism; more fundamental even than the first chapter of Genesis or the eighth chapter of Proverbs.'[2]

John asserts three things about Jesus as the Word of God in the opening two verses of the gospel:

1. Jesus Christ shares God's eternity. He was *In the beginning.* . . . By definition, God has no beginning. We can think back only to the moment of creation, *in the beginning*, and perhaps register a vague notion of God's life in himself 'before' time (*cf.* 17:5, 24: 'the glory I had with you before the world began . . . before the creation of the world'). John's contention is that at the point where we reach the boundary of all human conceptualizing we have to begin our speaking about Jesus Christ; he shares God's eternity; *he was with God in the beginning* (2). 'If we ask the fundamental question of the philosopher, "Why is there not

---

[2] E. C. Hoskyns, p. 137.

nothing?" the answer is that in the "beginning was the Word" '.[3] Although he lived within time as a human being he is not bound by time. He predates all existence; 'there never was when he was not' (Athanasius). However far back we set the beginning of things, and whatever model we employ to describe that origin, according to John, Jesus was present as the presiding Lord of that moment and event (*cf*. 3).

This truth has major implications for the way we conceive God. Since Jesus is the eternal Word of God (14), and since 'I [Jesus] and the Father are one' (10:30) and 'Anyone who has seen me [Jesus] has seen the Father' (14:9), God is always Jesus-like! 'God is Christlike and in Him is no unChristlikeness at all' (A. M. Ramsey). This is important for the way we read the Old Testament. The significance of this opening phrase of John is that the God who speaks in the Old Testament, who entered into covenant with his people Israel, and inspired and moved the prophets, was none other than the God known in Jesus Christ. God has not changed or evolved. Jesus Christ was always at the heart of God.

It also has implications for the way we understand God's electing his people to salvation (a truth we shall meet at a number of points in this gospel). The God who elects is not 'prior to' Jesus Christ. Hence there is no God 'behind the back' of Christ, so to speak, who may yet say 'no' to us on the day of judgment, despite our having heard Jesus say 'yes' to us as we embraced him as our Saviour. The Son no less than the Father is the electing God.

2. Jesus Christ was eternally with God (verse 1: *and the Word was with God*). *With* here is literally 'towards'. Many scholars have seen an indication in this preposition of an intimate relationship between God and the Word (or, in the common conceptuality of the gospel, between the Father and the Son). A. T. Robertson suggests 'the Word was face to face with God'.[4] Basil Atkinson[5] refers to a 'sense of home'; 'the Word was in God's home'. Certainly if the wisdom motif is part of the hinterland of the *logos* concept there is a moving sense of intimacy expressed in Proverbs 8:22, 30: 'The LORD possessed me at the beginning of his work,' (see footnote *c* in NIV); 'I was filled with delight day after day, rejoicing always in his presence.'

This may be pressing the limits of the text, but it certainly makes clear the distinct existence of the Word with respect to God. The

---

[3] L. Newbigin, p. 2.

[4] A. T. Robertson, *A Grammar of the Greek New Testament in the Light of Historical Research* (London, n.d.), p. 623; *cf*. R. Brown, 1, p. 3, who translates, 'in the presence of God'.

[5] B. F. C. Atkinson, *The Theology of Prepositions* (London, n.d.), p. 19.

Word is no mere 'emanation from God' as in much first-century thinking.

3. Jesus Christ is one with God ('the Logos was God . . .'; verse 1; *cf.* 1:18: 'God the Son . . .' [see footnote *f* in NIV]; 20:28: 'My Lord and my God'). This phrase unambiguously affirms the deity of Jesus Christ. He is God the Son, one in Godhead with the Father.[6] Some discussion has been engendered by the fact that 'God' here does not have a definite article, opening the way for some who deny the deity of Jesus Christ to claim that the correct translation is therefore adjectival rather than nominal, so, 'the Word was God-like', or even, 'divine'; *i.e.* the Word reflects divine or God-like qualities. Similarly others, such as Jehovah's Witnesses, attempt on the basis of this text to drive a wedge between the Father and Son, 'The Word was a god'.[7]

The grammatical issue has been thoroughly explored in recent years and the traditional translation has been shown to be entirely correct.[8] Apart from which, New Testament Greek has a perfectly usable word for 'divine', *theios*, which appears elsewhere in the New Testament. John chooses not to use it. His point is that there is no distinction in essence between God and the Word (or between the Father and the Son). Both are equal in Godhead and therefore equally to be honoured, adored and worshipped; and he says it straightforwardly, *the Word was God.* 'When John says "the Word was God", this must be understood in the light of Jewish pride in monotheism. Even though this writer regarded monotheism as a central tenet in his religion, he yet could not withhold from the Word the designation "God".'[9]

By putting the relationship thus, John is also avoiding the error of a complete identification of the two persons. To quote Tasker,

---

[6] *Cf.* also 1:18; 10:30; 14:9; and 1 John 5:20.

[7] *New World Translation* of John 1:1 (The Watch Tower Bible and Tract Society).

[8] *Cf. e.g.* D. A. Carson, *John*, p. 117, 'There are many places in the NT where the predicate noun has no article, and yet is specific. Even in this chapter, "You are the King of Israel" (1:49), has no article before "King" in the original; see also 8:39; 17:17; Rom. 14:17; Gal. 4:25; Rev. 1:20 . . . In fact if John had included the article he would have been saying something quite untrue. He would have been so identifying the Word with God that no divine being could exist apart from the Word', a denial of the immediately preceding phrase! Interestingly the Jehovah's Witness New World translation renders 1:49 'you are King of Israel'.

[9] L. Morris, *John*, p. 78. *Cf.* also comments of C. K. Barrett, p. 156: 'John intends that the whole Gospel be read in the light of this verse. The deeds and words of Jesus are the deeds and words of God; if this is not true the book is blasphemous.'

'the Word does not by himself make up the entire Godhead',[10] *i.e.* there is more to the Godhead than either the Father, or the Son. We need great care in using 'more' here since, as Augustine taught centuries ago, 'no two persons are greater than any one person';[11] *i.e.* the Father plus the Son is not greater in deity than the Father alone, or than the Son alone, since both, and both together with the Spirit, are one Godhead. At this point we confront the profound mystery of the Trinity and apprehension moves imperceptibly (but delightedly) into adoration.

What does this tremendous opening verse imply for our approach to Jesus Christ?

1. *The finality of Christ.* Jesus' place in the being of God is changeless. For evermore he is the Son in and with the Father, and hence the one in whom God is made known to us. In our time pluralism is increasingly the order of the day. This has arisen partly as political and community leaders, struggling with nations and societies torn apart by religious division, attempt to achieve a new social concord through affording equal status to the various world faiths. In addition the communications revolution has made it increasingly difficult to maintain isolation, and religious intolerance appears in many eyes as almost the ultimate form of sin. Due to these developments Christians come under considerable pressure at times to water down the great historic distinctives of the Christian faith, such as the deity of Christ. Certainly bigotry is never to be encouraged, and respect for those of other persuasions is always appropriate, but we cannot compromise the uniqueness of the revelation of Jesus Christ merely for the sake of an often vague communal harmony. He alone is God come to us. No other can stand alongside him or take his place. The revelation in Jesus Christ is the final revelation. In acknowledging him lies the seeds of true community.

2. *The mystery of Jesus Christ.* Since Jesus Christ is one with God in his being, he shares in the infinity and limitlessness of God. This does not mean we cannot claim to know him, or assert certain final truths about him, but it means that we do not have an exhaustive knowledge of him. This is John's concern as his gospel closes (*cf.* 20:30; 21:25) and it is implicit from the very first verse. We therefore know him, and yet there is always more to know, more to experience. This is why worship is fundamental to understanding, and why love and knowledge are inseparable.

3. *The centrality of Jesus Christ.* Because Jesus Christ is God

[10] R. V. G. Tasker, p. 45.
[11] Augustine, *On the Trinity*, LCC, vol. VIII (Westminster, 1955), bk. VIII, p. 39.

himself come to us, he must always be in the centre of our approach to God, our thinking about God, and our relating to God (14:6).

4. *The supremacy of Jesus Christ.* If Jesus Christ shares the nature of God, we are called to worship him without cessation, obey him without hesitation, love him without reservation and serve him without interruption. To him be all glory for ever.

2. Jesus Christ and the created universe

The eternal Word is here related to creation. John speaks of a two-fold relationship: origin and illumination.

1. Origin (1:3)

Through him all things were made. Love's instinct is to create; so out of the unique communion of love between 'God' and 'the Word' (or between 'the Father' and 'the Son'), the universe sprang into existence. John puts this fundamental truth of creation through the Word of God both positively (*Through him all things were made*) and negatively (*without him nothing was made that has been made*). This mediatorial role in creation is one which other New Testament passages similarly attribute to Christ.[1] We note further that while John asserts the intimate involvement of the Word in the creation of the world, he does not specify how this relates to the origin of the universe as described scientifically. His point is the essentially religious and doxological one – the greatness of Christ is shown by his being the creative mediator of the observable universe. Christ is therefore the unifying principle at the heart of all existence. 'The eventual goal of science is to provide a single theory that describes the whole universe.'[2] From the theological perspective, the theory is a person, Jesus Christ.

John stresses the all-inclusive range of the creative activity of the Word: *Through him all things were made* (3). This is apparently the reason for the repetition of the negative clause following, *without him nothing was made that has been made*. John is correcting some first-century notions of the origin of the universe which

---

[1] *Cf.* 1 Cor. 8:6; Col. 1:16; Heb. 1:2; possibly also Rev. 3:14; *cf.* Pr. 8:22f.

[2] Stephen Hawking, *A Brief History of Time* (Bantam, 1988), p. 10.

taught that it was shaped by God out of some pre-existing primeval 'stuff', which was in turn the explanation of the presence of evil in the universe. The net effect, however, was to reduce God's sovereignty in the world, since by this view there are two determining forces in the universe, God and primary matter.

John's statement about the creating Word is congruent with the notion of creation 'out of nothing'.[3] Creation 'out of nothing' means exactly what it says. The universe came to be, *not* out of some pre-existing material 'something', but out of 'nothing', non-existence, void. This truth implies the unqualifiable dependence of all things upon the Word of God; *i.e.* the Word is the sustaining and upholding principle of an irreducibly contingent universe.[4] It also means that the universe, while utterly dependent on God, is also fundamentally distinct from him. This is a crucial truth today. Much of New Age thought,[5] influenced by Hinduism and Buddhism, obliterates the distinction between God and the world,[6] leading to the deifying of nature and the claim that God can be experienced directly through nature. This experience of God is not of course in terms of a personal relationship with him, since God has no personal existence apart from the world. By contrast, biblical creation 'out of nothing' means that God is distinct from the world. As Father and Word (and Spirit) God in his full personal reality existed prior to the world. He is not dependent on the world for his existence and therefore, crucially, as a sovereignly free personal agent, he can enter into a personal relationship with his creatures within the world.

He is a God in whom we can 'believe', in the sense that John will explain throughout his gospel. In this stress on the breadth of the Word's creative act (*Through him all things . . . without him*

---

[3] *Creatio ex nihilo*; *cf.* Gn. 1:1f.; Ps. 33:6; Rom. 4:17; 1 Cor. 1:28; Heb. 11:3.

[4] *Cf.* Col. 1:16; Heb. 1:2.

[5] The name given to a broad movement in recent Western writing and consciousness. Elliot Miller suggests the following definition: 'The New Age movement is an extremely large, loosely structured network of organisations and individuals bound together by common values (based in mysticism and monism – the world view that "all is one") and a common vision (a coming new age of peace and mass enlightenment, the "Age of Aquarius"), *A Crash Course on the New Age Movement* (Monarch, 1989), p. 15. See also Karen Hoyt and the Spiritual Counterfeits Project, *The New Age Rage* (Revell, 1987); Russell Chandler, *Understanding the New Age* (Word, 1988).

[6] See M. Ferguson, *The Aquarian Conspiracy* (Tarcher, 1980), p. 100; G. Leonard, *The Transformation* (Tarcher, 1972), pp. 228f.; F. Capra, *The Turning Point* (Simon and Schuster, 1982), *passim*.

nothing) John is also addressing a first-century tendency to view Jesus as simply one of a series of intermediaries or emanations from God. A similar idea appears commonly in New Age writers, where Jesus is simply one of a series of spiritual masters who have been sent to bring enlightenment at different stages of human spiritual development.[7] John's point is that it is through Jesus alone that all things exist, whether physical planets or spiritual hierarchies. He towers above all and cannot be reduced to one of a series, whether as a stage in the process of human evolution or in the history of human ideas. 'Since he is fully divine, he cannot be reduced to an intermediate state; since he is a person he cannot be dissolved into an idea.'[8]

2. Illumination (1:4–5)

In him was life, and that life was the light of men. The light shines in the darkness. The fruit of the Word's activity in mediating creation was not just the coming into existence of the world 'in the beginning', but the emergence of life within it (4). We are driven beyond the initial act of creation to the Word's ongoing sustenance of the universe; the *logos* is the life-giver. Finally considered, all life derives from him (Acts 17:8, 'For in him we live and move and have our being'). 'There is no such thing as a godless person; he is too near every one of us' (Brunner).

This life John sees in terms of *light* (4), another elemental religious symbol, and another echo of Genesis chapter 1, as *the light shines in the darkness* (Gn. 1:3) in the act of creation.

John says three things about this *logos*-light. It offers illumination to every person – *that life was the light of men* (4); it shines in the context of *darkness* (5); and the *darkness has not overcome it* (5, NIV fn.). Traditionally this has been seen as a pointer to God's general revelation (so Calvin, for example, 'referring to the common light of Nature'[9]). John is alluding here to the Word's participation, in God's revealing himself universally to all people through conscience and in creation; a revelation which leaves them without excuse for their ignorance of God.

This is the first occurrence of one of the key themes of this gospel, 'bearing witness'. John the Baptist is particularly identified

---

[7] Levi, *The Aquarian Gospel of Jesus the Christ* (DeVorss and Co., 1907); F. LaGard Smith, *Out on a Broken Limb* (Harvest House, 1986), pp. 121f.; D. R. Groothuis, *Unmasking the New Age* (Inter-Varsity Press, 1986), ch. 7.

[8] R. Schnackenburg, 1, p. 421.

[9] J. Calvin, 1, p. 15. *Cf.* Ps. 19:1f.; Acts 14:17; 17:27; Rom. 1:15; 2:14.

with this activity.[10] But there are seven others who testify to the truth of God's self-disclosure in the Word made flesh; the Father,[11] the Son himself,[12] the Holy Spirit,[13] the works of Jesus,[14] the Scriptures,[15] assorted human witnesses,[16] and finally the evangelist himself.[17] In John's society witness-bearing was a serious matter and was the means of establishing the truth. It also involved commitment. 'Unless you commit yourself, unless you stake everything on the truth of what you say, you cannot be a witness.'[18]

From the fact that Jesus Christ was the agent of creation and is its continual sustainer at least three things follow. First, *the universe proclaims the greatness of Christ*. 'The heavens declare the glory of God; the skies proclaim the work of his hands.' (Ps. 19:1). Paul in Romans 1:20 similarly refers to God's power and Godhead being revealed through creation. John encourages us to apply these attributes to Christ. The heavens, and the earth, the macrocosmos and the microcosmos, declare the greatness of Christ.

> Jesus is Lord! Creation's voice proclaims it,
> For by his power each tree and flower was planned and made.
> Jesus is Lord! The universe declares it,
> Sun, moon and stars in heaven cry, Jesus is Lord!
>
> *David Mansell*

Secondly, *sin and evil do not qualify Christ's rule over the universe*. Evil's origin and presence in a world made through the Word remain a profound mystery to which the cross alone can speak, but no understanding of evil and the power of darkness is acceptable which qualifies Christ's ultimate sovereignty as the creative mediator of all that is. In the Bible, evil and Satan are taken with an impressive seriousness,[19] but never to the point of quenching the song of the angels, 'Holy, holy, holy ... for you created all things, and by your will they were created and have their being' (Rev. 4:8–11), or of qualifying the claim of the Son as he went to his sacrifice, 'Now ... the prince of this world will be driven out' (12:31).

In a commendable concern to do justice to the reality of the satanic order, and the seriousness of the Christian calling, we need to be alert to appearing to undermine Christ's universal creative sovereignty and Easter victory. 'Never forget', as Luther said, 'the devil is God's devil.' All authority in heaven and earth now belongs

---

[10] *Cf.* verses 19–34; 3:27–30; 5:35.   [11] 5:31f., 34, 37; 8:18.
[12] 8:14, 18, 37–38.   [13] 15:26; 16:14.   [14] 5:36; 10:25; 15:24.
[15] 5:39.   [16] 4:39; 12:17; 15:27.   [17] 19:35; 21:24.
[18] J. H. Oldham, *Life is Commitment* (London, 1953), p. 11, cited in L. Morris, *John*, p. 90.
[19] *Cf.* Eph. 6:12; 1 Pet. 5:8; 1 Jn. 5:19.

to the crucified and risen one (Mt. 28:18), in vindication of his primeval creative mastery. The full demonstration of his rule awaits his appearing, but its reality is already proclaimed in both creation and redemption.

Thirdly, *nature is to be respected and preserved.* Jesus Christ's agency of creation should significantly affect attitudes to the physical universe in general, and our response to its threatened destruction in particular. While we are not to worship the creation, as is the tendency in New Age and allied teaching (due as we saw to a lack of any doctrine of creation 'out of nothing'), we should certainly care about it and be actively involved in its preservation. John's prologue is a 'green' statement. That species are being exterminated, forests denuded, soil eroded, rivers and seas polluted and the ozone layer depleted, contradicts the creative action of our Lord Jesus Christ who called all things into being. Although affected by fallenness, they remain his personal handiwork. A lack of concern for our natural environment is a sign of a limited view of Christ, or of a spirituality which is more spiritual than Jesus and in need of balance and healing.

3. Jesus Christ and redemptive history

John now brings the ministry of the pre-incarnate Christ into relation with God's redeeming purpose in history. In a sense the rest of his gospel is an unpacking of this relationship. We can subdivide these verses into four sub-sections.

1. The preparation in Israel (1:6–13)

While John will refer shortly to the whole Old Testament period (*cf.* 17, 'the law was given through Moses') he concentrates here on the final phase of it, the ministry of John the Baptist. This brings him into step with the other evangelists and the early Christian preachers, who consistently see the Baptist as the immediate starting point for an account of Jesus' ministry.[1] John is described as a *witness* (*martys*), a title which belongs to all Christians (Acts 1:8). As such he is a model. He had a sense of personal commission; he was *sent from God* (6). His was a Christ-centred message; *a witness to the light* (8). His goal was specifically the winning of his hearers to personal faith, irrespective of their condition or attitude; *that through him all men might believe* (7).

What action of the Word is verse 9 referring to? Is this a further reference to the general revelation (as in verse 4) or has the evangelist moved on to special revelation – the revealing of the Word in the incarnation? There is actually a further uncertainty in that *coming into the world* can relate in the Greek construction to either *the light*, or to *all men/every man*. The former appears preferable, and is followed in the NIV translation. But is it the Word's becoming flesh that John has in view? Such is certainly the implication when Christ's *coming into the world* is referred to elsewhere in the gospel.[2] On

[1] *Cf.* Mt. 3:1f.; Mk. 1:1f.; Lk. 3:1f.; Acts 1:21–22; 10:37; 13:24f.
[2] *Cf.* 3:17; 6:33; 10:36.

the other hand we need to note the change from a present tense in verse 9 to a past tense in verse 11, where the historic mission of Jesus is plainly in view. If a universal witness is intended (general revelation), we are confronted with an implicit claim to deity. Jesus Christ confronts all people within the divine witness through creation and conscience.[3] The one before whom we shall stand on the judgment day (2 Cor. 5:10) will be no stranger; all people will have met him before.

John's witness was the immediate setting for *the coming into the world* of *the true light that gives light to every man* (9).

World (9) is a major term in John's writings.[4] Almost without exception 'world' has negative overtones; it is the 'world' organized in rebellion against God's rule and claim.[5] It was to this world that Christ came in person, but, in character, *his own did not receive him* (11).

People regularly exclaim at what they see as God's indifference to human tragedy and pain. If only God would appear and accept some responsibility or give some help, then perhaps they would recognize and follow him. In fact, as this gospel makes clear again and again, he is not indifferent; he does care. Indeed he could not care more, and it is because of this that he came. But when he came he was ignored. Nor, as Studdert-Kennedy surmises in his poem 'Indifference',[6] would it be different if he came again today.

When Jesus came to Birmingham they simply passed Him by,
They never hurt a hair of Him, they only let Him die;
For men had grown more tender, and they would not give
    Him pain,
They only just passed down the street, and left Him in the
    rain.

The world did not recognize him. It still does not.

But verse 11 points to an even deeper tragedy. *He came to that which was his own, but his own did not receive him. His own* here are his own people, Israel. It could be rendered 'his own home'.[7] There can be no more poignant expression of human folly and perversity than Israel's rejection of Christ (documented in the fol-

---

[3] Acts 14:15–17; 17:24–28; Rom. 1:18–21; 2:14–15.
[4] Of the 125 occurrences in the NT, 78 are in this gospel, 24 in John's letters, and 3 in Revelation. This compares with 8 in Matthew and 3 each in Mark and Luke.
[5] *Cf.* 7:7; 12:31; 14:30; 15:18; 17:25, *etc.*
[6] Woodbine Willie, *The Best of G. A. Studdert-Kennedy* (Hodder and Stoughton, 1947), p. 210.
[7] S. D. Gordon, *Quiet Talks on John's Gospel* (Revell, 1915), p. 87.

lowing chapters). In spite of all the centuries of waiting for their promised Messiah, when at last he appeared they not only dismissed his claim but instigated his destruction. It is a tragedy which brought tears to the eyes of Jesus (Lk. 13:14; 19:41), and to Paul 'unceasing anguish in my heart' (Rom. 9:2). It is a continuing tragedy expressed in Israel's 'hardening' towards Christ (Rom. 11:25). There is no ground here, however, for pointing the finger, for in all of this Israel only typifies the folly of the human heart universally. The continuing widespread rejection of Christ in our generation is a daily witness to the universal rebellion against the living God in which each of us is involved. It is also a sobering reminder of the inevitability of coming judgment.

The picture is not all negative, however. Some do believe, both in Israel and among the nations (12–13). John uses three synonyms to refer to this: *received him* (12), *believed* in his name (*i.e.* his person) (12); and being *born of God* (13). The gospel will reveal much more about this multifaceted reality as it unfolds.

Here in verse 12 is the first appearance of the phrase *believed in* in this gospel (*pisteuō eis*). It is a formula that recurs throughout.[8] 'Faith' is one of John's basic themes. Indeed the purpose of the gospel is to awaken faith (20:31). John characteristically associates the act of faith (*pisteuō*) with the preposition *eis* which means 'into, on to' (36 times in John, 3 times in 1 John, 8 times elsewhere in the New Testament). 'There is no real parallel in the LXX or in secular Greek.'[9] It is used both for believing in (on to) the Father (14:1) and for believing in (on to) Jesus. This construction reflects John's concern for the dynamic nature of faith: 'it involves much more than trust in Jesus or confidence in him, it is an acceptance of Jesus and of what he claims to be and a dedication of one's life to him'.[10] Here we note three features of this faith.

a. Its universal scope

'... *All who* ...' (12). John inhabited a world which confined its proffered 'salvation' to specific groups. Salvation could be had through philosophy, if one was intelligent; from the mystery cults, if one was among the initiated; by Jewish religion, if one had the right racial pedigree. By contrast, Christianity entered first-century society as a faith for everyone, irrespective of intelligence quotient,

---

[8] *E.g.* 3:16; 6:29; 7:38; 11:26; 14:1.

[9] R. Brown, 1, p. 512; *cf.* appendix I (9), pp. 512–513.

[10] R. Brown, 1, p. 513. *Cf.* W. Turner, 'The sense must be that the believer throws himself upon his Lord in loving, self-abandoning faith and trust.' *Expository Times*, LXIV, 1952–53, p. 51. See also L. Morris, *John*, pp. 335ff.

age, gender, race or religious background. In our increasingly pluralistic communities, it is one of the glories of Christianity to reaffirm this unqualified universalism – all who would believe may come.

b. The incredible status faith offers

... He gave the right to become children of God (12). In a world where rank counted for everything, and the majority of the population were slaves without rights or freedoms (or any prospect of ever acquiring them), the gospel carried immense appeal as a message which promised to all people, irrespective of rank, nothing less than personal membership within the family circle of God. Nobodies were in a moment transformed into somebodies. Even today, with all our vaunted rights and freedoms, so many people suffer from a crippling lack of self-worth, not least within the Christian community. How relevant therefore is a gospel which tells us that as Christians we are nothing less than the personally valued, dearly loved children of God, irrespective of how others may see us or even of how we see ourselves.

c. Faith's sovereign means

We shall have cause again in the course of the gospel to observe John's recognition of the complexity and mystery of a salvation which is both 'willed by man, and worked by God' (Schlatter). While both sides of the equation are asserted here (as they are throughout the gospel), the stress falls at this point on the sovereign action of God. Christians become such by being *born of God* (13). This birth is to be radically distinguished from human birth, with its human initiatives: 'natural descent' (lit. 'bloods', the notion that the act of procreation involved a mixing of blood); 'human decision' (lit. 'the will of the flesh', *i.e.* sexual desire); and 'a husband's will' (on the assumption that the male partner takes the initiative in sexual matters). All these are irrelevant in the case of spiritual rebirth; it is not something we can take into our own hands. We are *born of God*.

> I sought the Lord, and afterward I knew
> He moved my soul to seek him, seeking me;
> It was not I that found, O Saviour true.
> No, I was found of thee.
>
> I find, I walk, I love, but O the whole
> Of love is but my answer, Lord, to thee!

For thou wast long before-hand with my soul,
Always thou lovest me.

Anon.

2. The coming of Jesus (1:14)

The Word became flesh and made his dwelling among us. This
statement is one of the most significant and memorable ever
penned. Its implications are limitless. It has provided the church
over the centuries with a key to understanding the mystery of
Jesus Christ. It represents the heart and climax of the gospel. The
remaining twenty and a half chapters will be spent unfolding its
significance.

Jesus again appears as the divine *logos*, one with the Father in
divinity (1) and now one with us in humanity (14). The word *flesh*
(*sarx*) is a startling one. John deliberately bypasses 'man' or 'a
body'. ' "Flesh" stands for the whole person';[11] it refers to human
existence in its frailty and vulnerability (*cf.* Is. 40:6: 'All flesh is
grass . . .', RSV). Jesus identified with us to that degree. He made
our creaturely weakness his very own form of being (*cf.* Rom. 8:3:
'sending his own Son in the likeness of sinful man [flesh]'. In all
likelihood John is consciously combating early docetic ideas which
denied the true humanity of Jesus Christ. Paradoxically, such
denials, at least at the practical level, are more likely to be met
today among the orthodox than among the heretics, for whom
Jesus' deity rather than his humanity is the real difficulty.

The verb 'was made' (*egenetō*, from *ginomai*) 'expresses that a
person or thing changes its property and enters into a new condition, becomes something that it was not before'.[12] The tense is
aorist, implying a definite and completed action; there is no going
back upon the incarnation. The act of self-humbling on the part of
God is irreversible; he is eternally 'Emmanuel', God with us. God
the Son, without ceasing for a moment to be divine, has united to
himself a full human nature and become an authentic human
person, 'God with us'. In Jesus Christ, God 'was made man'.

No words can do justice to the height and depth of the truth
expressed here. Its enormity overwhelms the mind. C. S. Lewis
rightly refers to it as 'the Grand Miracle'.[13] Dorothy L. Sayers, in
a lyrical passage, observes that 'from the beginning of time until
now it is the only thing which has ever really happened . . . We
may call this doctrine exhilarating or we may call it devastating,

---

[11] R. Brown, p. 13.
[12] Cited in G. R. Beasley-Murray, pp. 13–14.
[13] C. S. Lewis, *Miracles* (Fontana, 1960), ch. xiv.

we may call it revelation or we may call it rubbish ... but if we call it dull then what in heaven's name is worthy to be called exciting?'[14]

> Lo, within a manger lies
> He who built the starry skies.
>
> *Edward Caswall*

> They all were looking for a King
> To slay their foes and lift them high.
> Thou cam'st, a little baby thing
> That made a woman cry.
>
> *George MacDonald*

Among the many implications of the 'Grand Miracle' are these:

1. *Salvation*. The incarnation directly addresses our need for salvation. As Anselm argued back in the eleventh century, our sin and fallenness imply that we cannot save ourselves. Only God can save us. But conversely, since it is we who have sinned, the repairing of our relationship with God must come from our side, from within our human life. Thus only God *can* save us; only we *should*. 'Since no one save God can make satisfaction for our sins, and no one save man ought to make it, it is necessary for a God-man to make it.'[15]

The coming of God in the flesh does not save us in itself; the death of the God-man is also required, as John will make very clear later. The incarnation, however, establishes the necessary precondition, and brings the healing of the great divide between God and his rebellious creatures into the realm of true possibility. In becoming one of us Jesus Christ is fitted to act on our behalf as Mediator and Redeemer.

2. *Affirmation*. The incarnation is a supreme affirmation of the value of human existence. For all our sin and fallenness, 'he abhors not the virgin's womb'. Our human life truly was the vehicle for God's life, our flesh contained the Word, our humanity was home for him who is for ever.

3. *Identification*. The enfleshment of the eternal Word demonstrates God's identification with us in our human life, and in particular in our weakness and suffering. There is no parallel anywhere else in the world's religions to the sympathetic presence of God in Christ sharing our human struggle with us. Here the gospel speaks

---

[14] Dorothy L. Sayers, *Creed or Chaos?* (Harcourt, Brace and Co., 1949), pp. 5, 7.

[15] Anselm, *Why God Became Man*, CC, vol. X (Westminster, 1956), ch. 6, p. 151.

with universal relevance, for the simple fact is, for the great mass of humanity, 'life is difficult'.[16] 'Come to me,' says Jesus 'all you who are weary and burdened, and I will give you rest' (Mt. 11:28).

4. *Adoration.* The greatness of this truth assaults the mind and staggers the imagination, but by that very fact also drives us to our knees in worship. 'Christmas can only be understood as a wonder.'[17]

> Who is He in yonder stall,
> At whose feet the shepherds fall?
> 'Tis the Lord! Oh, wondrous story!
> 'Tis the Lord, the King of glory!
> At His feet we humbly fall—
> Crown Him! crown Him, Lord of all!
>
> *B. R. Hanby*

John now personally identifies himself with this account of Jesus Christ, writing *We* (14). Though the distinction is not an absolute one, he moves from description (1–14a) to testimony and so stands consciously within the community of faith (*cf.* 12–13). To John has been given the unspeakable privilege of being among the 'eye-witnesses and servants of the word' (Lk. 1:2).

John's language (14b) reflects the events of the exodus from Egypt, and the revelation of God at Mount Sinai and in the tabernacle in the wilderness; happenings which dominated the faith of Israel from that day to the present. As God 'lived among' his people then, so the Word has come to live among us (14) now; literally 'pitched his tent among us'.[18] The word for 'dwell' and 'tent' are cognates of the Hebrew term š^ekînâ, which commonly refers to the revealed glory of God.[19] Hence, *we have seen his glory* (14). Just as the people in the Old Testament revelation had seen God's glory manifested in tabernacle and temple, so now God's glory is revealed in his coming in person as 'the One and Only (Son)' (18) to live among us in Jesus Christ. 'The evangelist sees the whole ministry of Jesus as a "tabernacling" in which the disciples again and again had glimpses of his glory.'[20]

Full of grace and truth (14) has similar Old Testament echoes. In Exodus 33:19, when revealing his nature in response to Moses' moving plea, 'show me your glory' (Ex. 33:18), God says, 'I will cause all my goodness to pass in front of you . . . I will have mercy

---

[16] M. Scott Peck, *The Road Less Traveled* (Touchstone, 1978), p. 15.
[17] K. Barth, *Christmas* (Oliver and Boyd, 1959), p. 18.
[18] *Cf.* Ex. 33:7–11; 40:34–38.
[19] *Cf.* Ex. 24:16; 40:34–35; 1 Ki. 8:11 – 11:21; 2 Chr. 7:1f.; *etc.*
[20] L. Newbigin, p. 8.

on whom I will have mercy, and I will have compassion on whom I will have compassion'; 'The LORD, the LORD, the compassionate and gracious God, slow to anger, abounding in love and faithfulness' (Ex. 34:6). Here, God's love is his covenant love, gracious and faithful (hence, 'true'). In Jesus Christ that identical grace and mercy, and that identical faithfulness and loyalty, are expressed for all who believe (14, 17).

3. The Baptist's testimony (1:15)

John the Baptist, whose ministry was the final stage in the historical preparation for redemption, is also the first witness to the coming of the Redeemer (15). John himself was a phenomenon in Israel in his day. His ministry engendered great excitement and his preaching had a marked impact on his hearers. In listening to John the people sensed that the long centuries of silence from God were now ending, the prophetic Word was again being heard in the land. But John is careful (*cf.* 19–34) to disavow any final significance for his ministry; he points rather to Christ who *was before me*. This covers both a temporal and an absolute precedence (16–17).

4. The church's witness (1:16–18)

The evangelist rounds off the prologue, this remarkable summary of the eternal glory of the 'Word made flesh', by testifying to what his coming has meant for the church, the community of faith. The one who was 'full of grace and truth' has shared the boundless riches of that divine fulness with his people, *grace upon grace* (RSV). This phrase is often understood as an unbroken series of 'grace gifts', so *one blessing after another* (NIV). 'All through life we are constantly receiving "Grace instead of Grace", for the Grace of Christ is triumphantly adequate to deal with any situation.'[21]

While this is a great truth which the New Testament elsewhere attests (*cf.* 2 Cor. 12:9), it is possible to take 'instead' (*anti*) in its more straightforward meaning of 'replacing one thing by another', and so view this phrase as asserting that the coming of God in his grace in Christ supersedes the grace of the 'old covenant' revelation. This interpretation can then be carried forward into verse 17, where the law given through Moses is in a sense set over against the *grace and truth* brought in Christ. This of course does not imply that the Old Testament revelation is set aside or the law abrogated. Rather it is fulfilled in Jesus Christ and thus remains in force. This is how John consistently sees the Old Testament throughout his gospel. This interpretation also enables the continuation of the note struck by John the Baptist (15) of Christ as the one who supersedes.

John rounds off this exposition of Christ's eternal significance with a great summary statement. *No-one has ever seen God, but God the One and Only [Son], who is at the Father's side, has made him known* (18). 'The absolute claim of the Christian revelation could not be put more definitively.'[22]

The manuscript reading for *God the . . . Only [Son]* (NIV mg.) is very strong, and, as the preferred reading, accords perfectly with the movement of thought in the 'prologue' as it reaches its conclusion. In doing so it returns to the point from which it began, the deity of the Word. In Jesus Christ God is known to us; in Jesus Christ God himself has come to us. He is *in the bosom of the Father* (18, RSV), the literal wording of *at the Father's side* (NIV). It is as if God has reached into his very being and plucked out his own heart in sending Christ to us.

Made him known is a verb from which we get the technical theological word 'exegesis', which refers to the clarifying of the meaning inherent in a text. Jesus Christ, John says, is the exegesis of God, the exposition of his hidden reality. Because he exists as the only-born, existing in the bosom of the Father, Jesus has unique authority to reveal the Father. The amazing claim of verse 18 is the basis for the discourses in the following chapters in which the Father is made known by Jesus. We note that as the prologue concludes, John moves imperceptibly from the 'God'-'Word' distinction to the 'Father'-'Son' distinction which dominates in the following chapters.

So concludes John's incomparable introduction which has carried us to the furthest horizons of time and the ultimate depths of the Godhead. He now moves to the theme which will occupy the greater part of his story, the ministry of the incarnate king, the 'Word made flesh'.

[22] R. Schnackenburg, 1, p. 278.

B. The ministry of the incarnate king
John 1:19 – 19:42

1:19–51

1. The inauguration

1. The beginning of the ministry (1:19–51)

a. The witness of John (1:19–34)

John the Baptist's witness to Jesus has already been stressed (*cf.* 1:6, 15); now it is filled out. John was something of a problem to the Jewish religious establishment. His religious pilgrimage had not been by official channels (Lk. 1:80). But, despite his unorthodox preparation and lifestyle, there were evident signs that God was at work in him.

The authorities are left with questions (1:24). There was considerable anticipation at that time that the promised *Messiah* (see below) might soon appear. Was John claiming to be he (20)? If not, where did John see himself among Old Testament figures expected to appear at the end of history? Elijah was anticipated in some form (Mal. 4:5). There was also the 'prophet like Moses' (21, see Dt. 18:15–18). John disavows these, and points instead to *the voice of one crying in the wilderness* (see also Is. 40:3), who is seen as the precursor of the promised Messiah (23, RSV).

Particular exception was taken to John's practice of baptizing penitents in preparation for the Messiah's coming. This involved an assumption of independent religious authority on John's part, especially when those baptized were in many cases circumcised Jews in good standing in the synagogue and temple (24–25). The Pharisees, as the self-proclaimed guardians of the religious life of the people and champions of the Torah, felt themselves particularly threatened by John's ministry at this point. John's self-designation in terms of Isaiah 40 is particularly appropriate, not only because of his wilderness location, but in the profounder sense that the later chapters of Isaiah proclaim the coming of God's kingdom in the graphic terms of a second exodus.

We should also note John's astonishing humility. 'John is only "a voice"; it is futile to try to get hold of the person behind the voice and fix him in a place in your scheme of things. There is nothing for you to get hold of. The speaker has no importance. He is not one of the *dramatis personae*. You must just listen to the voice.'[1] Despite the very tangible effects of his preaching ministry, and the consequent widespread respect he gained, he remains totally unaffected by his success. He is conscious only that he serves in preparation for the coming Messiah, beside whose ministry his own is almost totally insignificant (26). It is noteworthy that the one specified limitation on the service of slaves was the removal of the master's shoes. John states that he is unfit to perform even this se.vice for the Coming One.

The force of this section is better appreciated by examining the four titles which the evangelist applies to Jesus.

(i) Messiah (1:19–28)

The early decades of the first century was a time of intense speculation about the Messiah. Messiah literally means 'anointed one' (Gk. *Christos*), reflecting the designated means of appointing people to special tasks in the Old Testament period.[2] Anointing implied that the appointee was endowed with a special portion of God's Spirit for the task in question. There was no single ruling view of the Messiah in Jesus' day. Some thought he would bring peace, others stressed righteousness. Due to the Roman occupation many cast him in a military role and saw him as leading the overthrow of the Roman yoke and, beyond that, securing the world-wide prominence of the Jewish nation. For some he would be a clearly supernatural visitant from God, for others a human prince from David's line.

In denying that he himself was the Messiah, John bore clear witness that the 'anointed one' was nonetheless a hidden presence among them (26). John's identification of Jesus came at his baptism, when he saw the Spirit of God in dovelike form visibly descend upon Jesus and remain on him. The remaining was important, in contrast to earlier comings of the Spirit in the Old Testament period which were essentially spasmodic and temporary.[3] In verse 41 Andrew directly identifies Jesus as the Messiah, and Nathanael's declaration in verse 49, 'you are the King of Israel', would carry

[1] L. Newbigin, p. 13.
[2] *Cf.* Ex. 29:7; Lv. 8:30f.; 1 Sa. 16:13; 1 Ki 19:16.
[3] *E.g.* Samson, Jdg. 13:25; 15:14; or Saul, 1 Sa. 10:6; 19:23.

similar implications. Referred to Jesus this title points to three things:

Authority. The Messiah is generally a kingly figure embodying God's rule. The acclamation of Jesus as King will reappear throughout the gospel and find its surprising climax at the cross.[4] It is a title which confronts us with Jesus' claim to reign over our lives as King and Lord and calls for our whole-hearted submission to him.

Enabling. The Holy Spirit energizes Jesus. Luke makes more of this,[5] but it is certainly not absent from John here. Jesus has been affirmed in the prologue as an authentic human person (14), in a sense our model human. It is therefore most significant that his ministry was exercised in genuine dependence on the supernatural resources of the Holy Spirit. How much profounder our need of this anointing; 'The servant is not greater than his master.'

Fulfilment. The Messiah was prophesied throughout the Old Testament era under a range of images.[6] Jesus' messiahship therefore both underwrites the divine authority of the Old Testament writings, and also proclaims the lordship of God over human history.

(ii) Lamb of God (1:29, 36)

What did John the Baptist mean in giving Jesus this title? Some argue that John had in mind the warrior lamb of first-century Jewish apocalyptic writing, a figure of immense strength, who in Revelation 5:6 (*cf.* 17:14) is an image of the Lord Jesus Christ. This would accord with John's anticipation of the Messiah's function as judge (Mt. 3:7–12). Even if this be conceded, it is difficult to believe that the sacrificial aspects of the 'Lamb' title would have been absent from John's mind. We need to bear in mind the strong ethical note in his preaching, and his call for repentance followed by a rite of moral and spiritual import (baptism). As the gift of the Spirit through the Coming One and the fire of his judgment would both eclipse the Baptist's own contribution, it is certainly in keeping with John's message for him to have anticipated the messianic provision also of a more profound atonement for sin. Readers of the gospel with even a rudimentary knowledge of the Old Testament would have a number of pictures readily brought to mind: the lamb provided by God for Abraham (Gn. 22:8, 13); the Lamb of Isaiah 53 who was led to the slaughter for the sins of God's people; and perhaps most likely of all, the Passover Lamb of Exodus 12, which will be important for John the evangelist as he unveils the cross.[7]

---

[4] 1:49; 12:13; 18:36–37; 19:14, 19–21.   [5] Lk. 4:1, 14, 18; *cf.* Mt. 12:28.
[6] 2 Sa. 7:16; Ps. 2:2; 110:1; Is. 9:6f.; 11:1f.; Zc. 6:12; *etc.*
[7] *Cf.* Ex. 12:1–11, 43–47; John 19:14, 29, 36.

We should note also the *source* of this Lamb; he is provided by God himself (Gn. 22:7f.). We are utterly unable to provide for our own atonement; it is a gift. We note too the *significance* of it; the Lamb will 'take away' sin. In this connection the imagery of the scapegoat is particularly evocative. The priest laid his hands on the head of the hapless victim transferring the guilt of the people to the animal, and then the creature was released in the wilderness to proclaim the removal of guilt. Few aspects of the gospel need greater, or more frequent, reaffirmation than this one. How many people struggle for survival beneath crushing burdens of guilt! But Christ, the Lamb of God, really has borne it all for us! He says to us today, 'son [daughter], your sins are forgiven' (Mk. 2:5). 'Their sins and lawless acts I will remember no more' (Heb. 10:17). Finally there is the *scope* of the Lamb's ministry, 'The sins of the world.' Without any exception, every kind of sin and evil is covered. There is no sin too heinous, no wickedness too terrible, no habitual failure too often repeated, that it cannot be 'taken away' by Christ, our heavenly Lamb.

> Not all the blood of beasts
>   On Jewish altars slain,
> Could give the guilty conscience peace
>   Or wash away its stain.
>
> But Christ, the heavenly Lamb,
>   Takes all our sins away;
> A sacrifice of nobler Name,
>   And richer blood, than they.
>
> Believing, we rejoice
>   To see the curse remove;
> We bless the Lamb with cheerful voice,
>   And sing His wondrous love.
>
> *Isaac Watts*

(iii) Baptizer with the Spirit (1:32–33)

We noted above John's witness to Jesus as Messiah, the one whom the Spirit anoints. Here is the complementary truth – Jesus also dispenses the Spirit to his people. With the single exception of 1 Corinthians 12:13, the New Testament usage of 'baptism with/in the Spirit' is in connection with John's witness to Jesus.[8] Baptism is an initiatory experience. In the case of John the Baptist, it initiated its recipients into a readiness for the coming of the Messiah; in the New Testament church, baptism initiated into the family of

---

[8] *Cf.* Mt. 3:11; Mk. 1:8; Lk. 3:16; Jn. 1:33; Acts 1:5; 11:16.

God.[9] To entitle Jesus 'the baptizer with the Spirit' means primarily that he is the one through whom we are initiated into God's kingdom through receiving the life of God the Holy Spirit. In this sense it is a synonym of Jesus as the regenerator, the one through whom we are 'born again' (so 1:13; 3:1f.).

A further, secondary implication is possible. Bearing in mind that John's baptism was a public one and very likely by immersion,[10] it was clearly a critical experience for those who underwent it. That Jesus is 'the baptizer with the Spirit' implies possibilities in terms of our experience of God through him, which may, as God chooses, be similarly 'overwhelming'.

(iv) Son of God (1:34)

This title was given to Jesus at his baptism by the Father (Mt. 3:17; Lk. 3:22). It is central to that whole relationship in this gospel. The context is the Father's delighting in his Son: 'with him I am well pleased' (Mt. 3:17). There is a similar juxtaposition of these truths in 3:34–35. The Son as the recipient of the Spirit is the one the Father loves. As *Son of God*, Jesus brings delight to the heart of the Father, and also to our hearts as we follow him.

An alternative reading, 'chosen/elect of God', is preferred by some recent commentators, on the ground that the copyist would be much less likely to change from 'Son' to 'Chosen' than the other way round. While this is a possibility, the manuscript evidence for 'Son' is extremely strong, and the copyist may conceivably have been carried along by the associations with Jesus' baptism, indicated above, and inadvertently written 'Chosen', a title declared at the transfiguration in similar circumstances (Lk. 9:35).

At a time when there is increasing recognition of the critical importance of the child-parent relationship for the development of human personality, this gospel affords a wonderful, God-given model of what that special relationship can mean.[11]

---

[9] Mt. 28:18–19; Acts 2:41f.; 8:34f.; 16:30f.; Gal. 3:26f.

[10] Absolute certainty as to the mode is not possible. In favour of immersion are considerations such as the meaning of the word used for baptism throughout the New Testament, *baptizein*, which normally meant to dip, or drown (!); the place of administration (1:28) – every self-respecting hamlet in Palestine had a well, and if effusion was used visits to rivers would have been unnecessary; the presence of a model – proselyte baptism was by immersion (the admission rite for Gentiles who converted to Judaism, such as the significant company mentioned in Acts 2:5–11). For an alternative point of view see J. G. Davies, *The Architectural Setting of Baptism* (Barrie and Rockcliff, 1963).

[11] See also my comment on 5:17.

b. The call of the first disciples (1:35–51)

As in other gospels, the witness of the Baptist is followed by the calling of disciples. In this Jesus conforms to Jewish rabbinical models where teachers were traditionally surrounded by 'learners', which is what 'disciples' means. There is, however, a significant difference in Jesus' case. In Judaism the student was left to find a teacher for himself. Here, Jesus took the initiative.[12]

The noting of the time-link, *the next day . . .,* may be significant (*cf.* 1:29, 39, 43; 2:1). In running the events together, John presents Jesus' early ministry as a week-long activity culminating in the first sign at Cana in Galilee. Recalling the background of Genesis chapter 1 in the prologue, it is not inconceivable that John is consciously presenting the work of Jesus, the Word made flesh, as the week of re-creation, climaxed in the first of the signs which reveal his glory.

These verses also describe the earthing of the ministry of the divine Word in human life. The prologue lifted our vision to the vistas of eternity and the inner being of God. While all that is not forgotten or left behind, John now shows the glory of the eternal Word intersecting with ordinary folk in the midst of their everyday lives, people with deep human needs, like John's readers across the ages. Therein lies the wonder of Christ and the gospel. It brings together the heights of heaven and the depths of earth, the glories of God and the agonies of humanity.

A further preliminary question concerns the harmonizing of this account with the one given in the other gospels.[13] There appears no reason why the meeting with Jesus described by John here should not have preceded the more critical encounter described in the other gospels. Indeed the occurrence of this earlier contact helps explain the disciples' readiness to make the radical break, which the synoptic writers describe, apparently without opportunity to examine Jesus' credentials or to weigh the personal consequences.

John the Baptist's directing his followers to Jesus (35–36) expresses his belief that the ministry of the Messiah would supersede his own (26–27). It is noteworthy that his conviction at this point is carried through into action which hurt John personally. Andrew's going over to Jesus at John's instigation would cost John a loyal and gifted follower and, moreover, Andrew was the link to Peter, whose immense potential would have been recognized by John as it was by Jesus (42). Further, the other unnamed disciple

---

[12] J. Jeremias, *New Testament Theology* (SCM, 1971), 1, pp. 132f.
[13] *Cf.* Mt. 4:18–22; Mk. 1:14–20; Lk. 5:1–11.

also changed his allegiance, and he may well have been John the evangelist, hardly an 'also ran'! Yet John the Baptist deliberately encourages their transfer of allegiance to Jesus.

Here was a preacher who was prepared to live by the message he preached; which goes a long way to explain why he made such an impact, and why he was remembered with respect decades later when John composed his gospel. At a time when public trust in Christian leaders is at an all-time low, the world is in desperate need of preachers who are prepared to mortgage their personal ambitions and popularity out of a consuming concern for Jesus' pre-eminence and the advance of his cause, by whatever human instrument. The challenge of Nietzsche to Christians in public view has rarely been more pertinent – 'Show me you are redeemed and I will believe in your redeemer.'

This section is a demonstration of the claim in the prologue that, though in general Jesus was disbelieved among 'his own' people (11), there were, and are, the exceptions who 'believe' and find new life (12–13).

Coming to the text itself, it is significant that the description of the four disciples' commitment begins with a reiteration of Jesus' title, *Lamb of God* (36). On the likelihood that this title had strong sacrificial associations, John is reminding us, his readers, that to follow Jesus necessarily begins with a recognition of his Saviour-hood.

Another fundamental prerequisite is exposed in the question Jesus asks the two following disciples in verse 38, *What do you want?* Although on the surface a simple query about the reason for their evident interest in Jesus, it has deeper implications. Sooner or later when we begin to take Jesus seriously we face the same question: what do we really want with him, or from him? C. S. Lewis puts the issue with typical force, 'There comes a moment when the children who have been playing at burglars hush suddenly . . . was that a *real* footstep in the hall? There comes a moment when people who have been dabbling in religion ("man's search for God"!) suddenly draw back. Supposing we really found him? We never meant it to come to *that*! Worse still, supposing he had found us? So it is a sort of Rubicon. One goes across; or not. But if one does . . . one may be in for *anything*.'[14] Happily our motivation does not need to be perfectly disinterested for us to continue our pursuit of Jesus. Strictly there is no such thing as absolutely pure motive this side of heaven. But Jesus' question is a salutary challenge to hypocritical unreality. It is a searching question at every stage of life, and he has a disturbing habit of facing us

[14] C. S. Lewis, *Miracles* (Fontana, 1960), p. 98.

with it at every new crossroad of experience: 'What do you want?'

Note that Jesus does not press them for an immediate response, but gives them opportunity to spend time with him before making a commitment (39). This is a lesson for over-zealous Christian witnesses for whom the only valid response to the gospel is one made immediately upon hearing it presented. The parallel with the physical birth process is relevant at this point (*cf.* 13; 3:1f.); the crisis of birth is preceded in every case by a period of gestation. To force a birth prematurely may have as disastrous repercussions in the spiritual order as in the physical.

Each of the four cases of response to Jesus detailed in this section are distinct and Jesus' approach varies with each one, a reflection no doubt of the claim of 2:24–25 that 'he knew what was in a man'. Sensitive and skilled evangelists will need no reminder of the truth expressed here. Each potential disciple is an individual to be related to in a unique and distinct way. 'Laws' and 'methods' in personal evangelism may provide helpful tools, but the application must be individual in every case.

(i) Andrew (1:40–41)

Andrew is the first follower of Jesus to be identified by name (40). *Simon Peter's brother* would have identified him most clearly to John's readers, but the phrase also expresses Andrew's whole career – his relationship to Peter was his means of identification. Andrew is not alone. Many lives are lived in the shadow of another, whether a sibling, a 'rival', a colleague, or even a parent. However regrettable, it is a fact of daily experience for multitudes. It is good to be assured, even when the overshadowing is not dispelled with the passing of the years, as in Andrew's case, that God does not value one life more highly than another. He has no 'favourites'. Each of his children is 'special' to him.

Andrew's reaction to finding Jesus has been a classic model for Christian witness over the centuries (41). He began with his immediate family; witness, like charity, begins at home. With hindsight, Andrew's bringing Peter to Jesus was 'perhaps as great a service to the Church as any man ever did'.[15] Nor did his concern to bring others to Christ stop with Peter (*cf.* 6:8; 12:22).

Here lies the secret of the extraordinary spread of Christianity in the early centuries, as the historian Gibbon noted, 'it became the most sacred duty of a new convert to diffuse among his friends and relatives the inestimable blessings he had received'.[16] Statistics

[15] W. Temple, p. 28.

[16] E. Gibbon, *The Decline and Fall of the Roman Empire*, 6 vols. (Dent, 1954), chap. XV, pp. 430ff.

repeatedly demonstrate that while gospel preaching is undoubtedly important, personal witness and friendship continue to be the primary means by which people are brought to Christ.

(ii) Peter (1:42)

Peter, the second recruit identified, is addressed by Jesus in terms of the person he was to become (42). *Simon son of John*, his given name, would give place to *Cephas* (Aramaic; *Petros*, Greek), meaning 'rock' (*cf.* Mt. 16:17–19). It is striking how regularly Jesus approached people from the perspective of their potential.[17] Our concern to declare the sin and fallenness of those we witness to (which has its place, *cf.* 'though you are evil', Lk. 11:13) must not inhibit our recognition of the possibilities of grace ('know how to give good gifts', Lk. 11:13). The vision of future potential can be a deeply effective means to the realizing of that potential.

> Could'st thou in vision see
> Thyself the man God meant,
> Thou never more could'st be
> The man thou art, content.
>
> *Emerson*

(iii) Philip (1:43–45)

Philip is one of the less prominent disciples. Although one of the inner twelve (Lk. 6:14), this gospel is the source of almost all we know of him.[18] He usually appears in association with Andrew, and commonly in situations where he is somewhat out of his depth. This may explain why Jesus apparently took direct initiative in calling him (43b); left to himself, Philip might have been too reluctant to pursue his interest to the point of commitment. While this last comment probably runs the risk of building too much on the limited biographical information available to us, it is nonetheless appropriate to affirm that God's purpose also embraces 'background' personalities who live much of their lives at, or beyond, the limits of their capabilities. 'It is encouraging to reflect that Jesus went out of his way to find this perfectly ordinary Philip and to enlist him in the apostolic band.'[19] Whatever his limitations may have been, Philip shows himself to be an effective personal witness as he points his friend Nathanael to Christ (44). Philip's testifying to Jesus as *the one Moses wrote about in the Law, and about whom the prophets also wrote* (45), is 'probably a general statement that Jesus is the fulfillment of the whole Old Testament'.[20] It enables

---

[17] *Cf.* Lk. 5:10; Lk. 18:22; Jn. 1:47; 4:7; 6:70.   [18] 6:7; 12:21f.; 14:8f.
[19] L. Morris, *John*, p. 162.   [20] R. Brown, 1, p. 86.

John to refute any lingering suspicion from verses 16–17 that with the coming of Jesus the Old Testament revelation has ceased to have significance as an inspired record of the nature and acts of God.

Clearly Nazareth does not rate highly in the estimate of Nathanael (46). His prejudice is probably religious rather than domestic; Nazareth (unlike Bethlehem, Mi. 5:2) has no mention in the prophetic anticipation of the Messiah. No historical contradiction need be implied here (or in 7:41, 52). That Jesus was popularly believed to have been born in Nazareth does not deny his birth in Bethlehem, due to the special circumstances of the Roman census (Lk. 2:1–3). If this author may intrude a personal illustration, he is known as 'from Dundee', the place of his entire upbringing, but the fact, not widely known, is that due to temporary wartime evacuation he was born in Forfar, a small country town some miles from the city of Dundee. Philip's reply to Nathanael is undoubtedly the best one for handling prejudice: 'come and see' (for yourself) (46); meet for yourself the One who says still, 'touch me and see' (Lk. 24:39).

(iv) Nathanael (1:45–51)
Jesus' greeting of Nathanael is designed not only to capture his attention but also, by its penetrating insight, to throw him off guard. It is notable, in view of the following allusion to Genesis 28, that the quality with which Jesus sees Nathanael as most richly endowed, *viz.* guilelessness, is the one most clearly lacking in Jacob. Nathanael's admiring surprise is deepened by Jesus' further insight, *I saw you while you were still under the fig-tree* (48). It is not evident what exactly Jesus is referring to, but it clearly displays a miraculous knowledge of Nathanael's movements and evokes his profession of faith (49). *Son of God* could have messianic implications (2 Sa. 7:14; Ps. 2:7); however, the presence of the definite article points to the dimension which would certainly not be missed by John's readers, Jesus as one uniquely related to the Father. Jesus concludes by assuring Nathanael that there is a richer basis for his faith, yet to be disclosed, through his developing association with Jesus. The converse between heaven and earth witnessed by Jacob will be re-enacted before Nathanael's eyes (50–51). Indeed he will see *greater things* as the traffic between the two worlds attains its climax as Jesus' ministry moves to its conclusion. If, as some rabbis taught, Genesis 28:12 indicated that the angels were ascending and descending on 'him' (*i.e.* Jacob), Jesus, as the Word of God made flesh, is the new and supreme point at which God and humanity intersect.

This is the first occurrence in the gospel of the characteristic phrase *amēn, amēn*.[21] It commonly introduces a statement of special significance and solemnity, as here.

Jesus' self-designation, *Son of Man*, occurs frequently in the synoptic gospels. It is a common Hebraism for 'man'. It also occurs in the very important passage in Daniel 7:13f., in the apocalyptic vision of the heavenly Son of Man, who appears at the end of history on the clouds of heaven to exercise universal judgment and receive the worship of the nations. Jesus' use of the definite article when using the title of himself, as here, indicates that this is consistently the background to his understanding of it. The claim to such a role in the divine purposes is a staggering one, bordering on rampant megalomania in any ordinary mortal. But this, and similar claims recurring through the gospel, is wholly congruent with Jesus' divine nature. Here indeed faith can rest with security, seeing all that Jesus is, has done, and will finally accomplish. We echo Peter, 'to whom else can we go? . . . for we believe and are sure that you are the Christ, the Son of the Living God' (6:68 – 69, my translation).

The relevance of these paragraphs to our present experience is obvious. Christ the risen King continues to issue his summons, 'Follow me!' (*cf.* 21:19, 22). It echoes around the world today through the witnesses of Jesus among the nations. It reaches to overshadowed folks like Andrew; explosive, potential leaders like Peter; withdrawn, struggling characters like Philip; earnest, ingenuous souls like Nathanael; and to every other conceivable classification. Although the world still 'knows him not' (see 11), for all who commit themselves to him, the discovery waits to be made that the man who hails from Nazareth (46) is yet 'the meeting point between heaven's fullness and earth's need, even in the midst of the bustle and noise of our modern world'.[22]

> The angels keep their ancient places;
> Turn but a stone, and start a wing!
> 'Tis ye, 'tis your estrangèd faces
> That miss the many-splendoured thing.
>
> But (when so sad thou can'st not sadder)
> Cry: – and upon thy so sore loss
> Shall shine the traffic of Jacob's ladder,
> Pitched betwix Heaven and Charing Cross.
>
> *Francis Thompson*

---

[21] AV 'verily, verily . . .'; NIV *I tell you the truth* (*cf.* 3:5; 5:24; 6:26, 32, 53; *etc.*).

[22] G. R. Beasley-Murray, p. 30.

2:1 – 12:19

2. The procession

Chapter 2 opens a new section of the gospel, containing John's account of the public ministry of Jesus from its commencement in Galilee to its climax in Jerusalem. It is organized around seven miracles. John's word for them is 'signs' (*semeia*), which is his alternative to 'miracles' or 'wonders'. John does not of course have any reservation about the operation of the supernatural in respect of these mighty works of power. He is concerned, however, to see beyond the miracles to their significance; they are signs, *i.e.* special actions by Jesus which reveal his glory to those who believe and which confront others with the need to decide about Jesus.

It is worth observing that this understanding of Jesus' miracles is somewhat different from that of the synoptic evangelists. Their favourite words for the miracles, *dynameis*, acts of power, and *terata*, portents, miracles, occur in John not at all in the former case, and only once (4:48) in the case of the latter.

The distinction can be put in this way: for the synoptic writers Jesus' miracles are actual occasions of the incursion of the kingdom of God. 'Fundamentally [they] are acts by which Jesus establishes God's reign and defeats the reign of Satan.'[1] For John, the miracles, though no less real as historical acts of supernatural power, are more symbolic; they point beyond themselves to Jesus and his significance. Put more succinctly, the synoptic miracles are essentially eschatological, John's essentially christological. For John, faith based on miraculous signs is not regarded as satisfactory.[2] It is, however, at least a step beyond those who willfully refuse to even see the signs.[3]

One other aspect of the 'signs' is worth noting. Jesus commonly refers to them as 'works' (*erga*). 'Works' can also include his words

[1] R. Brown, 1, p. 524, *cf*. pp. 525–531.   [2] 2:23–25; 4:48; 6:26.
[3] 3:19–21; 12:37–41; *cf*. my comments on 4:43–54.

(*cf*. 14:10). The use of 'works' directly links the ministry of Jesus to that of the Father – 'My Father is always at his work to this very day, and I, too, am working' (5:17). So close is the union of Son with Father that the works of Jesus can be considered as the Father's works in him (14:10). Thus the signs, like the entire gospel, confront us with Jesus and the inescapable challenge, 'Who are you?' (8:25).

There is some consensus among commentators that the two events in chapter 2, the changing of the water into wine at Cana, and the cleansing of the temple in Jerusalem, establish the terms of Jesus' ministry. They also anticipate Christ's future work. 'To attend a marriage feast and to cleanse the temple were among the first acts of our Lord's ministry at his first coming. To purify the whole visible Church and hold a marriage supper will be among his first acts, when he comes again.'[4]

1. The first sign – Cana (2:1–11)

The opening phrase, *On the third day*, links the miracle directly with the events just described. We have noted the possibility of John's using a creation-week motif. More generally the linkage makes the point that the divisions which we make for purposes of exposition are only provisional at best. This gospel in the final analysis is like Jesus' undergarment, a 'seamless robe' which is 'woven in one piece from top to bottom' (see 19:23). There is further linkage possible in that the promise made to Nathanael of 'greater things' begins to find fulfilment immediately in the revelation of the glory of Jesus to his disciples (11).

Jesus' being invited to the wedding (2) is interesting – clearly he is not perceived as an antisocial killjoy, albeit there may have been a family link behind the invitation. Mary appears to have had some leading catering role. The depletion of the wine supply is probably explained by the duration of Jewish wedding celebrations, sometimes as long as a week. It was, however, a serious social *faux pas* and reflected poorly on the bridegroom. Lawsuits were not unknown in these circumstances.

Mary's sharing her dilemma with Jesus was possibly a habit bred of long years of family dependence, in the apparent absence of Joseph (Mk. 6:3). Her request, essentially informing him of the need, is a helpful model of *intercessory prayer*. (*Cf*. 11:3, 'the one you love is sick'; 2 Ki. 19:14). We all have a tendency to use prayer to dictate to God. Our part is to lay the need before him, and then trust him to respond as he wills. We also note that Mary's request

[4] J. C. Ryle, p. 36.

was followed by implicit obedience (5). Prayer without a willingness to obey is little better than faith without a willingness to work.[5]

Jesus' response to his mother (4) is surprising in two respects; his addressing her as 'woman', and his apparent hesitation about responding to her dilemma. The former is not as jarring as might appear. *Dear woman* (NIV) expresses the affectionate undertones; the identical word is used in a deeply caring moment (*cf.* 19:26). *Why do you involve me?*[6] contains a note of correction which cannot be eliminated. This exchange marks the transposing of Jesus' relationship to his mother, although still special, into a new key in the light of his Father's mission and the shadow of its finale. While that hour of his self-oblation is *not yet come*,[7] already its demand lies upon him. As a result, all previous relationships, not least his natural ones, must be revised. When Mary is prepared to adjust to this new order her plea is accepted. 'Mary approaches Jesus as his mother, and is reproached; . . . she responds as a believer, and her faith is honoured.'[8]

Jewish law required that hands be ceremonially washed before meals (6) and the vessels to be used also be cleansed (*cf.* Mark 7:3–4). Stone jars, being more impervious than earthenware, would be less likely to contract uncleanness (*cf.* Lv. 11:29–38).

The servants' obedience to Jesus' command (7–8) is rewarded (9), however irrelevant his directive must have appeared to the immediate crisis. The master of ceremonies' exclamation of surprise at the quality of this 'new wine' compared to that served earlier (10) takes us to the heart of the 'sign' and its meaning. The 'new wine' of the kingdom brought by Jesus contrasts with the old wine of Judaism. 'Jesus changes the water of Judaism into the wine of Christianity.'[9]

John has already claimed this contrast in the 'prologue' (1:17–18). The Word heard and preserved through the long centuries in Israel has been superseded in being fulfilled. 'The one Moses wrote about in the Law, and about whom the prophets also wrote' (1:45) has appeared among us; anticipation has been crowned by realization; the Word has become flesh (*cf.* Heb 1:1–2).

As far as the actual physical nature of the miracle is concerned there can be no doubt that what Jesus provided was real wine. It would be wrong, however, simply on this basis to theorize about the appropriateness or otherwise of the consumption of alcoholic beverages by disciples of Jesus today. There is no 'ground here for

---

[5] Jas. 2:16; *cf.* Jos. 7:10–13; 1 Tim. 2:8.   [6] W. Barclay, 1, p. 59.
[7] *Cf.* 7:30; 8:20; 12:23, 27; 13:1; 17:1.   [8] D. A. Carson, *John*, p. 173.
[9] L. Morris, *John*, p. 146.

conclusions regarding the degree of intoxication of the guests at this wedding'.[10] More generally, the accumulated human misery in every corner of the earth which results directly or indirectly from the immoderate use of alcohol puts the burden of proof on those who would advocate anything other than abstinence as the Christian stance in the late twentieth century.

Returning to the meaning of the sign, if we take the purifying function of the water as a specific expression of the transformation Jesus brings, the superiority of Jesus' gift is clear in at least three respects.

First, in terms of the achievement of purification, the law (1:17) could point the way, but gave no permanent relief to the conscience burdened by failure. Repeated rituals of cleansing were the limit of its solution (cf. Heb. 10:1–18). By contrast, Jesus, through his 'one sacrifice . . . has made perfect' and 'is able to save completely those who come to God through him' (Heb. 10:14; 7:25; Rom. 5:1; 8:1).

> Though your sins are like scarlet,
>   they shall be as white as snow;
> though they are red as crimson,
>   they shall be like wool. (Is. 1:18)

No deeper word can be spoken to our guilt than this.

Second, the law could give direction concerning purification but could not enable the worshipper to take the road it indicated. The holy life was set forth, the invitation to the feast was issued, but the realities of fallen human nature meant that the means of purification and cleansing had to be constantly on hand (Rom. 7:18, 'I can will what is right, but I cannot do it', RSV; cf. New American Standard Bible, 'the willing is present in me, but the doing of the good is not'). The prophets dreamed of God's one day overcoming this pervasive weakness of Judaism through the 'new covenant written on the heart', a covenant not just of prescription but of power (cf. Je. 31:31–34; Ezk. 36:25–27). Christ has brought this new covenant. Let Harold Morris speak for a liberated multitude, 'The promise of 2 Corinthians 5:17 is that a person in Christ becomes a new creature. That included Convict 62345. Old habits and attitudes were replaced as the Spirit of God worked in my life. The vengeance that I had nourished for five years and the rebellious spirit that had been a driving force in my life relaxed their grip when Christ took control. Little by little he replaced my hatred by his love. Sometimes I lay in the prison yard looking at the sky and relishing the joy and peace that I'd found in Christ. The bars and fences were still there, as were the guards with their high-

---

[10] C. K. Barrett, p. 193.

powered rifles. But I had an inner strength I'd never known before – the very presence of Christ.'[11] T. W. Manson makes the same glad affirmation: 'The living Christ still has two hands, one to point the way and the other held out to help us along. So the Christian ideal lies before us, not a remote and austere mountain peak, an ethical Everest, which we must scale by our own skill and endurance, but as a road on which we may walk with Christ as guide and friend.'[12]

Third, the law's insipidity is expressed at the point of inducement. Christ's new motivation of thankfulness and responding love is a far more compelling stimulus to obedience than the sheer imperative of the commandment. 'For the love of Christ controls us, . . . he died for all, that those who live might live no longer for themselves but for him who for their sake died and was raised' (2 Cor. 5:14–15, RSV). It was precisely this impulse that moved C. T. Studd to a lifetime of costly missionary service: 'If Jesus Christ be God, and died for me, then no sacrifice can be too great for me to make for Him'. But this miracle can happen again as the water of guilt, habitual failure and legalism, is transformed by the word of the risen Jesus into the wine of forgiveness, victory and joyful obedience.

The picture of the kingdom as a wedding feast has wide biblical support.[13] For all the reality of the struggles of faith, the pains of the world, and the warfare of the kingdom, Christ continues to invite us to celebrate with him.

Since this is the first of the miracles John records, a general comment is in order. The possibility of these miraculous acts of power is implicit in the opening statement of the gospel, 'Through him all things were made' (1:3). The all-creating Word cannot be held ransom by the constraints of his own creation. 'The modest water saw its God and blushed.'[14] These miracles also challenge the tendency in post-enlightenment western Christianity to 'spiritualize' the New Testament message, so that 'it is understood to be concerned with realities which operate only within the mental world – the interior world of human thinking, feeling and willing'.[15] These signs proclaim the direct presence and action of God in the external world of 'nature' and history. The reality of the incarnation should not thereby be minimized. Clearly some self-imposed limitations lie upon Jesus, as he himself testified: 'The Son can do nothing by himself; he can do only what he sees his Father doing'

---

[11] Harold Morris, *Twice Pardoned* (Focus on the Family, 1986), p. 96.
[12] T. W. Manson, *Ethics and the Gospel* (SCM, 1960), p. 68.
[13] Mt. 5:6; 8:11–12; Mk. 2:19; Lk. 22:15–18, 29–30a; *cf.* Is. 25:6; 55:1–2.
[14] W. Temple, p. 36.   [15] L. Newbigin, p. 24.

(5:19); 'The Word became flesh' (1:14). But the boundless energy of the Father is available to the Son, not for arbitrary demonstrations of power, but for 'signs' which reveal the Son's true glory.

2. The cleansing of the temple (2:12–25)

This section links naturally with the call of the first disciples and the turning of the water into wine. Following Jesus starts with the issues of purification from sin and the offering of true worship. More particularly, the insipidity of Judaism is now shown to be rooted in a fundamental spiritual apostasy which Jesus has come both to confront and reverse. The incident in itself is a sombre indication, this early in the gospel, of the forces of opposition which must be confronted before the triumphant purpose of God in Jesus can win its way to destined victory.

John is particularly concerned with the annual Jewish feasts in his record of Jesus' ministry. He uses the meaning of these feasts to throw into relief the claims Jesus makes and the fulfilment he brings to the promise inherent in Judaism. John mentions three Passovers in his gospel.[16] The Passover festival (13), deriving from the exodus from Egypt (*cf.* Ex. chapters 12–13), was celebrated primarily in the temple, the perceived 'seat' of the living God, and hence the source of the holiness both of the city and the nation. The cleansing of the temple which Jesus effects during the feast is an impressive statement both of his personal authority and of the crisis which his mission represented for Judaism.

Scholars have debated the question of historical reliability, raised by the fact that John at this point appears clearly out of step with the synoptic evangelists, each of whom likewise recounts a cleansing of the temple but uniformly sets this at the end of Jesus' ministry, during holy week.[17] There are three possibilities.

1. There was only one cleansing which chronologically took place, as in the synoptics, at the close of Jesus' ministry. It can perhaps be argued that John is not necessarily to be censured on that account, since his alleged concern is not for strict factual sequence, in our modern historiographical sense. By this view the theological meaning of this incident is primary, and so John sets it at a point in his narrative where this significance can be seen to maximum effect. Hence the ministry is launched by an affirmation of Jesus' renewal of the worship of Israel and his claim to be the new locus, as the Risen One, of all commerce between God and humanity.

[16] *Cf.* 2:13; 6:4; 11:55f.
[17] Mt. 21:12–17; Mk. 11:15–18; Lk. 19:45–46.

2. The synoptics are out of step with strict chronology; John is right, there was one 'cleansing' of the temple and it took place at the beginning of Jesus' ministry as recorded here. The synoptic writers made the change to suit *their* theological purposes.

3. There were two similar, though not identical, actions of cleansing on Jesus' part, reported correctly by all four evangelists though each records only one of them. There is certainly no inherent impossibility in this solution. The synoptic writers record a repetition of the miraculous feeding of a large crowd of people,[18] and Jesus was arguably 'anointed' on more than one occasion.[19] Further, there is an inherent appropriateness in this action at both 'ends' of Jesus' ministry. At the beginning, Jesus sees the worship of the nation through eyes newly kindled by the call of God and his nascent sense of mission. As the newly authorized Messiah King, he moves energetically to confront Israel's apostasy and recall it to a new submission to God (Mal. 3:1f.). At the end of the ministry Jesus comes, in the shadow of his looming self-sacrifice, to declare the final bankruptcy of a religion which has turned its back on its high and holy destiny in the interests of self-aggrandizement and empty legalism. Thus both accounts are contextually credible, besides which there is an objective attestation to the validity of John's witness here in the statements of the witnesses at Jesus' trial. Mark 14:58 (*cf.* Mt. 26:61) reproduces the saying of John 2:19, words which find no trace in the synoptic reports of a cleansing of the temple. Not for the first, or last, time John and the synoptics present complementary accounts.

The scene described in verse 14 is fully in keeping with Old Testament laws demanding animal sacrifice, and their stress on the awesome holiness of God to whom gifts should be made in appropriately 'holy' coinage;[20] hence the animal-sellers and the money-changers. While there is little doubt that at least some of the trading was corrupt, it is the cleansing recorded in the other gospels which more acutely raises that issue (*cf.* 'a den of robbers', Mk. 11:17). Here Jesus appears to be inveighing more against the presence of this trading, with all its hubbub, within the precincts of the house of God, a place dedicated to the prayerful seeking of God and the offering of awe-filled worship to his majestic name. So *How dare you turn my Father's house into a market!* (16). 'Instead of solemn dignity and the murmur of prayer there is the

[18] *Cf.* Mt. 14:13–21 with 15:29–39; Mk. 6:30–44 with 8:1–13.

[19] *Cf.* Mk. 14:1–11 with Lk. 7:36–50.

[20] The actual temple tax was paid in Tyrian shekels, used because of the high purity of their silver. The money changers charged a percentage for their service.

bellowing of cattle and the bleating of sheep. Instead of brokenness and contrition, holy adoration and prolonged petition, there is noisy commerce.'[21]

Jesus' response is, by any account, a physically violent one. Whether or not he actually struck any specific person or animal, verses 14–16 convey an ineffaceable picture of sustained physical threat. 'Gentle Jesus, meek and mild' is nowhere more inaccurate and unhistorical than here. Among the many epithets which might with justice be applied to Jesus, this incident makes it abundantly clear that 'mild' is not one of them; not ever!

Jesus is driven at this point by a burning, all-consuming zeal for the honour of his Father, and so awakens a recollection of the words of Psalm 69:9 in the minds of the astonished disciples (17). For Jesus the honour and glory of God are at stake, generally in the quality of the worship offered by his people, and specifically in their behaviour within the sacred precincts associated with his holy presence (18f.). The temple authorities, incensed by his action, demand to know his authorization (18). Significantly there is no hint of the slightest readiness to face Jesus' charge of dishonouring God by their temple commerce. Rather than 'proof' in terms of the fundamental moral congruence of Jesus' action with the holy character of God, they request tangible supernatural attestation in a miracle (18). It is a demand for the visible at the expense of the ethical.

Jesus' reply is suitably enigmatic. He offers them a visible attestation, albeit a somewhat puzzling one from their perspective. *Destroy this temple, and I will raise it again in three days* (19). *This temple* is deliberately ambiguous; referring either to a shrine for worship or to the shrine of God's dwelling place within a human person or body. The saying is parallel to words recorded in Matthew 12:38–40, 'no sign shall be given to it [this generation] except the sign of the prophet Jonah. For as Jonah was three days and three nights in the belly of [a huge fish], so will the Son of man be three days and three nights in the heart of the earth' (RSV). Jesus thus predicts his destruction at the hands of the Jewish authorities, and his glorious resurrection, the great sign which will authenticate both his claims and this specific action.

More generally, Jesus is looking beyond the age of temple worship (4:21–24) to the time when worship will be offered in the Holy Spirit on the basis of the sacrificial death of the Lamb of God, who is prefigured in the Passover victims which he had just evicted from the temple. He is claiming nothing less than the reconstituting of the entire worship of God's people around his

[21] D. A. Carson, *John*, p. 179.

own person and mission. The temple will pass into oblivion, not only because it is physically razed, but because it is spiritually obsolete. Jesus' body, offered up in sacrifice and raised up in power, will be the new temple where God and humanity, creator and creature, meet face to face. 'The action of Jesus is more than an example of prophetic protest against corrupt religion: it is a sign of the end of all religion.'[22]

The reference to *the miraculous signs he was doing* (23) anticipates the editorial comment at 20:31. John is selective, in the interests of bringing his readers to faith. We do not need to be given details of every sign or wonder Jesus performed, since a 'faith' based merely on these is ultimately inadequate. There is a deliberate parallel in the Greek construction here – the same verb is used for *believe* (23) and *entrust* (24); so perhaps it is better to read, 'they trusted in his name but he did not entrust himself to them'.[23] Jesus of all people will not be misled by outward professions of loyalty which do not involve true repentance and heart commitment. The claim to this knowledge of the human heart echoes Jeremiah 17:10, and is an implicit indicator of deity.

The 'cleansing of the temple' carries far-reaching implications for our understanding both of Jesus' mission and of the implications of becoming his disciples. As to the former, Jesus' action was an audacious one. There are echoes of Malachi 3 where, following the preparatory ministry of the forerunner ('See, I will send my messenger, who will prepare the way before me'; 1), the Messiah abruptly appears. ' "Then suddenly the Lord you are seeking will come to his temple; the messenger of the covenant, whom you desire, will come," says the Lord Almighty. But who can endure the day of his coming? Who can stand when he appears? For he will be like a refiner's fire' (1–2). Significantly, this refining action is related to the service of the Levites, who were especially concerned with the temple worship. More generally it is referred to those guilty of fraud and injustice (5).

For Jesus, worship is a matter of the gravest importance and as the messianic King he claims lordship over it. A significant proportion of the Bible is devoted to the regulation of worship and we are sadly misled if we imagine that the quality of what we offer in worship services, or the devotion with which we participate, are matters of peripheral importance. If 'Jesus is Lord', he claims the temple as a primary sphere of his rule. Modern-day worship which is irreverent, superficial, distraction-filled, cold, lifeless, sloppy, self-indulgent, hypocritical, ill-prepared or theologically inappropriate will likewise receive his censure, as will worship which

[22] L. Newbigin, p. 33.   [23] D. A. Carson, *John*, p. 184.

detracts from the honour and glory of the living God through a concern for performance and self-display on the part of those leading it. 'Judgment must begin at the House of God' (1 Pet. 4:17, my translation).

There is also a significant unveiling of the motivation of Jesus in his mission and ministry in this event. The yearning of his heart which explodes in this violent confrontation, is fuelled by his zeal for his Father's honour, an honour which he sees compromised by what was taking place in the temple. This motivation will surface again at later points (4:32, 34; 12:28; 17:4–5). Jesus' entire ministry is encapsulated in this incident, in its revelation of his awareness of unqualified personal identity with the Father, and a corresponding all-consuming sense of responsibility for his Father's honour in the world. Further, since dark forces are despoiling the Father's glory among his people, the incident embodies an uncalculating commitment to confront these powers, no matter the personal cost. This event represents a Judaean version of the Lukan account of Jesus in the synagogue in Nazareth at the outset of his later Galilean ministry (Lk. 4:13–21), where he states the content of his ministry in terms of Isaiah 61:1–2, the so-called 'Nazareth Manifesto'. The cleansing of the temple in Jerusalem has similar programmatic implications, as the succeeding chapters will indicate.

Jesus' motivation here has far-reaching significance for disciples then and now. A concern for God's honour will make us better (and more critical) worshippers, as we saw above. It will also promote a zeal for world-wide evangelism, for if all people are made in God's image for his glory (Gn. 1:26f.), then it is profoundly dishonouring to God that the great mass of them do not acknowledge him, or live in a manner which accords with his loving will. The temples of so many lives, which were created for the sole worship of God, are polluted by the idols of sin and evil and all manner of false notions about God. If to any degree we share Jesus' concern for God's glory, that fact should 'greatly distress' us, as it did Paul in Athens when he saw the city 'full of idols' (Acts 17:16). The Psalmist reflects a similar disturbance – 'Streams of tears flow from my eyes, for your law is not obeyed' (Ps. 119:136). As he saw, God's honour is diminished in the world by ungodly life-styles. 'I could not endure existence if Jesus were not glorified,' wrote Henry Martyn in his diary more than a century ago, and that concern drove him to invest his life in sacrificial missionary service in the Muslim world. It is a serious question whether the church in the western world has become so encased in the cocoon of material self-indulgence that the honour of God's name among the nations has become a matter of indifference, with the result that the burning, 'violent' zeal of Jesus, Paul, the Psalmist, or

Henry Martyn strike us as something of an embarrassment.

Jesus' action also demonstrates the need to confront evil, taking initiative to dispel the forces which dishonour God in human life at every level.

The much-quoted maxim attributed to Edmund Burke – 'the only thing necessary for the triumph of evil in the world is for good men to do nothing' – is to the point here. Jesus did not sit back and wait for a heavenly intervention. He took the initiative himself, just as later he would take the initiative in going to Jerusalem for the last time to confront the powers of darkness and to cast out their prince (12:31).

How far may such initiatives go? This passage has been frequently used as evidence of Jesus' support for the use of physical and military force to liberate the victims of oppressive political structures. Is Christ here the prototype of the political revolutionary or the 'freedom fighter' of modern liberation movements? Jesus' attitude to political agitation and revolutionary action has been much debated. The evidence that he endorsed such has simply not been shown from the gospels. It is true that at least one of his disciples was a zealot and, at least prior to following Jesus, belonged to the group in the Palestinian state dedicated to the violent overthrow of the Roman power. Some of Jesus' disciples owned and carried swords (Lk. 22:28; Jn. 18:10). Jesus was executed for claiming to oppose the Roman authority (19:12). The name 'zealot' comes from 'zeal', the term used here (17), in the course of an action which can certainly be interpreted as the work of a violent agitator.

All these points, however, need to be balanced. The disciples also included a tax collector whose job embodied and popularly symbolized a collaborationist position. Jesus disavowed the use of the sword.[24] The evidence supports the view that Jesus' real 'crime' was his claim to divinity and its implications. The political charges were trumped up by the Jewish leaders in order to win Pilate's approval for the execution. Further, Jesus' teaching is at points very clearly at odds with policies of violent revolution.[25] He taught and embodied the way of love and forgiveness (Mt. 5:44), and promised blessing on the peacemakers (Mt. 5:9). His temptation in the wilderness can be interpreted as, among other things, his rejection of the zealot option (Lk. 4:5f.). His kingdom, he tells Pilate, is not from this world, hence he deliberately did not, in military terms, mobilize his disciples (18:36).

If the gospel material does not lend support to violent revolutionary action, however, it equally does not underwrite a social and political quietism in face of forces which, in many parts of the world, desecrate and enslave human life. The disciple of Jesus who shares his zeal for God's honour in the world will necessarily be concerned about the plight of the poor world-wide, the oppression of totalitarian regimes of both right and left, the denial of rights, racial discrimination, the despair of the unemployed and other groups without proper social welfare, the street children of our great cities, the tragic victims of physical and emotional violence and the millions of unborn who are denied the right to life by 'easy' abortion. The list is endless, but disciples of the Jesus of this story will find themselves drawn into social and political initiatives on behalf of such as these, whoever and wherever they may be. The motive will no doubt include their larger good, but as this story makes clear, it can also embrace God's greater glory.

The section concludes with an impressive claim for Jesus: *he knew what was in a man* (25). This century has witnessed the dominance of Alexander Pope's maxim, 'the proper study of mankind is man'. In addition to the acceleration of the scientific analysis, in chemical and physical terms, of the human species, our time has also witnessed the emergence and burgeoning of the social sciences. Today, as never in our history, 'man/humanity' is under the microscope. Strikingly, for all our accumulated knowledge of ourselves, we have experienced an even deeper sense of alienation. Human personhood remains in many respects as great an enigma as it was to our primitive ancestors. The modern enigma is memorably captured by a contemporary writer:

This is my dilemma: I am dust and ashes; frail, wayward, a set of predetermined behavioral responses, riddled with fears, beset with needs, the quintessence of dust, and unto dust I shall return.

But there is something else in me. Dust I may be, but troubled dust. Dust that dreams. Dust that has strange premonitions of transfiguration, of a glory in store, a destiny prepared, an inheritance that will one day be my own. So my life is stretched out in a painful dialectic between ashes and glory, between weakness and transfiguration. I am a rebel to myself, an exasperating enigma, this strange duality of dust and glory.[26]

While these observations are not intended to dismiss the celebrated achievements of modern anthropology, John's claim that Jesus knows 'what is in' us demands attention and respect. What does Jesus teach us about the human person? At least two basic truths: the first is that we are morally flawed. His knowledge of

[26] Richard Holloway, cited in R. Chandler, *Understanding the New Age* (Word, 1989), p. 305.

us leads to his refusal to *commit himself* to us (24). We pollute God's temple; we refuse him true worship; he cannot trust us (*cf.* Lk. 11:13 'though you are evil'; Mk. 7:20f.). It was this estimate of us which took him to the cross to die for our sins. Only through his travelling that terrible road can we be saved.

The second basic truth Jesus teaches is that we are nonetheless infinitely valuable. Jesus' action in this incident was motivated not only by a zeal for his Father's glory, but also by a deep concern for his people and the renewal of their worship. It is this concern which would lead him to the establishment of a new worship in his risen body in anticipation of that time when worship is expressed in a new world where the temple is replaced by the Lord and the Lamb (Rev. 21:22; 22:6).

3. Conversation with Nicodemus (3:1–21)

The two incidents recorded in John 2 clarified the terms of Jesus' relationship to Israel's religious heritage: he brings the wine of the kingdom to the water of Judaism, and as the crucified and risen One he re-establishes and renews its worship. In the next section, containing the first of his extended discourses, he dialogues with one of Israel's teachers, clarifying the radical nature of the kingdom he is inaugurating. John 2 ended with an exposure of the inadequacy of a 'faith' based simply on miraculous signs (2:22f.). Nicodemus may be seen as a representative of this class of superficial respondents (*cf.* his reference to *miraculous signs* in his opening comment, 2:2). Note that, in interpreting this section, it is helpful to bear in mind John's stated aim (20:31) to teach his readers about Jesus and lead them to true faith in him.

Nicodemus comes with the best of credentials, a member of the Sanhedrin, a Pharisee (and therefore a zealot for the law and pure religion (1)) and a highly regarded teacher in Israel (10). His coming by night (2) may have been occasioned by the difficulty of finding time to talk with Jesus during the day. There may well have been an element of furtiveness, however, in his approach. Jesus was not likely to have been the kind of company he would be expected to keep. Nicodemus' approach, while not without some warmth (*cf.* 'Rabbi', a generous note since Jesus had not gone the official route to obtain accreditation as a teacher), is also somewhat patronizing (*cf. we know* – 'this is how we have judged your ministry to date').

Whatever the precise terms of his approach, Nicodemus is immediately rocked back on his heels by Jesus' rejoinder which unceremoniously exposes his spiritual need. *I tell you the truth* (Gk. *amēn, amēn;* cf. comments on 1:51), *no-one can see the kingdom of God unless he is born again.* The Greek word *anōthen*, here translated *again*, can also be rendered 'from above'. If rendered *again*, the emphasis is on the nature of the experience of entry into the kingdom (*born again*; 'it is a crisis akin to physical birth'). If rendered 'from above', the emphasis is on the origin of the experience. It is from the heavenly order, *i.e.* an essentially supernatural experience. 'Kingdom of God',[27] also rendered as 'kingdom of heaven',[28] is at the heart of Jesus' teaching as recorded in the gospels, 'In the thought of the kingdom of God Jesus lives, and works and dies.'[29] John's preferred category is 'eternal life', or 'life', which is a synonym for 'kingdom of God'. Literally it translates a phrase 'life of the age (to come)', *i.e.* the coming era when God would manifestly be king over Israel and the nations. 'Salvation' is another New Testament equivalent.[30]

As a devout and well-taught Jew, Nicodemus anticipated the arrival of the kingdom at the end of history. The uniqueness of Jesus' message and mission, which took Jews like Nicodemus completely by surprise, was the fact that with the arrival of the Messiah, the kingdom (eternal life) was *inaugurated but not consummated*. Thus there ensues an unexpected 'period between', when the kingdom has been established (eternal life is truly received), and yet the full realization of the kingdom (the full possession of eternal life) has still to take place. This 'period between' covers the lifetime of John's first-century readers and of those who read his gospel today, the period in which John seeks to 'do the work of an evangelist' by revealing the glory of Jesus and eliciting from his readers a faith-commitment to him (20:31), a commitment which will mean entry to the kingdom (receiving eternal life).

Jesus' statement in verse 3 of the terms of entry into the kingdom represented a further and even more shocking surprise as far as Nicodemus was concerned. As a devout, orthodox Jew he presumed that his place in the coming kingdom was assured, by virtue of his race and circumcision. Besides that, he was a leading religious professional, and moreover, a Pharisee and a member of the ruling council. There could be few Jews, if any, in the entire city that night whose credentials were more impressive as far as acceptance with God was concerned. Yet, Jesus tells him he needs to be *born again* (*anōthen*).[31]

In his response to this unexpected allegation (4), Nicodemus

[27] Verse 3, also 18:33; *cf.* 1:49; 19:14f.
[28] Especially in Matthew, *e.g.* 5:3; 13:11; 18:3.
[29] A. M. Hunter, *Introducing New Testament Theology* (SCM, 1957), p. 13.
[30] *Cf.* Lk. 19:9; Acts 16:30f.; 1 Tim. 2:3–4; *etc.*
[31] *Cf.* references to new birth; Tit. 3:5; 1 Pet. 1:3, 23; 2:2; 1 Jn. 2:29; 3:9; 4:7; 5:1, 18.

understands Jesus' words as implying a 'second birth', and that another physical one, with consequent absurdity. Jesus offers two helps to clarification, one biblical and the other meteorological (5–7). The former is a saying of much disputed interpretation, *no-one can enter the kingdom of God unless he is born of water and the Spirit* (5). In eliciting Jesus' meaning here, much depends on the historical context. His surprise at Nicodemus' difficulty with the concept of new birth (10) is the key to correct interpretation. Jesus obviously thinks Nicodemus has knowledge he should be drawing upon to understand the new birth, a clear pointer to Nicodemus' area of expertise, *viz.* the Old Testament, *cf. are you the teacher of Israel and you do not understand . . .* (10). (The 'the' in the original Greek may imply that Nicodemus was the leading theologian of his day). A clear Old Testament reference to a birth associated with water and Spirit is Ezekiel 36:25–27, which refers to the new order of the messianic age in which there will be a new experience of cleansing. There it states, 'I will sprinkle clean *water* on you, and you will be clean', as well as an experience of the Spirit, 'I will put my Spirit in you and move you to follow my decrees'. Jesus is therefore informing Nicodemus that this new day of cleansing and power anticipated by the prophet is now to hand, the long-awaited messianic age is now present. (By implication this is because the King, the Messiah – Jesus himself – is now present.) For entry to this kingdom, racial inheritance, circumcision, energetic law-keeping, acts of piety or scriptural knowledge, avail nothing. What is needed is the receiving of a new spiritual life from God (*cf.* 1:12–14) through personal faith in Jesus himself as the one who had come from God (3:14f.), and was to be *lifted up* as the object of faith. Significantly John the Baptist had also spoken of an experience of the Spirit in association with an act of cleansing (*cf.* Mt. 3:11). Jesus responds to Nicodemus' superior *we* of verse 2 with a *we* of his own in verse 11. Over against the partial, fluctuating viewpoints of the current Jewish teachers, Jesus sets the eternal truth of God from the lips of one who has seen 'heavenly things' at first hand as the *one who came from heaven* (13).

Jesus' second explanatory aid to Nicodemus is the wind and its essential mysteriousness (8). While today we have better knowledge of its origin and nature, we have no better mastery of its direction. Essentially therefore the new birth is from God; it is supernatural, beyond human control or exhaustive human knowledge. Like the wind, however, and despite its mysteriousness, its effects can be experienced at first hand.

Jesus then resorts to a further vivid Old Testament image to present Nicodemus with the invitation to experience this new life of the kingdom of God. (Since John did not write with quotation marks in his text, however, we cannot be sure where Jesus' words finish and John's editorial exposition begins.) Numbers 21:4–9 records the Israelites escaping physical death from a plague of serpents when they looked trustingly to a giant bronze serpent which Moses raised on a pole in the centre of their encampment. So, says Jesus, the Son of Man himself will be *lifted up*, and all who look trustingly to him will experience the eternal life of the kingdom. The verb *lifted up* is ambiguous – covering both exaltation and crucifixion. John makes much of this ambiguity later in the gospel.[32]

Verse 16 is the best-known and most often preached text in the entire Bible. It is a masterly and moving summary of the gospel, cast in terms of the love of God. The love of God was present (in the prologue) in the allusion to the 'grace' brought by the coming Word (1:14–17) and it is the silent presupposition of the entire ministry of the 'Word made flesh'. All that is so magnificently expounded in these chapters, as the glory of the Son is progressively revealed, is here traced back to its ultimate origin.

The *unfathomable depth* of the love of God is stressed: *God so loved. . . .* In his love, God went so far as to 'give (up)' his *one and only Son* (we should probably see here a reference to incarnation as well as crucifixion). The 'giving up' of Isaac by Abraham may lie in the background as a faint foreshadow of the sacrifice made in the heart of God.[33] If the depth of love is measured by the value of its gift, then God's love could not be greater, for his love-gift is his most precious possession – his only, eternally beloved Son. He could not love more. 'The true looking of faith is placing Christ before one's eyes and beholding in him the heart of God poured out in love.'[34]

The all-inclusive *scope* of God's love is also here. John's readers would have been familiar with the thought of God's special love for Israel, but in truth his love is (and always was) indiscriminate, embracing every man, woman and child. However astonishing this scope, John's primary wonder is probably the gracious embrace of God's love, for its object is *the world*, which John consistently sees as fallen and organized in rebellion against God.[35] It is against the background of the wickedness of the world, even more than its vastness, that God's love shines out most gloriously.

John moves on to the world's response to God's love in the gift of Jesus the Son. In an echo of 1:12, he notes that 'those who receive the Son, that is who believe in his name' (my translation),

[32] *Cf.*8:28; 12:32; *cf.* also Is. 52:13.   [33] *Cf.* Gn. 22, also Rom. 8:32.
[34] J.Calvin, 1, p. 74.
[35] See comment on 1:10

receive the new, endless, supernatural life of the kingdom of God. But this life is not automatic. Where the response is unbelief and rejection, the end result is unutterably solemn (verse 16 uses the word *perish*) a fate about which John will have more to say later in the chapter. This condemnation is not God's specific purpose; rather his purpose is salvation for all through faith in his Son.

The division between those who find *life* and those who *perish* is expanded in the following verses in terms of the vivid contrast between light and darkness. Jesus came as *light* (19). This picks up on the prologue[36] with its reference to the light-bringing ministry of the Word. The coming of the light forces a choice on every person (*cf.* Gn. 1:4). Darkness already reigns; the need of the world is a reality before the light comes. Indeed, as we have seen, it is precisely in his response to the darkness that God's love is so wonderfully expressed. In other biblical terms, 'all have sinned' (Rom. 3:23) and 'sin reigned' (Rom. 5:21).[37] The appearance of the light therefore precipitates a crisis. Tragically, in an astonishing act of self-destruction, multitudes refuse the light and continue to embrace the darkness; the supreme expression surely of the 'mystery of iniquity' (2 Thes. 2:7, AV). John, however, offers a certain rationale. The hatred of the light in the fallen human heart is fathered by a revulsion against being exposed by the light – *Everyone who does evil ... will not come into the light for fear that his deeds will be exposed* (20). By contrast, whoever 'lives by the truth' (lit. 'does the truth') is willing to have his deeds exposed, not to parade his own righteousness, but to allow Jesus, who is the light, to 'do the truth' through him (21).

To summarize:

1. In their essential moral lives prior to the hearing of the gospel, all people live in 'darkness'.

2. Believers are willing to open their lives to God's scrutiny, to 'come to the light'. This is painful, but a necessary preliminary step to finding salvation.

3. This 'coming to the light' leads, in the larger terms of verses 14–16, to 'believing in the Son', and in his sacrifice for our sins.

4. After 'coming to the light', believers live a new life expressing new moral power, but their 'open secret' is that the Light has now come and is the real, 'plainly' recognized source of this new life of 'doing the truth'. Believers live, therefore, as they are saved, by grace alone.

5. In contrast, by refusing the light of Christ, unbelievers face

---

[36] 1:4; *cf.* 8:12; ch. 9 *passim*.

[37] See Rom. 1:16 – 7:25 for an alternative exposition of the darkness/light theme using the broader categories of sin/grace.

the deepening of the condemnation already hanging over them because of their sinful lives.

6. Condemnation of unbelievers is not God's ultimate purpose, or by implication his pleasure, but is the solemn, negative result of the light coming into the world.

The dialogue with Nicodemus is a crucial section of the whole Bible, since it expresses most clearly the truth of regeneration by the Holy Spirit; the fact that it is by the secret, powerful operation of God the Spirit alone that one can experience salvation. *You must be born again.* In our interpretation we have shown that this teaching is anticipated in the Old Testament.[38] It is taught elsewhere in the New Testament,[39] and is also congruent with other New Testament images for salvation – entering the kingdom of God, believing in Christ, receiving eternal life, and the like. The specific contribution which regeneration by the Spirit makes to our understanding of salvation is in its stress on salvation as a supernatural work of God involving a radical change of nature. Only God can save. At a time when 'religion' is again generally in vogue, with ancient world faiths experiencing some resurgence, and new brands such as New Age appearing on the market, the idea that religion cannot save is as startling in our ears today as it was to the ears of religious Nicodemus. To experience God's salvation 'is not simply a matter of illumination; it is a matter of regeneration. It is not just new seeing, but new being'.[40] *You must be born again.*

This truth of new birth has far-reaching implications for those engaged in evangelism, for it teaches us that becoming a Christian is always a miracle. The Christian witness therefore will inevitably be a person of prayer, and churches which engage in evangelism with integrity will inevitably be prayerful churches, beseeching God for his intervention to enable dead people to be reborn. Salvation is of God, and no advance in Christian evangelistic methodology will ever eliminate or replace this. As truly today as in the first century, the key to effective mission *for* the living God is prayer *to* the living God. Only God can save.

Regeneration also makes clear the radical difference between Christians and non-Christians. We are either one or the other, born again, or dead in sins; we have come to the light, or are still in darkness; we are saved from condemnation, or under condemnation. There is no middle ground. We may not necessarily recall the details of our regeneration. That is not the primary issue, which is that we are now living in constant dependence on Jesus Christ

[38] *Cf.* Is. 32:15–20; 44:3; Ezk. 36:25–27; 39:29; Joel 2:28.
[39] Tit. 3:5; 1 Pet. 1:3, 23; 1 Jn. 2:29; 3:9; 4:7; 5:1, 14, 18.
[40] L. Newbigin, p. 38.

as our living Lord and Saviour and growing in our spiritual life, which is God's ever-renewed gift.

4. John the Baptist and Jesus (3:22–36)

Jesus now embarks on a more general preaching and teaching ministry in the Judean region. His proclamation apparently includes invitation; those responding are baptized (22). Though Jesus is not recorded as performing baptism at later points in his ministry (possibly in order to distinguish his ministry from that of John? *cf.* 4:1–3), he would later endorse it without qualification (Mt. 28:18f.). Practising baptism at this point generally enabled Jesus to express his affirmation of John the Baptist's preparatory ministry, which was continuing (23). More particularly, baptism, especially if by immersion, expressed most fittingly the radical life-change involved in response to Jesus. Further, if our interpretation of 'water and the Spirit' (5) is correct (*viz.* an allusion to Ezk. 36:25–27) then baptism in water was an obvious vehicle to convey entry to the new life of the promised kingdom.

Not surprisingly, with all this varied religious activity going on, controversy broke out, initially between followers of John the Baptist and a particular Jew, but spilling over into a potential rivalry between John and Jesus (26). John is sensitive to the inappropriateness of rivalry and the damage it would do (as is Jesus *cf.* 4:3), and seeks to defuse the situation in four ways.

1. He cites a maxim: *a man can receive only what is given him from heaven* (27). Jesus repeats a form of this to Pilate in 19:11, explaining Pilate's present power over Jesus. God's sovereign rule means that ministers are allocated by him as he pleases and for his purposes.[41]

2. He resumes his earlier stance (28) and refocuses on Jesus. This affirmation of Jesus' unique and pre-eminent role enables John to reaffirm his own position as one *sent ahead* of Jesus as his servant.

3. John uses the vivid image of a wedding to re-express the emotion he feels towards Jesus and his commitment to the task he has been given to do for his Messiah (29). He, like the bridegroom's friend, does not seek pre-eminence – it is not his day! Rather he rejoices at the union of the bridegroom with his chosen bride. The reference to Jesus as a bridegroom has echoes of Old Testament passages depicting Israel as God's bride,[42] and anticipates later New Testament teaching on Jesus as the bridegroom of the church.[43]

---

[41] *Cf.* Ps. 75:6–7; 1 Cor. 4:7.
[42] Is. 62:4–5; Je. 2:2; Ho. 2:16–20.
[43] 2 Cor. 11:2; Eph. 5:25–27; Rev. 21:2, 9; 22:17.

Used of Jesus against this background, it is another clear pointer to his deity (*cf.* Mk. 2:18–20).

4. He states a great principle of ministry. *He must become greater; I must become less* (30). Jesus must advance into the centre of the stage and John must retire to the wings, as the Messiah assumes his rightful rule in his kingdom and the bridegroom takes increasing claim over his bride. Few greater motto texts for ministry have ever been uttered. 'Only a great man can accept his own demise with joy.'[44]

Each of these four points has its relevance when we are tempted to thoughts of jealousy.

Verses 31–36 appear to represent the evangelist's further comments, drawing out the implications of the Baptist's contrast of the two ministries, and expounding more fully the pre-eminence of Christ. This pre-eminence is threefold.

First, Christ's is a pre-eminence of *origin*. Jesus is *from above* (31), *i.e.* from heaven, from the very presence and heart of God. By contrast, John is *from the earth*, a human, derived from a human process of generation. Jesus is therefore over all human ministers and witnesses.

Second, Christ's is a pre-eminence of *word* (32–34). Because Jesus is sent from the very presence of God, *he testifies to what he has seen and heard* (32). The words he speaks are God's words. Because God is truthful and the very expression of truth, so too are the words of the one who has come from him. In further guarantee of this truthfulness, the Spirit of God is given to the Son *without limit* (34), in contrast to the more fitful and spasmodic giving of the Spirit to witnesses and preachers in the Old Testament period.[45] John the Baptist is probably to be included in this Old Testament company. He stands in the line of the prophets, the last and greatest of them all (Mt. 11:11–14). They all passed on God's Word as it has been variously given them. Jesus, however, *is* God's Word come among us.

Third, Christ's is a pre-eminence of *resource* (35). Not only is the Spirit given to Jesus but, because he is the beloved Son of the Father, everything which the Father possesses has been made available to him – *and has placed everything in his hands* (35). It may be in keeping with the movement of thought here to recall that the Baptist, like all ministers and witnesses, must fast and petition for resources.[46] Jesus by contrast has all things immediately at his disposal.

---

[44] R. Fredrikson, p. 90.
[45] *Cf.* comments and passages alluded to at 1:32–33.
[46] *Cf.* Mk. 2:18f.; Lk. 11:1.

Verse 36 is a fitting summary statement to a chapter in which the cruciality of Jesus' mission for human salvation has been expressed. What is at stake in the ministry of the Son is nothing less than the bringing of salvation to the world. Jesus is the one from heaven, come from the loving heart of God to the world to offer salvation to everyone who will believe in him. Believing in him brings eternal life, a rebirth into a new order by the Spirit, the personal reception of the supernatural, endless life of the kingdom of God. Conversely, and there is no third alternative, all who do not come to the Son for this life, but reject him and his salvation, consign themselves to the most terrible of judgments – they *will not see life* (36; cf. 3). Rather they will 'see' the wrath of God.

The wrath of God is a difficult notion to hold together with the love of God, also affirmed in this chapter (16). The place from which to view these divine perfections in their mutual relationship is the cross, to which John will bring us before long. At this point, however, we should note that the Bible in general, and Jesus in particular, take the wrath of God with an awesome seriousness. For Jesus, God's wrath is not the outworking of some impersonal principle of retribution. It is a personal reality. God personally resists those who resist him. Further, God's wrath, unlike our fitful and often uncontrolled emotion, is without sin or error in its exercise. The cleansing of the temple (2:12–17) gives some glimpse of the righteous wrath of him who *comes from heaven* and who *testifies to what he has seen and heard* (31–32, cf. Rev. 19:1–3, where 'the wrath of the Lamb', 6–16, is extolled by the host of heaven). God is not endlessly passive about the presence of evil in his world, or the despite it does to his great glory. If we are regularly able to express wrath in reaction to acts of extreme brutality or injustice, how much more is that felt by him whose love for the brutalized and oppressed is so much more than ours! God is not mocked – 'It is a dreadful thing to fall into the hands of the living God' (Heb. 10:31; Gal. 6:7–8).

Paul in Romans chapter 1 recognizes that the wrath of God is already to be seen at work in his 'giving up' people to the bitter fruit of their evil choices (Rom. 1:24, 26, 28). That, however, is only the faintest foreshadowing of 'the wrath to come'. 'Kiss the Son, lest he be angry and you be destroyed in your way, for his wrath can flare up in a moment. Blessed are all those who take refuge in him' (Ps. 2:12). While we have opportunity we are to embrace the Son by believing in him, beseeching him for his mercy and the new life of his eternal kingdom. While we have opportunity we should urge others to do likewise in response to his great and eternal love, for his wrath is real and is coming.

5. The mission to Samaria (4:1–42)

This next section finds Jesus once again in conversation. The contrast with his partner in chapter 3 could hardly be greater. Nicodemus was a Jewish male, a highly learned teacher, a Pharisee scrupulous in his adherence to all the tenets of the law, and as a member of the Sanhedrin a person of considerable public repute and authority. His new conversation partner by contrast is a Samaritan female, illiterate (necessarily so since women were shut out from educational opportunities), with a lifestyle in flagrant contradiction to the law, and therefore publicly despised and ostracized. Yet, 'both needed Jesus'.[47]

What is also striking about the two dialogues is Jesus' remarkable ability to be 'at home' with each and to present the good news of salvation meaningfully and attractively to them. There are other echoes from chapter 3, in that water is again used to symbolize spiritual blessing, and more generally Jesus appears once more as the fulfiller of Old Testament promises, though a fulfilment which sends the old religious order into a fundamentally new orbit.

Verses 1–3 have already received comment. Competitiveness is not to be tolerated in the service of God, even if that means one leader moving away. So Jesus returns north to Galilee (4), which meant passing through Samaria *en route*. John notes Jesus' physical weariness: 'the Word became flesh' (1:14). Not for the first or last time in his gospel John reminds us that the heights of christological confession are balanced by the realities of human limitation.[48]

Jesus' request (7) invited censure on two accounts – she was a woman, and a Samaritan. Regarding relations with Samaritans, John's editorial comment in verse 9 says it all: *Jews do not associate with Samaritans*. The reasons were historical, dating from the division of the kingdom after the death of Solomon (1 Ki. 12:1–24) and the annexation of the northern territory by the Assyrians in 722–721 BC. The Assyrians resettled the area with foreigners (2 Ki. 17:24–41) which meant a loss of both racial and religious purity from the standpoint of the Judaeans in the south. The religious divide was deepened when the Samaritans (as they came to be called) built their own temple at Mount Gerezim around 400 BC. On the issue of gender prejudice, male Jewish attitudes at the time are reflected in the following rabbinic citations: 'One should not talk with a woman on the street, not even with his own wife, and certainly not with somebody else's wife, because of the gossip of men,' and 'It is forbidden to give a woman any greeting.'

[47] D. A. Carson, *John*, p. 216.
[48] *Cf.* 11:25 with 35; 19:30 with 28.

Jesus' request was a simple and sincere one; he was thirsty (7). Not for the first time Jesus' point of contact with a 'seeker' was a confession of personal need (*cf.* Lk. 5:1–3; 19:5). The living water which Jesus holds out to the woman was a particularly vivid image in an arid country like Palestine. But there are possibly Old Testament themes in the background in addition. Ezekiel 36:25–27 has already been seen to underlie the teaching on the 'new birth' of 'water and Spirit' (3:3, 5). God himself is a 'fountain of living waters' (Je. 2:13; 17:13, RSV), and there are also first-century rabbinic references to show that at times both the law (the Torah) and the Holy Spirit were referred to using this image. The image of 'living water' for Jesus' gift of eternal life continues to strike a chord. Over against the dissatisfying lifestyle of modern hedonistic culture, Jesus still issues his invitation: 'if anyone is thirsty, let him come to me and drink' (see 10–13).

The sheer satisfaction of that living water can rarely have been more authentically stated than in this testimony of Malcolm Muggeridge:

> I may, I suppose, regard myself, or pass for being, a relatively successful man. People occasionally stare at me in the streets – that's fame. I can fairly easily earn enough to qualify for admission to the higher slopes of the Inland Revenue – that's success. Furnished with money and a little fame even the elderly, if they care to, may partake of trendy diversions – that's pleasure. It might happen once in a while that something I said or wrote was sufficiently heeded for me to persuade myself that it represented a serious impact on our time – that's fulfilment. Yet I say to you, and I beg you to believe me, multiply these tiny triumphs by a million, add them all together, and they are nothing – less than nothing, a positive impediment – measured against one draught of that living water Christ offers to the spiritually thirsty, irrespective of who or what they are.[49]

The woman, like Nicodemus (though probably with more excuse), misunderstands Jesus' allusion, however, thinking in merely physical terms of some 'magic' water source which would dispense with the need for laborious drawing (11–12, 15). Jesus' penetrating request that she bring her husband (16) elicits her evasive, but truthful, reply that she had no husband (since the Jewish law did not recognize a common-law arrangement). Serial marriage was not altogether frowned upon, though the rabbis generally taught that three marriages were the maximum allowable. The

---

[49] M. Muggeridge, cited in J. Gladstone, *Living with Style* (Welch, 1986), p. 85.

deeper point is that Jesus brought to her awareness the relational desert in which she was living. His offer of *a spring of water welling up to eternal life* must have appeared wonderfully attractive. The woman, by now 'caught' because of Jesus' obviously supernatural knowledge of her, raises the issue of the Jewish-Samaritan division.

The author recalls similar recourse to the 'religious question' (in this case the relationship between Protestants and Roman Catholics), when presenting the gospel in Ulster. In neither case need this be viewed as deliberately evasive. Faced with the claims of Christ we all, understandably, want some awareness of what following Jesus will imply for our present relationships, particularly so in a religiously polarized community.

Jesus' response (21–24) includes some of his most basic teaching on worship (*cf.* comments below). The Samaritans confined 'Scripture' to the Pentateuch, which gave them no loyalty to the account of David's decision to build a temple for the Lord in Jerusalem (1 Ch. 17:1–15). The Samaritans had a messianic anticipation based on the Pentateuch, so they anticipated the *Taheb* (meaning 'converter'), who, in the terms of Deuteronomy 18:15–18, would be a second Moses, revealing the truth, restoring true belief and renewing true worship. Jesus informs the startled woman that she is speaking with the Promised One in person: *I who speak to you am he* (26). This statement possibly reflects Jesus' divine consciousness (*cf.* Temple's rendering, 'I that am talking to you, I Aм').[50]

While this story sounds deeper notes than the provision of a model for personal evangelism, it would be remiss to omit all comment on that aspect. Jesus has much to teach about sharing our faith. Among the most obvious points to note are these:

1. His *relevance*. The whole conversation is couched in terms which the woman could understand. Even when Jesus attempts to take her beyond present experience by talking about *eternal life*, his teaching is shaped by her experience (so, *living water*), and she is given handles from her experience to help her grasp it.

2. His *humanity* and naturalness. At no point is Jesus 'odd'. The conversation appears to flow easily, despite the major social taboos which Jesus is breaking and the profoundly disparate lifestyles of the participants. Jesus is clearly 'at ease' with her, which frees her to confront her deepest needs.

3. His *knowledge*. He is well aware not only of the woman's lifestyle and background, but also of the finer points of the historic relationship between the Jews and the Samaritans, and so can relate competently to her questions. While clearly supernatural dimensions appear in the story, much of Jesus' knowledge had come

[50] W. Temple, p. 64.

from dedicated study of the Scriptures in his early years and his willingness to acquaint himself with the social and religious history of his people.

4. His moral *integrity* and directness. What Jesus offers her is no 'easy believism'. The effects of the fall in her life are not swept under the carpet. The woman's response to Jesus' invitation was an emotional one, but it was also moral, involving new relationships and a new sensitivity to her behaviour.

5. His *positive presentation*. Although the moral needs of the woman are confronted and the call to repentance is issued, Jesus' presentation is a thoroughly positive and winsome one. He plainly tells the woman what she is offered, *viz.* eternal life, and he takes pains to ensure that she grasps the full terms of it.

6. His *refusal to be side-tracked*. Jesus' goal is clear and he keeps it in sight, *viz.* the woman's putting her faith in him. The question concerning the Jew/Samaritan divide is not dismissed, but neither is it allowed to deflect Jesus.

7. His *compassion* and sensitivity. Through the entire conversation Jesus deals with her as a person in her own right, with her unique history and special longings. She emerges in the account as a credible character with personal dignity – because Jesus treats her as such. Simply put, Jesus loved her and was prepared to breach age-old conventions to reach her. Our failures in evangelism are so often failures in love. Nothing is so guaranteed to draw others to share our *living water* than an awareness that we genuinely care about them. 'People want to know that we care before they care about what we know.'

The disciples' astonishment at Jesus conversing with the woman reflects their conformity to the sexual prejudices of their society; risking the scandal involved in speaking with a woman, especially one like this, was simply not to be tolerated.

The woman *leaving her water jar* as she hurried to share her discovery with her fellow-townsfolk is a nice eye-witness touch (28). Despite her likely unpopularity, due to her questionable character, they are moved to investigate (30). There are no more attractive evangelists than those who have newly discovered Jesus.

Jesus, meanwhile, shares with the disciples some basic realities of his mission. He talks about its essential character (34) as an act of obedience, the doing and completing of all the Father had called him to do. He speaks of the consuming satisfaction of his mission (34). The service of the kingdom is like a food which sustains and fulfils. He observes his mission's urgent opportunity (35–36). As Jesus has just demonstrated in his winning of the Samaritan woman, the time for reaping is at hand. All the generations of preparation within the life of Israel, the witness of seers, prophets, priests and leaders, culminating in the ministry of John the Baptist, have brought the harvest to fruition. The day of reaping is at hand, with its attendant joys.[51] *Four months more and then the harvest* was probably a proverb.[52] Finally, Jesus refers to the necessary partnership of his mission: *One sows and another reaps* (37). Jesus is probably thinking specifically of John the Baptist, who had ministered recently in this area (3:23). His point is that there is a partnership in mission; none is sufficient to him or herself; we need each other; it is the church that can reach the world.

The saying *I sent you* (38) anticipates the disciples' mission, which will be a major theme of chapters 13–17 of the gospel and will find specific focus after the resurrection (*cf.* 20:21; 21:1–23). It also makes the point, however, that the mission of Jesus and that of the disciples are indissolubly linked.

The section concludes with the response of the whole community as they progress from the woman's testimony (*what you said*), to their own living experience (*we have heard for ourselves and . . . know*; 42). Their title for Jesus, *Saviour of the world*, is a great and stirring one. Known in the pagan world of the first century, it was given to various Greek gods, and the emperor in Rome was likewise acclaimed. Philo in North Africa spoke of God as 'Saviour of the universe', and the later chapters of Isaiah clearly enunciate that role for God without actually using the specific words:

> Turn to me and be saved,
> all you ends of the earth;
> for I am God, and there is no other.[53]

On the lips of the Samaritans, however, it has its own special nuance. For centuries they have been told they were shut out from God's mercy, second-class people in the eyes of the Jewish leadership down in Jerusalem. As long as they clung stubbornly to their own tradition and religious credentials, the stigma continued to apply. But now at last the Promised One had come, born of the stock of David, a Jew by race, but one who had also come for them. The excluded were included, the circle of God's purpose embraced them too! Having experienced the inclusive love of Jesus for them despite their disadvantages, it was not a difficult step for the Samaritans to arrive at the conviction that this same love was big enough, wide enough and undiscriminating enough to embrace the whole world.

---

[51] *Cf.* Ps. 126:5–6; Is. 9:3; 55:12.

[52] For biblical references to the motif of harvest in relation to the kingdom of God *cf.* Is. 27:12; Joel 3:13; Mt. 4:19; 7:16–19; 13:24–30; Rev. 14:14–16.

[53] Is. 45:22; *cf.* also Is. 43:3, 11; 63:8–9.

Today we can affirm this as never before through all the long centuries since the Samaritans made their claim. It has become visible in this twentieth century in what Stephen Neill has called the 'unquestionably new fact of our time',[54] the worldwide church of Jesus Christ embracing people from every continent and all the major people groups of the earth. And so we unite our song of thanksgiving with these Samaritans – *this man really is the Saviour of the world.*

In the light of Jesus' teaching in verses 21–24, a final theme for comment is *worship*. In response to the issue of the correct location for worship, Jesus makes a number of points which are timeless in their application.

First, the critical hour (NIV's *time* in verse 21 is literally 'hour') for human worship of God is about to dawn. What is this? 'Hour' in John's gospel consistently means the hour of Jesus' exaltation through death and resurrection.[55] This impending crisis will throw the whole course of human relationship with God into a new dimension, rendering location, whether Jerusalem or Mount Gerezim, an obsolete issue. Jesus here goes a step beyond his statement in 2:19, where the raising of the temple of his body is the 'sign' which authorizes his cleansing of Israel's worship. Here he states clearly that the destroying and raising of his body will in fact lead to the replacing of the temple worship by a new *spirit and truth* worship, based on his sacrifice and living presence.

Second, the revelation given in the Old Testament (22), which has been preserved and cherished by the Jews, *is* valid, and gives a true knowledge of God. Hence, despite their periodic apostasy, the Jews remain the historic vehicle for the coming of God's salvation to the world. Jesus' messianic renewal of worship will therefore be based on the Old Testament revelation and will affirm it while transforming it.

Third (23–24), the time of true worship is now at hand (because by implication Jesus, the Son and Messiah, is now at hand). This is a worship in *spirit and truth*. He is the truth. He receives and dispenses the Spirit to all who believe in him, a dispensing experienced as a second birth. True worship is accordingly the worship offered through the Son and in living faith-union with him by means of the Holy Spirit.

The same conclusion is reached by another route in verse 24. The spiritual nature of God (*God is spirit*), means self-evidently that we cannot relate to God satisfactorily in physical terms. He is invisible and intangible and hence beyond our immediate sense-

---

[54] S. Neill, *A History of Christian Missions* (Pelican, 1964), p. 559.
[55] *Cf.* 7:30; 8:20; 12:23, 27; 13:1; 17:1.

apprehension. For God to be known and focused by us, thus making worship possible, he must take initiative to disclose himself to us. This he has done initially in the Old Testament Scriptures (verse 22, the Jews 'know' whom they are worshipping). But the further and fuller revelation of God is now at hand in the Son who makes the Father known (1:18). Hence, we reach the same conclusion. True and satisfactory worship is worship offered in and through Jesus Christ; only through the truth he embodies, and the Spirit he imparts, can we know God and worship him.

Worship is one of the great preoccupations in the churches today, and sadly a frequent cause of division. This section has something to teach about hindrances to true worship. It is hindered first by *wrong practices*. The woman illustrates this principle. Until her life is put right and its failures addressed, true worship cannot happen for her. This was Israel's error right through the Old Testament period, the assumption that if the externals of worship were in place, God would be satisfied. He was not, and is not today: *cf.* 'Even though you bring me burnt offerings and grain offerings, I will not accept them . . . Away with the noise of your songs! . . . But let justice roll on like a river, righteousness like a never-failing stream!' (Am. 5:22–24).[56] This is not to imply that worship is possible only for perfect people, but God does seek a sincere and humble dependence upon him and a genuine commitment to live in obedience to him. 'The sacrifices of God are a broken spirit; a broken and contrite heart, O God, you will not despise' (Ps. 51:17).

Secondly, worship is hindered by *wrong priorities*. In essence this was the error of the Jews and Samaritans who were locked in conflict over where worship should take place, largely unaware that the long-awaited Messiah, who was sent to renew their entire relationship with God, was at that very time in their midst. It is not difficult to conclude that the church today stands in danger of a similar imbalance. Issues are endlessly debated, such as the type of music to be used in worship. Should hands be raised or kept down? Should one particular form of words be used, or should there be complete spontaneity? And should worship be led by one leader or should many participate? These look suspiciously like the issue raised by the woman in this passage. They are concerned with form rather than content. In fact it is beyond question that true and sincere worship can be and is offered using *each* of the alternatives mentioned above. It is also true that insincere and unworthy worship is offered using *each* of these same alternatives. Decisions about form are often in essence matters of taste and temperament and should be seen as such. One of the implications of the fact that

[56] *Cf.* Am. 4:1–5; Is. 58:2–14.

God is spirit is that no form can ever be made the absolute one. No worship form can, or ever will, meet every need. If it did it would detract from the glory that is God's alone. The true priority is the content of worship, a worship from the heart which truly exalts God.

A third barrier is *wrong perceptions*, particularly about who God is and about our relationship to him. Since God is spirit we can worship him truly only as we bring our worship to the test of his self-revelation in his Word. Worship should therefore be Bible-centred, and at the same time Christ-centred, for he is the heart of the biblical writings, the truth embodied (14:6), and the one through whom the Spirit is given (7:37–39). One clear implication is where worship is not explicitly through Jesus Christ, it falls under our Lord's description of worship of *what you do not know*. If that is said of Samaritan worship which was based, at least in part, on the Old Testament, how much more must it be said of the worship in non-Christian traditions. Only in and through Jesus Christ, the Son who alone is 'at the Father's side', can the Father be truly known and worshipped.

There is finally in these verses a *supreme incentive* to worship. *They are the kind of worshippers . . . the Father seeks* (23), and nothing so encourages our approach to him than to realize this. Our worship, incredible as it may appear in our eyes, matters immensely to him. He gave his only Son to make it possible. 'To you . . . he has said, "Seek my face!" ' (Ps: 27:8 mg.). If we truly believe that, then we shall echo back from full and exultant hearts, 'Your face, Lord, I will seek.'

> We taste thee, O thou living bread,
>   And long to feast upon thee still;
> We drink of thee, the fountain-head,
>   And thirst our souls from thee to fill.
>
> *Bernard of Clairvaux*

6. The second sign – healing the official's son (4:43–54)

The previous section climaxed with the great declaration – Jesus is the 'Saviour of the world' (42). This title foreshadows Jesus' future reception by the Gentile nations (*cf.* 1:12, 'to all who received him . . .'). By contrast, in this following section, John anticipates the coming crisis of the rejection of Jesus by the Jews (*cf.* 1:11, 'his own did not receive him') both in his native Galilee (*cf.* verse 44) and even more so in Jerusalem (5:16).

This story of the healing of the official's son is a pointer to the nature of true faith. It has certain superficial similarities to the healing of the centurion's servant in the synoptic gospels.[57] The differences, however, are marked and clearly relate to a different occasion and miracle. We recall Jesus' stated intention (*cf.* 4:1) to escape from the unworthy rivalries which had developed *vis-à-vis* John the Baptist by returning north to Galilee (43). This he now accomplishes. The welcome he receives is outwardly a warm one (45). Jesus at this point is a 'native son' in Galilee, and his impact in the sophisticated southern city of Jerusalem would be guaranteed to strike a positive note in his fellow northerners, particularly as a number of them had apparently made the trip to the feast at the same time and had witnessed his miracles there (45).

He returns to Cana, the scene of his first 'sign', and is met by a man in great personal anguish. The individual concerned is simply described as *a royal official*, probably on Herod's payroll. His anxiety is a deeply human one: his son is dangerously ill at home in Capernaum, some twenty miles away. Jesus' earlier miracle at Cana is quite probably known to the father and, on the basis of this 'faith' in the supernatural power of Jesus, he beseeches him to come to his home and perform a healing miracle on his boy who was apparently, by this stage, at death's door. Jesus' rejoinder seems at first blush surprisingly brusque: *Unless you people see miraculous signs . . . you will never believe* (48). It is possible, however, to construe this as a challenge to the father to exercise faith in the miraculous power of God operating through Jesus.

If an element of apparent rebuke is present, there is a similarly unpromising response recorded in his reaction to his mother (2:4) and the Syrophoenician woman (Mk. 7:27). As in the other cases cited, the apparent refusal provokes a fuller and more earnest request, *Sir, come down before my child dies* (49). It is not a moment for discussion of the niceties of faith; action is needed! Action follows though in the form of a promise, *You may go. Your son will live* (50). It proves sufficient; the official *took Jesus at his word* (50), and departed forthwith to his home.

The journey would have required a night stop, and so it is not until the following day that he encounters his servants on the way to meet him with the good news that his son has indeed recovered (51). A check as to timing confirms the cure as synchronous with the word spoken by Jesus (52). On the basis of this clear miracle of healing, the official and his household profess faith, presumably that Jesus is the promised Messiah of Israel (53). This second 'sign' thus builds on the first. Jesus' glory is revealed in his mastery of the personal afflictions which threaten human life, as well as of the inanimate forces of nature.

[57] *Cf.* Mt. 8:5–13; Lk. 7:2–10.

The lessons of this passage concern the *meaning of faith*. John has already argued for *the cruciality of faith* for salvation.[58] Here its necessity is again underscored (54) for the operation of Jesus' power. That faith (on the human side) is the crucial ingredient is demonstrated by the fact that the lad, whose desperate need Jesus met, is never at any point in his physical presence. At that point the miracle is parallel to our own situation. Like the boy, we have never physically met Jesus but that does not limit his ability to minister to our needs. Rather, it creates the context in which faith operates.

This story also clarifies *the nature of faith*. Jesus exposes the limits of a 'faith' based merely on miracles and signs. He will not commit himself to those who respond only at that level (48; *cf.* 2:23). True, this level is where many people begin in their relationship to God. 'If you will answer my prayer, give me this thing I am asking for, do this miracle for me, then I will believe in you.' The request may concern the provision of a life-partner, an employment opportunity, the resolution of some conflict, the elimination of the consequences of failure or escape from some acute danger. The list is endless. It says much for the graciousness of the Lord that these 'prayers' are sometimes answered, not nearly as infrequently as verse 48 might lead one to anticipate.

Faith based on signs and miracles must not be mistaken for true faith, however, which is why Jesus does not encourage it. It fails to honour God, since by it he serves us rather than the other way round. We are left with the mistaken notion that we are in a position to dictate terms to him. Miraculous signs and miraculous answers to prayer, such as modelled here, may have a certain value as a starting point, making us aware of God's reality, but they remain sterile unless they lead on to a concern for the Christ to whom they point, and whose glory they signify (2:11). Beyond the miracles we seek the Lord who works them. It is in obeying his commands and trusting his promises (50) that true faith is expressed. Now we have ceased to dictate the terms of our relationship – we exist for him, not he for us. Now we 'believe' (53).

This leads to the third aspect of faith highlighted here, its *development*. There is a notable progression in the official's response to Jesus, from seeking *miraculous signs* (48) to taking *Jesus at his word* (50), to believing (53). Faith is a living thing which grows and develops. While it may have its crisis of final commitment, it also has its period of maturation. Or, using the image of chapter 3, it has its time of gestation before the crisis of birth. It is heartening

[58] *Cf.* 1:12; 3:14–18, 36; 4:41–42.

to observe Jesus' willingness to struggle with the official as his faith grew, even though that meant appearing at first to refuse his heart-felt request.

In a sense something even greater was at stake in this encounter with Jesus than simply the healing of the boy. There was the healing of the father also, a healing of spirit, which, having been obtained, was the means of blessing to his entire family (53). It is *this* final treasure that Jesus seeks and he is prepared to allow us to experience deep affliction in the process of obtaining it. 'It was good for me to be afflicted so that I might learn your decrees' (Ps. 119:71; *cf.* Heb. 12:11).

There is also teaching here with respect to *prayer*. The *passion of prayer* is exemplified by the official. His terrible anxiety drives him to make the long journey to Cana to meet with Jesus. We do not have difficulty identifying with the official at this point. But how little of such passion characterizes our prayers in the normal run of things. Jacob's 'I will not let you go unless you bless me' (Gn. 32:26) is language largely foreign to our intercessions.

This passion led to a dogged *persistence* which is a further mark of true prayer. Jesus taught such in several of his parables (*cf.* Lk. 11:5–12; 18:1–8), and history is replete with examples of those who through patient faith and prayer 'conquered kingdoms, administered justice, and obtained what was promised' (Heb. 11:33).

Here also is the *practicality* of prayer. The man is facing a crisis in his domestic life and he brings it to Jesus. Jesus does not set limits to what we may bring to him. The principle which governs our petitions is the principle of all loving, 'If it concerns you then it concerns me.' 'In *everything*, by prayer' (Phil. 4:6, my italics), includes all the practical needs and struggles of our daily round.

This story, however, also demonstrates in a remarkable way the *power* of prayer, for the request is granted and the son is healed. The supernatural power of God is released in answer to the pleading of this one man, and at that a man of limited understanding. That the healing was physical, as in several of the other 'signs', should not be overlooked (*cf.* 5:8; 9:7). The Creator is well able to renew his creation, as may please him. The latter phrase, however, remains critical for all prayers for healing. That God *can* heal is not in question; whether he will, and if so by what means and over what span of time, are matters for his determining. His power is real; his will is love; his love is wise. But what rich encouragement is here, for so many of the problems we face are not cured by merely human remedies! We need the intervention of God. Nothing less can heal the deadly diseases of the human heart in our generation. But God has not changed. His Son is still the healing Christ. He waits to be entreated.

Finally this paragraph points us again to *Christ himself*. These 'signs' are intended to 'reveal his glory' (2:11). Here we see the utter sufficiency of his grace; for those at a distance, as well as for those nearby; for those who do not seek it for themselves, as well as for those who do; for the needs of the body, as well as for the needs of the spirit; for those who are young, as well as for those who are mature. Christ is enough.

7. The third sign – healing the lame man (5:1–15)

A further healing miracle takes place on the Sabbath and immediately becomes the occasion of an extended dialogue between Jesus and the religious leaders in Jerusalem, a discussion which on their part hardens into a commitment to get rid of him (18). The setting is another 'feast', not named, because presumably there is no special link to be made between the feast in question and the miracle sign to be recounted. A pool with the requisite five colonnades, and located in the north quarter of the old city, has been confidently identified by archaeologists as the pool in question, a salutary reminder that we are dealing with history, not idealized legend or mere fable.

The manuscript evidence is poor for verses 3b and 4 and they should be omitted (as in NIV). Later copyists apparently thought it would be helpful to the reader to explain why the sick gathered there. That the pool was fed by some natural spring which had spa-like healing properties is perfectly credible. The popular explanation invoked the visitation of an angel (*cf.* NIV footnote *b*), and added (7) that the first into the water when it was disturbed by the spring would receive some physical benefit.

We are not told what brought Jesus to the pool, nor even, more tantalizingly, what drew him to this one invalid out of the many present. What is particularly notable about the man is that his need was a long-standing one. He had been paralyzed, or generally unable to walk, for no less than thirty-eight years. While we need not think of him as having necessarily spent the entire period in that one spot, the picture is nonetheless a sobering one. Here we confront another category of problem, the long, lingering need which reaches back across many years and may even cast a malignant shadow over the entire landscape of our past. The reality of such need is more regularly identified today through the insights of psychology and analysis in relation to personality traits. In a quite basic sense we all suffer to some degree from the hurts and errors of yesterday. In some people's experience, however, the shadow is particularly dark and overwhelming. Like this man by the pool they lie emotionally and relationally paralyzed. From this perspective Jesus' question, *Do you want to get well?* is a penetrating one. 'An eastern beggar often loses a good living by being cured' (Finlay). Cure has its implications, particularly when the need is so long-standing that a whole way of life has been built up around it. Jesus' question needs to be faced by all who would be delivered. Are we ready for the implications, including possibly repenting of sin and expressing a new loyalty to Christ (14)?

The man's reply to Jesus (7) is not particularly encouraging, being in essence a complaint about lacking someone to get him into the pool at the requisite moment. He is still locked up inside his own need and thinking of a 'cure' by the popular means. Nonetheless Jesus extends his healing power to this unattractive character – *Get up! . . . and walk* (8). The verb for *get up* (8, *egeire*) will be used again in the following dialogue for the life-bringing effect of Jesus' call at the last day (28–29); the miracle exemplifies it. But in relation to the nature of the need identified above, the message is clear and gloriously relevant. Jesus can relate to long-standing need.

Jesus' command to take his bed home in witness to the reality of his cure brings conflict with the authorities. The day of the healing was the Sabbath and carrying one's bed was a breach of the law of Sabbath observance. Strictly, there was no contravention of the written commandment (*cf.* Ex. 20:8–11), which was generally interpreted as a prohibition of performing one's daily occupation on the Sabbath. Since the man was not a furniture remover, he could not be accused of 'working' in that sense.

The oral traditions, however, which the Pharisees cherished, amplified the written law into an elaborate jurisprudence which significantly extended its range. With respect to the Sabbath, thirty-nine categories of work were identified which breached the Sabbath law. These included carrying anything, except in cases of compassion. Lesslie Newbigin's observation helps us appreciate the vehemence of their reaction: 'The law of the sabbatical rest was perhaps the most important of all the bulwarks by which Judaism was protected from erosion by the encompassing paganism.'[59] In practice the letter of the law had come to dominate its spirit. Outward conformity replaced heart commitment. They lost sight of the ultimate purpose of the law, its modelling a life which pleased God and witnessed to his gracious choice of Israel. The law became an end in itself. It is notable that when *the Jews* (10) confront the man, they do not show any interest in the wonder of his recovery with all its implications for his future lifestyle, nor do they appear in the least open to the significance of his healing as a pointer to who Jesus was.

[59] L. Newbigin, p. 64.

The man's personal limitations are reflected in his unawareness of who has healed him. In his ignorance he represents the great mass of our race who do not acknowledge or worship God and yet daily receive his benefits of health and strength, the providential ordering of the universe, the protection afforded by the 'order' of human society, as well as the daily restraining of the full potential of evil in the world and the full effects of the fall in personal life, to say nothing of the patience with which God delays the day of his just judgments (2 Pet. 3:1f.). When Jesus meets the man again, possibly at some time removed from the healing, he warns him of the need to respond to the grace of God in his life by repenting of his sin, lest he face a worse fate. This *something worse* is most probably a reference to the coming last judgment (*cf.* Lk. 12:4f.; 13:1–5). The link between sickness and sin was clearly established in the popular mind, as it commonly is today. Jesus confronts it again in chapter 9, which records his encounter with the man blind from birth, and where he disavows any universal law of cause and effect. Sickness in individual cases is not invariably linked to sin, though it *may* be the cause of it, and in this case it was.

Whether the man retained any degree of gratitude to Jesus is impossible to assess. He certainly wastes no time in informing the authorities of the identity of his mysterious benefactor, the instigator of his Sabbath-breaking. The man does not appear in a good light in this story, either before or after his healing, a timely reminder that physical healing in itself is no guarantee of spiritual healing. Being freed from our affliction may not lead to a godlier or better life. It is a further indicator that God's gifts are finally *grace* gifts, *i.e.* they are shared with the unworthy. This man does nothing to 'earn' his cure, but God does not require such, particularly in the dispensing of his supreme gift of eternal life. Precisely this is the glory of his gift; it is for sinners, not saints; it is for us all.

Identified as a Sabbath-breaker, Jesus becomes the object of a more focused antagonism. The authorities begin to move to 'persecute' (16) and 'kill' him (18). This hardening of attitude is due to the claim Jesus makes in defence of his 'liberal' approach to the Sabbath (17) — 'My Father is always at his work to this very day, and I, too, am working' (17). This saying marks the first major occasion in the gospel where Jesus' claim to a unique relationship to 'the Father' surfaces in the text. It is therefore an appropriate point to recognize that the 'Father' image is suffering a degree of eclipse in much contemporary Christian consciousness.

There are at least three contributory reasons for this eclipse:

1. 'Father' is a gender word which puts it under suspicion with those seeking a less sexist formulation of Christian faith.

2. The experience of fatherhood has been a poor one for many people. Their fathers were abusive, or alcoholic, or left the family through divorce, or were largely absent through workaholism or the sheer demands of career; so its associations are not especially positive or helpful.

3. Those whose faith is largely shaped by a vital personal experience of Jesus, and the living ministry of the Holy Spirit, although orthodox Trinitarians in their theological convictions, often find little place in devotion or practice for 'the God and Father of our Lord Jesus Christ' (1 Pet. 1:3).

The loss of the 'father' image is a serious one. Certainly sexism needs to be addressed, and the feminine qualities of God as taught in Scripture recognized, but not to the degree of jettisoning the fundamental categories of biblical revelation. Certainly 'father' has negative resonances in some people's experience, but that is not in itself an argument for discarding this image, which is sanctioned by the experience and language of the Son of God. Rather it is an argument for recovering the image in its pure and perfect form. Our fundamental human need for a true 'fathering' is answered finally, and precisely, by our relationship with the only perfect Father, from whom all other fatherhood derives (Eph. 3:15 mg.). Certainly, as this gospel so clearly teaches, Jesus Christ must for ever be at the centre of our vision of God, but God is Father as well as Son (and Spirit). To omit the Father in worship and experience can engender a form of Christianity which is weak on the providence and sovereignty of God, has limited engagement with the responsibilities of Christian citizenship, and lacks a mature historical perspective. Against this background, John's gospel, with its pervasive 'Father – Son' language, can serve both as a relevant model of true parenting, and also as a timely summons to rehabilitate this great God-given image.

Notably at this point Jesus does not challenge their rabbinic extensions of the letter of Old Testament law as he did, for example, in the Sermon on the Mount (cf. Mt. 5:21–48). That ground was available to him in this controversy, but he reaches beyond it to remind them that God himself goes beyond the letter of the Sabbath law in working to constantly sustain the world, and in acting with grace towards needy people on the Sabbath; a truth which in general the rabbis conceded. Jesus is asserting that his 'work' of healing, which led to a breach of their oral tradition, was a work of mercy which imitated the gracious Sabbath work of God. Implicit in the claim is a self-consciousness of the most audacious and revolutionary kind. Jesus is claiming a unique identity with the Father, a fact not lost on his hearers (18), which provokes their hardening commitment to eliminate him.

97

8. Sabbath controversies and testimonies (5:16–47)

a. Sabbath controversies (5:16–30)

In this section Jesus further clarifies his special relationship to the Father and expounds some of its implications. His claims are astonishing in their range and carry corresponding challenges to the mind and heart. He has defended his Sabbath healing by appealing to the identity of his work with the work of the Father (17). In response, the Jews have accused Jesus of the blasphemy of claiming equality with God in the sense of setting himself up in rivalry to God (18). It was the lure of just such a rivaling equality which was the occasion of the fall (Gn. 3:5). If that were in Jesus' mind, the Jews have the best grounds for their accusation. But Jesus is not claiming 'equality with God' in the sense of being a second rival deity. Rather it is an equality expressed as a unity in which the Son is so utterly submitted to the Father that the two are one in the works that they do; *the Son can do nothing by himself* (19). Jesus places no limit on his dependence on the Father. 'The Father is God sending and commanding, the Son is God sent and obedient.'[60]

Put another way, we are not concerned here with a bare monotheism but with a rich Trinitarianism.[61] This unique *inter-relationship* of revealing and imitating (19) is rooted in the mutual love of Father and Son. Thus the revelation of God in the Son is finally grounded, not only in the love of God for the world (3:16) – a love which moves the Father to impart himself to sinners, but also in the eternal love of the Father for the Son – a love which moves the Father to reveal his deeds to the Son. *The Father loves the Son and shows him all he does* (20). This is holy ground indeed.

Such a christology of personal subordination does not imply any reduction of being on the Son's part, since he who does what the Father alone can do is also divine. The divine prerogatives of the Son are expounded in the following verses. Jesus refers to them as *greater things* (20), and so they are in comparison with the healing miracle at the pool, though they also stand in some relationship to it.

1. *The Son will raise the dead* at the end of the age (21, 25, 28f.). Typically this is a work in which the Father also shares (21). The same verb as appears in verse 8 with respect to the lame man is used for this eschatological 'raising' in verses 28–29. The power of

[60] C. K. Barrett, p. 468.
[61] *Cf.* also the references to the ministry of the Holy Spirit, 14:15–17; 16:5–15; *etc.*

Jesus in bringing life to the 'dead' limbs of the man at the pool is the identical power which will one day call the dead of every generation into life from the power of death. Further, this power is already at work. The voice of the Son is sounding in the world; 'whoever hears my word and believes him who sent me has eternal life and will not be condemned; he has crossed over from death to life' (24). The resurrection life which the Son will confer at the end of time is already imparted here and now to those who respond to the voice of the Son. This amazing claim of Jesus will be vindicated in the raising of Lazarus in chapter 11.

2. *The Son will be the judge of all people* at the end of the age (22, 27, 29–30). This is another supreme prerogative of deity. As creator, God holds all his creatures accountable to him; he is by definition 'the Judge of all' (Gn. 18:25). Jesus, however, has been appointed to judge (27).

The use of *Son of Man* in this connection is the only instance in the gospel where the title lacks the definite article in the Greek text (verse 27, literally, has simply 'son of man'). Some see here a recognition of Jesus' humanity, since the title can be used of human beings generally. It accordingly affirms his fitness to act as our judge because he had lived our human life. While there may be validity in this interpretation, it should be noted that the seminal use of 'son of man' in Daniel 7:13 also lacks the definite article. It is difficult to believe that this saying in the ears of a Jewish audience, or of someone versed in the Old Testament, would not have had clear overtones of Daniel. This is particularly so since the Son of Man in Daniel 7 appears in the judgment context of the seating of the heavenly court and the opening of the books (Dn. 7:10).

The note of judgment is also struck in the preceding story, as Jesus warns the man who was healed about the moral implications of what has been done for him. 'Stop sinning or something worse may happen to you' (14). The 'something worse' is his standing at the end before the Son of Man, as one who had personally received his healing grace and yet not changed his lifestyle in the light of it. Jesus the Judge will come.

These two functions referred by the Father to Jesus are awesome in their implication and it is impossible to remain neutral in the face of Jesus' claims. In C. S. Lewis' often cited words,

> In the mouth of any speaker who is not God, these words would imply what I can only regard as a silliness and conceit unrivalled by any character in history. . . . You must make your choice. Either this man was, and is, the Son of God; or else a madman or something worse. You can shut him up for a fool, you can

spit at him and kill him as a demon; or you can fall at his feet and call him Lord and God.[62]

Those claiming to have chosen the last-mentioned option to call him Lord and God must face the question: What difference is this making in my life? Since he is the Son who will raise us in the face of the destructive power of death, and since he is the one before whom we shall stand at the great assizes, it is certainly incumbent upon us to pay more than lip-service to the principle he himself embodied with respect to his Father; cf. 19, *whatever the Father does the Son also does*.

b. Testimonies concerning the Son (5:31–47)

Jesus' staggering claims raise acutely the question of his right to make them. He addresses that issue in the concluding paragraph of the chapter. First he disavows a purely personal authority (31). The Son who defers in all things to the Father is not likely to act independently of him in the supremely critical issue of his authority; his teacher is none other than the Father himself (32, 37, 43). The Father's authorizing of the Son is mediated through three channels.

(i) The witness of John the Baptist (5:33–35)[63]

John's testimony was a 'human' one and therefore not of ultimate importance, yet Jesus mentions it *that you may be saved* (34). Jesus reminds the Jews that many of them, and some of their leaders, had been prepared to listen to John and enjoy his *light* (35). Go back there, Jesus is saying. Begin where you were previously ready to make some response. Recall John's message of repentance, and his pointing to me as one who was to come (1:26f.).

Human testimony to Jesus continues to be significant, not least in the form of preaching in which, as with John the Baptist, the call to repentance is articulated and the hearer directed to Christ. One of the great religious portraits on the continent of Europe is Grunewald's 'John the Baptist'. It had a profound impact on Karl Barth, who, not infrequently, referred to it in his writing. The striking feature of the painting is its focus on the pointing index finger of John as he directs attention to Christ on the cross. In that image is captured the classic calling of the preacher, and so understood there can be no greater privilege given to mortals. Thomas Carlyle's comment glows with life in this context – 'Who, having been called to be a preacher, would stoop to be a king?'

[62] C. S. Lewis, *Mere Christianity* (Macmillan, 1952), pp. 55–56.
[63] *Cf.* 1:7,15, 19, 26; 3:27ff.

Who indeed? Charles Wesley caught the mood:

> Happy, if with my latest breath
> I may but gasp His name:
> Preach Him to all, and cry in death,
> "Behold, behold the Lamb!"

Lest we glamorize the preacher's role unduly, however, it is well to recall that the preacher of whom Jesus speaks – John the Baptist – was put to the sword in Herod's dungeon!

Giving witness to Jesus, in the sense of pointing to him, however, is the privilege of every disciple. Statistics prove repeatedly that the most regularly used means for people coming to Christ is the testimony of others who have found him for themselves, thereby modelling D. T. Niles' classical definition of evangelism, 'one beggar telling another beggar where to find bread'.

(ii) The witness of the miracles (5:36)

John prefers to call the miracles 'signs'. These are 'weightier' than John's witness (36), particularly as they encompass Jesus' entire mission, including not only miracles but also his death and resurrection. Indeed, in principle, they embrace the whole unending and world-transforming work of the risen Lord as he moves on through the ages and among the nations, saving, renewing, healing, liberating, inspiring, lifting, comforting and directing all who come to God by him. *The very work that the Father has given me to finish . . . testifies that the Father has sent me* (36).

The witness of the miracles remains a weighty one. Even at the historical level there is great difficulty in giving any explanation for the whole fact of Jesus Christ which is less than the confession articulated at the conclusion of the gospel, 'Lord and God' (20:28). The Father has set his seal of approval to the work of Jesus (36).

(iii) The witness of the Scriptures (5:38–40, 46).

This reference is preceded by an allusion to the Father: 'You have never heard his voice nor seen his form' (37). By implication the unseen God has spoken and disclosed himself in the written Scriptures. Jesus concedes that the Jewish leaders diligently study the sacred writings (39), but their study is unfruitful because the student is not looking for Christ in the Scripture. It is not the Scriptures as such, or mastery of them at the literary level, which will give eternal life (39). The Son alone gives life, but he is met in the Scriptures.

At root, the Jews miss him there because of a prior decision, *you refuse to come to me* (40). The problem in the end is in the will and heart rather than in the mind. That Jesus should speak of the

Old Testament as *the Scriptures that testify about me*, and on that basis condemn the Jews for their conscious rejection of him, is even more pertinent for those who have the additional and fuller witness of the New Testament. How much less excuse have we today if we neglect the clear witness of God's written Word! Correspondingly, how important is the ministry of Bible societies, and other agencies such as the Gideons International, in putting this supreme testimony to Jesus into the hands of the nations! Nor need we be fearful for the Bible in that process. C. H. Spurgeon's retort, when asked how he would defend the Bible, is to the point. 'Defend the Bible? – I'd as soon defend a lion!' The Bible remains 'the cradle of Christ' (Luther).

Jesus concludes with a scathing exposure of the Jewish leaders for their refusal to come to him for the life he offered (42–47). Their fundamental failure lay in esteeming human praise above God's praise (44). Theirs was a religion of human merit, one which seeks salvation through obeying the commandments (39). This explains their paranoic defence of the finer points of the written and oral law, and their conflict with Jesus (16) in the beginning. It was a thoroughly human religious system, permitting no real place for the living God (37) or for considerations of the awful predicament of the human spirit in his presence, engulfed by the destructive power of sin (40). Thus other messianic pretenders would be welcomed whose credentials were purely self-generated (43). They would be accepted because they spoke the same language and sought the same goals. Jesus alone pointed them beyond the merely human to the divine. *I have come in my Father's name* (43). In his person they met the absolute demand of the Almighty, lifting them beyond the relativities of human merit and summoning them to cast themselves on his grace alone. But such concepts were beyond them.

Devastatingly, their chief accuser was the Moses whose name they so revered (45). There is some evidence that many Jews believed that Moses' intercession for the people of God[64] was continued in the heavens, and hence that Moses was their guarantor with God. If so, then Jesus' comment here is the more terrible. Moses their saviour is in fact their accuser and judge, possibly because he had pointed to Jesus (Dt. 18:15), but more probably because the covenant with God born at Mount Sinai is now fulfilled in the new covenant in the Son and his gift of the Spirit (3:1ff.). Those who thought they had most, in fact have least. The Son alone is the way to the Father, but they will not come to him to find life.

[64] Ex. 32:30–32; 33:7–11; 34:34f.

9. The fourth sign – feeding the five thousand (6:1–15)

The time-link to the previous section is vague: *Some time after this* (1). The reference to the Passover in verse 4 gives an indicator of duration. A year has passed since the cleansing of the temple (2:13f.). During this time Jesus has ministered largely in and around Galilee, as described by the other three evangelists. This sixth chapter is the only section of teaching in this gospel which is set in the Galilee region. The Galileans were a distinct type, peasants living close to the soil and labouring hard for a subsistence wage. The primary issues for them are the down-to-earth matters of food and the means of livelihood. This was in contrast to the more sophisticated audiences Jesus had encountered in the south, whose concerns were more theoretical: the fulfilment of scriptural prophecies, wrangling about the law and the theological implications of Jesus' claim.

The feeding of the five thousand is the only 'sign', other than the cross and resurrection, to appear in all four gospels, indicating its importance in the minds of the first Christian witnesses. Like the audiences in the south, the Galileans are also attracted by Jesus' miracles (*cf.* 2:23f.; 4:48).

As the synoptics make clear (*cf.* Mk. 6:31), Jesus is seeking privacy at this point. The disciples have just returned from a highly successful preaching tour and are also in need of rest. Jesus takes them to the hills to the east of the sea of Galilee, the area known today as the Golan Heights. Verse 3 refers to *the* hillside, which may imply an often visited spot.

The crowd get wind of Jesus' whereabouts and follow him round the head of the lake. Jesus is seated among the disciples as they approach. The reference to the Passover (4) is critical for the interpretation of this section. 'The movement from the miracle to the discourse, from Jesus to Moses, and above all from bread to flesh is almost unintelligible unless the reference to the Passover picks up 1:29,35, anticipates 19:36, and governs the whole narrative.'[65] We should also note that the Passover was a great patriotic festival which stirred the Jews' sense of national identity.

Jesus accepts the invasion of his vacation and ministers to the crowd (*cf.* Mk. 6:34). The passing of time raises acutely the question of food and provides Jesus with an opportunity to test the disciples, Philip in particular. He was from nearby Bethsaida and was perhaps the spokesman conveying the disciples' consensus that they had a major problem on their hands. Alternatively, knowing the district better than the others he would be cognizant of the fact that there

[65] E. C. Hoskyns, p. 281.

103

was no local food source to draw upon. Philip thinks only in terms of the immediate reality of limited resources and makes his calculations accordingly. *Eight months' wages* would buy only a morsel all round (7). Over against Philip's gloomy estimate, Jesus remains unperturbed since *he already had in mind what he was going to do* (6).

This comment is capable of the widest application. Our Lord still surveys the needy world with compassion, just as he surveys the micro-world of our personal affairs. He is not without plans. He 'already has in mind what he will do' in our time and generation, and just as surely with the tangled threads of our personal present and future.

Andrew comes into the picture, to somewhat greater effect than Philip, producing *a boy with five small barley loaves and two small fish* (9). The lad has brought a meal with him, the loaves being small rolls or scones, and the fish no more than titbits. John alone mentions the boy in this personal way, a nice eye-witness touch recalling another one in Mark (the 'green' grass, Mk. 6:39), which later detail incidentally confirms the time as around Passover, the only 'green' period of the year in Palestine. Beside the crowd, which with five thousand males alone would probably have totalled at least double that number, such a resource is pitiful in the extreme, as Andrew is not slow to point out (9). But on the basis of this tiny contribution the Master proceeds to make arrangements for a general feeding of the multitude. After thanksgiving the miracle happens. He *distributed . . . as much as they wanted* (11). The multitude is fed, and satisfied too! The word for 'giving thanks' in verse 11 is *eucharistein*, from which 'Eucharist' is derived, a common term for the Lord's Supper. Too much should not be read into that, however, as it is a fairly common word and John uses terms with some freedom.

Jesus commands that the scraps not be wasted and twelve baskets are filled (12f.). Preservation of this kind of leftovers was a Jewish custom. Jesus here, however, gives his dominical support to a concern for conservation which has many points of application today. Whatever the immediate stimulus, Jesus' directive under-writes our revulsion at the destruction of excess food in a hungry world, as at the wastage of human skills and energy in unemployment, and also more general concerns to reduce waste through recycling. It is a sombre comment on our world that it has taken the threat of environmental pollution, and our planet's diminishing ability to sustain life, rather than a moral repugnance at waste in general, to awaken a concern for conservation.

The twelve baskets may be a fortuitous indicator of Jesus' ability to more than meet the needs of his whole people (*cf.* the twelve tribes of Israel), but more generally makes the point that 'after all have been satisfied there is more left over than there was at the beginning'.[66] Jesus' resources are without limit; he can meet all our needs and more.

The sequel to the miracle is significant and anticipates the dialogue which will follow. The crowd, buoyed up in their nationalistic aspirations by the Passover celebration, see in Jesus the fulfilment of Deuteronomy 18:15–19, *Surely this is the Prophet who is to come into the world* (14). While this Old Testament passage anticipates a prophetic figure rather than the messianic King, they immediately cast Jesus in the later role (15). The Passover had been instituted during Israel's wilderness wandering, when God had fed his people supernaturally with manna from heaven. The setting was again a 'wilderness' area, where Moses had spoken of the 'prophet' who would come. Surely this was he, a 'second Moses', their long-awaited deliverer. 'It was the custom of Messianic pretenders in Jesus' time to seek credibility by either re-enacting or matching O.T. miracles.'[67]

Jesus, however, will have none of it and *withdrew again to a mountain by himself* (15). Some manuscripts read 'fled back', which a number of commentators think is probably the original reading, copyists arguably making the change to tone down the embarrassing picture of Jesus in flight. Certainly Jesus' rejection of their attempts to set him at the head of a revolutionary mob is an abrupt and decisive one. We can perhaps detect here an echo of the earlier temptation (*cf.* Mt. 4:8f.) to pursue a political route to his kingdom, or perhaps at a deeper level, a messiahship which would by-pass the cross and leave the dominion of darkness intact. We can recall a similar revulsion at Peter's commendation of just such a course at Caesarea Philippi: *cf.* Matthew 16:23, 'Get behind me, Satan!' The disturbing effect of this experience may be reflected also in Jesus' desire to be alone again with the Father as he 'sends' the disciples away,[68] probably to protect them from the insidious influence of this nationalistic fervour.

The application of the miracle is made in the discourse which follows, where Jesus presents himself as the bread of life, the satisfier of the hunger of the human heart (6:25–59).

At this point, we note how vividly this story expresses the ministry challenge facing the disciples of Christ in our generation. Today, as never before, we are confronted by the crowds. World

---

[66] R. Bultmann, p. 213.

[67] J. R. Michaels, p. 102.

[68] The word used in Matthew and Mark is a very strong one, 'compelled'; *cf.* Mk. 6:45 (my translation).

population levels will explode through the six billion mark by early next century, and the sheer human reality of the needy masses is an everyday fact for ministry, particularly in the teeming cities and mega-cities of the globe. It is therefore significant to note that Christ faces the crowd and makes his disciples face them also (5). We regularly struggle against that. J. H. Bavinck touches something deep in most of our hearts when he writes:

> People wish to remain quiet, in the peaceful little Church under the high Gothic arches; they would brood about God and be preoccupied with the needs of their own souls. They do not want to be shocked by the bewildering idea that there are still many hundreds of millions of people who have never heard the gospel.[69]

But Jesus will not let us brood, he challenges us with the need, both for the 'bread of life' as in Bavinck's quotation, and also for material bread, and every other kind of need that cries out to be met.

Faced with the need, Jesus still asks us individually, and also as church communities, *Where shall we buy bread for these people to eat?* (5). This is a *test* of Philip (6); nor is that accidental. Jesus regularly tests his people. We cannot simply 'amble along' with Jesus, for he is concerned more for our growth than for our comfort. To walk with Jesus means climbing.[70]

Sadly, our response to the Lord's testing is too often the same as Philip's. We measure the need, quantify our inadequate resources, and resign in hopelessness. It is all beyond us; the need cannot be met. Even when, like Andrew, we identify some limited resource, the possibilities are not significantly improved. *How far will they go among so many?* (9). But this assembling of our resources is a key to the divine provision, for Jesus is not discouraged, as we are, by what we have to offer. Indeed, if we will put it into his hands he will still 'give thanks' for it, a wonder in itself. Our instinct is to put ourselves down and demean what we have to give, particularly when measuring it against raw human need. But Christ is thankful for us! And if we will believe sufficiently in his gifting to trust him with our whole selves, he will take us, break us as need be (Mk. 6:41), and offer us to the Father as in his hands the miracle is repeated, the resource multiplied, and a multitude fed.

---

[69] J. H. Bavinck, *An Introduction to the Science of Missions* (Presbyterian and Reformed, 1960), p. 277.

[70] *Cf.* Heb. 12:10: 'God disciplines us for our good, that we may share in his holiness.' *Cf.* Heb. 12:4–12; also 1 Pet. 1:6–7.

The key, beyond our believing in God's ability and will to use us, lies in the wholeheartedness of our surrender to him. William Booth's secret is an open one. Asked to explain the phenomenal impact of his life, he replied, 'For the last eighty years God has had all that there is of William Booth.' Through him Christ fed a multitude.

10. The fifth sign – walking on the water (6:16–24)

Before the miracle of the loaves is discussed, a further 'sign' takes place, which also appears following the feeding miracle in the synoptic gospels (Mt. 14:22–36; Mk. 6:45–52). The disciples are alone in the boat in the darkness when a storm blows up, as was frequently the case on the lake of Galilee. There is a mood of discouragement underlined by John's observation that *it was dark* (17).

Here is discipleship without the discerned presence of the Lord, and, recalling the traditional image of the church as a boat, it is not difficult to make application. In many parts of the world today, particularly in the West, it would be difficult to find a more telling picture of the church. Here is a small handful of people, seemingly remote from the land where most people live their lives, apparently irrelevant to the great issues confronting the world. It is tossed by the winds of secularism without and controversy and uncertainty within, out of touch with its point of departure, unsure of its whereabouts, and with no clear destination ahead. All the while its members, like the disciples in the story, strain at the oars of good works and ministry, making no apparent headway in the process. Crucially, they have no manifest conviction that Jesus, the Head and Lord of the church, is anywhere in sight. 'It is dark.'

Suddenly, Jesus is seen, or at least an approaching figure is observed walking on the waves towards them (19). Some commentators, who have difficulty with the miraculous, think they find a 'let-out' here, as the Greek of verse 19, *walking on the water*, can be rendered 'by the water'. The suggestion is that the boat has never gone far from shore and Jesus appears walking along the shore line to encourage them. The difficulty with that interpretation lies in its complete inability to account for their terror (19). Besides, if this is not a miraculous appearance of Jesus, then it is difficult to see why the incident is included at this point, bearing in mind the theological undertow of the story. The traditional interpretation is much to be preferred, not least because it corresponds to the accounts in the other gospels where the ambiguity in meaning does not arise (*cf.* Mt. 14:24; Mk. 6:47). At first the disciples do not recognize him and are terrified, experienced sailors as they are. Clearly something extraordinary is occurring. The disciples are apparently more afraid of the Saviour than they are of the storm.

There are occasions when Jesus' coming seems only to intensify our troubles. That was to be Peter's experience later as Jesus faced him, painfully, with his failure (21:15ff.). It was Paul's experience when he responded to the call of Christ to go to Macedonia and found himself a bloodied victim in a Roman prison (Acts 16:9 with 24). Christ's coming can divide as well as unite (Mt. 10:34–39); it can bring rejection rather than acceptance (15:18–21).

So Jesus comes to them (19). They have never been out of his sight, even if he may have been out of theirs (Mk 6:48). His commitment is unconditional; the church, whatever its limitations, will never be abandoned. He stills the disciples' fear with his word of greeting, *It is I; don't be afraid* (or, more literally, 'stop being afraid', 20). The words *It is I* translate the Greek *egō eimi*, which in other contexts is the divine self-affirmation so often reproduced in this gospel, 'I am'.[71] The words would of course be natural enough in this context as a means of Jesus' identifying himself. It is difficult, however, to believe that John does not intend us to see more here, particularly if we recall the Passover background. The deliverance of the Israelites from Egypt led to the wilderness wandering and their supernatural sustenance by means of the manna. That wilderness experience, however, was reached by way of the Red Sea and the supreme demonstration of the majesty of God as he parted the waters for his people (Ex. 12–14). Jesus appears here as Lord of the waves and the seas, the personal manifestation of the Almighty who walked upon the waters at the Red Sea. 'The waters saw you, O God, the waters saw you and writhed; ... Your path led through the sea, your way through the mighty waters' (Ps. 77:16,19). A similar passage in Psalm 107 concludes, 'He stilled the storm to a whisper; the waves of the sea were hushed. They were glad when it grew calm, and he guided them to their desired haven' (29–30).

This 'arrival' is apparently a further miracle, for *immediately* on Jesus entering the boat they find themselves at their destination (21). The appropriateness is well caught by Godet:

> One can scarcely imagine, indeed, that after an act of power so magnificent and so kingly as Jesus walking on the waters he should have seated himself in the boat and the voyage have been laboriously continued by the stroke of the oar. At the moment Jesus set foot on the boat he communicated to it the force

[71] *Cf.* 6:35; 8:24, 58; 10:14; 15:1; 18:5.

victorious over gravity and space, which had just been so strikingly displayed in his own person.[72]

So Christ's presence brings renewed hope and power to his dispirited church, and, where needed, to individual lives. The last word does not lie with the world, no matter how threatening its manifestations. Jesus still comes walking upon the waves, and in a recovered experience of his presence, the church, for all its internal failings, may yet sweep upon its way, and at the last be carried by its triumphant Lord on to that 'eternal shore' for which we are destined.

Verses 22–26 relate the surprise of the crowd at not finding Jesus on the east side of the lake where the miracle of the loaves had taken place. Only one boat had made the crossing and Jesus had not been aboard when it set sail, of that they were sure. He plainly was no longer in the vicinity, however, and so they return to Capernaum, his place of residence at this point, to try and find him. They go, the text says, *in search of Jesus* (24), and that helpfully sets the scene for the long discourse which follows in which the mystery of Jesus' person is further explored.

11. Discourse on the bread of life (6:25–71)

This long section contains some of the profoundest teaching in this gospel concerning the significance of Jesus. It has been the centre of considerable debate due to the vividness of Jesus' language, particularly in verses 53–58, where many have detected overtones of the Lord's Supper. In order to expound this section it is useful to divide it into sections. One way of doing this is to follow the indication in verse 59 that this material was shared as Jesus taught in the Capernaum synagogue. We may therefore assume a move into the synagogue somewhere around verse 25, following his return from the lake. The discourse can be seen developing naturally within the synagogue worship where the occasional interchange, such as recorded here, was not unknown. With that didactic setting in mind we propose the following division:

a. The congregation who do not believe (26–29)
b. The preacher who calls for faith (30–35)
c. The congregation who do believe (36–59)
    (i)   Their security (36–40)
    (ii)   Their destiny (41–51)
    (iii) Their identity (52–59)
d. The cost of discipleship (60–71)

[72] F. L. Godet, p. 573.

a. The congregation who do not believe (6:26–29)

Jesus confronts the Galileans with their error. Basically they are materialists (26). Their real interest in Jesus lies in his feeding their bellies, so that they no longer had to work for their food. They are so obsessed with the material world that they are not able to see that the true blessing which God is offering them is not on that level at all. It is the *food that endures to eternal life* (27), the gift of the Son of Man whom God himself has affirmed – *On him God the Father has placed his seal of approval* (27). (This affirmation is a possible allusion to Jesus' baptism, but more probably to the general consciousness of the divine favour to which Jesus repeatedly testifies).

Jesus' confrontation provokes the congregation to ask what it is that God wants them to do (28). Jesus points them to the true food, faith in *the one he has sent* (29). But as 'earthy' Galileans they are still operating with essentially materialistic agendas. They lack any awareness of the higher and deeper needs of the heart. For them God's blessings are a free food supply and a political Messiah who will rid them of their hated Roman overlords. Their concern is with what they can do to help the cause along.

Galileans are still met around Christian congregations today. They are down-to-earth folks who 'don't go in for this Bible study and prayer stuff', or who don't believe in 'taking religion too far'. They are 'practical Christians' who 'live in the real world', and whose motto text is 'God helps those who help themselves'. To all such Jesus says, *The work of God is this: to believe in the one he has sent* (29). At this point Jesus and Paul stand side by side: 'we maintain that a man is justified by faith apart from observing the law' (Rom. 3:28). 'By grace you have been saved, through faith . . . not by works' (Eph. 2:8f.).

b. The preacher who calls for faith (6:30–35)

Jesus' invitation to believe in him is met by a request that he demonstrate his credentials, further evidence of how little they have responded to his truth (30). One might have assumed that the feeding of the crowd was a sufficient confirmatory sign, but apparently not. Possibly some of the congregation were not part of the crowd who had been fed. They cite Moses' sign, the manna from heaven (31), though again Jesus would appear to have amply met such a criterion. Jesus again corrects their misunderstanding. The source of the manna was not Moses but God, his Father, and that God, the God of Moses, was now among them giving them the true bread. This was the one who *comes down from heaven*, Jesus himself (33). In apparent expression of some stirring of spiritual desire they ask for this bread from heaven, though how earthbound their understanding remains will emerge as the conversation continues.

In response to their request Jesus makes the great claim of verse 35, *I am the bread of life. He who comes to me will never go hungry, and he who believes in me will never be thirsty.* This is the first of the notable 'I am' sayings in this gospel, in which we hear a clear echo of the divine self-definition in Exodus 3:14: 'I AM WHO I AM.' While the synoptic writers do not contain these precise titles, their substance is present in other sayings which reflect a similar awareness on Jesus' part of his unique position in the relationship of humanity to God. The saying enshrines the essence of Jesus' message – he is the answer to the needs of the human heart. *The bread of life* implies the fundamental, elemental role Jesus claims to fulfil in relation to the yearning of the human spirit. For Jesus' audience bread was 'the staff of life', the primary source of nourishment, as it continues to be for millions in Third World countries. But since bread is a basic food universally, there is also the implicit claim that he fulfils this role for everyone. Caviar, like cake and confectionery, is for the few, but bread is for all. He is 'the Saviour of the world' (4:42).

The bread of life also points to the satisfying nature of Jesus. This is drawn out in the corollary, *never go hungry* and *never be thirsty*. All other breads, like the manna in the wilderness, leave a sense of dissatisfaction. The inner ache is not permanently assuaged; we hunger again. By contrast Jesus, once tasted, obviates the need for further satisfaction. As Jesus had said to the woman in 4:14, 'whoever drinks the water I give him will never thirst', so now he says to the Galileans, *he who believes in me will never be thirsty.* Jesus alone can satisfy the heart. In a society which has experimented to the point of satiation with every form of material, physical and spiritual palliative to fill the inner emptiness of its heart, Jesus' invitation comes with wonderful relevance – *He who comes to me will never go hungry . . . will never be thirsty.*

c. The congregation who do believe (6:36–58)

Jesus turns from the Galileans with their materialistic preoccupations to those who will truly respond to the invitation he issues to the world. He tells us three things about them.

(i) Their security (6:36–40)

They are 'given' to the Son by the Father (37, 39). God's sovereignty is asserted in this saying, an emphasis which we will meet regularly in this gospel.[73] As elsewhere in Scripture, this does not imply a denial of the cruciality of faith for salvation, nor of the need to proclaim the gospel to the world and to urge all to believe. Jesus is patently engaged in just such an endeavour in this passage. But God 'who works out everything in conformity with the purpose of his will' (Eph. 1:11) is also at work in human response to the work of his Son. The apparent temporal priority of the Father's ownership, *all that the Father gives me* (37), needs to be understood in terms of the time sequence necessitated by Jesus' incarnation. As we noted in our comments on 1:1, the Son is eternally one with the Father. Election is necessarily also the work of the Son, as he acknowledges within the gospel (6:60; 15:16). His people having been given to him, the Son for his part undertakes to keep and protect all of them. This is simply part of his full obedience to the Father's will (38, 40).

The 'keeping' ministry of the Son will include securing his own people at the judgment at the end (39). To look to Jesus Christ is to have the confidence of being 'raised up' at the last day (40). Eternal life with God in eternity is, in this sense, already given to the believer in Jesus. Our decision to follow him (*who looks* to him is how it is vividly expressed in verse 40) is a response which is rooted in God's everlasting purposes. God has claimed us from the beginning; the Son will raise us at the end; we belong to eternity.

> Long before time began you were part of his plan.
> Let no fear cloud your brow; he will not forsake you now!

(ii) Their destiny (6:41-51)

Jesus tells us about the *destiny* of those who believe in him. The Galileans' response to Jesus' claim to have 'come down from heaven' (38) is typically materialistic. They knew Jesus' parents. How can he have come from heaven? (42). Jesus in reply reaffirms that only the Father can enable someone to respond to the Son (44). He speaks of the inner illumination which God gives, citing from the Old Testament, *They will all be taught by God* (45), which is a paraphrase of Isaiah 54:13. Jesus is the one who has come from God. He alone has 'seen' the Father, and so he alone can give this true inner illumination which brings a knowledge of the Father (46). Old Testament revelation was therefore valid, but limited. Like the manna in the wilderness, supernatural gift as it was, it did not absolve from death (49). Jesus, as the true bread of God, gives everlasting life to those who believe in him (51). This is the destiny of his true disciples, the conquest of death. They will

[73] Cf. 6:44; 10:26-29; 15:16; 17:2, 6, 9, 24.

be 'raised up' (44) and live for ever with him beyond death (47, 50–51). Jesus then carries the metaphor of bread a step further by urging that the bread has to be 'eaten' to give life (51). We should observe the clearly sacrificial language in verse 51: ... *my flesh, which I will give for the life of the world.*

(iii) Their identity (6:52–59)

This brings Jesus through to his vivid exposition of the *identity* of those who truly believe. He uses the language of consumption. Faith is like eating the flesh and drinking the blood of Jesus himself. Clearly the sacrifice of the cross is in his mind. We cannot forget that he is already proclaimed as 'the Lamb of God' (1:29), and the one who will be 'lifted up', as was the serpent (3:14). His broken body, and blood poured out, on the cross, need to be personally appropriated in an act of faith in Jesus which is akin to the personal act of eating food (53–57). This will produce a communion between Christ and his believing disciple parallel to the communion of Father and Son, which underlies the salvation that the Son will offer, the eternal life which will triumph over death (54, 58).

Not surprisingly, many interpreters have seen here an endorsement of the supreme importance of the sacrament of the Lord's Supper. It has to be said, however, that there is no explicit reference to it in this passage. Jesus' concern appears to be with his present congregation, confronting them with their errors and pointing them to the true way to find life from God. Essentially their need is to believe in him as the one the Father has sent as a sacrifice for the sin of the world. The eating of his flesh and drinking of his blood would appear a vivid, even shocking, illustration of what 'believing' in him implies. In its 'earthiness', however, the image is ideally suited to the materialistic mind-set of his audience, the more so since many of them had so recently eaten the miraculous bread which Jesus had provided. It is perhaps to the point to note that 'everlasting life' is attributed to faith in verse 47, and to eating and drinking in verse 54, an implicit pointer to the latter as a picture of the former; *cf.* Augustine, 'Believe and you have eaten.' Interpreting the passage in this way, however, does not preclude our recognizing that Jesus' imagery came to life in a new way in the later experience of the church as it shared the meal Jesus instituted 'on the night he was betrayed' (1 Cor. 11:23). This section is certainly not out of place when read in the context of the Lord's Supper, provided we never lose sight of the cruciality of faith, both for coming to Christ and for the renewal of our communion with him in the feast he has instituted.

113

d. The cost of discipleship (6:60–71)

John now conveys to us the reaction to this teaching in the Capernaum synagogue. It was overwhelmingly negative; many who were 'disciples' turned back (66). We need to assume that 'disciple' is used at this point to refer to all those who were prepared to associate with Jesus. They find his teaching *hard*. Presumably this refers not only to his offensive language about 'eating his flesh', and the like, but also to his earlier claim to have 'come down from heaven' (38). Some of them were offended by his unwillingness to assume the role of a socio-political Messiah who would feed their bellies and liberate their nation.

Far from easing his demands or reducing his claims in the light of their discomfort, Jesus assures them of greater cause for offence which lies in the future, *viz*. that he will *'ascend to where he was before'* (62). If they find this teaching offensive now, how will they cope when it is actualized, and the Messiah's flesh and blood are sacrificed before their eyes in his glorious, kingly enthronement? *The flesh counts for nothing* (63) does not imply that Jesus' sacrifice in the flesh is less than utterly necessary. It implies rather that the grasping of the significance of his teaching, and hence of the sacrifice of the Son of Man, is a gracious gift of God by his Spirit (63). As for Nicodemus with all his theological sophistication, so for the Galileans with their down-to-earth practicality – birth from above, in water and Spirit, is necessary for salvation. *The Spirit gives life* (63). *This*, he emphasizes, *is why I told you that no-one can come to me unless the Father has enabled him* (65).

Jesus is not overwhelmed by the loss of commitment on the part of many who had professed some allegiance to him. He knows about human response to him (64; *cf.* 2:25), and he is unshaken in his confidence that through it all God's purpose is being fulfilled (65). This moment represents a decisive turning point for the crowds in Galilee. A year from now, as the Passover is celebrated once more in Jerusalem, the Messiah will die on a cross, forsaken and alone.

Jesus then invites the twelve to clarify their position (67). Peter typically speaks for them. He reaffirms their loyalty on the grounds that, since Jesus alone has the words of eternal life, there is no other to turn to. Peter confesses that *We believe and know that you are the Holy One of God* (69). We should note the reference to Jesus' **words** here (*cf.* 63). The Spirit of the kingdom of God is encountered in the words of Jesus as well as in his deeds. Here, as elsewhere, Word and Spirit are drawn together, because Jesus and his words are drawn together. There is no Christ other than the Christ of the Scriptures. He is met in his words, and in the inspired

114

biblical writings within which context alone can his words and deeds be understood and interpreted. Peter's confession, *the Holy One of God* (69), is an exalted one, since 'holy' refers to that which belongs uniquely to God. Hence 'Jesus stands over against the world as the One who comes from the other world and belongs to God.'[74]

Lest the disciples seek the basis of their adherence to Jesus in their own insight or ability, Jesus reminds them that their being with him rests finally on his sovereign choice of them (70). Yet even that does not guarantee a true loyalty for, he states, *one of you is a devil!* (cf. 13:2, 27). Here we encounter the mystery of sin and unbelief as it interfaces with the purpose of God. That Judas was personally chosen in order to do the work of the betrayer is unthinkable, yet Jesus, who knows all hearts, recognized the terrible possibility within Judas, even as he afforded him the supreme and surpassing privilege of belonging to the twelve. The only true security is in having no security except the mercy of God. 'To believe is to have been brought to the place where one knows that one has to rely completely on Jesus, and on Jesus alone.'[75]

This concluding paragraph of the chapter vividly expresses the cost of following Jesus. Being a true believer will involve going the way of the cross, as Jesus will indicate: 'unless a grain of wheat falls to the ground and dies . . .' (12:24). Among other things, that will mean remaining true to Jesus when he and his word are dismissed. Being a true believer will mean following him loyally when his truth is hard to understand and even harder to apply, when his claims seem largely contradicted by tangible realities, and when the multitudes turn away from him and we find ourselves part of a small and ostracized minority. It will mean being loyal too when, among the company of the 'faithful', we discover the work of the evil one in those who, in life and word, betray their Lord. On the other side, however, we shall not be completely alone, for others too will be loyal, and confession of Jesus will be made by those who also know there is no other to whom they can go. Jesus himself will remain there for us, moving on his appointed way to his destined glory, and on the road giving his Holy Spirit and the assurance of eternal life to those whom he has chosen. But, when all these are weighed, the cost is real, and he does not shield us from it. Will you also go away?

[74] R. Bultmann, p. 449.   [75] L. Newbigin, p. 90.

12. The feast of tabernacles I (7:1–52)

Discourses at the feast of tabernacles

With the conclusion of the 'bread of life' discourse in Capernaum we arrive at the long central section of the gospel, encompassing chapters 7 to 10. This covers the final year of Jesus' ministry, from the second Passover at which he fed the crowd, to the third Passover during which he was crucified. This last year of ministry is itself punctuated by two other feasts, that of tabernacles (7:2) and dedication (10:22). The material in these chapters comprises, largely, loosely connected paragraphs consisting sometimes of straightforward teaching, sometimes of questions and Jesus' response to them, and sometimes of significant events. While systematic order is not possible, the themes of the feasts provide a certain coherence and we shall use this in exposition, though other divisions are certainly possible.

If we take the feast of tabernacles as our 'peg' for the sections which follow, we arrive at an outline of this order:

Prelude (7:1–13)
Feast of tabernacles – discourse 1 (7:1–39)
 postscript (7:40–52)
Excursus – The woman taken in adultery (7:53 – 8:11)
Feast of tabernacles – discourse 2 (8:12–59)
 postscript (9:1–41)
Feast of tabernacles – discourse 3 (10:1–21)

Prelude (7:1–13)

Jesus continues in the north because the south has become dangerous for him. He is not unprepared to face the challenge there. Indeed, he is ready to give up his life at Jerusalem, and will do so, but only at the right moment, when his 'hour' has come (7:30). 'By going to Jerusalem, Jesus will indeed show himself to "the world", in the widest sense; Jerusalem is the place where he must be "lifted up" so that all without distinction may be drawn to him.'[75]

His *brothers* (3) (presumably his natural, younger brothers), reproach him for remaining in the comparative obscurity of the north. Recognizing his power to perform miracles, they urge him to use it at the feast in Jerusalem (3–4). Possibly they are aware of his flagging support and are encouraging him to stage a spectacular

---

[75] F. F. Bruce, p. 171; Jn. 3:14f.; 12:32.

show at the feast to revive his popularity. Whatever their motives, Jesus is not to be drawn. He probably detects in their plea the erroneous attitude to miracles that he has already encountered on numerous occasions.[76] Hunger for spectacular signs is the enemy of real faith, since it leaves the fallen, self-centred heart untouched and unrebuked. The attitude of his brothers is the attitude of the rebellious world. Hence for them *any time is right* (6) for doing things, whether going up to the feast, or whatever. They know nothing of the hatred of the world with which Jesus has to grapple (7). The world cannot hate them because they belong to it; it does not hate its own.

Some comment on the feast of tabernacles is in order at this point. Instituted in the Old Testament, it was associated with the ingathering of harvest.[77] The feast ran for seven days and was reputedly the most popular of all the annual festivals. It commemorated the provision of God for his people in the wilderness, and the celebrants were required to recall that historical period by living during the feast in temporary structures of leaves and branches. A special feature was the water-drawing and lamp-lighting rite, which was performed each day in the temple and upon which, as we shall see, Jesus drew in his teaching. During the festival the people gave thanks for the rainfall which nourished the harvest, but also looked forward to that coming day when God's Spirit would be poured out at the coming of the kingdom of God.

There are those who see a difficulty in reconciling Jesus' expressed refusal to go to the feast (8) with his eventual attendance (10). The NIV inserts *yet* in verse 8, which is not inappropriate. Jesus must wait for the Father's direction. He will do only what the Father shows him (5:20). When he does set out for the feast, he goes in a manner which is the opposite of that recommended by his brothers, *in secret* (10). The crowds at the feast express a wide variety of views of Jesus, from the mild *He is a good man*, to the much more adversarial *he deceives the people* (12). This latter echoes Deuteronomy 13:1–6 and was a capital offence if proven. It was the typical later Jewish view of Jesus, and John would be aware that some of his readers had been influenced by it.

Discourse 1 (7:14–39)

The material is partly in the form of dialogue and so the title, 'discourse', may be misleading. Jesus *is* conveying truth in a fairly straightforward manner, however, and so the title can stand.

---

[76] *Cf.* 2:23; 4:48; *etc.*   [77] Ex. 23:16; Lv. 23:33–43; Dt. 16:13–15.

(i) The character of his teaching (7:15–18)

This straightforward aspect is reflected in the astonishment of the Jews as he begins to teach. Jesus' learning amazes them, particularly his command of the Old Testament, since he had never studied at the rabbinic centres of learning (15). 'The evangelist would see something intensely dramatic in this picture of the Jews confronted by the Incarnate Logos and yet treating him as an "uneducated fellow"!'[78] In Mark 1:22 it is the sheer authority of Jesus which amazes the audience. That is hardly lacking here. Indeed, the question of authority underlies his comment in verse 16. Jesus clarifies the source of his learning by referring them to *him who sent me* (16). His identity with the Father gives him access to the Father's knowledge. But Jesus also offers a means of testing the validity of his teaching and the claim implicit in it, obedience. *If anyone chooses to do God's will, he will find out.* (17). There is no way of testing a claim to divine revelation other than this one. Nor is the situation different in principle for *any* claim to ultimate authority. Since by definition there *can* be no higher authority, there is no external criterion by which such claims can be tested; they must be self-authenticating. Only by submitting to God with complete willingness to do his will are we in a position to evaluate Jesus' claim. But when we *do* come in that attitude, Jesus asserts, we shall discover that Jesus' teaching is indeed the very truth of God, and therefore that Jesus is who he claims to be, the divine Son who is one with the Father.

In contrast to other teachers who are motivated by their fallen hearts, and hence by a desire for their own personal honour (18), Jesus seeks only the honour of the Father who sent him, and is therefore *a man of truth* about whom there is *nothing false* (18). This last claim is especially noteworthy. In general experience, the holier a person, the greater his or her sense of personal moral failure. Against the accumulated centuries of human experience, and the universal confession of the continual need for forgiveness, Jesus' claim to absolute integrity appears as gross insensitivity at best, and towering arrogance at worst. What are we to make of one for whom such claims express the essence of his moral life?

(ii) The connections of his teaching (7:19–36)

In his teaching Jesus establishes connections at two levels, first with Judaism (19–24), then with his Father as the source and goal of his life (25–36).

---

[78] C. H. C. MacGregor, *The Gospel of John* (Hodder and Stoughton, n.d.), cited by L. Morris, *John*, p. 405, who adds that 'it is a highly ironical situation'.

As far as Judaism was concerned, the issue is his attitude to the law. The Jews in Jerusalem have not forgotten his last visit when he had, in their minds, encouraged the breaking of the Sabbath law (5:1–15). Jesus accuses the Jews of breaking the law themselves by their plots to kill him, a clear breach of the commandment not to murder (19; cf. Ex. 20:13). He then presents a tightly reasoned argument in support of his action (21–24). He points out that they regularly break the letter of the Sabbath law when they circumcise children on the Sabbath (22), effectively conceding that the command to circumcise takes precedence (as it did historically in terms of the time of its inauguration) over the law of the Sabbath instituted at Sinai (22). But if the cutting of one small part of the body is acceptable on the Sabbath in the interests of the covenant being fulfilled, how much more defensible was Jesus' healing a whole person on the Sabbath (23). His action was in fullest accord with the healing and redeeming purposes which lie at the heart of the old covenant. Thus, far from being the enemy of Judaism and the law, Jesus is, in fact, the one in whom the historic purpose of Judaism is affirmed by being fulfilled.

As for Jesus' connections with the Father, the Jews express hesitation about him because his human origins are apparently well enough known, whereas the Messiah when he came would, according to popular belief, appear without warning (27). Jesus neither accepts nor refutes this view. Rather, he simply points out that though they may indeed be aware of his human origins, these do not in fact disclose his true origin. He has come from the Father who is true (28, *true* equals real; he is the living God), and who is unknown by them, despite all their protestations to the contrary. 'The language is simple; the claim is august.'[79] This audacious claim incenses the authorities, who attempt to seize him, but are frustrated. We are not told the ostensible reason for that. Possibly they were inhibited by the strength of Jesus' popular support at this point. The underlying reason is given; *his time* had not yet come (30). The Father's time has not yet arrived, though it is not far off. The expression of popular admiration of Jesus, *When the Christ comes, will he do more . . . than this man?* (31), drives the authorities to more official action. The chief priests and Pharisees (not always the best of friends) unite to dispatch the temple police to arrest him (32).

Having established his relationship to his Father as far as his *origin* is concerned (28–29), Jesus speaks of that relationship in terms of his *goal*. *I go to the one who sent me* (33). As a result they will not be able to find him (34). The crowds, misunderstanding as

[79] F. F. Bruce, p. 178.

always, imagine Jesus to be referring to some anticipated mission journey, perhaps to the scattered groups of Jews among the Gentile nations (35). They are not wrong to think that Jesus has mission plans for these, and indeed for the Gentile nations too. These plans, however, will be fulfilled by his going to the Father, through death and resurrection, with the consequent outpouring of the Spirit, and the world mission of the disciple community, the church.

So Jesus moves steadfastly and deliberately forward in the will of the Father who directs his every movement. He is utterly secure from the machinations of the authorities until the hour appointed in eternity when he will go home to the Father's side, there to direct through his Spirit the realization of all his purposes across the ages.

(iii)   The content of Jesus' teaching (7:37–39)

While we have to reckon with a time delay between the last statements and those we include in this section, the setting remains the feast of tabernacles, and that now becomes critical.

Dramatically, John tells us that *On the last and greatest day of the Feast, Jesus stood and said in a loud voice, 'If anyone is thirsty, let him come to me and drink. Whoever believes in me, as the Scripture has said, streams of living water will flow from within him'* (37–38). The controversies are laid aside for a moment as Jesus opens his heart in this impassioned appeal. It is deeply moving to visualize the Saviour standing in the temple among the crowds of pilgrims, probably in the proximity of the altar where the water from the Pool of Siloam was poured each morning, calling on all who would to come to him and to receive the life-giving blessing of the Spirit. The imagery also picks up on that used in chapter 4 (13–14).

The correct reading of this passage is debated. Since the alternatives affect the interpretation, it will be necessary to take some account of the discussion. The original manuscript of John did not contain punctuation marks, and while that does not affect the sense in the great majority of instances, occasionally, as here, there is room for some ambiguity. The traditional reading of verses 37 and 38 implies that Jesus is promising that whoever comes to him (believes in him) will be given a drink to quench his or her thirst. This is the Holy Spirit, who will be like a living, springing river within the heart (lit. belly) of the believer. If, however, the break in verse 38 occurs after *me* in the middle of the verse, rather than after *him* at the end of the verse, the sense becomes (as in the NIV margin), *If anyone is thirsty, let him come to me. And let him drink, who believes in me. As the Scripture has said, streams of living water will flow from within him.* The important difference is that this second format, detaching as it does the *streams of living water* from the promise to the believer, allows the *him* in verse 38 to refer to Christ rather than to the believer. The river flows from the Lord. The support in the manuscripts, and among interpreters, is fairly equally balanced between the two possibilities. D. A. Carson, in his recent discussion (which comes down finally on the side of the traditional, first alternative), helpfully notes the considerable common ground shared by both interpretations. Provided one keeps clearly in mind that Jesus is the ultimate source of the Spirit by either interpretation, and therefore that there is no ground here for believers claiming for themselves some inner, personal source of spiritual power independent of their relationship to Christ, the consequences of whichever option one follows do not appear overwhelmingly significant.[80] This writer inclines to the margin reading in that it accords somewhat better with the essential thrust of the passage: Jesus appealing to all to come to *him*, and the consequent truth that *he* is the one through whose glorification the Spirit would be given (39).

Jesus claims to be the source of the blessings anticipated at the feast. As he is glorified by being 'lifted up' on the cross, the Spirit will be poured out, and the rivers of God's blessing will flow into a thirsty and parched world (19:34; 20:22). John adds the comment that *the Spirit had not yet been given*, thereby denying neither the Spirit's presence in Jesus, nor his work in inspiring the prophets and writers of the Old Testament, but arguing that his full outpouring must await the glorifying of Jesus.

Postscript (7:40–52)

The concluding paragraph lists a variety of reactions to Jesus. Possibly due to his claim to be the giver of living water, some of his hearers are reminded of Moses giving water from the rock to the people in the wilderness, and hence of Moses' prophecy of a 'prophet like me' (40; *cf.* Dt. 18:15; and comment on 6:14). Others wonder if he is the long-awaited Messiah (41; the Jews largely distinguished these figures). Difficulty with the messianic identification is expressed because of Jesus' reputed Galilean origin (41). The Messiah, the Scriptures made clear, was of David's line and from Bethlehem.[81] It is arguable that John is writing with tongue in cheek here. He knows, as does the whole early church, that Jesus is indeed *from David's family*.[82] But this is

---

[80] D. A. Carson, *John*, pp. 323f.
[81] 42; 2 Sa. 7:12–16; Ps. 89:3–4; Is. 9:7; 55:3; Mi. 5:2.
[82] *Cf.* Mt. 1:1; Lk. 3:31; Rom. 1:3; 2 Tim. 2:8.

not common knowledge in Jerusalem. As always, Jesus provokes division (43).

The temple police meanwhile return to their masters. Unlike the Roman soldiers who could be counted upon to carry out orders, with physical brutality if necessary, these were basically peaceable men, more an order of stewards than law enforcers. As Levites and religious men they are impressed, even overwhelmed. *No-one ever spoke the way this man does* (46). This was an entirely valid assessment, but it gets them no hearing with the Pharisees. Instead they are handed a threefold rebuttal. The first is that they themselves are *deceived* (47). The second rebuttal is that none of the rulers or the Pharisees have believed in Jesus (48); a claim which is immediately refuted by Nicodemus (50; John is grinning again).[83] The third is that the *mob* around the temple, who have supported Jesus, are cursed (49), since they do not follow or study the law like the Pharisees. They are an ignorant rabble whose views are to be discounted. Contemporary sources confirm this contempt for the common people on the part of these first-century Jewish leaders. At this point Nicodemus finds the courage to challenge their dismissal of Jesus, citing the widely acknowledged right of the accused to make due representation (50–51). He too is summarily dismissed with another appeal to Jesus' Galilean origin (52).

So ends Jesus' first discourse at the feast of tabernacles. Another will follow; but in the meantime we pause with the important statements of verses 37–39 concerning Jesus' gift of the Spirit.

We note firstly the *nature* of the gift. Jesus here, in the context of the feast, links the gift to the coming of God's promised kingdom.[84] The gift of the Spirit is not something strange, a sheer phenomenon unrelated to God's historic purposes. It is in fact the precise fulfilment of these purposes.

Jesus speaks powerfully also about the *means* by which the Spirit will be given. It will be through the 'glorifying' of Jesus. His Easter victory will be the means for the releasing of the Spirit. This was to be literally perceived by John at the cross, when the spear-thrust produced an emission of blood and water (*cf.* on 19:34f., water the symbol, as here, of the Spirit). This link between the 'glorifying' and the gift is expressed again in Jesus' 'breathing' the Spirit (20:22), and in Peter's explanation of the coming of the Spirit at Pentecost: 'this Jesus . . . Exalted to the right hand of God, he has received . . . the promised Holy Spirit and has poured out . . .' (Acts 2:33). Paul can pray, therefore, that the church at Ephesus will experience the identical power that raised and exalted Jesus (Eph. 1:17–21).

---

[83] R. V. G. Tasker, p. 109.
[84] *Cf.* 3:3–5; Is. 44:3f.; Je. 31:31; Ezk. 36:24–27.

He prays rightly, according to this text, for that is who the Spirit is.

We are encouraged also to note the *range* of this gifting: *If anyone is thirsty* (37), *whoever believes* (38). The gift of the rivers of living water is for every believer as surely as is forgiveness, justification, adoption and all the other blessings of salvation.

Finally we note the *impressiveness* of Jesus' image – streams of water. It is a striking enough metaphor in a culture where water is plentiful and rivers a common-place. It is the more impressive in an arid country like Palestine, where rivers were the very source of life. Christ's gift of the Spirit to his church is not niggardly but expansive. Our generation has seen a major reiteration of the ministry of the Spirit in the churches, sadly one which has often proved divisive. In that context this passage says two things.

1. It validates the Spirit's ministry. We dare not, in the interests of peace and the maintenance of the status quo, close our ears to Jesus' wooing invitation. His heart cries out to give us his best gift. He longs to send the Spirit to bring life and fruitfulness to our arid and barren world.

2. It establishes important safeguards for interpreting the Spirit's ministry. The Spirit is bound in the closest possible way to Jesus (an even more explicit identification if the margin reading is followed). The Spirit is given in the context of the glorifying of Jesus, and it is ever so. The heart to which the Spirit is largely given is not the heart that hungers for personal manifestations of power or Holy Ghost ego trips, but the one which yearns and thirsts and pleads for the glorifying of our Lord Jesus Christ. For this reason above all we plead, '*Veni, Creator Spiritus!*'

> O Spirit of the living God,
>> In all the fullness of thy grace,
> Where'er the foot of man hath trod,
>> Descend on our apostate race.
>
> Baptize the nations; far and nigh
>> The triumphs of the cross record;
> The name of Jesus glorify,
>> Till every kindred call him Lord.
>
> *James Montgomery*

13. Excursus – the woman taken in adultery (7:53 – 8:11)

It will be noted that this story is introduced in the NIV text by the comment 'The earliest and most reliable manuscripts and other ancient witnesses do not have . . .'. It is in point of fact absent from virtually all early Greek manuscripts, and from very many in the other language groups. None of the early church fathers who wrote commentaries on John's gospel include it. There can be no real doubt that it was not an original part of John. One or two manuscripts include it in Luke after 21:38. This may be a clue to its origin, as the passage has some textual affinities with the language of Luke's gospel. The hesitation over this paragraph may have been partly due to its content, as on the surface at least it appears to express a liberal attitude towards sexual sin on Jesus' part. The spirit of the passage, however, is such that its place within the gospel corpus has been universally accepted. 'There is nothing in the story itself, or its language, that would forbid us to think of it as an early story concerning Jesus.'[85] Its placement at this point in John, while certainly without justification in terms of the manuscript evidence, may have a certain appropriateness. 'The theme of judgment is strong in chapters 7–8, and the story could well be regarded as illustrative of 7:24 and 8:15–16.'[86]

The essence of the story is a carefully baited trap set for Jesus (6) by the *teachers of the law and the Pharisees* (a grouping without echo in John but common in the synoptics). A woman caught in the very act of adultery is paraded. What does Jesus teach should be done with her? The law pronounced stoning, they allege. It has been shown that the word for 'adultery' here implied that she was a married woman. Deuteronomy 22:22 does call for the death penalty in cases of proven adultery, though the man concerned should also be a victim, and the method of execution is not prescribed. In Jesus' day, interpretation may have varied somewhat from the strict letter. The issue is clear. The law was perceived to teach capital punishment in this case. The evidence of her wrongdoing is conclusive. What will Jesus do about it?

The trap is a clever one. To refuse to uphold the stoning would clearly confirm the authorities' suspicions, already aroused by matters like his attitude to the Sabbath, that Jesus stood light to the law. If that were established, then he is a self-proclaimed heretic and their rejection of him is clearly justified. On the other hand, his compassion for the downtrodden and the lawless is known. A hard-line judgment in this case would have discredited him in the eyes of the common people.

There may also have been another hook on their line, in that advocating stoning, in strict conformity with the Jewish law, might have brought down on Jesus' head the wrath of the Roman authorities because of their jealous retention of the right to execute.

[85] R. Brown, 1, p. 335.   [86] G. R. Beasley-Murray, p. 144.

Jesus' response is significant, though we have some difficulty at this remove knowing exactly what to make of it. He made no reply but *bent down and started to write on the ground with his finger* (6). Ingenious suggestions have been made as to what Jesus might have been writing. Certainly it was a dramatic gesture which would have heightened considerably the tension of the moment. It may be worth observing that Jesus elsewhere uses the image of 'the finger of God' (Lk. 11:20) to refer to his exercise of divine authority. It was with 'God's finger' that the law had been written on the tablets of stone at Sinai (*cf.* Ex. 32:16). Whatever we make of his action, Jesus' words are certainly clear enough. *If any one of you is without sin, let him be the first to throw a stone at her* (7).

This statement took into account the special role which the witnesses of the sin were required to fulfil; their responsibility was to initiate the stoning. Accordingly they needed to be appropriate witnesses who had neither connived in any way in the sin, nor been backward in trying to prevent it. If, as was very probably the case, the witnesses had been part of the framing of the woman, their consciences now had opportunity to convict them. By this reply, however, Jesus is not standing lightly to the law. He is in effect giving his permission for the stoning to begin, though only under valid moral conditions.

Jesus' saying is a particularly impressive example of his astonishing wisdom in dealing with his critics, a characteristic which has been reflected again and again in the dialogues we have been examining. In him truly 'are hidden all the treasures of wisdom and knowledge' (Col. 2:3). Jesus' statement ought not to be seen to imply that the law can be enforced only by moral paragons, nor that one cannot pass a judgment on moral issues, or on sexual moral issues in particular, unless one is untainted by any history of wrong deeds or desires. Jesus *is* confronting us, however, with the need for consistency in passing judgment. The sword of judgment is double-edged. In judging others we judge ourselves, and an unwillingness to pronounce judgment on ourselves undercuts our right to pronounce it on others. Put more generally, God's call to all of us, all of the time, is to live holy, godly lives. *Any* deviation from that should concern us, as much in ourselves as in others.

An additional point is that the law prescribed the death penalty as much for the man concerned as for the woman. The male adulterer's absence from the story is critical. It makes clear that this is also a story of male chauvinism, which was reflected widely in practice in the application of the law. As in his teaching on divorce (*cf.* Mt. 19:1–10), so here with respect to adultery, Jesus refuses to allow the woman concerned to be disadvantaged.

125

The impact of Jesus' challenge is overwhelming. One by one they slip away. At last Jesus is left with the woman and addresses her for the first time. Since apparently she has no accusers, neither will he accuse – *neither do I condemn you, . . . go now and leave your life of sin* (11).

This passage has much to say to a world living in the aftermath of the sexual revolution. Sexual activity before, alongside and outside marriage is today a fact of social life in both Western and Third World countries. Nor is the phenomenon met only outside the church. All Christian disciples have to come to terms with a society where pressures towards promiscuity are subtle and unrelenting. In that context this story is first of all a plea for understanding. Blanket condemnation gets no support from this passage. True, the pulpit needs urgently and repeatedly to clarify the Christian norm of sexual sanctity and commend its benefits, not least the honouring of the God whose will these standards reflect. In its handling of the individual who has failed, however, the church in its pastoral mission needs to move with the greatest sensitivity and understanding.

Secondly, we need to declare tirelessly the reality of God's forgiving grace. It is surely a remarkable fact that he who is the embodiment of divine holiness, the 'I AM' who met the people of God at Sinai in fire and thunder (Ex. 19:16ff.), should say to a self-confessed sinner with the guilt of the broken commandment heavy on her conscience, *neither do I condemn you*. Here is the miracle of the grace of God. There is no greater wonder than this. The turning of water into wine, the healing of a dying lad by a word, the feeding of five thousand and more with a snack lunch, the walking on a storm-tossed sea; none of these, nor all of them together, compares with this, that Jesus said *neither do I condemn you*. In this sentence, and in the heart of mercy which lay behind it, is all our hope and all our salvation for ever.

Thirdly, Jesus summons the woman to a new obedience to the law – *Go now and leave your life of sin*. It is a mistake to interpret this story as though sin is unimportant. Jesus upheld the law here, even to the point of setting in motion the application of its judgments. Furthermore, while his forgiving the woman is not conditional on repentance, he clearly sees her repentance as the natural outcome of it. Forgiveness does not operate in some non-moral sphere 'above' the moral law. There is no such place, for all realms, whether above or below, are the place of the presence of the living God who distinguishes between right and wrong and who is always the holy one, even as he is also the merciful and forgiving one. To be able to say *neither do I condemn you* cost Jesus the hell of Calvary. 'Sin scorches us when it comes under the light of forgiveness.'[87] To receive the Lord's mercy means living henceforth for the Lord's glory. 'Mercy from God calls for life unto God.'[88]

14. The feast of tabernacles II (8:12–59)

a. Two kinds of teacher – discourse 2 (8:12–30)

If we omit 8:1–12 (see comments above), and also 7:40–53 which comments on reactions to Jesus' teaching, this section follows on smoothly from 7:39.

We noted earlier that Jesus claimed to fulfil the water element in the feast of tabernacles' rituals. The feast had another symbol, light. At the end of the first day in the 'court of women' (which is the probable location of Jesus' teaching, indicated at verse 20) four golden lamps were lit amid great rejoicing. Singing and celebration with music and dancing continued through the nights of the feast, with the light in the temple illuminating the entire city. In this setting, Jesus' claim in verse 12 stands out boldly: *I am the light of the world. Whoever follows me will never walk in darkness, but have the light of life.* As the feast ends and the lights are extinguished, Jesus proclaims himself as the true light of the people of God, and not only of Israel, but of the whole world! 'A claim of cosmic significance.'[89]

Light is a rich Old Testament symbol. The exodus background to the feast would prompt memories of the pillar of cloud and fire by which God led the people in their journey (Ex. 13:21–22). The Psalmist had taught that 'the Lord is my light' (Ps. 27:1). The coming age of the kingdom would be a time when 'the Servant of the Lord' would be as 'a light for the Gentiles, that you may bring my salvation to the ends of the earth' (Is. 49:6) and when God himself would be his people's light (Is. 60:19–22; Rev. 21:3–4). Zechariah had depicted a union of light and living waters, a perfect reflection of the two symbols of the feast, and of the corresponding claims of Jesus in these discourses (Zc. 14:5b–7). This passage may even have been part of the liturgical readings during the feast.

The reaction to Jesus' tremendous claim is predictably critical. The Pharisees confront him directly. *Here you are, appearing as your own witness; your testimony is not valid* (13). There are two specific points here, and a more general one which is a key to interpreting the section. First, they are probably citing Jesus' own criteria for truthfulness: 'if I testify about myself, my testimony is not valid' (5:31). But they have once again misunderstood him, for

[87] K. Barth, *Credo* (Hodder and Stoughton, 1936), p. 45.
[88] G. R. Beasley-Murray, p. 147.   [89] L. Newbigin, p. 102.

Jesus' point is the one he will make again here, that his witness is not by himself to himself, but for the Father to the Father, and crucially *with* the Father.

Secondly, the Pharisees are certainly also alluding to the Old Testament requirement that claims be corroborated by supportive witness (Dt. 17:6; 19:15), thereby highlighting one of the most distinctive features of Jesus' teaching ministry, *viz.* his assumption of direct personal authority. This was in direct contrast to the rabbinic method which involved regular appeal to supportive authorities. True, Jesus respected the Old Testament and repeatedly cited its words, but even here he came as one who fulfilled these Scriptures and so was sovereignly free in his handling of their witness.

Jesus' defence of his method and the authority which underlay it is fourfold.

1. He appeals to his mission (14). He knows where he has come from and where he is going. He is the one sent into the world by the Father and engaged in a mission for him which will culminate in his exaltation.

2. He appeals directly to his Father's presence with him (16): *I am not alone. I stand with the Father, who sent me.* Literally this last sentence is simply 'I and the Father . . .', expressing the relationship which is the heartbeat of Jesus' life, as this gospel testifies repeatedly. There can be no higher claim. His unity with the Father means that his teaching and judgment are those of the Father. This claim demands decision; either we accept this and believe, or reject it and disbelieve.

3. He appeals to his divine origin. *I am not from this world* (23). He does not, like his opponents, originate from this present order; he speaks from the standpoint of one who has come from the heavenly world.

4. He appeals to his future 'lifting up' (28). This impending exaltation of the Son of Man will significantly vindicate his teaching. At that time *you will know that I am [the one I claim to be] and that I do nothing on my own but speak just what the Father has taught me* (28).

Jesus' unique consciousness of his unity with the Father is also reflected in his use of the phrase *I am: cf.* 24, *if you do not believe that I am . . . you will indeed die in your sins*, and 28, *When you have lifted up the Son of Man, then you will know that I am.* We met this earlier at 6:35 and shall meet it again in verse 58 of this chapter, (and at 13:19 and possibly 18:6). With the Mosaic and exodus setting for this discourse it is difficult not to see here an allusion to Exodus 3:14, the self-definition of God: 'say to the Israelites: I AM has sent me to you.' In the Septuagint the Greek reads, 'I am the one who is' (*egō eimi ho ōn*), which has led many scholars to identify a further background strand to Jesus' claim in the later chapters of Isaiah, with 43:10 as particularly pertinent. 'You are my witnesses, ... and my servant whom I have chosen, so that you may know and believe me and understand that I am he.'[90]

We can draw these threads together in the assertion that Jesus' authority lies in his unique relationship to the Father. He shares with the Father a unity of being (*cf.* 10:30, 'I and the Father are one'), expressed in verse 16 as simply *I ... with the Father*. This intimacy of communion rooted in Jesus' divine origin (23) is expressed in his mission in the world (12) in which he *always [does] what pleases* the Father (29). This utter submission to the Father will culminate in his self-oblation at the cross, which will be nothing other than his exaltation in the Father's presence and the final vindication of his mission and claims (28).

> Words which in a human being would look like exaggerated arrogance, can take no other form in the mouth of the eschatological revealer who alone has brought knowledge of the Father (1:18). Anyone looking for a picture of the earthly Jesus will be offended by the Johannine Christ.[91]

This is the teacher who addressed the Pharisees and the listening crowds of pilgrims at the feast of tabernacles, and who confronts us today with his uncompromising claim, *I am the light of the world* (12). By contrast, there is the other kind of teacher represented by the Pharisees. Jesus characterizes them in five ways.

1. They are ignorant of Jesus' mission (14). They have *no idea where I come from or where I am going*. For such teachers Jesus is not understood; his mission is opaque. They see only the outward form of it and judge it as unimpressive, a verdict which would find ample apparent justification as he took his leave of them on the cross.

2. They judge by merely human standards (15). Because they do not experience the intimate oneness with the Father that Jesus knows, they are left at the mercy of their purely human judgments.

3. They are ignorant of Jesus' person, and therefore also of the person of the Father (19). The order here is important. *If you knew me, you would know my Father also*. As the teachers of Israel, professing to know God and to be the official guardians of his truth, they were, in fact (and the irony could hardly be greater), strangers to the living God. The possibility of knowing God, how-

---

[90] *Egō eimi; cf.* Is. 41:4; 43:13, 25; 46:4; 48:12.
[91] R. Schnackenburg, 2, pp. 192f.

ever, is now open to them in Jesus (24), if they will believe in him. There is no other way at all to the Father except through the Son.

4. Accordingly, since they do not know God, they cannot go to where Jesus will go after death (21). The heavenly order from which Jesus has come, and to which he will return, is barred to them. They will *die in [their] sin* (21).

5. They are *of this world*, unlike Jesus who is *not of this world* (23). Their horizons are limited by their nature. Their merely human judgments reflect the reality that they are merely worldly men. They have never been reborn from above.

The claim Jesus makes in verse 12 is an uncompromising one. He is the light of the world who *alone* reveals the Father of light. Today the unifying of the globe through the communications revolution, and the accompanying renewed concern to eliminate communal and international conflict, have rekindled hopes of harmonizing all the great world religions. Surely, it is urged, no one religion can claim unique precedence. To assert that the Christian path is the only way to God, or that Jesus is the only Saviour, sounds to the modern consciousness both arrogant and indefensible. While the older East–West confrontation in its more acute form may have passed, other polarizations will no doubt continue to arise. For humanity to survive in our increasingly crowded and unified planet, we shall need 'a new way of thinking' (Einstein), involving, it is claimed, a tolerant acceptance of the equal insights of all, not least in the religious sphere. All religions have some light to share with the great human family, we are told. Jesus has much to offer, maybe more than any other. But his light is not exclusive. Muhammad too must speak to us, and the Buddha, and the Hindu scriptures, to say nothing of the older native religions.

While the Christian will certainly identify with the goal of world community, and with the elimination of ancient prejudices in every sphere, including religion, there is a point beyond which the Christian cannot go. Jesus stands alone, because of who he is. In him alone God in person has come to us and made himself known to us. Further, as we shall see later in the gospel, he alone has atoned for our human sin through his unique sacrifice. He alone therefore is the way to God. Whatever insights other religions may have to contribute, they cannot bring us to God. Even Judaism, as Jesus meets it here, the religion which developed in the closest proximity to the revelation of God in the Old Testament Scriptures, shows in general no recognition of the true God in Jesus. *If you knew me, you would know my Father* (19), but if you do not come to me, *you will die in your sin* (21).

There is, however, a wonderful invitation inherent in Jesus' claim. *All* may come to him, for he is the light *of the world*. To do that we must first admit our darkness for 'none will ever present themselves to Christ to be enlightened save those who have known both that this world is darkness and that they themselves are altogether blind'.[92] But if we are ready to admit that need, Christ stands ready to give the light of salvation to all who will believe in him as Saviour and Lord.

The contrasts drawn here between Jesus and the Pharisees hold a challenge for all who feel called to teach in Christ's service. John Oman drew a distinction once between those who speak 'with authority' and those who speak 'with authorities'. The Pharisees belonged to the latter group. As teachers it is possible to support our material with the most thorough research and scholarship and yet to lack the distinctive authority of the Christian teacher. This observation is not intended as an advocacy of sloppy or careless teaching. God does not encourage shoddy workmanship. 'God forbid that I should give to the Lord that which cost me nothing' (2 Sa. 24:24, my translation).

There is another dimension, however, as far as teaching with authority is concerned. Jesus supremely embodied it. 'He taught them as one who had authority, not as the teachers of the law (Mk. 1:22). The secret in Jesus' case was his total submission to the Father's will – *I always do what pleases him* (29). Authority is the child of obedience. When we reflect a like submission we shall be able to testify as he did, *The one who sent me is with me* (29), and others will know that it is so, and be moved, as some were at the feast, to *put their faith in him* (Jesus) (30).

Lest the demand of this last application overwhelm us we can recall that there is an objective content, a divinely provided syllabus for our teaching. Happily, we are not asked to share with the world merely our own fragmentary knowledge or limited experience. Here, as elsewhere, the grace of God reigns, and here also our weakness and insufficiency may yet be the vehicle of his power and glory. He still uses sinners and can speak, even through us, the Word of his grace.

b. Truths for disciples – discourse 2 (8:31–47)

Part two of this second tabernacles discourse, unlike the first part, is not initiated by a claim of Jesus, but arises spontaneously from the response to his earlier teaching. His exposition of his authority resulted, as we saw, in many putting their faith in him (30). Jesus now addresses these aspiring disciples, and encourages them to

[92] J. Calvin, 1, p. 210.

continue in their new path by 'holding on' to his teaching.[93] To do so will bring them a knowledge of the truth which will set them free (31). 'Remaining in the truth' is the mark of the true disciple.[94] 'Those who falsely proclaim they believe give way from the very start, or at least in the middle of the race, whereas (true) believers persevere to the winning-post.'[95]

Sadly, these disciples are quickly shown to be more of that 'rocky places' group (cf. Mt. 13:20f.) which we have already met in this gospel (2:23f.; 6:61f.). Jesus' claim to set them free carries the negative implication that prior to their response to Jesus they had been in bondage. This they proceed to contest vehemently (33). They desire Jesus' gift of life as an additional adornment to the moral and spiritual status they presume to possess already by virtue of their Jewish inheritance. But Christ can never be had as an addition to our natural attainments, a part-Saviour who complements our personal achievements. He is the Saviour only of the desperate who have nowhere else to turn and no other on which to call.

Jesus clarifies the nature of their bondage. It is a bondage to sin (34), which only Jesus, as the eternal Son of God, is qualified to break. The inadequacy of their response is now clearly disclosed (37–47). Their true father is not God but the devil. They have no room for Jesus' word (37); they are ready to kill Jesus (37, 40); they do not love Jesus although he has come from God (42); they are unable to hear what Jesus is saying to them (43); and they refuse to believe in Jesus although they cannot prove him guilty of wrong-doing (45–46). In general they show the twin characteristics of the devil; *lies*, in that they reject the truth of Jesus; and *murder*, in that they seek the death of Jesus (44–45). In all of this they demonstrate that they *do not belong to God* (47).

These verses represent a damning indictment of human nature. As Reinhold Niebuhr remarked a generation ago, no amount of contrary evidence seems to disturb humanity's good opinion of itself. But the evidence is there on every hand in our own period, from the horrors of Auschwitz and a thousand other war-time hells, through the killing fields of Cambodia and the wasted millions of Stalin's Gulag, besides the daily toll of gratuitous violence, rape, abuse, abortion, torture, and murder in every corner of the globe. Jesus' view of human nature in these verses has been, and continues to be, abundantly verified in experience.

---

[93] Verse 31; the Greek verb is *menō*, commonly rendered 'remain'; cf. ch. 15, *passim*.
[94] 1 Jn. 2:19; 2 Jn. 9; 3 Jn. 3.   [95] J. Calvin, 1, p. 221.

(i) 'Of human bondage'

In his unveiling of the human heart Jesus reaches beyond the specific acts of sin, to which he will turn in a moment, to the root cause, the principle of sin, what Paul was to call 'the sinful nature' (Rom. 7:18, 23; cf. Mk. 7:21f.). We do not become sinners because we commit sins; we commit sins because we are sinners, i.e. we have fallen, sin-oriented hearts. It is this that goes towards explaining why Jesus disavows the political option as far as his messiahship is concerned. A political saviour leaves the root problem unaddressed. The fallen heart accompanies the revolution and will express itself within the new order in new bondages and oppressions. There is no freedom if the individual heart is not set free. All of which does not mean a political quietism. God is a God of justice, and so political structures which flout justice and despoil his creatures, who were made for freedom and dignity, dishonour God and cry out for change. But the real need cannot be met at the political level. Jesus traces the ultimate source of evil in the heart back to the devil. He alludes here clearly to the fall (44, cf. Gn. 3:1f.) where Satan's twin qualities of murder and falsehood were exposed. He is a murderer because he robbed Adam and Eve and all of us of the original gift of eternal life (Rom. 5:12f.). Death is Satan's handiwork, from the beginning in Eden until the last moment before the return of the Lord. Furthermore, he is a liar. He lied to Adam and Eve in Eden and he still lives in all lies; it is his native expression (44).

Jesus' unveiling of a hidden level of spiritual antipathy behind the behaviour of his opponents (a level even beyond the machinations of their inner, fallen natures) is salutary. This is more so because his audience consists of religious people who are professing a desire to follow him. In Christian living, as in Christian ministry, the terms are the same for us as they were for Jesus and the apostles: 'For our struggle is not against flesh and blood, but against the rulers, against the authorities, against the powers of this dark world and against the spiritual forces of evil in the heavenly realm' (Eph. 6:12). To ignore Jesus' unveiling of that enemy is to invite disaster. Earnest protestation and practice of religion on the one hand, and the plotting of murder and the embracing of lies on the other, are not incompatible. The Jews here are adamant about their religious credentials. God himself is, they claim, their only Father (39, 41). No doubt many of them gave expression to their religion by energetic works of piety. This feast they are celebrating is indicative. Yet they are at the same time plotting the destruction of God's Son. Religion as such is no guarantee of sanctity. Over against this sombre picture, however, we set Christ's new freedom.

(ii) Christ's freedom
This freedom comes from Jesus personally. *If the Son sets you free* . . . (36). We can characterize it further.

It is *a gift, not a pedigree* (33–37). This freedom cannot be had from our religious background, a succession of race or family, or from anything inherent in ourselves. It is given personally by Jesus himself.

It is *eternal, not temporary* (35). Jesus who gives this freedom is the eternal Son who lives for ever, and hence his gift sets us, in union with him, within the eternal life of God.

It is *expressed in obedience, not independence* (35). The recipient becomes a loving, obedient child within God's family.

It was Martin Luther's insight that the human person is made to serve. He depicted the human will as a horse whose choices are limited to who will be its rider, whether God or the devil.[96] The notion of the radically independent individual who can do as he or she may please without reference to any other authority, an image regularly celebrated in modern post-Enlightenment culture, is in fact a man of straw. This 'free' person is a myth who never existed and who never will. We are radically, incurably and eternally dependent beings who were made to serve. Our freedom is not the freedom to do as we want, but the freedom *from* being controlled by our fallen hearts *to* do as God wants. 'True freedom is not the liberty to do anything we please, but the liberty to do what we ought; and it is genuine liberty because doing what we ought now pleases us.'[97]

c. Greater than Abraham – discourse 2 (8:48–59)

The remaining verses (48–59) of this discourse comprise a dialogue arising out of Jesus' denunciation of the Jews. He is accused of being a Samaritan, a very deep insult (48, *cf.* comments on 4:4). This may reflect their resentment at his appearing to question their pure religious inheritance, rather as the Samaritans did. The further accusation of demon possession (48) is repeated in the gospel at other points.[98] Jesus defends his motivation as being the complete opposite to demon possession. His passion is to serve the living God, and to further his honour (49). His own glory is a matter for the Father, who seeks the Son's glory in the present, and will realize it in the future at the judgment when those who have kept Jesus' word will pass into eternal life (51).

[96] M. Luther, *The Bondage of the Will*, LCC, Vol. XVII (Westminster, 1969), p. 140.
[97] D. A. Carson, *John*, p. 350.   [98] *Cf.* 7:20; 8:52; 10:20.

The vitriol of the Jews here should not surprise us, even on the part of some who had so recently professed to follow Jesus. The human heart is seldom so spiteful as when it perceives its self-esteem threatened. There is almost nothing we will cling to with greater vehemence than the props by which we bolster our self-image. Further, the treatment meted out to Jesus here is a timely reminder of what is involved in identifying with him and his truth in a fallen world of falsehood. Jesus was quite clear about the implications. 'A student is not above his teacher, nor a servant above his master... If the head of the house has been called Beelzebub, how much more the members of his household!' (Mt. 10:24f.).[99] It is never easy, of course, to come to terms with others' rejection of us, particularly when our treatment of them has been above reproach (*cf*. 'Can any of you prove me guilty?', 46). It is, however, the inevitable result of being on Jesus' side.

> Once let a Christian take up the cross and follow Christ, there is no lie too monstrous, and no story too absurd for some to tell against him, and for others to believe. But let the Christian take comfort from the thought that he is only drinking the cup which his blessed Master drank before him.[100]

Jesus replies to the accusations with an astonishing claim, *if anyone keeps my word, he will never see death* (51). He is not suggesting that his disciples will never experience physical dissolution. Rather, they will never have to confront death in its terror as the occasion of final separation from God; death as the curse of sin. This claim Jesus will enact in chapter 11 at the grave of Lazarus. *Are you greater than . . . Abraham?* is the astonished query of the Jews. *Who do you think you are?* (53). Before answering that question directly Jesus reaffirms his claim to know the Father. The Father is the key to who he is (55). He is the one the Father has sent into the world, in fulfilment of the ancient promises to Israel. These promises Abraham embraced in faith; he in that sense *rejoiced at the thought of seeing my day*.

Jesus' reference to Abraham's 'rejoicing' may be an oblique echo of the feast, with its note of celebration. As they have celebrated in anticipation the coming of the water and light of the kingdom, so Abraham celebrated in anticipation of Jesus' coming. The tense of the verb implies a specific moment of celebration, most probably the birth of Isaac, the son of promise (Gn. 21:1f.) in whom the original promise to bless the world was realized (Gn. 12:3). Some commentators have suggested that Abraham's rejoicing is a reference to his viewing the mission of Jesus from the perspective of

---

[99] *Cf*. Mt. 24:9; Jn. 15:18; 2 Tim. 3:12.   [100] J. C. Ryle, p. 165.

paradise. This is probably not in mind, though one needs to weigh Jesus' strong sense of the aliveness of the patriarchs.[101] Not for the first time the Jews interpret Jesus literally, understanding him as claiming to have been present on earth in Abraham's time (57) although he is not yet fifty years old. To this, Jesus makes the majestic reply, *I tell you the truth, . . . before Abraham was born, I AM!* (58, my emphasis). A conscious reflection of the Old Testament self-designation of God is evident. We are again at the burning bush in Exodus 3:14, and with the prophetic vision of Isaiah 41:4, 'I, the LORD – with the first of them and with the last – I AM HE' (my emphasis), or Isaiah 43:10, 'Yes, and from the ancient days, I AM HE' (my translation).

That Jesus' words are a claim to deity is certainly the perception of his hearers. *At this, they picked up stones to stone him* (59), presumably because his words represented a supreme blasphemy of the holy name of God, and required to be dealt with in the terms of Deuteronomy. 'If a prophet . . . appears among you . . . and he says, "Let us follow other gods" . . . That prophet . . . must be put to death . . . do not yield to him or listen to him. Show him no pity . . . Stone him to death, because he tried to turn you away from the LORD your God' (Dt. 13:1–10). In the light of this reaction, Brown's comment is entirely appropriate, 'No clearer implication of divinity is found in the gospel tradition.'[102]

He is the eternal Christ sharing the everlasting life of the Father, the changeless Lord who towers over history, Master of time, Ruler of the ages, undiminished by the passing of the centuries, 'the same yesterday and today and for ever' (Heb. 13:8). To a generation conscious of the brevity of life, and in a culture where time is replacing money as the commodity of highest value, we feel constantly threatened by time's flow. It runs through our fingers and escapes us no matter how frantically we try to fill it and hold it back. But Christ has all time in his hands; and as we rest our lives in him our fragile, ephemeral consciousness finds meaning and permanence. He is still able to 'save them to the uttermost' (Heb. 7:25, AV) all who come to God through him.

15. The sixth sign – healing the blind man: postscript (9:1–41)

This chapter is the most unified of the gospel. It gathers entirely round a healing 'sign', the giving of sight to the man born blind. The feast of tabernacles with its 'festival of light' continues in the background. One of the marks of the coming of the messianic age

---

[101] Lk. 20:37, '. . . not the God of the dead . . .'; Mk. 12:24–27.
[102] R. Brown, 1, p. 367.

is the receiving of sight by the blind (Is. 29:18; 35:5). Verse 5 makes an explicit connection with Jesus' earlier claim (8:12), *I am the light of the world*. In this chapter we learn again that the coming of the light has a twofold effect. It brings salvation to those who are blind (6–38), and brings the shadow of judgment to those who will not come to the light (*cf.* 39–41).

The opening verses set the scene. *A man blind from birth* (1). Who is responsible? For the disciples, as for the Jews of the time and for many others since, the answer is simple. Personal suffering of this nature is due to personal sin. The only uncertainty concerns who is directly responsible. Since the sin concerned must have been congenital, the options were either that this man committed it during his antenatal life in the womb, or his parents had committed it before his birth. While the Bible allows a general relationship between suffering and sin, due to the fall (*cf.* Gn. 3; Rom. 5:12f.), it refuses to permit the principle to be individualized in every case. Sin has produced a suffering world, but an individual's personal suffering is not always attributable to his or her personal sin. Sometimes of course it may be, as when suffering results from drunken driving or sexual promiscuity. But Scripture refuses to universalize such instances. This was the issue between Job and his friends, and the lesson of the book of Job is God's dismissal of that simplistic theology of suffering. It is here dismissed by Jesus.

This simplistic view is met today, however, in much 'popular religion' which lives in fear of breaking the rules lest some punishment be visited. Specifically it is expressed in Hinduism with its doctrine of *karma*, the notion that the immortal soul has to go on working out, in a whole series of lives, the consequences of its actions, so that good is rewarded by a 'higher' life in the next reincarnation, and evil punished by a 'lower'. Hindu thought would therefore offer a further possible answer to the implied question in verse 2: 'Did he sin in a previous life?'[103] This eastern idea has permeated the West through the New Age movement, which in many of its popularizers embraces the idea of multiple lives, and links what happened in previous existences to problems faced in the here and now.[104] The Bible fundamentally rejects such notions.

[103] A few rabbis in North Africa argued in somewhat similar terms concerning the soul's antenatal life.

[104] J. Head and S. L. Cranston, eds., *Reincarnation: The Phoenix Fire Mystery* (Julian, 1977); N. L. Geisler and J. Yutaka Amano, *The Reincarnation Sensation* (Tyndale, 1986). S. MacLaine, *Out on a Limb* (Bantam, 1983); R. Chandler, *Understanding the New Age* (Word, 1988), pp. 262–269; F. LaGard Smith, *Out on a Broken Limb* (Harvest House), pp. 69f.

Each person is a distinct individual, made in God's image and confronted with the call to believe in Christ. Each is responsible to God for his or her life and will give account to him personally beyond death (Heb. 10:29f.). Jesus' expression of urgency in verse 4 indicates how incompatible with his teaching such ideas are. The time is urgent precisely because we have only this one life in which to work for God. There are no further 'lives'.

The attempt to establish a simplistic correspondence between sin and suffering also resurfaces in certain theologies of healing. Thus for a sick person to be made well it is necessary for them to repent of their sins, or their unbelief, or their broken relationships, or their lack of faith, or their unwillingness to praise and thank God for their illness, and so on. There is a grain of truth here in that sickness *may* have some relationship to some sinful situation in the past, dealing with which may, correspondingly, be a factor in the healing process. But when that insight is universalized so that all sickness is related to sin, and the whole burden for the healing falls squarely upon the invalid, then not only is a wrong theology being applied but an inhumane and God-dishonouring assault is being waged on the hapless sufferer.

All our Lord will venture is that in this case *the work of God might be displayed in his life* (3). Jesus already knows the way in which this man will become a 'sign', revealing the glory of the one sent by God. This also, however, should not be elevated to a universal principle. It is true that in many cases where suffering is submitted to God then God's work *is* displayed, possibly by a healing or deliverance, as here, or alternatively by a courageous acceptance of the suffering, enabling a discovery of God's strength in our weakness, as was Paul's experience (2 Cor. 12:7–10). But in the end there is a dimension in suffering which defies all 'explanation'. In a fallen world, exhaustive explanations are in principle not available. The nearest we come to plumbing the mystery is at the cross, and even there a 'why?' could not be suppressed (Mt. 27:46). 'We can "make sense" of a dark world only by believing in the one who came to be the "light of the world".'[105]

The existence of human suffering and blindness is a call to work, not simply to reflect (4). Jesus links the disciples with himself in referring to his work, an anticipation of his teaching in chapters 13–16. In a larger sense, it anticipates the coming ages when the risen Lord would be at work in the world through his people. For Jesus himself, but also for his disciples in every age, there is an urgency to be reckoned with (4). 'As the shortness of daylight stirs labourers to industry, that they may not be overtaken by the

[105] L. Newbigin, p. 120.

darkness of night in the middle of their work, so when we see that a short time of life is allotted to us we should be ashamed of lazing in idleness.'[106] It is a similarly diligent attitude that is commended in Jesus' parable in Matthew 24:45–51. On his return, the Master expects to find his servants busily applying themselves to the tasks he has allotted them. *Night is coming*; and, as for Jesus, so for us, there are some things which will not keep until after this life is ended. Therefore we 'must' work.

Jesus proceeds to heal the blind beggar, using a mudpack made from saliva (6). There were primitive beliefs in the first century concerning the magical powers of the saliva of heroic figures. No reason for Jesus' using this method is given. Indeed, we are not told why he should use means at all when a word had sufficed in previous acts of healing (*cf*. 4:50, 53). Perhaps the man needed to be involved in the healing process by some simple act of obedience to Jesus. Early writers saw a link between the ground used in the mudpack and the dust from which Adam was formed (Gn. 2:7).[107] The Pool's meaning (Siloam = Sent), is surely not coincidental from John's perspective. Consistently in this gospel Jesus is the 'sent one' of the Father. As such he wields the Father's re-creating power. The man having obeyed the command to wash in Siloam *came home seeing* (7). Again Jesus appears as a fulfiller. 'The waters of Siloam disappear in the living water of Christ.'[108]

The man is now subject to a series of interviews, first by his neighbours, who are not even sure he is the same person (8–9). He is called upon to 'tell his story' of his healing but of course cannot identify Jesus, as he has never 'set eyes' on him (11–12). The neighbours bring the man to the Pharisees, concerned no doubt to have some help in understanding this astonishing miracle (13). It is at this point we learn that the healing had taken place on the Sabbath. From the strictest Pharisaical standpoint, Jesus had infringed the Sabbath tradition (not Scripture!) at two, probably three, points. First, he had healed on the Sabbath, which was permissible only when life was in danger. Patently it was not so in this case. Second, in making the mud he had kneaded on the Sabbath, which was specifically forbidden. Third, he had anointed the man's eyes, which the stricter teachers also proscribed.

The Pharisees take the matter with due seriousness, which was no less than it deserved in view of the greatness of the sign performed. They conduct three interviews, first with the man (13–17);

---

[106] J. Calvin, 1, p. 240.

[107] *Cf*. 'He who made man out of earth cures him with earth.' Quesnel, cited in Hoskyns, p. 353.

[108] E. C. Hoskyns, p. 355.

secondly with his parents (18–23); and thirdly with the man for a second time (24–34). The man's account of what happened is so persuasive that some of the Pharisees are clearly impressed. *How can a sinner do such . . . ?* (16). For the others, however, Jesus' breach of the Sabbath traditions is enough to damn him. Good men do not break the Sabbath which God has instituted. Jesus breaks the Sabbath, *ergo* Jesus is not a good man (16). It was all so tidy. No hint here of any openness to review what might have been God's purpose in giving the Sabbath, or to face the possibility that the God who had given the Sabbath had further things to reveal. Their God was petrified in the past.

The man, asked to take sides in their dispute by giving *his* view of Jesus, is not daunted. *He is a prophet* (17), probably the highest category he could muster at this point. He sides with the pro-Jesus camp. The Pharisees in their scepticism are still not inclined to believe that the man is really telling the truth, and so decide to seek corroboration from his parents (18). The parents confirm the miracle but are evasive on how, or through whom, it has happened (20–21). The reason is given. To agree that he is the Messiah means excommunication from the synagogue (22). While such hardened rejection of the followers of Jesus became more common among Jews by the time John wrote his gospel, there is no reason to believe that this ban was not applied on a limited local scale during the years of his public ministry. That Jesus stirred up considerable hatred is plain from the historical fact of his crucifixion; that it could take this form is certainly not incredible.

The parents would not have been the first, or the last, who have trimmed the sails of their conviction to the passing breeze. Sadly so, since this surely was a moment for standing with their son in his wonderful new liberation. Perhaps the implications of having a 'seeing son' were not uniformly positive. Begging was, after all, a fairly lucrative source of income in some cases, and the man certainly comes across in the story as a person of considerable initiative and likely therefore to have done well in his begging. Perhaps, in defence of his parents, it needs to be said that being excommunicated from synagogue worship was an extremely serious penalty in that fiercely religious culture. It meant a far-reaching reduction of social as well as religious life and, in their eyes, probably forfeiture of standing with God. The man himself, however, was ready to pay that price (*cf.* 34).

The beggar is recalled for a second hearing (24). The command to *Give glory to God* (24) echoes the summons to Achan (Jos. 7:19), and therefore probably implies, 'Own up and show that you recognize the truthfulness of God by admitting that this prophet of yours is in fact a transgressor of the law, and hence a common sinner,' rather than, 'Give God glory for this miracle, instead of attributing it to this prophet of yours whom we know to be a sinner because he breaks the law.' This draws from the healed man the wonderfully authentic response, *Whether he is a sinner or not, I don't know. One thing I do know. I was blind but now I see!* (25). They are concerned with the finer points of the law and what constituted a breach of it. The man is concerned with the overwhelming reality of his healing. Now he can see, life has been totally transformed. The encounter at this point is a classical expression of the clash between the theoretical and the experiential worlds; not for the first or last time the experiential wins hands down.

The amazing spirit shown by the man is a vivid contrast to the rather flat and submissive attitude to the authorities shown by the man we met in chapter 5 who was healed at the Pool (*cf.* 5:11, 15). This in itself helps authenticate these encounters. Both men, and particularly this one, stand out as credible characters in their own right. It also underlines the variety of the people to whom Jesus ministered. They were very different, yet his grace and healing mercy are available equally for both.

The Pharisees resort to asking for a further account of the healing, which provokes the man to a superb piece of repartee: *Do you want to become his disciples, too?* (implying perhaps that he himself is ready to be counted one; 27). The fundamental issue is thereby brought to the surface. *We are disciples of Moses! We know that God spoke to Moses, but as for this fellow, . . .* (28–29). This was the bottom line in their controversy with Jesus. Their real commitment was to their tradition and to the law of Moses which was its heart. Their commitment to Moses or, more correctly, as they rightly insist, God speaking to and through Moses (29), was valid enough. God *did* speak to him, and what he wrote and conveyed was indeed God's very Word, still authoritative since God had not changed. Their failure lay in the way they viewed and used the law. They did not see it in its covenantal framework, as the way of life appropriate to those who belonged to God solely on the basis of his grace. So understood, the law was a 'grace-law', to be kept out of gratitude for grace received, and not as the means of securing standing with God. They were committed to the ten commandments of Exodus 20:3–17, but had overlooked verse 2, which is the critical context, 'I am the LORD your God, who brought you out of Egypt, out of the land of slavery.' The law was for those who lived by the merciful deliverance of God alone. Because they had lost this context, their zeal for the law committed them to a religion of merit, in which the letter of the law and its meticulous observance, along with all the additional oral requirements, became the essence and end of everything in their religious universe.

This shrinking of horizon also meant that they could think of the Messiah only as a second Moses, who, like themselves, would be a zealot for the letter of the commandments. All God's purposes were therefore ossified around the written law. As a result they could not recognize a Messiah who, as the living presence of God among them, claimed the freedom, as the lawgiver, to reinterpret the law in terms of the further and fuller purposes of God. This included the right to embody the 'more important matters of the law' (Mt. 23:23), not least its 'mercy', as he had done so beautifully, in the renewal of hope, health and usefulness to the blind beggar. From their blinkered viewpoint such a Messiah was unrecognizable. He did not appear to follow Moses, so he could not be from God.

No-one can ponder the tragedy of the Pharisees without asking deep and disturbing questions. Here were men who revered the Scriptures and were zealots for pious behaviour and practices, such as prayer and fasting. They were frequently in worship and gave most sacrificially to God's work. Yet they were among the principal instruments in the hands of Satan in having Jesus destroyed. The Pharisees are not an extinct breed. Whenever we find ourselves valuing the letter of God's law above its spirit; whenever we find ourselves unable to rejoice in the saving and renewing of lives simply because the instrument used was not someone who dots all the i's and crosses all the t's of our theological group; whenever we lose the daily, hourly sense of joy in the grace of God by which alone we know him and live before him, then we need to beware. 'Lord, is it I?' The only security against Pharisaism is grace, which is perhaps the reason the Lord may from time to time permit us to stumble in our Christian walk so that we may have opportunity to rediscover it. Luther's observation, 'there is no cure for spiritual pride like a little over-eating, over-sleeping or over-drinking' is to the point; spiritual Pharisaism may be similarly cured.

The man's final thrust is to express amazement at their professed ignorance of Jesus, in view of the extraordinary power of the miracle he performed (30–32). This evokes their final, angry dismissal: *You were steeped in sin at birth* – a tacit acknowledgment of the validity of the miracle (34; John again has his tongue in his cheek!).

Jesus seeks to minister to the man and help him to fuller understanding. *Do you believe in the Son of Man?* (35). The reference here is to the figure of Daniel 7, the one who will exercise judgment, appropriate in view of Jesus' following comments. What matters almost more than the title is Jesus identifying himself as the one in whom the beggar should now believe. Seeing Jesus for the first time, and having experienced his delivering power at first hand, he is ready to commit himself. *Lord, I believe* (38). *Worshipped* (NIV) may be, strictly speaking, more than the verb in verse 38 will carry. He 'prostrated himself' is more accurate, yet it is impossible to think that worship is not implicit. Jesus certainly does not disavow it.[109]

The Son of Man then pronounces his summary of the entire incident and the subsequent exchanges. *For judgment I have come into this world, so that the blind will see and those who see will become blind* (39). At first blush this appears a direct contradiction of 3:17. The texts, however, are surely reconcilable. Jesus did not come specifically and primarily to condemn or to effect damning judgment. He came primarily and specifically to save sinners in this lost and fallen world. But his coming results *both* in salvation *and* in judgment. The light shines in the darkness. Those who welcome it are delivered into the light, but those who refuse it turn away into a deeper darkness (39). The same light both dispels darkness and casts shadows. The Pharisees, overhearing, query its relation to themselves: *Are we blind too?* (40). If they were without any moral responsibility for their response to Jesus, the light of the world, they would indeed be 'blind', with a 'good' blindness in contrast to their present plight. But since they actually are responsible and yet reject the light, their *guilt remains*, a terrible condition (41).

This incident is an important illustration for John of the meaning of faith.

1. We note that the man expresses the human condition prior to meeting Christ – *blind from birth* (1). Part of the implication of being born into a fallen world is that we have no natural spiritual perception, *cf.* 'their thinking became futile and their foolish hearts were darkened' (Rom. 1:21). 'The blind man represents fallen humanity languishing in the darkness of ignorance and sin without hope of salvation.'[110]

2. The man, however, also eloquently models the way of salvation, the turning from darkness to the light of the world. We note the growth in the healed man's perception. From *The man they call Jesus* (11), he moves on to *He is a prophet* (17), *he opened my eyes* (30), he is *from God* (33), and finally to, '*Lord, I believe,*' *and he worshipped him* (38). Faith is a journey towards Jesus up

---

[109] In complete contrast to his followers when similarly honoured; *cf.* Acts 3:12; 10:26; 14:14–15.

[110] Loisy, cited in Hoskyns, p. 355.

to the point of commitment to him as Lord. When that happens sight is born. And we know that it is so.

3. The man also illustrates the repercussions of coming to believe in Jesus. They may be highly upsetting both for ourselves and our families. The difference in our perspective and outlook may be a rebuke to those around us, bringing to the surface attitudes which we would prefer had been left hidden. Christ can cause division (Mt. 10:34–36), and we need to be ready for it. Whether we can articulate the reality of what Jesus has done for us to the satisfaction of others may be doubtful. In the end we may simply have to testify – *One thing I do know. I was blind but now I see!*

> Loud mockers in the roaring street
> Say Christ is crucified again.
> Twice pierced his gospel-bearing feet,
> Twice broken his great heart in vain.
> I hear, and to myself I smile,
> For Christ talks with me all the while.
>
> *Anon.*

Though such witness be unsophisticated it can be effective, and bring pleasure to the heart of God.

4. The story expresses the division which the coming of Jesus produces (39). To those who respond by coming to the light (3:20–21), casting themselves upon the mercy of Christ, his light shines savingly and renewingly. But those are judged who refuse to come to the light, stubbornly clinging to the light that they claim is already in them. They go out into the darkness in which no light will ever shine.

> Light of the world, for ever, ever shining,
>   There is no change in thee.
> True light of life, all joy and health enshrining,
>   Thou canst not fade nor flee.
>
> Light of the world, undimming and unsetting,
>   O shine each mist away!
> Banish the fear, the falsehood and the fretting;
>   Be our unchanging day.
>
> *Horatius Bonar*

16. The feast of tabernacles III (10:1–21)

The first half of chapter 10 continues in the setting of the feast of tabernacles and concludes the great central teaching section of the gospel. There are two sub-divisions. In the first, Jesus illuminates the distinctiveness of his ministry (1–18), and, in the second, reactions to his teaching are identified (19–21). Links to the immediately preceding section are clear. There is no break in the flow of the discourse at verse 1, and the reaction in verse 21 is specifically related to the healing of the blind man. There is also continuity in the content of the sermon. The Pharisees' treatment of the formerly blind man in verse 34 is not simply an expression of their personal blindness. It also represents a grievous dereliction of duty on their part. As the spiritual leaders of Israel they are responsible for the flock of God (a regular Old Testament image for the nation, cf. Ps. 81:1).

The passage is parabolic in form and Jesus uses several images somewhat interchangeably. Calvin wisely counsels against trying to tie the metaphors down too tightly. 'Let us be content with the general view that Christ likens the Church to a sheepfold in which God assembles his people, and compares himself to the door since he is the only entrance to the Church.'[111] Jesus' imagery would have been familiar in a society where sheep-farming was a staple of the economy. The 'fold' or pen was probably a large, communal enclosure where several flocks were herded for safety at night. The calling of the sheep in the morning (3) would be crucial as each shepherd assembled his own flock from the larger herd in the fold. During the night a guard would be hired (3, the *watchman*). He would remain at the only door to the enclosure. Robbers could enter only by scaling the enclosure. The guard would admit only the true shepherds by the door when they arrived in the morning.

There is a rich Old Testament background to this imagery, most obviously Ezekiel 34:1–31, which is essentially an indictment of the false leaders, the 'shepherds' of God's people. These have failed to care for the sheep by not feeding them, or helping those in various sorts of need. They even cloth themselves 'with the wool and slaughter the choice animals' (Ezk. 34:3). As a result the nation is plundered by its enemies. God makes two promises. In the first, he himself will come and be the shepherd of his sheep, rescuing and regathering his scattered flock and passing judgment on both false shepherds (10) and, where appropriate, on his sheep (16–21). The second promise is that he will appoint a new shepherd. 'I will place over them one shepherd, my servant David, and he will tend them; ... and be their shepherd. I the LORD will be their God, and my servant David will be prince among them' (Ezk. 34:23–24). It is significant that this passage has such close links, both textually and thematically, with the promise of the new covenant in the

[111] J. Calvin, 1, p. 259.

heart, and with the cleansing streams of the coming of the Spirit in Ezekiel 36. False shepherds are also denounced in Isaiah 56:9–12; Jeremiah 23:1–4; 25:32–38 and Zechariah 11. God is the shepherd of Israel in Psalms 23:1; 80:1 and Isaiah 40:11. In collating the biblical background we must not omit the shepherding imagery in Jesus' teaching as recorded in the synoptics.[112]

The discourse naturally divides into two parts, 1–5 and 7–18, separated by a reference to Jesus' *figure of speech*, and his hearers' failure to understand (6).

a. Discourse 3 (10:1–5)

Jesus contrasts himself with the false shepherds with whom he has just tangled, and whose dereliction has been apparent in the case of the newly healed blind-man. He identifies five features of *his shepherding* which show him to be a 'true' shepherd.

1. The appointment he receives. Jesus enters upon his task in the right way. He is appointed by the Father, not self-appointed like the false shepherds of his day (1–2).

2. The response he evokes. *The sheep listen to his voice* (3). It is true that many refused to listen, but the common people heard him gladly (Mk. 12:37), and 'All that the Father gives me will come to me' (6:37). So the beggar has responded, 'Lord, I believe' (9:38).

3. The call he issues. *He calls his own sheep by name* (3). Bernard observes, 'It is still common for Eastern shepherds to give particular names to their sheep descriptive of some trait or characteristic of the animal, as Long-ears, White-nose, *etc.*'[113] It is in personal terms that he calls his followers today.

4. The direction he provides. *He . . . leads them out* (3). Jesus is the guide of his people. To follow him is not to walk in darkness but to have the light of life (8:12). The Pharisees saw their strength lying precisely at this point. They had the law and its application in their hands so were competent to teach people how to live. But they failed to provide guidance because for them living meant 'following the rules'. By contrast, Jesus teaches that living means following a Master ('Follow me', 1:43; 21:19, 22). True, there are rules which reflect his character, but the essence is a living relationship with a living Lord. This guidance will be amplified by the gift of the Spirit, who will 'guide you into all truth' (16:13).

5. The obedience he elicits. *His sheep follow him because they know his voice* (4). Jesus is recognized by *his own* and they gladly give him the rule of their lives.

---

[112] Mt. 9:36; 18:12–14; Mk. 6:34; 14:27; Lk. 15:1–7.
[113] J. H. Bernard, 1, p. 350.

By contrast with the true Shepherd, the 'thieves and robbers' stand self-condemned. They attempt to enter by another way, setting themselves up as leaders. As a result they are false shepherds whom the sheep of Christ do not recognize and from whom they will run away (5).

b. Discourse 3 (10:7–18)

At this point Jesus' imagery becomes more difficult to keep track of. In this section he is both the gate to the enclosure and also the shepherd. We can summarize his teaching as follows.

(i) Jesus reveals the blessings which his shepherding brings to the flock (10:9–10)
The first is 'salvation' – from the threats and dangers which surround the flock, but also from the lostness brought about by sin (*cf.* the imagery of Jesus' parable in Lk. 15:1–6, 'I have found my lost sheep'). This salvation is expressed positively as 'knowing' the shepherd (14). Jesus is the gate to this salvation (9; *cf.* Ps. 118:20). By implication there is no other.

The second blessing for the flock is to *come in and go out and find pasture* (9), an image of security and nurture. The sheep are under the shepherd's care and grow through nourishment by the food he provides. We note that the security is provided by the proximity to the shepherd, not by the walls of the enclosure.

When the people of Christ have forgotten this and tried to secure unity or safety by building walls around themselves, the results have not been encouraging. The walls have either been so comprehensive as to enclose a number of wolves along with the sheep (with disastrous consequences for the sheep) or they have been so restrictive as to exclude more sheep than they enclose.[114]

The blessings of the shepherd are defined more generally in verse 10, *life . . . to the full*. This echoes earlier witness to the new life Jesus brings.[115] It may also hark back to the first of Jesus' signs at Cana which proclaimed him the one who brought the joy of the kingdom to the arid legalism of Judaism. *Life . . . to the full* is the eternal life of the kingdom, with all its rich biblical imagery.[116] It is glimpsed briefly in Eden, and seen in vision in Revelation as a

[114] F. F. Bruce, p. 228.
[115] *Cf.* 3:1–5; 4:14; 5:24–26; 6:33–35; 7:37–38.
[116] *Cf.* Is. 35:1–10; 51:1–16; 55:12–13; 60:1–22; 65:17–25; Joel 3:1–21; Am. 9:13–15; Mi. 4:1–5; Zc. 14:1–21.

city coming down from God, the holy dwelling of God with his people. It is the life for which we were created.

(ii) Jesus speaks of how these blessings are won (10:11–15)
For the kingdom to come, and for its new life to be made available, the shepherd must suffer. Shepherding is a hard, demanding and costly life, in contrast to the perception of most western Christians (excepting farmers!) influenced by memories of cuddly lambs. David experienced this cost when defending his flock from the attacks of wild animals (1 Sa. 17:34–35). The true shepherd is the *good* one who endangers himself if called upon (11, 14). Some commentators, recognizing that *kalos*, 'good', has overtones of beauty, prefer 'noble shepherd',[117] or 'worthy'[118] or 'model'.[119]

Jesus is predicting Calvary. His love for his own will lead him inexorably to sacrifice himself for them. The good shepherd is also the Lamb of God. It is this element which marks off Jesus' exposition of the shepherd theme from its Old Testament taproots. 'The unique feature in the Johannine picture of the shepherd is his willingness to die for the sheep.'[120] The preposition *for* (11) indicates the underlying rationale of the shepherd's action. The sheep are in danger and under threat; the shepherd acts on their behalf for their deliverance. It is here that Jesus makes good his claim to be the *good* (or 'noble') shepherd, unlike the *hired hand* (12). The latter may be a reference, beyond the present Jewish religious leadership, to others who have come before him, professing to be the Messiah, and hence also to others who will subsequently make the same claim (Mt. 24:5). Jesus embodies the goodness and nobility of a love that could not let us go, even to the point of bearing our guilt, in all its horrendous implications, on Calvary. Truly,

> None of the ransomed ever knew
>   How deep were the waters crossed,
> Or how dark the night that the Lord passed through
>   Ere he found the sheep that was lost.
>   *Elizabeth C. Clephane*

Jesus presents himself here as the true leader of his people. His claim has an echo of Moses' prayer for a leader to succeed him. 'Let the LORD, the God of the spirits of all flesh, appoint a man over the congregation, who shall go out before them and come in before them, who shall lead them out and bring them in; that the

---

[117] D. A. Carson, *John*, p. 386; G. R. Beasley-Murray, p. 170.
[118] D. A. Carson, *John*, p. 386.
[119] R. Brown, 1, p. 386.
[120] *Ibid.*, p. 398.

congregation of the LORD may not be as sheep which have no shepherd' (Nu. 27:16f., RSV). The man so appointed was Joshua, but when we recall that the Greek for 'Joshua' is 'Jesus', we can imagine any reader familiar with the Old Testament being directed to the 'greater than Joshua', Jesus the Christ. In his self-sacrifice for the sheep, Jesus presents the true model for leadership. The aim of many leaders today is their own glory. Not truly loving those they lead, they use them as a means to their own personal satisfaction. It is the leadership of the hireling, not of the shepherd. This principle is certainly not confined to the church. Leadership, whether in political life, industry, business, or community, follows one of these two routes. Either it is directed to the self-life of the leader, or it is directed selflessly for the good of those who are led. The former is the way of the world, which leads to death; the latter is the way of Jesus, which leads to life.

(iii)   Jesus indicates who these blessings are for (10:16)
The *other sheep* are those Jesus will call from beyond *this sheep pen* (or, better, 'flock', see below). Since the 'flock' is Israel, according to Old Testament imagery, this can be a reference only to the Gentile church: the millions who over the ages would fall under the spell of Jesus, hear his voice and, through his sacrifice for their sins, receive a share in the new abundant life of his kingdom.

There are moments in Jesus' ministry when his focus seems narrowed to Israel, just as there are similar moments in the Old Testament story. But the true and stated goal both of the Old Testament revelation (*cf.* Gn. 1 – 11; 12:3; Is. 49:6), and of Jesus' ministry (Mt. 28:18f.), is the whole world. The God who created all people, and who loves all equally, sends the offer of his salvation to all the peoples of the earth, that all may believe and then unite together in the one great 'flock' of Jesus, the 'good shepherd' ('fold', 16, AV, was a basic mistranslation). It is a dream captured in the vision of John on Patmos:

> After this I looked, and behold, a great multitude which no man could number, from every nation, from all tribes and peoples and tongues, standing before the throne and before the Lamb . . . crying out with a loud voice, 'Salvation belongs to our God who sits upon the throne, and to the Lamb!' (Rev. 7:9–10, RSV).

Jesus concludes by taking us behind this self-sacrifice (which will produce the new, united flock from all the nations), to the eternal love of Father and Son which is its source (10:17–18). He makes four points.

149

1. The self-sacrifice *of* the Son is related to the Father's love *for* the Son (17). The Father loves the Son because the Son loves us unto death. This is a remarkable revelation. Our need, and Christ's gracious response to it, is the occasion of the drawing forth of the Father's love for his Son. This does not mean that the Father's loving the Son is contingent upon Christ's loving us. Rather, the love of Father for Son, and of Son for Father, is antecedent to all our experience of his grace, and is indeed its ultimate basis. Yet that love finds a fulfilment in the heart of God as the Son gives himself to us. What he uttered at Jesus' baptism, the Father utters with greater vehemence at the cross towards which the baptism pointed: 'This is my Son, whom I love; with him I am well pleased' (Mt. 3:17).

2. The sacrifice of Jesus for us was a voluntary one. *No-one takes [my life] from me, but I lay it down* (18). Thus the control, as far as Jesus' sacrifice is concerned, lies not with Judas, or Caiaphas, or Pilate, or the Sanhedrin, but with Jesus himself. He gave himself freely.

3. Jesus' vision embraces not just his death but also the resurrection which will follow it (18). Indeed, the death itself is a form of exaltation which demands the resurrection as its necessary sequel. In this profound sense it was indeed 'impossible for death to keep its hold on him' (Acts 2:24).

4. All of this Jesus will do in obedience (18). He who is eternally one with the Father is also the Son who always obeys the Father. In that mutuality lies not only the mystery of the inner life of the Trinity, but also the secret of his mission.

c. *The sequel (10:19–21)*

Once again there is division because of Jesus, perhaps all the sharper as he moves closer to his 'hour'. The attribution of demonic inspiration to Jesus (20) has occurred before.[121] The readiness with which the authorities now resort to this judgment bears witness to their increasing frustration. In this accusation they come close to the unforgivable sin (Mt. 12:24–32); *viz.* the deliberate, sustained closing of the heart to the clear witness of the Holy Spirit of truth.[122] The accusation is evidence also of a deepening resolve on the part of Jesus' opponents, a resolute closing of the eyes to the light, which sadly can have only one conclusion in a moral universe, a descent into darkness, unbroken and eternal.

[121] *Cf.* 8:48; 10:21; *cf.* Lk. 11:15f.
[122] For further comment on 'the unforgivable sin', *cf.* the author's *Know the Truth* (IVP, 1982), p. 109.

What are *we* to make of this person? How are we to handle these unparalleled claims and the extraordinary consciousness which underlies them? A unique self-consciousness runs right through these dialogues, and permeates the entire portrait of Jesus in this gospel, which is, we recall, a book replete with eye-witness elements, which attained universal acceptance among Jesus' contemporaries. This 'mind', however, is not unique to John. The Jesus of the synoptic gospels makes similar staggering claims and evidences a parallel self-consciousness.[123]

The picture hangs together. To push it back on to the evangelists by referring it to their 'creative genius' or the like only begs the question. As has been remarked, 'It would take a Jesus to invent a Jesus.' We cannot stand back in serene judgment on these Jews. What are *we* to make of him? The choice is inescapable. Is he, as he claims, from God, or the deluded victim of some 'obsession'? We too must choose. Everything without exception hangs on our response.

17. The feast of dedication (10:22–42)

Our study of the gospel to this point will have alerted us not to take a 'feast' reference as a mere piece of local colour. Unlike the other feasts which had ancient biblical roots, this particular feast had its origin in comparatively recent history. In 167 BC, when the Syrian Emperor, Antiochus Epiphanes, was attempting to establish uniformity of worship throughout his empire, he desecrated the temple in Jerusalem by erecting an altar to Zeus. In a heroic struggle, Judas Maccabaeus led an ultimately successful revolt against the Syrians, and in December 164 BC the temple was reconsecrated in an eight-day celebration. This became an annual, joyous commemoration of the victory and the restored freedom of worship. Unlike the other feasts it did not involve pilgrimage to Jerusalem, but could be celebrated at home. Held during the December period (hence *winter*; 22), it was therefore about three months after the tabernacles feast, but often associated with it in the popular mind. One specific overlap was the use of lights. In this case it celebrated the restoration of the light of freedom.

The reference to 'winter' may be symbolic, as John's use of 'darkness' is elsewhere (*cf.* 1:5; 13:30). Certainly the chill winds of unbelief and rejection had begun to blow in earnest among the Jewish religious leadership. The temperature at that time of year also probably dictated the location of Jesus' teaching. *Solomon's*

---

[123] *Cf.* Mt. 4:19; 5:17, 22, 28; 9:2; 10:37; 11:6f., 25–30; 12:40–42; Mk. 13:26; 14:22, 62; Lk. 4:21; 18:22; 20:17; *etc.*

Colonnade was surrounded by arched pillars on four sides and would afford shelter from the cold winds. It would be the scene of the meetings of the earliest Christian believers a few months hence (Acts 5:12).

This visit was Jesus' final period of ministry in Jerusalem before his 'processional' move on the city at the Passover four months later. The brevity of his reported encounter and its concluding threat of violence are in keeping. The time is running out for Jesus, and he knows it. The 'hour' appointed by his Father will soon be at hand, but until that hour strikes he must 'finish the work' he has been given to do. Jerusalem must be given one further opportunity to embrace the light before the 'hour of darkness' arrives.

Jesus' debate with the Jews gathers around two titles: 'Messiah', verses 24–30; and 'Son of God', verses 31–39.

a. Messiah (10:24–30)

The Jews attempt to confront Jesus, *How long will you keep us in suspense?* (24) is probably not as good a translation as 'How long do you intend to annoy us?',[124] reflecting an attitude of hostility on the part of those who have made up their minds about Jesus, and are looking only for further grounds on which to accuse him. Jesus refuses to state categorically in the course of a public proclamation that he is the Messiah (though he is not reticent with individuals, *cf.* 4:26). The most probable reason is that their political and military understanding of the messianic role made it impossible to make the claim openly. The feast of dedication and its reminders of the heroic leadership of Judas Maccabaeus would do nothing to reduce this understanding. Jesus himself is patently assured that he is the Messiah foretold by Scripture, but it is evident that the Jews were in no state of mind to recognize and receive such a deliverer. Jesus can do no more than point them to the twin witnesses which he had already supplied – his works (*miracles*, 25), and his words (27). But they have rejected them, *because you are not my sheep* (26).

Jesus' repetition of the shepherding metaphor, used in the tabernacles III discourse (1–18), has caused some interpreters to assume that John has artificially introduced a break in the teaching to accommodate the feast of dedication. There is no reason, however, why Jesus should not use the same material in different contexts with new applications. No travelling preacher, then or since, has shown any reticence about doing so, nor have they usually encount-

[124] C. K. Barrett, p. 380.

ered rejection on that ground. Besides, Jesus' reference to his sheep perfectly fits the point he is concerned to make to the Jews here (12), that their antipathy to him lies in their being closed to the call of the Father through him. More generally, they are finally powerless to prevent the true flock of the Messiah coming to the shepherd and following him. In standing against Jesus they are in fact dashing themselves against the inviolable and indestructible purposes of God. The shepherd imagery also makes sense in response to their question (24), for one of the supreme Old Testament images of the Messiah was David, the shepherd king of Israel.

In the course of his reply (25–30) Jesus refers to some of the supreme privileges of those who believe in him.

1. They are a *summoned* group. *My sheep listen to my voice* (27). The call of Christ has brought them into a new relationship with him (*I know them*); a relationship which in turn leads to a new lifestyle (*they follow me*). The proof of faith is obedience. 'Only he who truly obeys truly believes.'[125]

2. They are a *gifted* group. The gift they receive is *eternal life* (28). All who believe will live; the new life of the kingdom is theirs. No longer a part of this passing 'world', under the power of the evil one, *they shall never perish* (28). They are part of the permanent.

3. They are a *secured* group: *no-one can snatch them out of my Father's hand* (29). Christ's people are his possession. He has committed himself to them even as they for their part have, however falteringly, committed themselves to him. In this too the Father and the Son are one (30). The 'flock' has been given to the Son by the Father and he stands behind the Son in his guardianship of the flock. Hence the forces of opposition and destruction have to confront the awesome and limitless power of the Father, who is 'greater than all'. No profounder security is conceivable for the follower of Jesus.

> Christ declares that his people 'will never perish'. Weak as they are they will all be saved. Not one of them shall be lost and cast away: not one of them shall miss heaven. If they err, they shall be brought back; if they fall, they shall be raised. The enemies of their soul may be strong and mighty, but their Saviour is mightier; and none shall pluck them out of their Saviour's hand.[126]

[125] E. Brunner, *The Doctrine of the Church, Faith and the Consummation* (Lutterworth, 1960), p. 299.

[126] J. C. Ryle, p. 193.

153

Jesus' specifying the reason for the Jewish leaders' failure to believe in him as *you are not my sheep* confronts us with the mystery of divine election and human unbelief. In stressing the call of the Son and the gifting of the Father, Jesus does not eliminate the leaders' culpability for their rejection of him. Their responsibility is the unuttered premise of every word of judgment he pronounces. But behind and through their response God is also at work. The salvation that is worked by humans is also willed by God. If we find ourselves among the flock who have heard the Shepherd's voice, it is not because those who do not believe are greater sinners, for our hearts also incline to the darkness. We also resist coming to the light lest our deeds be exposed (3:20). Only by the sovereign mercy of God are we found among the company of the 'believers' in Jesus. But, like the election of Jesus, our election is always to service and sacrifice (*cf.* Is. 42:1, 6f.). To receive his grace is to be committed to the sharing of the message of that grace with all the world. The chosen are the commissioned.[127]

The final matter for comment is the claim *I and the Father are one* (30). It should be clear from the context that it is an essentially functional unity which Jesus is referring to here. The Father and Son are one in the mission of the Son, and hence those whom the Son calls and undertakes to protect are simultaneously the concern of the Father. The widespread use of this text in the early Christological controversies is therefore somewhat misplaced. It would also be a mistake, however, to ignore this statement as far as our understanding of the person of Christ is concerned. This unity of action is finally inseparable from a unity of persons. To assert, as Jesus does here, that he is so at one with the living God that his action is the action of God in and through him, is necessarily to say something about the way in which God and Jesus are related. A claim such as this reflects no merely human consciousness. It is nothing other than a 'word made flesh' consciousness. It is certainly not exceeding the limits of this text, therefore, to establish a connection with the prologue and the confession there of the deity of Christ. Schnackenberg comments, 'In these words ("I and the Father are one") we are given a glimpse of the metaphysical depths contained in the relationship between Jesus and the Father.'[128]

b. Son of God (10:31–39)

Whatever our view today of the claim of Jesus in verse 30, its implications are clear enough for his audience: *the Jews picked up stones to stone him* (31). In defence, Jesus reminds them of his

[127] See comments at 1:1 and 6:37   [128] R. Schnackenburg, 2, p. 308.

many 'great' miracles.[129] The Jews will have none of it. Jesus' crime is clear – *blasphemy, because you, a mere man, claim to be God* (33). The Greek here, 'make yourself God', is significant and also ironic, for this is precisely what Jesus is *not* guilty of doing. He is not a mere man who is aspiring to 'become as God', a repetition of the primal sin of Adam in Eden. Jesus has totally renounced any claim for himself. He is only who the Father appoints him to be. He is not bent on his own glory, but seeks only the glory of the Father. He did not grasp at equality with God (Phil. 2:6).

In effect, Jesus is calling the Jews to a revision of their understanding of God. Their radical and uncompromising monotheism implied that any claim to deity represented, necessarily, a claim to rival God, as a second God. Hence the charge of blasphemy inevitably followed. By contrast, Jesus presents them with a God who possesses an internal richness of being, a God able therefore to appear in person among them as 'the Father's Son' without thereby abdicating or compromising his majestic Godhead. The God who had appeared on Sinai was now 'God a second time' in the one who confronted them as 'the Son of the Father'. God was not an undifferentiated monad but a multi-person Trinity.

Jesus' defence against their accusation of blasphemy is to refer them back to the Old Testament Scriptures (34), to Psalm 82:6. (Note that 'law' includes the Psalms.) The exact object of the reference to 'gods' in this text was debated by the Jews, and still is. Three main identifications of the 'gods' have been advocated: the judges of Israel, the angels of God, or the Israelite recipients of the Word of God addressed in the Psalm. The third appears the most straightforward. Jesus may be hinting that since the receiving of the 'Word of God' through the prophets was sufficient to ennoble the recipients to the rank of 'sons of God', how much more appropriately is that title referred to him who is 'the Word of God' in the flesh. More generally, Jesus is arguing that if the title had some relevance to mere men in the Old Testament period, it can hardly be thought too exalted a title for him *whom the Father set apart as his very own and sent into the world* (36). The reference to 'setting apart' (36) is noteworthy. The root of the verb is the idea of holiness, or dedication. Here again Jesus is the fulfiller of the feasts of Israel. The feast of dedication celebrated the rededicating of the temple as the sanctuary of the living God. Jesus is the one whom the Father has 'dedicated' from all eternity as the meeting place of God and humanity, the sanctuary in and through whom the living God may be approached and worshipped.

---

[129] The Greek is *kalos*, the same adjective used with 'shepherd' in verses 11 and 14. 'Noble' might again be appropriate, even 'beautiful', or 'fine'.

We note too Jesus' passing affirmation of the veracity and trust-worthiness of the written Scriptures which *cannot be broken* (35). 'Wherever the Scripture speaks plainly on any subject, there can be no more question about it. The case is settled and decided. Every jot and tittle of Scripture is true, and must be received as conclusive.'[130]

Jesus also appeals once more to the 'works' which point clearly to the Father's presence with, and in, him (29). But they will not tolerate it. The end of the road has been reached. They grope for their stones, but he *escaped their grasp* (39). His hour has not yet come, though come it will, and soon. Never again, however, will he present himself to them as the fulfiller of their feasts, the messianic King and life-giver. Henceforth he will come only as the fulfiller of the Passover, 'despised and rejected' by them, that through that very rejection he may become a 'light to the Gentiles' (Is. 53:3; 49:6).

c. 10:40–42

Jesus withdraws from the city north-eastwards to the vicinity identified as the place where John the Baptist had his great ministry and bore witness to Jesus (40). The location is debated. The issue is linked to the location of the 'Bethany' referred to in 1:28 as the site of John the Baptist's early ministry. It is clear that it was not the Bethany close to Jerusalem where Jesus' seventh sign would shortly be performed. Some recent opinion favours the territory known as Batenea in Philip's tetrarchy, where Jesus began his mission. Others favour Transjordan (see below on 11:6).

The welcome he receives there, as '*many believed*' (42), no doubt fortified him for the final conflict ahead. They remembered John the Baptist there, the supreme human witness to Jesus. *Though John never performed a miraculous sign, all that John said about [Jesus] was true* (41). In a society where the performing of miracles was seen as essential to divine authorization, John's failure to perform such said much about the impact of his life at other levels. No greater testimonial to a witness could be penned. 'All that he said about Jesus was true.' Let every teacher, preacher and witness aspire to the same.

18. The seventh sign – the raising of Lazarus (11:1–57)

The 'revealing of his glory' (1:18) through the 'signs' (2:11) now reaches its final stage with the greatest 'sign', the raising of Lazarus

---

[130] J. C. Ryle, p. 196.

from the dead, an action which will lead inexorably on to the all-surpassing 'sign' of the death and resurrection of Jesus himself. It is helpful to sub-divide the chapter as follows.

a. The sickness and death of Lazarus of Bethany (1–16)
b. The meetings with Martha and Mary and Jesus' grief (17–37)
c. The raising of Lazarus from the dead (38–44)
d. The Sanhedrin's decision to have Jesus killed (45–57)

a. The sickness and death of Lazarus of Bethany (11:1–16)

Jesus has withdrawn from Jerusalem prior to his return to the city for the final Passover, as was noted in 10:40. His preparation for that supremely demanding crisis is interrupted by an urgent request for help. This comes from a family especially close to him, living at Bethany, a few miles south east of Jerusalem. The family consists of two sisters, Martha and Mary, and their brother, Lazarus. John identifies Mary as *the same one who poured perfume on the Lord and wiped his feet with her hair* (2). This anticipates what we learn about her in the next chapter (12:1–8), and the description is no doubt to distinguish her from other Marys in the gospel (*cf.* 19:25–26; 20:1). It may also indicate that John's first-century readers are already familiar with the incident and have some knowledge of the Christian story.

It is usually presumed that Lazarus and his sisters were resident in the same household, though in fact the text does not state that. If Lazarus was a man of mature years, as by all accounts he appears to have been, then he would almost certainly have been married and living in his own home, though within the village. This may explain the comment in 12:2 where, at the dinner given in Jesus' honour by the sisters, Lazarus is explicitly identified among the guests, an unnecessary detail if the dinner was being served in his own home. The unity of the family is patent, however, so when their brother falls seriously ill the sisters send to Jesus for help. Their message is somewhat oblique – *Lord, the one you love is sick* (3). It may be that they were informed of his recent encounter with the authorities in Jerusalem, and recognized that to bring him again to the vicinity of the city would be dangerous. Certainly Thomas is in no doubt about the folly of such a journey in these circumstances (16). The wording may be a conscious compromise. Perhaps they are also aware of Jesus having healed on a previous occasion by means of a word, without his physical presence being necessary (4:43–54). The title given to Jesus, *Lord*, probably renders the Aramaic for 'rabbi' (*cf.* 28; 20:16). As D. A. Carson observes,

157

the message 'hints at friendships and relationships that are barely explored in the Gospels, and suggests that some at least felt peculiarly loved by him'.[131]

Jesus responds to the message by making two comments on the illness of Lazarus, and by deliberately choosing to stay *where he was two more days* (6). His first comment is that the sickness will not prove fatal in the long run (4). Some see this as a recognition that Lazarus was not in fact dead at this point and that Jesus hoped he could still be cured. This appears to conflict, however, with the evident control of events which Jesus exercises at every point in this incident. It is therefore better to interpret this initial reaction as setting the scene for what follows. Lazarus, a beloved and valued friend, has succumbed to the power of sickness, the emissary of the 'god of this world'. But the power of sickness, this manifestation of the fall, will not have the final say. The final outcome (Jesus' second comment), will be life, not death, therein manifesting the glory of the Son, the dethroning of the god of this world,[132] and the further glory of the Father through him (4).

Jesus' attitude to sickness here is parallel to 9:3: the sickness provides a platform so that the 'work of God might be displayed in his life'. What is true here at the level of physical illness can be extended to all the trials we face as Christian disciples. Our natural response is to rebel against them as alien intruders, which must be expelled from our lives as quickly and painlessly as possible by every means available, including God's miraculous intervention. With hindsight, however, another perspective is possible. We can offer our trials to God for him either to remove or retain as *he* pleases, thereby bringing glory to his name and deepening our faith, and possibly that of others too.

Joni Eareckson Tada, a paraplegic sufferer, authentically expresses this second alternative. 'I do not care if I am confined to this wheelchair provided from it I can bring glory to God.'[133] The same conviction is expressed more generally by Hudson Taylor. 'Trials afford God a platform for his working in our lives. Without them I would never know how kind, how powerful, how gracious he is.' While we may feel daunted by the heights of devotion reflected in these quotations, we can all make a beginning in our present pains by offering them consciously to God for his using. From such small seeds a new maturity can blossom.

According to verse 6, Jesus, receiving the news of Lazarus' con-

---

[131] D. A. Carson, *John*, p. 406.
[132] *Cf.* comment below on 'deeply moved', verses 33 and 38.
[133] Joni Eareckson Tada and Steve Estes, *A Step Further* (Zondervan, 1978), p. 41.

dition, deliberately remained where he was for two further days before making any response. This is in no way a contradiction of his love for the family (5).[134] Why the two days' delay? Our answer will necessarily touch the issue of Jesus' precise whereabouts. The traditional location is in Transjordan, which would set him within a day or so's journey from Bethany. By this view Lazarus died almost as soon as the messenger set off for Jesus. His delay in that case has two possible explanations. *Either* he is unwilling to allow his movements to be determined merely by his natural desire to hurry to Bethany as soon as possible. (He is at the command of the Father and must wait for the Father's timing for a move back to the proximity of Jerusalem.) *Or* Jesus waited to ensure that by the time he arrived at Bethany Lazarus would have been dead four days (*cf.* 17). The reason for this timing will be indicated below (*cf.* comment on 17).

If, however, Jesus had withdrawn all the way to Batenea, which was a good four days' journey to the north east, the reconstruction in that case has Jesus receiving the message about Lazarus at a time when Lazarus is still alive. The statement in verse 4, *This sickness will not end in death*, then belongs to the point where Lazarus is still hanging on to life. Two days later, Jesus, perceiving by supernatural means that Lazarus has died, proceeds on his journey of four days to reach Bethany and raise him again.

A location at further remove from Jerusalem fits the need for Jesus to escape the city entirely at this point. *Let us go back to Judea* (7) appears to imply a significant change of location. The synoptics, however, appear to locate John's early ministry in some proximation to Jerusalem (*cf.* Mt. 3:1–5). The Batenea location would also necessitate Jesus modifying his plans in view of the unforeseen deterioration in Lazarus' condition. It also leaves somewhat unexplained the evangelist's drawing attention to the two-day delay. In all this we necessarily deal in suppositions. The essential issue appears to be that Jesus does not respond immediately to the sisters' plea, with the result that by the time he arrives at Bethany Lazarus has been dead for four days.

The delays of God are clearly part of the biblical record. One may ask at the most basic level why the effects of the fall were not addressed more immediately, or more particularly why so many centuries preceded the coming of the Redeemer. We can likewise ask why the Lord delays his return, with all its concomitant blessings. True, Peter addresses that in terms of God's patient grace

---

[134] NIV makes the link between Jesus' love and his delay a direct one. *Yet when he heard . . .*; the Greek, however, simply says, 'When therefore he heard . . .'

which gives sinners further opportunity to repent (2 Pet. 3:9). But even limited contact with the pain and anguish of so many human lives world-wide makes the question inescapable. Many find the question of delays raised for them personally as they pray through long years for some particular need, perhaps some personal disability they seek freedom from, or a loved one for whose salvation they yearn. Others struggle with some promise of God which remains unfulfilled after weary years of waiting.

This story teaches us two things about God's delays. The first is that they are inevitable. Since we are mere finite creatures, we are necessarily largely unaware of the circumstances which surround the events taking place in our lives and those of others, as well as the consequences which result from them. Only God is omniscient. Further, since our desires are not fully renewed, even if we were aware of all the implications, there is no guarantee that we would choose only what was for the highest good for ourselves and others. Our imperfect desires also make us want immediate answers, and render us unprepared for the patient ripening of God's plans. His delays, however, do not contradict his love (*cf.* 5). He loves us as fully and as truly when he remains in Transjordan (or Batenea), ministering to others' needs, as when he journeys to Bethany to minister to ours. The second point about God's delays is that they are not final. He will come, in his own time and way. No doubt that will frequently be later than we would have chosen. From his divine perspective, however, it will be the right time. God is the best of time-keepers. He created time; he is never late for his appointments.

The delay concluded, Jesus gives the order to go to Bethany (15). The disciples are well aware of the danger there and remind him of it (8). In response Jesus warns against over-estimating the danger. Just as there is daylight as well as darkness, and journeys are always possible if the right hour is chosen, so while the darkness of opposition is looming there is still time to 'do the work of him who sent me' (9:4). Further, since he is the light of this world, the disciples, if they keep close to him, will have light to walk by also.

Jesus announces that Lazarus has died, first metaphorically (11) and than directly (14). 'Sleep', while used of death in the Old Testament, as, for example, 'Amaziah rested [slept] with his fathers' (2 Ki. 14:22), was not a common way of referring to it, which perhaps explains the disciples' failure to grasp the import. The use of this metaphor by Jesus, both here and in the raising of Jairus' daughter, (Mk. 5:39) set the trend for later Christian usage (*cf.* Acts 7:60; 1 Thes. 4:13). As a metaphor for death it need not imply the end of all consciousness following the moment of death.

In Scripture, sleep is regularly a very 'active' experience.[135] Primarily, 'sleep' implies the truth of the recovery of consciousness after death.

> When I go down to the grave, I can say like so many others that I have finished my day's work; but I cannot say that I have finished my life. Another day's work will begin the next morning. The tomb is not a blind alley – it is a thoroughfare. It closes with the twilight to open with the dawn.
>
> *Victor Hugo*

Jesus reiterates that this death of Lazarus is a 'good death' about which he is personally glad, *so that you may believe* (15). The pain and anguish of the family are still of less worth than the nourishing of the faith of both the family and the attendant disciples. Once again the cruciality of faith is stressed.

Let us go to him (15). *Him*, we note, is a person, not a corpse. As spokesperson, Thomas reflects a whole-heartedness which will find later expression (*cf.* 20:28). He also unwittingly lays out the terms of following Jesus: *Let us also go, . . . that we may die with him.* The invitation to follow Jesus is precisely that. 'If anyone would come after me, he must deny himself and take up his cross and follow me' (Mk. 8:34). 'When Jesus calls a man to follow him he bids him come and die.'[136] The disciples, however, have still to learn this lesson in experience. A fiery crucible awaits them before they too will walk the way of the cross.

b. The meetings with Martha and Mary and Jesus' grief (11:17–37)

Verse 17 brings us directly to the time-frame of this sign. Whatever our view of the geographical sub-plot it is clear that Jesus' moment of arrival is deliberately designed so that *Lazarus had already been in the tomb for four days* (17). The reason for this must now be explored.

There is good rabbinic evidence for a Jewish belief that, for three days after death, the soul of the deceased person 'hovered' around the body seeking re-entry. On the fourth day, 'when it sees the colour of its face has changed (*i.e.* that decomposition has commenced) then it goes away and leaves it'.[137] This evidence is from the third century and so some caution needs to be exercised in

---

[135] *Cf.* Gn. 28:11–15; Dn. 7:1f.; Mt. 1:20.

[136] D. Bonhoeffer, *The Cost of Discipleship* (Macmillan, 1963), p. 99.

[137] H. L. Strack-Billerbeck, *Kommentar zum Neuen Testament aus Talmud und Midrasch* (C. H. Beck, 1926–61), 2, pp. 544f.

assuming that it was held generally in Jesus' day. Hoskyns, however, finds a more general cultural support for the distinction
between the third and fourth days. Hospitality in the East allowed
visitors a stay of three days' duration, a day to rest, a day for
fellowship and a day for departure. To stay on for a fourth day
was a very serious breach of etiquette. A similar distinction between
the third and fourth days was apparently later used by some Christians to test the validity of a travelling prophet. True prophets would
be on their way by the end of the third day. Those staying longer
were spongers on Christian hospitality.[138] There is a similar conviction in the ancient Persian religion, Zoroastrianism, that on the
morning of the fourth day after death the soul finally abandons the
body and passes over the bridge Cinvat, where the good and evil
are separated from each other. Hoskyns describes the belief in
this distinction as 'widespread' among the Jews of that period.[139]
Edersheim mentions that Jewish mourning customs viewed the first
three days after death as being for the greatest and most intense
mourning, during which the dead person was still present to witness
the grief of his or her family and friends.[140]

Turning to strictly biblical data, we should note the importance
of the third day after death, especially significant in respect of the
resurrection of Jesus (cf. Ho. 6:2; cf. 20:1). The time of Jesus'
arrival, therefore, coincided with the conclusion of the first three
intense days of mourning, the period when the soul has left the
body beyond any recall and decomposition had set in. Jesus deliberately withholds his succour until the enemy he is confronting has
assumed a fullness of authority and destructiveness. The greater the
challenge, the greater the miracle, and the greater the strengthening
of his followers' faith as a result; and above all, the greater the
glory accruing to his Father through it.

The presence of mourners reflected the Jewish custom. Rabbis
taught the solemn duty of comforting mourners, and the sisters
clearly had a significant company of friends in the nearby city,
probably confirming the impression (cf. 12:3) that theirs was a
family of some means.

Although the character details given in the gospels are meagre,
the sisters' reactions appear at least congruent with what we derive
from Luke's cameo of the home (Lk. 10:38–42). Martha, arguably
the older, takes immediate initiative to meet Jesus while Mary,

---

[138] *The Didache*, 12, Ancient Christian Writers, tr. J. Kleist (Newman,
1984), p. 23.
[139] E. C. Hoskyns, p. 199.
[140] A. Edersheim, *The Life and Times of Jesus the Messiah* (Eerdmans,
1984), 2, pp. 318–320.

more dependent and spiritually intuitive, waits for Jesus' initiative (20). Martha immediately addresses Jesus, *Lord* (*cf.* 3), . . . *if you had been here, my brother would not have died* (21). This almost appears as a rebuke for his tardiness in responding to the message, and hence by implication lays on Jesus some measure of responsibility for Lazarus' death. On the other hand, she may simply be indicating that she believes that had Jesus been able to be there he would have saved Lazarus from death. However her opening words are to be construed (and it should be noted that Mary was to repeat them; 32), her next words appear in a different and more hopeful tone. *But I know that even now God will give you whatever you ask* (22). This strikes a positive note, as though she is quite ready to believe in the astounding miracle which is shortly to take place. The statement has to be qualified, however, in view of verse 24, and more especially verse 39, where Martha objects to the opening of the tomb. Perhaps she is simply saying that as a person with unique intercessory power, Jesus will still be able to bring hope to the family even in face of the enormous tragedy of their brother's death.

Jesus' immediate reassurance of Lazarus' future resurrection (23) calls forth Martha's confession: *I know he will rise again in the resurrection at the last day* (24). Here Martha identifies with the larger hope of Judaism. Over against the Sadducean party, incorporating many of the leading clerics of the day, which trenchantly denied the resurrection of the dead (*cf.* Mk. 12:18–27), Martha, like the Pharisees, believes that God will not leave his own to pass for ever into oblivion. Lazarus will rise when the messianic kingdom dawns at the general resurrection on the last day (24).

Jesus' remarkable reply, *I am the resurrection and the life*, is a culmination of the unfolding revelation in the preceding chapters. Jesus has been revealed as the giver of life, in a number of ways. Materially, he gives life to water, making it wine. Spiritually, he offers the new spiritual life of the kingdom of God to Nicodemus, and the life which springs up within a person satisfying all thirst, to the woman of Samaria. Physically, he imparts life to a dying boy, a long-standing physical paralytic, and a man born blind. He is the good shepherd who has come to give life 'to the full' (10:10). The life he brings is primarily 'eternal life' (literally 'life of the age'), the life of the long-awaited kingdom of God. Jesus now fills out these claims to their fullest proportion. The life he gives is nothing less than the indestructible life of the resurrection, the very life of the deathless God himself. Moreover, it is his gift here and now. Martha believes in some such life at the distant horizon of history when the Messiah eventually appears. Jesus invites her to reshape her hope radically. Resurrection life which triumphs over death is not confined to the distant future, but is present here and now in him who is the Resurrection, the embodiment of the promised life and salvation of God. To believe in Jesus means that death lies defeated. True, there may be a moment of physical dissolution (*though he dies*, 25), but in fact that will not be 'death', the elimination of hope and the reduction of existence to a mere shadowy beyond. For the believer, the present reality is the eternal life of God received through faith in Jesus. Can Martha rise to that level of faith?

Perhaps not fully. Yet she can affirm that Jesus is the Messiah, the *Son of God, who was to come into the world* (27). *Son* here may simply represent a messianic title.[141] Readers of this gospel will know by this time that the title has new depths of meaning in terms of Jesus' unique oneness with the Father, in his mission and person (see the comment on 1:49; on *come into the world*, see the comment on 1:19).

Jesus then invites Mary to meet him. She responds with haste (29), followed, it would appear, by a number of her sorrowing friends (30–31). Mary's demeanor is less composed than Martha's. Her greater sense of spiritual intimacy with Jesus (cf. Lk. 10:39, 42) may have given her a greater freedom to share her deepest feelings. Prostrating herself before Jesus (32), she utters the same regret as Martha, *Lord, if you had been here . . .*, and bursts into tears (33), a response which is immediately echoed in the mourning friends who have accompanied her (33).

Jesus' reaction is profound, and in some degree surprising. *He was deeply moved in spirit and troubled* (33). Jesus is not remote from the sufferings of his fellow humans. The fact that he is one with us in humanity means that he is one with us in agony. So *Jesus wept* (35); paradoxically, the shortest text in the Bible is one of its most eloquent. (The tense is aorist, expressing a definite action, hence 'Jesus burst into tears'.)[142] John's point in verse 33 is that the tears were not the professional tears of the hired mourner or of the inwardly detached spectator. Jesus is one with us in our need; he feels our pain; he lives our experience from the inside; his tears at that moment authentically expressed the emotion of his heart.

The further and somewhat unexpected element in John's description of Jesus' reaction is in the verb in verses 33, and 38, translated

---

[141] Passages such as 1 Sa. 26:17,21,25; 2 Sa. 7:14 and Ps. 2:7 all link sonship with the Davidic messianic hope.

[142] E. C. Hoskyns, p. 403; G. R. Beasley-Murray, p. 182; F. F. Bruce, p. 246.

deeply moved in the NIV. This word (*embrimaomai*), when used outside the Bible, can refer to the snorting of horses; applied to human emotion it invariably speaks of anger! We may cite Schnackenberg, 'The word, *embrimasthai* ... indicates an outburst of anger, and any attempt to interpret it in terms of an internal emotional upset caused by grief, pain or sympathy is illegitimate.'[143] Thus G. R. Beasley-Murray offers in translation: 'Jesus ... became angry in spirit,'[144] and D. A. Carson suggests: 'He was outraged in spirit ...'.[145] B. B. Warfield comments forcefully: 'What John tells us, in point of fact, is that Jesus approached the grave of Lazarus in a state, not of uncontrollable grief but of inexpressible anger. True, he did also respond with tears (35), but the emotion which tore his breast and clamoured for utterance was just rage.'[146] Once again in this gospel, as at the cleansing of the temple (2:15), we encounter the 'wrath of the Lamb'.

What caused Jesus' anger at this moment? Among the suggestions that have been offered are that he is annoyed that the miracle of the raising of Lazarus is thus thrust upon him, or that he is angry at the hypocritical grief of the mourners around Mary who do not really enter into her pain. More plausibly, Jesus' anger is related to the unbelief expressed in the uncontrolled grief of Mary and her friends. 'The one who always does what pleases his Father (8:29) is indignant when faced with attitudes which are not governed by the truths the Father has revealed.'[147] This is well said and may be the truth of it, though if it is, it carries the most sobering implications for our response to God. For if even our grief in the face of acute personal loss, seemingly legitimized by Jesus' own tears, is sufficient to arouse the violent anger of the Son of God then the implications for his assessment of other areas of our Christian lives are sombre indeed. For this writer this interpretation is accordingly too harsh.

Can we not see here the presence of another dimension? B. B. Warfield articulates it memorably: 'The spectacle of the distress of Mary and her companions enraged Jesus because it brought poignantly home to his consciousness the evil of death, its unnaturalness, its "violent tyranny" (Calvin). In Mary's grief he sees and feels the misery of the whole race and burns with rage against the oppressor of men. It is death that is the object of his wrath, and behind death him who has the power of death, and whom he had

---

[143] R. Schnackenburg, 2, p. 335.   [144] G. R. Beasley-Murray, p. 415.
[145] D. A. Carson, *John*, p. 415.
[146] B. B. Warfield, 'The Emotional Life of our Lord', in *The Person and Work of Christ* (Presbyterian and Reformed, 1950), p. 115.
[147] D. A. Carson, *John*, p. 416.

come into the world to destroy. Tears of sympathy may fill his eyes, but that is incidental – his soul is held by rage, and he advances to the tomb, in Calvin's words, "as a champion who prepares for conflict".[148] Like the farmer in his parable, Jesus can pronounce this verdict: 'An enemy did this' (Mt. 13:28). That enemy he has come to slay.

The watching Jews respond with two observations. They take Jesus' reaction as indicative of the depth of his love for Lazarus. He is a true friend; he weeps at his passing (36). That was true, of course, but, as we have noted, the factors operating at this moment are profounder than mere human affection, worthy as that may be. Their other observation was to wonder at the apparent helplessness of Jesus before this tragedy. He had seemed able to cope with all other eventualities; could he not somehow have prevented this? (37). Is this then the limit of Jesus' power? Some trials he can deal with, some sicknesses he can cure, some human tragedies do indeed yield to his word of power, but there are others concerning which we sadly conclude that 'he could not'. Were that to be the case then all our hopes are finally vacuous. A 'so far . . .' Saviour is in the end no Saviour at all.

On the first reaction the Jews are right, though their understanding is superficial. On the second, they could not be more wrong! Jesus proceeds immediately to demonstrate how wrong they are, and how wrong every other has been over the centuries who has set limits to the possibilities and power of Jesus Christ.

c. The raising of Lazarus from the dead (11:38–44)

Arriving at the tomb, Jesus, again visibly swept by a tempest of anger, commands its opening (39). Martha, clearly unable to rise to this ultimate challenge to faith, remonstrates with Jesus. The soul has departed (the Greek lacks a masculine reference; there is no longer a 'he' there), the body is putrefying (39). Jesus reminds her of his promise (cf. 4), presumably repeated to the sisters, that all this would end in the glorifying of God. Jesus' first sign at Cana was the beginning of the revelation of the glory of God in him. Here in the seventh sign that glory is manifest in its fullest and most authentic manner. Truly here we can echo John's own witness, 'we have seen his glory' (1:14).

A vocalized prayer to the Father follows (41–42). In making it Jesus recognizes that its purpose is for those standing by. He himself is in such constant communion that his prayer is his life. In all his thoughts he stands constantly in his Father's presence. In

[148] B. B. Warfield, *op. cit.*, pp. 116f.

the confidence deriving from that position he can express thanks that his petition for the raising of Lazurus, like all his petitions, is truly heard.

These verses teach a number of lessons about prayer. Here is its *focus – Father*. The title is constantly on Jesus' lips, but it has a peculiar force in this setting. We cannot forget his astonishing invitation, 'When you pray, say: "Father . . ." ' (Lk. 11:2). Here also is the *confidence* of prayer – *you always hear me*. True, this is spoken by the sinless Son of God, but let the struggling soul take heart. He is a God defined by his alertness to our cries. 'O you who hear prayer . . .' (Ps. 65:2). 'Does he who implanted the ear not hear?' (Ps. 94:9).

Jesus' words also touch on the *style* of prayer. It was uttered for the sake of the crowd around. Not all prayer is to be private, even relatively spontaneous, as in this case. D. A. Carson appropriately comments, 'It is not foreign to the spirit of this passage to remark that public prayers, though like private prayers addressed to God, must be crafted with the public in mind.'[149] Sadly, many who have the high responsibility of leading prayer in public worship are moved by the principle that, while to preach in public demands diligent preparation, to pray in public requires none, and such is even a mark of unspirituality. Undue formality in public prayers is certainly undesirable, but no less is the wordy rambling of those who give no prayerful preparation of heart and mind to the holy work of leading fellow sinners into the very presence of God.

Jesus' prayer also touches the *fruit* of prayer, which is faith. As God hears our cries and graciously grants our requests the result is the enriching of faith. In the remembering of God's past faithfulness our faith grows.

Finally, these words also represent a great *inducement* to pray. While our prayers are often hampered by the realization that our sins separate between us and our God so that 'he will not hear' us (Is. 59:2), that is never so with Jesus. Our great intercessor, who has gone into the presence of God for us, and who 'always lives to intercede' for his people (Heb. 7:25), is constantly heard in the heavens. He still says to the Father, *I thank you that you have heard me*. So our feeble requests, presented in his name, are gathered within the encircling arms of his great intercession, and placed upon the heart of the Father by him who ever lives to pray for us.

The prayer having been offered, the moment has arrived! Jesus cries, *Lazarus, come out!* (43) and, incredibly, *The dead man came out*. 'He speaks, and, listening to his voice, New life the dead

---

[149] D. A. Carson, p. 418.

receive . . .'[150] 'As the sheep hear the voice of the good shepherd when he calls them by name, and leads them out of the cramped sheepfold (10:3), so Lazarus is immediately drawn forth from the grave by the word of Jesus.'[151]

The grave clothes still bind him. According to Jewish custom the body would not have been fully mummified, but rather wrapped round with a large linen cloth and tied at hands and feet with further strips. The head would have been wrapped in a separate face napkin to keep the jaw in place. So bound, a living person could still shuffle or hop, as Lazarus apparently now proceeded to do (44). Jesus orders his releasing (44). Lazarus is again among the living; death has been robbed of its prey. Faith in Jesus as the one sent by the Father and the embodiment of the resurrection life of God is attained (42). The Son has revealed the Father's glory and in that revealing has *himself received glory* as the one sent by the Father (40).

In that very triumph, however, lie the seeds of the coming 'defeat'. For the raising of Lazarus from the dead is the final provocation of Jesus' enemies (45–57), and the sealing of his own death at their hands. But in that too – in that above all – will the Father's purpose find fulfilment, and the Son bring the supreme glory to the Father by finishing the work he has been given to do.

The raising of Lazarus from the dead is an astonishing miracle and, not surprisingly, has provoked considerable controversy. Those operating with a narrowly naturalistic view of the universe dismiss it out of hand as pure legend. Dead men do not rise in a closed universe; therefore Lazarus did not rise. Other critics, though coming to the same negative conclusion in the end, attempt to attribute some authenticity to the gospel material by suggesting that the story is an idealized 'write-up' of the parable of Dives and Lazarus in Luke 16. The recurrence of the name is certainly noteworthy, though Lazarus was not an especially uncommon name in first-century Palestine. Besides, there appears no reason why, in the period of oral tradition when the accounts of the deeds and teaching of Jesus were circulating widely, the name might not just as plausibly have become attached to the parable than the other way round. More generally, the radical revision of the material necessary to bring the incident into line with the parable is daunting. This is to say nothing of the implications for the integrity of the evangelist, and of the churches (who had many links with the first generation of 'eye-witnesses . . . of the word' (Lk. 1:2). where this gospel was received and affirmed. In addition, the synoptic

[150] From Charles Wesley's hymn 'O for a thousand tongues, to sing'.
[151] E. C. Hoskyns, p. 407.

gospels recount at least two other cases where Jesus raised people from the dead (Mk. 5:21–43; Lk. 7:11–15), and the signs of the messianic ministry of Jesus reported to John the Baptist include the fact that 'the dead are raised' (Mt. 11:4; Lk. 7:22). On the premise of the living Creator God there can be no objection in principle to the authenticity of this account. Lazarus was raised.

The miracle is so striking a manifestation of the authority of Jesus that it fittingly appears in John's record as the seventh and last sign leading into the final climactic sign of the cross and resurrection. It is therefore right to pause and identify some of its more obvious implications.

(i) The shadow(s) of God's love

This derives from the experience of the sisters. Faced with the critical illness of their brother they inform Jesus of the situation, and then experience the anguish of Lazarus' death before ever Jesus appears on the scene. Their joint testimony is eloquent. 'If you had been here, my brother would not have died.' In fact, as the record makes abundantly clear, the sisters and Lazarus were deeply loved by Jesus (3, 5). Yet in love he withholds himself and allows them to pass through their hour of dereliction before he comes to them to meet their need. The reason for it is not hidden. 'I am glad . . . so that you may believe' (15). 'It is for God's glory so that God's Son may be glorified through it' (4); . . . *for the benefit of the people . . . that they may believe* (42). The nature of the love of God for us is thereby revealed. It is not the love of an indulgent parent who gives in to every whim of the child. In the end that is not 'love' for the child but a form of self-love in the parent. Despite the massive propaganda to the contrary, our Lord's purpose for us is not to make us happy, but to make us holy. He loves us too much to leave us part-saved, part-remade, part-sanctified. He wills our holiness, and since 'suffering produces . . .' (Rom. 5:3),[152] we may expect him in his love for us to allow things in our lives which, in our self-centred pursuit of happiness, we ourselves would exclude. Yet even in the shadow of his love there is always mercy. Our sorrows are shared by him; he comes to us in our pain. The end of it all is not only his glory, which needs no further justifying, but also our good. 'There is no joy like the joy of holiness' (R. Murray McCheyne).

(ii) The sympathy of Jesus

This passage uncovers the fullness of Jesus' humanity as almost no other within the New Testament gospels. 'Sympathy' literally

---

[152] *Cf.* Heb. 12:11; 1 Pet. 1:6–7.

means 'feeling along with', and that is who this passage unveils to us – a Saviour who shares our feelings!

We live in a world swept by great emotions: pity, anger, joy, hatred, desire, rage, love, grief, regret ... At times our personal world is invaded by these storms, lifting us to heights of ecstasy, or more often plunging us into depths of agony. In such moments the familiar landmarks lose their power to direct us. We seem not even to know ourselves. But Jesus is there. He has been this way already; he understands.

> 'Tis the weakness in strength, that I cry for!
>   my flesh, that I seek
> In the Godhead! I seek and I find it. O Saul,
>   it shall be.
> A Face like my face that receives thee; a Man
>   like to me,
> Thou shalt love and be loved by, for ever: a
>   Hand like this hand
> Shall throw open the gates of new life to thee!
>   See the Christ stand.
>
> *From* Saul, *Robert Browning*

(iii) *The authority of Christ*

In the raising of Lazarus the full implications of the union of the Son and the Father in the mission of God to the world become apparent. So absolute is the Son's commitment to the glorifying of the Father in that mission, that there is nothing which the Father will refuse him (41–42; 13:3; 17:2). Accordingly the Son is invested with all authority in heaven and earth. Nothing is withheld from him, not even the power of life and death.

In making reference to the Son's authority over death, however, we should note (as this story goes out of its way to make plain) that it includes his mastery of the processes of dissolution and decay. He is Lord of death in the *fullness* of its power. We try regularly to insulate ourselves from the repugnant aspects of death, the physical and mental destruction which it commonly entails. No-one who has watched a loved one changed almost out of recognition, before death has finally brought its welcome release, needs any further words of description. But the thrust of this story is that Christ's authority extends there also. That too we can bring to him. Our hope as Christians is a fleshly, bodily hope. 'My body also will rest secure, ... nor will you let your Holy One see decay' (Ps. 16:10). Christ's rule extends over the flesh, and his promise is nothing less than the renewing of all that he has made.

(iv) Hope in face of death

Patently the loser in this story is death, and 'him who holds the power of death – that is, the devil' (Heb. 2:14). In this sense the story anticipates the resurrection of Jesus himself. Lazarus represents not merely the dead in general, but in particular the long-forgotten dead, those who have dissolved and disappeared, the decomposed. In the raising of Lazarus Jesus made good his claim, 'for a time is coming when all who are in their graves will hear his voice and come out' (5:28). The devil's power, though real, is limited. His reign in death (Rom. 5:17) is only temporary.

Death is the universal fact, the final horizon that conditions all our human dreams and purposes. 'The paths of glory lead but to the grave'. Sooner or later every person experiences the numbing shock of bereavement and the long shadow it casts over the future. Humanly there is nothing to add. *C'est la vie*. Precisely at this point the realities of faith shine most brightly. Compare these two testimonies. The first is death as viewed by Lord Bertrand Russell, the witness of *unbelief*. 'There is darkness without, and when I die there will be darkness within. There is no splendour, no vastness anywhere, only triviality for a moment, and then nothing.' The second is the witness of *belief*, death as seen by Kohlbrugge, the nineteenth-century Lutheran theologian and preacher. 'When I die – I do not die anymore, however – and someone finds my skull, let this skull still preach to him and say: I have no eyes, nevertheless I see Him; though I have no lips, I kiss Him; I have no tongue, yet I sing praise to Him with all who call upon His name. I am a hard skull, yet I am wholly softened and melted in His love; I lay here exposed on God's Acre, yet I am there in Paradise! All suffering is forgotten! His great love has done this for us when for us He carried His cross and went out to Golgotha.' In Christ, through their faith in him, the dead are alive. Though the form and location of their existence is in most respects hidden from us, the reality of their continued life is sure.

Many Christians and people of goodwill can echo Martha's creed in verse 24, respecting her brother. 'I know he will rise again in the resurrection at the last day.' But Christ takes us beyond that. We are not simply to believe that in some vague future moment those we have loved and lost awhile will be raised up with us. That is true, but it did not need the coming of Jesus to produce that conviction, as Martha's testimony makes clear (24). Jesus' coming means we can go beyond that conviction in two ways.

1. In the coming crisis of his ministry, his death and resurrection, which is foreshadowed here, a certainty of eternal life is attained which would not be possible without these great events.

2. Jesus makes the possession of eternal life a fact of present

171

experience. Thus the Christian can be characterized, as the martyrs of Jesus in every age bear moving witness, by a radiant assurance of the life of glory begun here and now through faith-union with Jesus, 'the resurrection and the life' (25).

(v) The offer of Jesus

Christ as the Lord of life and death still invites the world to come to him. Death is inevitable for all of us, but Christ has won the victory over death, and shares that victory with all who repent and believe in him as their Saviour and Lord. To respond to Christ's invitation is to surrender our independence. But to 'die' in this sense is to begin to live. As for Jesus, so for us, death leads to resurrection. 'He is no fool who gives away what he cannot keep in order to gain what he cannot lose' (Jim Elliot). 'I am the resurrection and the life. He who believes in me will live, even though he dies; and whoever lives and believes in me will never die. Do you believe this?' (25–26).

d. The Sanhedrin's decision to have Jesus killed (11:45–57)

As is so frequently the case, Jesus' words and actions cause division. For 'many' of the friends of Mary (Martha's too, one would presume, though she is not mentioned at this point), witnessing the raising of Lazarus was the awakening of their faith in Jesus (45). Here is a faith related to a miracle which is not called in question. Perhaps its authenticity is indicated by the clear reference to believing *in him*. Their faith reached beyond the miracle worker to the Messiah and Saviour. *Some of them* (46), were less loyal friends and reported all in the ears of the Pharisees. While this might be construed positively as encouraging the Pharisees to revise their negative judgment of Jesus, that likelihood is probably not warranted by the text. The effect was to harden the opposition.

A meeting of the Sanhedrin was summoned (47). The Sanhedrin was the central court of the Jewish people at the time, operating under Roman jurisdiction. It was concerned with the political and religious life of Israel on a day-to-day basis and had absolute authority within the limits permitted by Rome (cf. on 18:31). Chaired by the high priest, it consisted of seventy or so members. It mainly comprised the Sadducean party, though the Pharisees were an important minority group. Various shades of theological opinion were reflected within it. Some of the more socially influential members were not especially religious.

They met in an atmosphere of alarm. Clearly their strategy of confronting Jesus, challenging his teaching, and trying to discredit him with the people, was getting them nowhere. The miracles were continuing unabated, now apparently including even the raising of the dead. Jesus clearly had much support among the masses, and that was likely to grow rather than diminish. The outcome could well be an abortive popular rising which the Romans would speedily and ruthlessly put down, and in the process impose direct rule, with possible further desecration, if not destruction, of the temple.

The language in which the views are expressed, *our place and our nation* (48), indicates that the overriding concern was not national but personal. Such developments would destroy the *status quo* by which they, the Sanhedrin, had power and privilege within the state. That simply could not be permitted. Thus the guardians of the sacred traditions of Israel were reduced to the level of political functionaries, to be met any day of the week in the parliaments and board rooms of the world. The primary issue is not one of principle but of expediency. Right has become equated with the avoidance of trouble and the preservation of their hold on power. Thus the cause of the living God, the glory of the age-old revelation from the patriarchs through the Red Sea and Mount Sinai, is all mortgaged in one sorry impassioned hour to save their political skins. The possibility that Jesus may in fact be authentic is not raised, even though the veracity of his miracles is universally conceded (47). That the common people for once might have a sound religious instinct is also left unconsidered. Jesus is a threat, a cancer on the body of the nation, that must be cut away if 'health' is to be recovered.

Paradoxically, by their attempt to preserve the *status quo* the Sanhedrin contribute to its overthrow, for the elimination of Jesus will in time become part of the political and social ferment which will finally bring upon their heads the very destruction they dread. But, through it all, the purposes of the God of their fathers will find new occasion and undreamed-of fulfilment. 'These small and frightened men, clothed in the robes of authority which are in fact only a covering for pitiful weakness, are the unwitting instruments of a mighty divine purpose.'[153] The outcome of their deliberations is expressed by the high priest, Caiaphas, son-in-law of the still widely influential Annas (see comment on 18:13). Appointed to office in AD 18, Caiaphas continued until AD 36, when he was deposed at the same time as Pilate, the Roman procurator. *That year* (49) is probably 'that unique and special year'. John is well aware, like any other Jew of Palestine at the time, that Caiaphas was in office for much longer than a single year.

---

[153] L. Newbigin, pp. 146f.

Caiaphas' proposal is a cynical one. Jesus has become a threat to their well-being and that of the nation as a whole. He must go. Much better *that one man die for the people than that the whole nation perish* (50). While John often relates sayings which have deeper levels of meaning, leaving the reader to uncover the further significance, on this occasion he draws it out. In this saying Caiaphas is an unwitting prophet as well as a priest, for in it he proclaims the substitutionary death of Jesus. The model of the lambs slaughtered daily in the temple ritual to redeem the lives of the worshippers becomes the basis of the political strategy of the Sanhedrin. Jesus is to be offered up for the saving of Israel, one man for the nation. That was nothing less than the truth. And not just for Israel, for he will die as the sacrificial substitute for the sins of the world. Thereby the saving and uniting of the people of God among all the nations and in every age will be accomplished (51). 'The high priest fears for the destruction of the temple, but does not know that Jesus is himself the true temple and that though the Jews will indeed destroy that temple it will be raised up to become the place to which all the nations of the earth will come to worship, as the prophets had foretold.'[154] The die is cast, so *from that day on they plotted to take his life* (53).

Jesus moves out of range to Ephraim, probably the modern village of Et-Taiyibeh, about twelve miles to the north of Jerusalem (54). He does not dread the Sanhedrin, but the timing of the critical confrontation will be in his hands, not theirs. And so the Passover arrives, the hour of crisis. The early worshippers enquire after him in his usual teaching sites around the temple area. Will he come to the feast (56)? And if he does, will the authorities succeed in their known commitment to eliminate him?

There is an atmosphere of tension in the air, as well there might be. As the pilgrims prepare to sacrifice the Passover lamb in commemoration of God's gracious liberation from slavery, so God's own true Lamb is prepared and ready at the Father's summons to offer himself in bloody sacrifice for the sins of the world. In that act he will win a new and everlasting freedom for his people, thereby fulfilling and rendering obsolete this and every Jewish feast till the end of time.

19. Anointing at Bethany (12:1–11)

In this chapter John permits us to feel the tension building as Jesus leaves his retreat at Ephraim and begins his final march on Jerusalem. It is just over a week before the Passover will begin (1)

---

[154] L. Newbigin, p. 146.

and Jesus chooses to break his journey at Bethany. The scene of his recent supreme act of vindication by the Father, it will provide him with further encouragement as he prepares for the fearful trial ahead. So Jesus *arrived at Bethany* (1).

A public meal is held in his honour, with Martha, predictably, among the servers, and Lazarus among the guests (2). Thus Jesus' public ministry, which began for John at the wedding feast in Cana, moves to its close with another social occasion at Bethany. The mood, however, is strikingly different. At Cana, Jesus and the disciples had attended in the anticipation of their newly launched mission, the bringing of the sparkling new wine of the kingdom to the tired, insipid waters of Judaism. The mood was buoyant, even exuberant. Here the tone is significantly different. Dark, heavy clouds are massing on the horizon; there is a burden in the heart of Jesus. The celebration is muted. The talk is of burial rather than renewal.

Yet even here the note of optimism is not excluded, for this *is* a celebration. We cannot entirely lose the perspective of hope expressed in the meal, and its promise of the coming day when those from north and south, east and west will sit down together in the kingdom of God. Lazarus' presence is also significant, the symbol of Jesus' ministry in its divine authority. But, as always, it was a 'sign spoken against', and so before the account is completed we will learn of plotting against Lazarus too (10–11).

The warm conviviality of the meal is interrupted as Mary comes up behind Jesus as he reclines in the customary manner, his head close to the low central table where the food was laid. In an act of moving devotion she approaches Jesus and, breaking open a bottle of very expensive perfume, anoints his feet (3). Nard is an oil-like perfume extracted from the root and spike of the nard plant, grown in India; definitely not one of the lower-quality brands sold at the Bethany supermarket!

This incident has parallels in the other gospels. Luke describes an anointing which has only partial points of contact and is viewed by many as an account of a different incident much earlier in Jesus' ministry (Lk. 7:36–39). Matthew and Mark, however, appear to be describing the same event (*cf.* Mt. 26:6–13; Mk. 14:3–9). The most obvious point of seeming contradiction concerns which part of Jesus' body Mary anoints. John speaks specifically of the feet, Matthew and Mark of the head, of Jesus. In fact, as D. A. Carson points out, the amount of nard used was considerable and hence the anointing was likely to have extended beyond either the head or the feet. Significantly in Matthew's and Mark's accounts, Jesus refers to Mary's having anointed his 'body' for burial (Mt. 26:12; Mk. 14:8).

175

Mary's using her hair to wipe Jesus' feet (3) echoes the earlier incident Luke records, and may even be in conscious imitation of it, since the earlier act is likely to have been retold among Jesus' followers. A woman unbinding her hair was regarded as most unseemly, so Mary is clearly moved by deepest feelings of loyalty in being willing to brave the inevitable social disapproval. The effect on the atmosphere is immediate and pervasive as the whole house fills with the fragrance of Mary's deed, both physically and emotionally (3).

Not all are pleased, however. The synoptic writers refer to the indignation of 'the disciples' at the wasteful extravagance of Mary's action. John focuses on the ringleader of the discontent, Judas (4). 'Judas is the type of man who has money on his mind all the while. He views everything from the aspect of pecuniary value.'[155] He is referred to as *Judas Iscariot, who was later to betray him*, reflecting no doubt 'the shocking force of hindsight'.[156]

The value of the perfume was indeed enormous, equivalent to the total annual salary of an average or above-average wage-earner (5). And now it was all gone, in a society where the evidences of abject poverty were on every hand and starvation never far from the door for most households. Some degree of sympathy with Judas is, at first sight, not entirely misplaced. There are certainly no grounds for the assumption that in his place we would not have shared his reservations. But Judas has deeper and darker motives. As the treasurer of the disciple band he apparently was not above helping himself from the revenues in his charge (6). The value of this perfume would certainly have given him rich pickings. John's implication is that this pilfering had already become a settled trait in Judas and perhaps throws some light on his betrayal of Jesus, which, when all is said and done, was for a significant monetary price. Avarice had already, apparently, invaded his soul. Before ever there was a betrayal of Jesus' person there was a betrayal of Jesus' trust. Judas' acting as treasurer would certainly have been with the approval of Jesus, if not by his direct appointment. Presumably he had some aptitude in this area, since clearly others might have been chosen, like Matthew, with a proven experience of monetary affairs behind them. Possibly because 'Temptation commonly comes to us through that for which we are naturally fitted',[157] the task was given to Judas, and with it the trust of his colleagues and above all that of Jesus. And he woefully, and wickedly, betrayed it.

[155] W. Hendriksen, 2, p. 177.
[156] D. A. Carson, *John*, pp. 428ff.   [157] E. F. Westcott, p. 177.

Jesus defends Mary – *it was intended* (7). There was a divine purpose in her deed, the preparation of Jesus' body for the day of his burial! With this utterance the atmosphere must have chilled considerably. But Jesus spoke truly, for if the timing of the incident at *six days* before the Passover is noted (1), then, exactly one week from that Saturday evening, Jesus' body, anointed for a second time, would lie in the cool and silence of a tomb in a Jerusalem garden. The Greek of verse 7 is somewhat unclear. The NIV's *It was intended that she should save this perfume for the day of my burial*, however, appears to reflect the sense well enough. See Matthew 26:10: 'Why are you bothering this woman? She has done a beautiful thing to me.' It is impossible to know to what extent Mary understood the significance of her action. Commentators divide and clearly dogmatism is out of place. Our view will appear below.

You will always have the poor among you (8) has occasioned comment. Two extremes are to be avoided in interpretation. On the one hand Jesus is *not* teaching that giving to the poor has no place in a disciple's financial obligations. The very existence of the alms bag among a group whose leader professed to have 'nowhere to lay his head' (Lk. 9:58), and whose material legacy was only the clothes he wore to execution, speaks powerfully to every follower of Jesus of the obligation of sacrificial giving to the less fortunate. 'The poor you will always have with you, and you can [and should] help them any time you want' (Mk. 14:7). On the other hand Jesus is certainly not minimizing the centrality of his personal, self-sacrificing mission for the sins of the world. It is his all-consuming consecration to that costly mission which brings Jesus to this feast, as Mary perceives, and for which perception she is commended (7). The cross must control every aspect of the disciple's life, including alms-giving. Jesus is not presenting us with the competing loyalties of 'spiritual' versus 'material' giving. It is a prime case of both/and, rather than either/or, with each at the proper occasion, and all in the light of the cross.

The real challenge presented in Jesus' statement, however, is motivational. Our giving to the poor, or for the preaching of the gospel, is finally sterile if motivated in either case from a desire to attain merit before God. What Jesus brings is the radically new motivation of gratitude. His journey to Jerusalem to offer himself for lost sinners brings those who have despaired of earning God's favour the free gift of salvation. Those saved by his grace become his debtors, in gratitude making available for his service all they possess. 'Devotion to Jesus and gratitude for his sacrifice will lead in fact to a service of the poor (which will always be needed) in a manner quite different from a legally required almsgiving. It will

177

be in fact part of the fragrance of the gospel which is destined to fill the whole world.'[158]

In the following verses we note the two-edged effect of the miracle of the raising of Lazarus. For many it brought new and persuasive grounds for believing (11). For the chief priests it extended their 'hit list', as Lazarus also becomes a target of their prejudiced minds (10). This illustrates well the uncontrollable reality of sin. Once we surrender to expediency as the rule of action, we are in the grip of a current which will sweep us on without mercy. First Jesus must die, then Lazarus, later Stephen, and then James. It has been rightly observed that he who would sup with the devil had best ensure he is supping with an exceedingly long spoon. 'Everyone who sins' becomes 'a slave to sin' (8:34).

This action of Mary represents a model for service of Jesus in every generation. It is in the first place the fruit of a *humble spirit*. To anoint Jesus' feet she assumed a posture of subservience. Significantly, Mary is mentioned three times in the gospels and always in association with Jesus' feet. Thus she 'sat at the Lord's feet' (Lk. 10:39), to listen to his teaching; she 'fell at [Jesus'] feet' (Jn. 11:32), to indicate her dependence; now she anoints Jesus' feet to express her devotion. True service for Jesus springs from a whole-hearted commitment to him as Lord. The feet of Jesus is where service for him begins.

Secondly, Mary shows a *perceptive heart*. Although the full significance of her action is possibly hidden from her, it was 'right' because she perceived something of the mind of Jesus. Despite the festive nature of the occasion Mary senses his *true* spirit, and feels in her own soul the chill of the dark waters in which Jesus must soon be immersed (Lk. 12:50). The secret of Mary's insight is an open one. She 'sat at the Lord's feet listening to what he said' (Lk. 10:39). Here is the path to the heart of Jesus, open to all disciples. As we make it a priority to spend time at Jesus' feet listening to his Word (and it needs the whole Bible to interpret his Word) we begin to attune with Jesus' mind and discern how, where, and in what ways we can serve him. The encouragement of this incident is that our acts of devotion genuinely 'serve him'. Within the wonder of God's condescension to us in Jesus Christ is his ability – the Almighty who has need of nothing (Acts 17:25) – to allow us to minister to him in ways which bring delight to his heart, and further his cause in the world. Hence to Mary is given the surpassing privilege, a 'share in the consecration of Jesus to the royal service of his passion by which the saving sovereignty of God will be won for the world'.[159]

[158] L. Newbigin, p. 151.   [159] G. R. Beasley-Murray, p. 209.

Thirdly, Mary's was a *timely act*. *It was intended* (7) that the perfume be kept for this moment. Had she kept it for another time the opportunity would have passed. Life is full of uncertainties; we 'do not even know what will happen tomorrow' (Jas. 4:13f.). So 'as we have opportunity, let us do good' (Gal. 6:10), or, in Jesus' own words, 'We must work the works of him who sent me, while it is day; night comes, when no one can work' (9:4, RSV). William Barclay tells the poignant story of Thomas Carlyle and his remorse at failing to appreciate his long-suffering wife while she was alive. 'If only I could see her but once more, were it but for five minutes, to let her know that I always loved her. She never did know it, never.'[160] *Now* is the time to serve Jesus.

Fourthly, Mary's action was *sharply criticized*. There is a note of realism here. While Jesus may approve, others may not – even among the inner circle of Jesus' disciples. The opposition *may* arise from hearts which follow this present world, like Judas, and for whom our Christian work and ministry seem a sheer waste. It also may arise, however, from fellow-disciples, possibly rebuked by our spirit of sacrifice, or with their own agendas for our time, talents or treasure. We need fortitude in serving Jesus.

Fifthly, perhaps the most notable quality of Mary's action was its *extravagance*. It was an amazingly generous gift (even if the family was relatively wealthy, as the number of mourners from Jerusalem [11:19], and the expensiveness of the perfume, would suggest). Mary, however, gave it away; poured it all out for her Master.

There is a prudence which is rightly part of the Christian mind-set. Extremes and extravagances do not often work the will of God, perhaps because they are often fed, not by genuine devotion, but by ego factors in the Christian or church concerned. Nonetheless Jesus merits the richest treasures of our self-giving. It is possible to become so circumspect and balanced in our Christian profession that we lose touch with the extravagance of a heart like Mary's. In the service of Jesus there is indeed a 'time to keep', but there is also 'a time to throw away' (Ec. 3:6), for the glory and honour of him who is worthy of all our love and devotion.

Finally, Mary's service was *fruitful*. *The house was filled with the fragrance of the perfume* (3). The synoptics record Jesus saying in assessment, 'wherever the gospel is preached throughout the world, what she has done will also be told' (Mk. 14:9). Thus a simple act of devotion has become a light to multitudes in every corner of the earth. Sincere service of Jesus, however much it may be opposed, has a capacity to touch and bless other lives, a capacity

---

[160] W. Barclay, 2, pp. 112f.

which is missing from acts of merely legalistic piety. Others will be blessed when we serve Jesus; perhaps, as in Mary's case, far beyond our dreams. For what is done for Christ, however humble, becomes part of the indestructible. 'Anyone who gives you a cup of water in my name because you belong to Christ will certainly not lose his reward' (Mk. 9:41). 'Let nothing move you as you busy yourselves in the Lord's work. Be sure that nothing you do for him is ever lost or ever wasted' (1 Cor. 15:58, JBP).

20. The triumphal entry (12:12–19)

Like a monarch processing to his coronation, or a conqueror marching to his victory, Jesus leaves Bethany behind him and advances on Jerusalem. The synoptic writers tell with what heaviness of spirit Jesus made that final journey up to the city as, breasting the Mount of Olives and seeing the city lying below him, he burst into tears and wept for its tragic unbelief and coming decimation (Lk. 19:41). But foremost in John is the enthusiastic welcome of the 'Palm Sunday' pilgrims.

The Passover crowds were enormous by any standards, as pilgrims gathered from all over Palestine and from every corner of the Mediterranean world. Josephus, the first-century Jewish historian, gives an attendance figure for a Passover of over two and a half million, some thirty years later. Some travelled up with Jesus from Bethany and the surrounding villages (17), others went out from the city to meet him (13). Their welcome was expressed both in deed and word. The active part consisted in waving palm branches (13). From the time of the Maccabees, palms had been a recognized symbol of the Jewish state. They appear both on the coins struck by the Jews during their revolutionary struggle against the Romans, and in the coinage struck by the Romans after the revolution was put down. The action of the crowd therefore testifies to deep nationalistic fervour among the pilgrims. Their words, or shouts of welcome, incorporate Scripture (13). *Hosanna* literally means 'Give salvation now!' This is a quotation from Psalm 118:25, which was part of the Hallel, the section of Psalms (113–118 in our Psalter) sung daily during the feast of tabernacles. When 'Hosanna' was reached during the singing of the Hallel, every male worshipper waved his 'lulah' (a bunch of willow and myrtle tied with palm).

The words *Blessed is he who comes . . .* (13, Ps. 118:25–26) were widely understood as a reference to the Coming One, the Messiah. This messianic meaning is explicit in the following words, *Blessed is the King of Israel!*, which were not part of the Psalm, but show how the crowd were understanding it. This nationalistic and messianic fervour was fuelled, as John tells us, by the raising of

Lazarus, which was widely reported to the crowd coming out from the city by those travelling with Jesus (17). Jesus is hailed as the 'King who is the conqueror of death'.[161]

Faced with the nationalistic politicization of the messianic title, as he had been in Galilee (*cf.* 6:15), Jesus again takes corrective action. In Galilee he withdrew into the hills, in Jerusalem he mounts a donkey! Unlike the synoptic writers John does not detail Jesus' careful planning for this symbolic action (*cf.* Mk. 11:1–8). Its meaning, however, is crystal clear. He *is* the King of Israel, but not like Judas Maccabaeus who entered the city on a war-horse (Is. 31:1–3), nor like Solomon (1 Ki. 4:26). Rather he is the King of whom Zechariah had prophesied, who comes, 'gentle and riding on a donkey' (Zc. 9:9), who 'will take away the chariots from Ephraim and the war-horses from Jerusalem', and through whom 'the battle-bow will be broken. He will proclaim peace to the nations. His rule will extend from sea to sea and from the River [*i.e.* the Euphrates] to the ends of the earth' (Zc. 9:10). Jesus deliberately de-militarizes their vision and declares the nature of his messianic rule; a rule of peace, gentleness and universal tolerance. 'Nothing further from a Zealotic view of the Messiah could be imagined.'[162] The disciples did not understand Jesus' purpose until later (16). It took his 'glorification', through death and resurrection (and the gift of the Spirit which flowed from it), to open their eyes.

The Pharisees look on with dismay (19). Their attempt to contain Jesus' influence appears completely ineffective. *Look how the whole world has gone after him*! (19). Only the Sanhedrin's policy of judicial execution will meet the need, but they will need to be extremely careful in implementing it.

John strikes a note here which will become more pronounced in the following chapters: Jesus is King. His kingship is of a unique order. To express it Jesus must disappoint the nationalistic aspirations of his fellow Jews. But King he is, and no confederacy of the powers of evil, whether Sanhedrin, Caiaphas, Annas, Pilate, Rome, Judas and the prince of this world, can wrest that authority from him. He moves majestically forward in procession to his throne, a throne constructed by his enemies, the throne of the cross!

Accordingly the triumphal entry is an exposition of the nature of Jesus' kingship. In the first place, negatively, it is *non-military*. The imagery in Zechariah is framed as a conscious alternative to militaristic rule. True, the kingdom of Jesus will have military and political implications, for it must reflect the righteous and just character of the God who is King over all. But as a 'gentle' kingdom

[161] G. R. Beasley-Murray, p. 209.   [162] *Ibid.*

it will uphold the rights of the vulnerable and the oppressed, and afford no easy sanction to militaristic means for achieving these ends. Similarly, the King who rides into Jerusalem clothed in the mantle of Zechariah's prophecy is possessed of a larger dream than Israelite nationalism. *King of Israel!* they shout, and it is true, for such he is, but he is more than that, for his reign 'will extend from sea to sea and . . . to the ends of the earth' (Zc. 9:10). As Israel's king he will not subscribe to their narrow nationalism, for temple and city will both perish, and circumcision as the sign of entry to the people of God will give place to faith, modelled in the Old Testament (Rom. 4:1–25; Heb. 11:1–40), and embodied in all those from every nation who express personal trust in this strange King crowned upon a cross of sacrifice.

There is no sanction here either, for nationalistic visions in our own day which limit global obligations, or which glorify our national heritage to the exclusion of the nations beyond our borders, of whatever colour, race or creed for whom as truly the King has come, died and risen.

Positively, this paragraph also proclaims Jesus as the King of *peace*, whose coming drives out fear (*cf. Do not be afraid*, 15) and whose ways are ways of mercy, gentleness and forgiveness. To establish his kingdom and realize these ideals, however, will be costly. It will mean riding on 'in lowly pomp . . . to die'.[163] For these ideals are no merely human possibility. Jesus' mission is nothing less than the supernatural inbreaking of God in the death and rising of the Son and the outpouring of the Spirit. The ideals of the kingdom can be realized only where the King is enthroned. The righteousness, peace and joy of the kingdom are possible only 'in the Holy Spirit' (Rom. 14:17).

Further, it is a *divisive* kingship which Jesus declares on Palm Sunday. Some will welcome him with enthusiasm, though much fewer than appears on the surface, once the true nature of his claims are laid bare. Others, however, will plot his downfall. For the 'world' is a fallen territory where a rival power, the 'prince of this world', holds his unauthorized sway. The coming of the King therefore produces the conflict of the kingdoms; light confronts darkness, life encounters death. For the coming of the King means the usurping of our rebel kingdoms, and the denial of our sinful independence. In its starkest terms, it means that we face death before we can know life. Not surprisingly, many are not drawn to that option, and choose to resist. Each of us must take sides. There is no neutrality, though 'All that the Father gives me will come to me' (6:37).

[163] From Henry Hart Milman's hymn 'Ride on! ride on in majesty!'

Lastly, it is as a *universal* King that Jesus comes; the King whom *the whole world has gone after* (19). This is of course an exaggeration, though appropriate enough in the mouths of the Pharisees in these circumstances. But, as so often in John, the truth is spoken in ignorance. The *'world'* has indeed gone after Jesus, not only because of the variety of races represented among those Palm Sunday pilgrims, a variety immediately embodied in some searching Greeks (20); not only indeed because of the multitude who at Pentecost would become the nucleus of the new-born church (Acts 2:9–11); and not only even because of the impressive spread of the church among the Gentile nations when John wrote his gospel. The *world has gone after* Jesus also because of the international Christian community of our time, numbering (nominally at least) more than a third of the human race, and increasing among the nations with every hour – anticipating that coming day when the Lamb, who is the King, will be acclaimed upon his throne as the one who with his blood 'purchased [people] for God from every tribe and language and people and nation' (Rev. 5:9).

12:20 – 19:42

3. The coronation

1. Anticipation (12:20–50)

We arrive at one of the profoundest and most demanding sections of the entire gospel. There are depths here which defy all sounding. 'The whole world' which has gone after Jesus is embodied in the Greeks who seek him (20f.). Some commentators propose a gap of several days between verses 19 and 20, during which, according to the synoptic accounts, Jesus cleansed the temple, specifically the 'court of the Gentiles' where the money changers had their booths (*cf.* Lk. 19:45–48). Some commentators speculate that those Greeks could have witnessed that scene and been impressed by it. John says nothing which excludes this reconstruction.

The Greeks represent the many sensitive and thoughtful non-Jews in the first century who were attracted to Judaism. They were drawn by the simplicity and credibility of its theology. Compared with the multiple deities of Greek and pagan religion the monotheism of Israel was attractive and persuasive. Judaism also appealed at the moral level, where its strong ethical emphasis on obedience to the law of God, centred in the great moral imperatives of the decalogue, was clearly superior to the often questionable behaviour of the Greek deities, and the general tendency in popular religion to separate religion from morality. The Greeks are possibly uncertain about Jesus' attitude to Gentiles and so approach him through Philip (21), an understandable choice among the disciples due to his Galilean roots and the likelihood of his having spoken Greek. Philip, possibly sharing their uncertainty, or simply because he did not find personal initiative easy, seeks out his colleague, Andrew (*cf.* 1:44; 6:5–9).

The request of the Greeks to see (*i.e.* talk seriously with) him is like an exploding fuse in the mind of Jesus. *The hour has come* (23). Right through the preceding chapters the 'hour' has been 'not yet'.[1] The 'not yet' is over; the 'now' has arrived. So John brings us to the central crisis of the gospel, and the goal of the entire mission of Jesus, and does so by the middle of the twelfth chapter!

No clearer indication of the centrality of the cross and resurrection could be given. Christian faith is Easter faith. In this connection it is astonishing to reflect that there have been interpretations of Christianity, claiming genuine validity, which have tried to limit the message and significance of Jesus to his moral teaching, and to reduce his 'kingdom' to the ethical principles within his proclamation. In other words, they attempted to conclude the ministry of Jesus at the beginning of Holy Week, eliminate the resurrection, and permit no significance to the cross beyond its being an outstanding example of self-giving love. What is even more astonishing is that such unbiblical and fallacious versions of Christianity are still embraced at times within the churches.

The 'hour', however, is not a bare point in time but a moment filled with meaning; *the hour has come for the Son of Man to be glorified* (23). He whom the Father had consecrated and sent into the world, whose food is doing the will of him who sent him and finishing his work, now brings final glory to the Father in a supreme act of obedience unto death. In this action the Father will reciprocally crown the Son with glory. 'In that act the glory which is the flaming heart of the universe is revealed.'[2] God's 'glory' (Gk. *doxa*) is the manifestation of his divine majesty (*cf.* Ex. 16:7–10). This glory was revealed in Jesus' ministry (1:14), not least in his acts of power.[3] To 'glorify God' (*cf.* 12:28; 13:31f.) is therefore so to relate to him that he is afforded the honour due to him as God. To *be glorified* hence simply means to be honoured. Referred, as here, to Jesus (23), it implies the renouncing of any independent glory on his part (*cf.* 5:41; 7:18). His honour is attained only in the context of his utter submission to, and zeal for, the Father's glory through him (13:31). Thus he glorifies the Father by becoming personally transparent, like a window or lens through which the Father's glory is seen and focused.

Jesus' glorification is through death. He is as a grain of wheat which must fall into the earth and die there before he can become fruitful in the Father's purpose (24). The glory will not be produced by 'a linear extension either of Jewish religious enthusiasm or of Greek intellectual curiosity. There is no straight road from these to God and his glory'.[4] Rather it is by an act of supreme self-abnegation that the glory of God will be revealed and the kingdom become available for the world.

---

[1] 2:4; 4:21, 23; 7:30; 8:20.   [2] L. Newbigin, p. 156.
[3] 2:11; 11:40; 17:4.   [4] L. Newbigin, p. 155.

Later, Paul discovered the way of the cross, the deepest truth of the Christian gospel, to be 'a stumbling-block to Jews and foolishness to Greeks' (1 Cor. 1:23). It still is. The 'Jews' abound who would achieve the kingdom of human brotherhood and peace by the road of religious piety and moral effort. Their faith in the possibilities of unregenerate human nature is apparently boundless. A new political 'world order' beyond the superpower confrontation of the last half-century, a new amalgam of the great historic religious traditions, and before long the kingdom will be ours. The 'Greeks' are likewise still with us. The human intellect, unaided by divine revelation, is still capable of determining ultimate questions. The enquiring mind still holds the key, not only to judge ultimate reality, but to harness the forces of nature and create a new world of prosperity and peace. For 'Jews' and 'Greeks' the cross remains incomprehensible and repugnant. To believe that only through that blood-stained gibbet can the meaning of existence be discovered, and the life for which we were made experienced in its fullness, is still widely dismissed as unacceptably narrow-minded, ethically dubious, intellectually naive, and religiously intolerant. The choice lies before the world. Jesus, however, still points the way to glorification by the narrow and only way of the cross.

The link made by Jesus between glorification and crucifixion is fundamental to John's presentation of the Easter drama. The death and resurrection of Jesus are not divisible into a defeat at Calvary which was righted by the subsequent powerful, victorious act of the resurrection. Rather, *both* death and resurrection represent one inseparable event in which Jesus achieves the glory of God. The same truth appears in verses 31–32, in the deliberate ambiguity of *lifted up*. Thus while the glory of God is also revealed in the resurrection, (13:31–32; 17:1, 5) the essence of the glorifying of God lies in the cross itself.[5] Behind this revolutionary understanding may well lie the description in Isaiah 52:13 of the 'Servant of the Lord' who will suffer for God's people so profoundly that 'his appearance was so disfigured beyond that of any man and his form marred beyond human likeness' (52:14), yet who is simultaneously 'raised and lifted up and highly exalted' (52:13). The crucified is the King!

If this identity between glorification and crucifixion is valid it is no mark of Christian maturity to focus almost exclusively on the risen and ascended Christ and upon the Spirit, the life-gift of the exalted one, as is the tendency in our modern-day expressions of Christian faith and worship. Certainly the cross is not ignored today in the church. There can be little question,

[5] *Cf.* 1:14; 8:50, 54; 12:28; 13:31–32.

however, that the primary emphases lie elsewhere. John would ask us to think, and to look, again.

That the glory of God is attained through death is true not only for the Saviour but also for his disciples, as verses 25 and 26 make clear. This is relevant at two levels, salvation and service. To receive eternal life, the harvest which ripens from the buried seed of the Son of Man, we must 'hate' life in this world (25). The strong verb here draws upon a Hebrew idiom which contrasts by expressing the most extreme instance.[6] Jesus is not advocating world-abnegation. Nonetheless the force of his challenge must not be diluted. Faith in Jesus involves dying to all the blandishments and attractions of this passing world order.[7] To follow Jesus as Lord and King means ceasing to follow the lords and kings of the world. Like John the Baptist before him, Jesus plainly informs us that without repentance from sin, and in particular the sin that overvalues the world and its applause (cf. 43), there can be no salvation.

The alternative to this 'death' is a solemn one. To cling to life is ultimately to lose it for ever (25). But the compensations are overwhelming: *where I am, my servant also will be* (26) – the guaranteed presence of Christ on the way beside us, and the promise of being honoured by the Father, here and hereafter. Jesus' promise is that the Father will vindicate his disciple's act of self-sacrifice just as he will fully vindicate the self-sacrifice of Jesus himself (26).

This 'life through death' principle also touches our Christian service. It is in fact 'the law of the Kingdom of God'.[8] Fruitfulness is costly. It is in dying that we become life-givers. Paul expresses it: 'We who are alive are always being given over to death for Jesus' sake, so that his life may be revealed in our mortal body. So then, death is at work in us, but life is at work in you' (2 Cor. 4:11–12). Through a combination of inward struggles, trying circumstances, opposition from the enemies of the gospel, and our wrestling with God-permitted weaknesses, we, like Paul, are to learn to 'die every day' (1 Cor. 15:31). The seed must perish for the harvest to be produced.

> O Cross that liftest up my head,
>   I dare not ask to fly from thee:
> I lay in dust life's glory dead,
> And from the ground there blossoms red
>   Life that shall endless be.
>
> *George Matheson*

---

[6] *Cf.* Gn. 29:30–31; Dt. 21:15; Mt. 10:37; Lk. 14:26; Rom. 9:13.
[7] Mk. 8:35; *cf.* Mt. 10:39; Lk. 9:24.   [8] G. R. Beasley-Murray, p. 211.

The realization of his imminent suffering breaks over Jesus (27): *Now my heart is troubled*. The verb is a strong one, signifying shock, agitation, even revulsion. We recall Hebrews 5:7, referring to Jesus' 'loud cries and tears', and more specifically 'the agony in the Garden'. 'Being in anguish, he prayed more earnestly, and his sweat was like drops of blood falling to the ground' (Lk. 22:44). This parallel to Gethsemane is strengthened if the words *Father, save me from this hour* (27) do not form a question indicating a mere possibility (as in the NIV and RSV). The Greek is perfectly capable of being translated as a direct petition, *Father*, (please) *save me from this hour*. The context here, *viz.* the agony of Jesus faced with the impending horror of his death, makes sense of a prayer to evade the 'baptism' of suffering which awaits him (Lk. 12:50). No less than the prayer in Gethsemane, this is a petition to be permitted to bypass the cross. The implications of granting this plea are unthinkable, for the whole purpose of God in salvation would be thwarted, the mission of the Son as the Sent One of the Father unfulfilled, the prince of this world left unjudged, and sinners abandoned to face the just deserts of their sins in eternity.

John does not recount the 'agony in the Garden'; in a sense he has no need. This says it all. Or, alternatively, it says nothing, for there are depths here which go beyond all description or imagining. In contrast to Socrates who, faced with death in Athens because of his teaching, spent his last moments before drinking the hemlock in convivial conversation with his friends, Jesus faces death with extreme agitation and revulsion. Why? We can but surmise. Death for Jesus is not a natural event, the simple termination of a purely natural process. For Jesus, living within the biblical world, we are not mere hominids but creatures of God, made in his image, and as the objects of his providential care and redemptive love, we have absolute worth. Our dying therefore has singular significance; it is value-laden. For we were made to live for ever. Death is therefore 'unnatural', a usurper which has overtaken God's creation and sown its foul seed among the good planting of the Lord. God is not, however, excluded from our dying, for death is the 'wages of sin', the judgment of God upon our rebellion against him. Death proclaims that there is nothing in our lives which is finally fit to endure to eternity. It is 'guilt made visible' (Rahner), the 'sacrament of sin' (Denney). In death God meets us as Judge, and it is this element which explains Jesus' recoiling in horror in the face of it. In his death he must take the place of those to whom he has come to bring life. He must die their death in order to free them from death for ever.

In the terrible imagery of Gethsemane (*cf.* 18:11), Jesus must 'drink the cup' the Father has given him. The cup is a familiar Old Testament image. It is the cup of God's wrath,[9] hence Jesus' horror! For in his death he must not only face the reality of human finitude, the ending of his mission, the mockery of his enemies in whose eyes he will die a failure, and in addition the appalling physical and mental sufferings of death by crucifixion. Beyond all that he must also face the Father himself, the one to whom he has been inseparably bound for all eternity, not in the warm embrace of his everlasting love, but in the terror of his holy and righteous wrath. He must in fact become the object of divine rejection, the bearer of the implacable antipathy to sin and evil of the ever-living God. He was *troubled* (27). Indeed, he had reason to be.

Even as he starts back in fear from the terror of the cross which lies before him, however, he senses once more behind him the thrust of the divine purpose which has brought him to this hour of crisis. *No, it was for this very reason I came to this hour* (27). Here is the equivalent to Gethsemane's 'Yet not as I will, but as you will' (Mt. 26:39). The truth here extends far beyond our feeble imaginings, as God wrestles with God on the brink of Golgotha. The gospel may be simple, but it is not superficial. It may be free, but it is not cheap.

As Jesus agonizes in that awful moment, caught as it were in the vice of his awful destiny, there emerges from the depths of his spirit a great yearning cry which lays bare the ultimate passion of his being – *Father, glorify your name!* (28). This plea of Jesus is in fact the identical petition set at the head of the prayer he taught his disciples, 'Father, hallowed be your Name'. Indeed, R. Brown goes further and suggests that 'the first three petitions of the Lord's Prayer are synonymous.'[10] The sanctifying of God's name, his being reverenced as the Holy One, the inbreaking of his kingdom, and the doing of his will on earth as in heaven, are precisely the realities which underlie the glorifying of God. There is no greater prayer. In truth there can be no other prayer, for all our other petitions find their justification and achieve their requested end only as they promote and extend the Father's glory.

Not surprisingly the prayer is immediately answered from heaven. *I have glorified it, and will glorify it again* (28). The audible response is a witness to the crowd standing by (30), though many of them do not understand it (29). That which is clear and articulate to Jesus is only a noise in the ears of those who are not in tune with the Father. The message of the Father is twofold (28). It affirms the Father's approval of the ministry of the Son; in his obedience and mission the Father has truly been glorified. It further

---

[9] Is. 51:17–22; Je. 25:15–28; Zc. 12:2.   [10] R. Brown, 2, p. 476.

expresses the Father's promise that in the Son's impending obedience unto death, that purpose will be fulfilled again and the Father again glorified. It is nothing less than the disclosure of the absolute commitment in the heart of God to realize himself as Lord in the mission of Jesus.

Jesus completes this remarkable series of statements with an exposition of the meaning of the cross (30–32). His death will achieve four things.

1. It will pass judgment on the world, in two senses (31). First, it will expose the sin of the race. 'Since the Son of Man is sent by God into the world as his representative and agent, rejection of the Son of Man is rejection of God himself. In the murder of the Son of Man sin is exposed in its most dreadful form.'[11] This is the record, that God in his love sent his Son into the world, and the world in its rebellion hung him up to die. Thus the cross judges the world and within that lies the judgment of every one of us. But secondly, in the wonder of the divine love of God, the Son comes not simply as the representative and agent of the Father, but as the representative of God's rebellious subjects. In the cross he reveals not only the guilt which makes judgment necessary, but, as the guilty one in place of the guilty, he bears the judgment for us.

2. Jesus' death will 'drive out' the prince of this world (31). This event on Golgotha, which to the unenlightened onlooker will appear the most thoroughgoing victory for Satan, is in fact his utter defeat. In the cross he is driven out, because there Jesus carries to conclusion his perfect obedience as man to the will of God, and thereby smashes the chains of guilt and condemnation with which the evil one has bound the children of Adam since the fall. 'The Holiness of Christ is the one thing damnable to the devil's power, and that holiness is consummated in the cross, hence the cross is the destruction of the evil one.'[12]

Most commentators note the image of another Johannine passage, Revelation 12, where Satan is 'hurled down' (Rev. 12:10), overcome 'by the blood of the Lamb and by the word of their testimony'. John of course is not in ignorance that to this hour 'the whole world is under the control of the evil one' (1 Jn. 5:19). But the cross has broken Satan, 'his doom is writ' (Luther), the wound in the heart of evil is mortal. The kingdoms of this world are destined to become the kingdoms of our God and of his Christ (Rev. 11:15). The church in its ministry between the ages must never forget this note of victory. Jesus is King.

3. Jesus's death will exalt him (32). The verb *lifted up* is ambigu-

---

[11] G. R. Beasley-Murray, p. 213.

[12] P. T. Forsyth, *The Glorious Gospel* (London, n.d.), p. 6.

ous. The reference is to 'lifting up' in crucifixion (as John immediately makes clear, verse 33), but it can also refer to 'lifting up' in exaltation. Paradoxically both are present. For the elevation on to the cross is to be understood as the exalting of the one who reigns. The cross is a throne, his crucifixion is his coronation; he reigns from the tree. 'His being glorified is not a reward or recompense for his crucifixion; it inheres in his crucifixion.'[13]

4. The death of Christ, he says, *will draw all men to myself* (32). These words probably have in mind not simply the elevated posture which enables the crucified to be seen by distant watchers, but the spreadeagling of the arms of the crucified (*cf.* 21:18) which poignantly expresses his embrace of the world. The promise of worldwide harvest has already been given, in the Samaritans who believe in 'the Saviour of the world' (4:42), in the anticipation of the bringing of the 'other sheep' into the fold of God's people (10:16), and in the Greeks who seek Jesus (12:21), the first fruits of the 'whole world' who will indeed 'go after him' (12:19). Here is the means to this universal harvest, 'the lifting up of the Son of Man'. The harvest will be great and will be gathered from the nations, but first the corn of wheat must fall into the ground and perish. In perishing, however, he will 'bring forth much fruit', nothing less than the church of the firstborn from all the nations and all the ages of the world.

This astonishing teaching demands response. Surprisingly, the response is apparently meagre; a further question (34) is all that is recorded, though in essence a profound one. Since the Old Testament taught the eternity of the Messiah, how can Jesus be the Messiah if he is to be 'lifted up'? More generally, how could they believe in a crucified Messiah?

For the Old Testament Scriptures in view, see the footnote below for examples.[14] The view that the Messiah would establish an unending kingdom was a commonplace. This difficulty of reconciling his claims with his cross was a real one, not only for Jesus' audience, but also for John's first-century readership. Many Jews, attracted to Jesus on other grounds, struggled understandably with his rejection by his own people, and with his shameful death at the hands of the Gentiles. Jesus does not offer a direct response to his audience's question. He has given it already. The kingdom he brings *is* eternal, the life he offers *is* eternal life. For it to be made available, however, the prince of this world must be confronted and his enslaving hold upon the human heart broken through the final and perfect obedience of the Son of Man. The guilt of the ages cannot be swept

[13] F. F. Bruce, p. 267.
[14] Ps. 72:17, or Ps. 89:35–37; Is. 9:7; Ezk. 37:25.

under the carpet but must be drawn out into the light and judged. The Son of Man must die in order to reign for ever. So, instead of yet further reiteration of his unique relationship to the everlasting one, Jesus confronts them for a last time with his claim and invitation. He is the light who has come into the world (35). He is still with them. If they will but put their trust in him they will themselves become sons of light (36). But the time of opportunity is almost at an end – *just a little while longer* (35). And the alternative is solemn indeed. If they will not come to the light, he tells them, darkness will overtake them, and they will not know where they are going (35).

These sobering possibilities complete Jesus' public ministry as John records it. He will share a further block of Jesus' sayings before the chapter closes, but these consist essentially of a general appeal. Our Lord's final word is a most solemn warning. To refuse to come to him means being shut out from the light for ever.

There is an urgency in this last appeal of Jesus from which the modern church does well to learn. The days when sermons on hell and its conditions were the staple diet of the evangelical pulpit have long since departed. Their going is not wholly to be regretted. Fear of hell-fire is certainly not the primary motive for seeking Christ's salvation. Besides, such preaching often concentrated on the damnation of the lost in a manner that left the saved smugly secure and unchallenged concerning the profound moral and ethical implications of living a 'saved' life. We would not turn back the clock in this respect even if we could. Yet the warning note which Jesus strikes here is always relevant. The implications of turning away from the light of God are terrible in the extreme, and Jesus is concerned that people be clearly aware of them. We are certainly to draw men and women towards God's salvation by all God-honouring inducements. We are certainly authorized to bear witness with full hearts to the completeness of the salvation which Christ has won for sinners, and the joys beyond compare which await those who cast themselves upon his mercy. In addition, however, we dare not fail to warn them that the redeemer is also a judge, that sin unrepented is sin condemned, and that it is, and will be when the King returns, 'a dreadful thing to fall into the hands of the living God' (Heb. 10:31). While people have opportunity, we are to speak, and plead, as did our Saviour: *You are going to have the light just a little while longer ... before darkness overtakes you ... Put your trust in the light while you have it* (35–36).

Verses 37–50 is a concluding summary of John's account of Jesus' public ministry. From 13:1 Jesus is no longer the public preacher of the good news of salvation, and the revealer of the glory of God through the signs of the kingdom. He is rather the instructor of his disciples (13–16), the intercessor with the Father (17), and the Lamb of God, crucified and raised again for the sins of the world (18–21). In particular John does two things. He addresses the unbelief of the Jews (37–43), and then provides a succinct summary of the message which the Jews, and all unbelievers since, reject.

The unbelief of the Jews, and their religious leaders in particular, has been a minor motif throughout the story. There is evidence that it continued to be a major issue in later decades, since one of the biggest stumbling blocks in the path to commitment to Jesus as Messiah for many of John's contemporaries was the failure of the Jewish people to recognize him as such, during the course of his ministry. John has already indicated their rejection of Jesus due to their unwillingness to 'come into the light for fear that [their] deeds will be exposed' (3:20). He has just recounted Jesus' solemn teaching on the cost of commitment (24–26). He now adds two further reasons for their unbelief.

First, Jesus has been rejected because God has so willed it. This sounds like extreme predestinarianism, but John, as we shall see, modifies that in certain respects. His main point (and therefore God's main point, since John is writing under the special inspiration of the Holy Spirit), however, is that human unbelief cannot escape from the all-embracing purposes of God. *How* this is so certainly escapes us; *that* it is so John does not hesitate to affirm, and neither ought we.

John cites two Old Testament passages in support, Isaiah 6:10 and Isaiah 53:1. The latter is particularly apt coming on the heels of verse 31, for the Servant passage from which it is culled represents the sufferer as 'lifted up and highly exalted' (Is. 52:13). The former refers to God's call to the prophet to proclaim his word, even though the result will be the hardening of the hearts of the people against his message. The same passage is used with similar import in the synoptic gospels to account for the failure of Jesus' listeners to comprehend the parables of the kingdom (Mk. 4:12). Paul also refers to the Isaiah 53:1 passage along with others of like implication as he wrestles with the identical issue of Jewish unbelief in Romans 9 – 11.

There is certainly an element of irony in the terms of Isaiah's call. His ministry would appear fruitless, seeming only to confirm the people in their headlong flight to judgment. Nonetheless John's use of the passage is clear enough. God is not excluded from the response people make to his claims upon them. As he acts in grace to enable and support the faith of those who believe, so he acts to confirm judicially the rejection of those who choose the path of unbelief. This does not, for John, eliminate human responsibility, as his repeated references through the gospel to the challenge of faith indicate, among which Jesus' appeal for faith in this passage is a particularly clear example (44–50). Further, as with Israel in Isaiah's time, there is a remnant who believe, even among the Jewish leaders (42). Finally, as John goes on to show, God will use this very rejection to fulfil his purposes of salvation (20:30). More specifically, since Isaiah *saw Jesus' glory and spoke about him* (41), the rejection of Jesus by Israel was foretold in these Old Testament passages, and so is not outside God's eternal purpose.

Isaiah's seeing *Jesus' glory* (41) has occasioned comment. It can be taken to mean that Isaiah prophesied concerning Jesus' ministry, and in that sense 'saw' and 'spoke about' him. Alternatively, John may be thinking of the pre-incarnate Christ (*cf.* so Paul in 1 Cor. 10:4), either as part of the divine glory in Isaiah 6:1f., or as foreshadowed in the sacrifice on the altar by which the prophet was cleansed (Is. 6:6–7). This Sent One cannot be confined to the period of his earthly mission. He is eternal, and the glory he reveals is the glory of 'the One and Only, who is at the Father's side' (1:18), which he shared with the Father 'before the world began' (17:5).

The unbelief of the Jews was not complete, even among the rulers (42). John is thinking here no doubt of Nicodemus, and probably also of Joseph of Arimathea, who is shortly to enter the story as a 'believer' (19:38). Clearly there were others, however, apparently even less willing to make a stand. Their faith remained dormant, and possibly abortive in the end, because of their fear.

This brings John to the second reason for the lack of recognition of Jesus, particularly on the part of the religious leaders (42–43). It would have meant expulsion from the synagogue, and that price was too high. At root their failure to confess Jesus was, as he had earlier noted (5:44), a preference for human praise over the praise of God. Calvin comments that they were bound by the 'golden shackles of earthly honours' and thus kept from honouring God.[15] In this they stand in stark contrast to Jesus, who consistently disavowed all honour except that of his Father.[16] Many of John's readers would have faced the same dilemma, and it is no different today. Following Jesus is costly. Those who expect the Lord to own their names on the judgment day, he expects to own his name now before a watching world (Mk. 8:38). There is no such thing as a totally secret disciple.

Verses 44–50 are described by C. H. Dodd as 'the content of the kerygma of Jesus'.[17] That is to overstate the case. This paragraph,

[15] J. Calvin, 2, p. 49.   [16] 7:18; 8:29; 8:50.
[17] C. H. Dodd, *Fourth Gospel*, p. 382. The 'kerygma' is the theological term for the message which is preached.

however, certainly sounds many of the primary notes of his message. First, Jesus has been sent by the Father (44) and fully obeys him (49). Secondly, Jesus is uniquely one with the Father. To see and hear him is to see and hear the Father (45, 49, 50). Thirdly, Jesus is the light of the world. To come to him and believe in him is to receive the light of salvation (46, 47b, 50). Fourthly, to reject Jesus means choosing to *stay in darkness* and to face future judgment (46, 48). Fifthly, this judgment will be by the words Jesus has spoken, because they are the Father's very words (48b–50). Sixthly, conversely, to follow Jesus' words brings eternal life (50).

We note finally that John mentions the manner, as well as the content, of his proclamation (*what to say and how to say it*; 49). That manner is stated: *Jesus cried out* (44). This verb is also used at the tomb of Lazarus, 'Jesus called in a loud voice, "Lazarus, come out!" ' (11:43). At times Jesus was quiet and subdued (Mt. 12:19f.). At other times, as here, he was vehement and compelling. In the manner of his speech no less than in its content he was the servant of his Father.

The vehemence of Jesus' appeal at this point is wholly credible as his public ministry concludes. The challenge to those who are called to proclaim the good news of Christ, however, is a deep one. Richard Baxter's complaint bears reflection.

> I marvel how I can preach . . . slightly and coldly, how I can let men alone in their sins, and that I do not go to them and beseech them for the Lord's sake to repent, however they take it, and whatever pains or trouble it should cost me. I seldom come out of the pulpit but my conscience smiteth me that I have been no more serious and fervent. It accuseth me . . . 'Shoulds't thou not weep over such a people, and shoulds't not thy tears interrupt thy words? Shoulds't thou not cry aloud and show them their transgressions and entreat and beseech them as for life and death?'[18]

Preachers with cold hearts will never warm and awaken the consciences of their hearers. Preaching is more than delivering a message from God; it is delivering a message from God in a manner consistent with that content. The message concerns the fire of God's love, and the fire of his judgment, and hence can be authentically proclaimed only by hearts kindled with the fire of the Holy Spirit. False emotionalism, and the unrealistic dramatization of the message, do not honour the Lord, and tend only to alienate non-Christians further. But there is a true engagement of the heart in preaching, and in our everyday witnessing opportunities, which is

[18] R. Baxter, *The Reformed Pastor* (SCM, 1956), p. 110.

195

stamped with sincerity, and which is an authentic reflection of the heart of the God whose gospel we proclaim. God is looking today for preachers who, like his Son, will 'cry out'.

2. Instruction (13:1 – 16:33)

John signals the beginning of a major new section of the gospel in three ways. First, the Passover has now arrived. Another feast implies a new phase in the ministry of Jesus, providing John with a key to interpret the events of Jesus' death and resurrection (19:14; 19:36). Secondly, the 'hour' has come (1; the NIV misses this with *the time*, the Greek is 'hour', *hora*). We have already noted the significance of this word, and its role in building a sense of climax in the gospel. Thirdly, while the disciples have not been neglected to this point, Jesus has been largely preoccupied with outsiders. This section signals a change of focus as Jesus turns to 'his own' and shows them his love.

a. The foot-washing (13:1–17)

The setting is a meal shared with the disciples. The precise nature of this meal and its relationship both to the Passover family meal, and to the Last Supper described in the synoptic gospels, has long been debated.[19] The many points of parallel to the synoptic descriptions make it highly likely that this was the same occasion. We shall attempt further justification of this interpretation later.

As the meal gets underway an astonishing scene is enacted. Proper etiquette, generally more important in the East than in the West, taught that guests, begrimed from journeying through the dusty streets, should, on arrival, have their feet washed by a slave. This was a particularly humble task, included in a list of works which a Jewish slave should not be required to perform.[20] As they commence the meal with feet as yet unwashed, since apparently none of the disciples are prepared to fulfil the duty (one does not wash the feet of peers!), Jesus himself rises, divests himself of his outer clothing,[21] girds himself with a towel, and proceeds to wash and then dry his disciples' feet. Peter characteristically cannot contain himself and trenchantly resists the approach of Jesus (6, 8). Jesus overcomes his resistance by assuring him that only the washed belong to him (7, 9). Peter must submit in trust; there is a deeper

---

[19] Cf. Mk. 14:12–26; Lk. 22:1–38.

[20] See Midrash Mekilta on Ex. 21:2; also Strack–Billerbeck, I, 707; cited in Beasley-Murray, p. 233 *et al.*

[21] The verbs here are identical to those used in 10:18.

meaning to Jesus' action which he will realize later. Peter's reaction is typically whole-hearted: *Not just my feet but my hands and my head as well!* (9).

With the hindsight of the cross we can appreciate what Jesus is doing (7). He is performing a symbolic prefigurement of his cleansing sacrifice at Calvary. Viewed in this way the foot-washing uncovers a number of aspects of the death of Christ.

(i)   The incomparable love which underlies it

Verse 1 refers to Christ's love which he now reveals to its *full extent*. This phrase can also be translated 'to the very end', *i.e.* a temporal reference. The qualitative meaning is probably to be preferred. Significantly there is no real break between verses 1 and 2. Thus the 'love to the limit' is now expressed in the foot-washing which, as Jesus indicates to Peter, points directly to his 'later' action, his self-humbling to death. 'This is love: not that we loved God, but that he loved us and sent his Son as an atoning sacrifice for our sins' (1 Jn. 4:10). In the end there is no explanation of the cross other than the love of God. There can be no other, for we certainly do not deserve it and can never earn it.

(ii)   The sinister coalition which effects it

Judas is part of the company sharing the meal and hence among those whose feet Jesus washes. His heart, however, is elsewhere. It has been invaded by Satan (2). John does not imply that Judas is a helpless pawn in the hands of the evil one; he was prompted, not propelled. But Judas' resistance of Jesus, his surrender to the spirit of avarice, his thwarted ambition, his disenchantment with Jesus' disavowal of political power, or whatever else was the taproot of his decision to betray his Master, gave the devil an opportunity. Having closed his heart to the light, Judas found himself the servant of darkness.

There is the solemnest of warnings here. Not all who profess to follow Jesus are truly 'his own'. Even some who receive the outward washing of Christ are still unwashed in heart. This is obviously applicable to the Christian sacraments. Baptism and the Lord's Supper, though powerful means of grace to the committed, cannot in themselves impart salvation. Satan is ever seeking hearts which have closed themselves to the light (1 Pet. 5:8). Our safety lies only in keeping close to Jesus and daily allowing the light of his Word to expose and correct us.

(iii)   The hidden sovereignty which directs it

The death of Jesus will take place only at *the hour* (1), the time, which the Father had ordained and for which the Son waited. The

197

initiative remains with God. Verse 3 expresses this sovereignty of God in the death of Jesus in terms of the unqualified authority which the Father has committed to the Son. *All things* means just that. His rule is complete; his lordship is absolute. Thus the other actors in the drama of his death, Judas, Annas, Caiaphas, Pilate and the mob, act within the purpose of God. Their failure, rebellion and sin are but the occasion for the revealing of love's triumph.

(iv) The inescapable challenge which arises from it
This challenge is both personal and corporate. At the personal level the challenge is reflected in Jesus' words to Peter, *Unless I wash you, you have no part with me.* In the wonder of his self-giving love Jesus stoops to the cross, and, as God's Passover lamb, submits to slaughter on our behalf, to wash us clean from all our moral filth and guilt. The question then becomes, has Christ washed us? How that happens is illustrated in these verses. Like Peter, as long as we imagine we can get by without Christ's cleansing we cannot be saved. Pride must perish. We are helpless sinners for whom no amount of good works, religious exercises, or Christian ministries can atone. Only the blood of Christ can save us – his sacrifice offered for us on the cross, and received by an act of simple, personal faith. So we come to Christ and allow him to wash us. There is literally no sin which he cannot cleanse in this way. All guilt can be forgiven; even sins we would be ashamed to admit to any other person. 'The blood of Jesus, his Son, purifies us from all sin' (1 Jn. 1:7).

The challenge of this incident is an ongoing one. When Peter offers his hands and head as well as his feet for cleansing, Jesus uses the opportunity to develop the symbol of the foot-washing in a different way. He distinguishes between a once-for-all cleansing, as when having a bath (10), and the continual washing of more specific areas of the body soiled in the regular course of things, like our hands. Certain manuscripts omit the phrase *needs only to wash his feet* from verse 10, and some recent scholars believe this abbreviated reading to be original. By this view Jesus is simply saying that when he washes us we are wholly clean, like a person who has had a bath. If, on the other hand, the interpreters who retain the phrase are correct, Jesus is using the imagery of washing to make a further point of application. There is a once-for-all cleansing when we become Christians as all our sins are judged and put away in the cross, but in the course of our ongoing Christian lives sin obtrudes daily. That sin too is to be cleansed through a daily coming to the Lord for his renewed washing.

There is also a communal challenge in Jesus' action which he proceeds to draw out in verses 12–17. Jesus has given not only a vivid illustration of the way of salvation, but also a powerful demonstration of the secret of communion. Jesus is our Teacher and Lord (14). *Lord* (*kyrios*) is a term of supreme authority. For at least some of the disciples, at this point, the title may have not meant much more than 'master'. Jesus' immediate assumption of their obligation to imitate him (14), however, points to the fuller dimensions of the title which were to surface unambiguously at 20:28, where it is linked to 'God'. Paul in Philippians 2 calls it 'the name that is above every other name'. In other New Testament usage it has clear overtones of deity.[22] The greater the title which Jesus uses, the greater the challenge of his action. If he has acted thus, stooping in humility to serve us by washing us through his cross, how much more ought we to be ready to wash the feet of even the lowest and meanest of his followers. Conversely, to refuse to do so through pride is to proclaim ourselves superior to Jesus our Master, which is unthinkable!

Whether this verse is a sufficient basis for the practice of foot-washing becoming a regular ordinance of the church is probably doubtful. It was not seen in these terms in the early centuries. With the exception of 1 Timothy 5:10 there is no other New Testament reference to it, and there the reference appears social rather than sacramental. The accompanying *attitude*, however, permits no exception. Humility is a universal Christian virtue to be expressed through sincere and costly service of others in Christ's name. Christian churches and fellowships are possible only where this attitude is expressed. They have no promise of permanence where it is lacking.

In a world desperately searching for the secret of community this passage speaks most powerfully. The personal and communal applications, however, cannot be separated. It is those who have been humbled at the cross, and come to Christ as helpless sinners seeking his cleansing, who are the raw material of the community of humble servants. The cross is both the way of salvation and the key to community. There is a close parallel here to the teaching of verses 34 and 35 which also draws a parallel between Jesus' relationship to us, 'as I have loved you' (34), and our relationships to each other, 'love one another' (34).

We ought, finally, to note the link which is made in verse 13 between Jesus as our *Teacher* and Jesus as our *Lord*. They belong together. One of the primary expressions of our submission to Jesus as our 'Lord' is our willingness to allow him to be our 'Teacher'. In practice that means the unreserved submission of our minds to his truth, allowing his words, standards, values, attitudes,

---

[22] *Cf.* Rom. 1:4; 10:9; 1 Cor. 8:6; 2 Cor. 4:5; 12:8.

commandments, example and teaching to rule our thoughts and determine our convictions. Thus, for example, Jesus' attitude of respect for, and submission to, the Scriptures (*cf.* 'The Scripture cannot be broken', 10:35) becomes normative for us. Simply, if Jesus is not our Teacher, he is not our Lord.

b. The coming of the night – Judas (13:18–30)

Within the intimacy of Jesus' sharing with 'his own' (1), a shadow lingers: 'not every one [of you] is clean' (11). The presence of a traitor has already been reported.[23] This demonic intrusion is now confronted, though, as ever, in love.

Fundamental to Jesus' engagement with the devil is the assurance that he remains Lord (3), and thus will use evil for his purposes. So, even this terrible demonic assault, the snatching away of one of 'his own' from the shepherd's near presence, is anticipated in the Scriptures (*cf.* 18; Psalm 41:9). The biblical image is a vivid one: *He who shares my bread has lifted up his heel against me* (18). 'To show the bottom of one's foot to someone in the Near East is a mark of contempt.'[24] It is associated with the kick of a horse, vicious and unexpected. But Jesus is not taken by surprise or outflanked by betrayal, nor should the disciples be (19). Rather, Jesus' uncovering of the traitor is further evidence that he is 'I Aм', the all-sufficient object of their faith (19). The Greek literally says *I am*, and in John we are alerted to the deeper meaning of this phrase. 'Despite the incomprehensible fact of the betrayal, Jesus continued to be the one sent by God, and, after the event has taken place, it will be clear that the disciple's betrayal and the plan devised by Satan even served Jesus' exaltation.'[25]

Although Judas' apostasy does not take Jesus by surprise, he is deeply affected by it: *Jesus was troubled in spirit* (21). The verb is *tarassō* (*cf.* comments on 11:33). It is used in 5:7 of the turbulence of the pool at Bethesda when the waters bubbled and convulsed due to an inrush from a hidden spring (also in Acts 17:8–13 for the agitation of a violent crowd). As in 11:33 Jesus expresses discomfort before the destructive activity of Satan. Although the victor over the devil and all his works (13:3; 12:31), Jesus does not face him in serene detachment. As with the abuse of the temple, the desecration of the Holy Place (2:13–17), so with the desecration of the temples of human lives, Jesus is profoundly agitated. It is a disturbance of mind his disciples are called to imitate. The confession 'Jesus is Lord' must not lead to a triumphalistic detachment

---

[23] 6:70–71; 12:4; 13:2.   [24] R. Brown, 2, p. 554.
[25] R. Schnackenburg, 3, p. 26.

from the world but rather to an appalled dismay that his lordship is contested, and a commitment to mission to the world in the name of its Lord (20).

Jesus' reference to the sending of the disciples (20) is in terms which anticipate 17:18 and 20:21. This is a key statement for the interpretation of the entire block of teaching which will follow (chapters 13 – 16). These 'upper-room discourses' have been commonly interpreted in terms of the intimate communion between Jesus and the disciples prior to his departure from them. While there is evident validity in that approach, it has frequently failed to recognize that the real context of these chapters is the impending mission of the disciples to the world. Those addressed are not just disciples but apostles (lit. = 'sent ones'). The analogy for these chapters is not a final farewell meeting between Jesus and his friends before his being snatched from them by death, a kind of spiritual deathbed scene with all the pathos engendered by such associations. Rather, the analogy is that of a commanding officer giving his troops final instructions and encouragement on the eve of a most dangerous mission in which he will lead them.

The parallel Jesus draws between the mission of the Son, sent into the world by the Father (*whoever accepts me accepts the one who sent me*), and the disciples' mission, sent into the world by the Son (*whoever accepts anyone I send accepts me*), is a crucial one and anticipates the identical parallel in 17–18 and 20–21. Up to this point in the gospel the first of these two missions has dominated the scene, *viz.* the mission of the Son sent by the Father (the only clear exception being 4:35–38). Now, the second mission comes increasingly into focus beside the first, not in any sense to replace it, as we shall see, and still less to rival it, but rather to carry it forward under new conditions. For the mission of Jesus as the 'Sent One' of the Father is not exhausted by his impending sacrifice, but will continue in the mission of 'his own'. The 'hour' which is now striking for the climax of the mission of Jesus is also the 'hour' for the launching of the mission of the church.

First, however, the traitor must be confronted. *One of you is going to betray me* (21). The opening words are *I tell you the truth* ('verily, verily', AV), a statement of great solemnity. The stunned silence precipitated by the saying is predictably broken by Peter, inviting the *disciple whom Jesus loved*, and who is reclining next to him, to enquire to whom Jesus is referring (23–24).

This is the first explicit reference to this disciple in the gospel, though not the last.[26] In 21:24 he is identified as the writer of the gospel. Traditionally he has been viewed as the apostle John, an

---

[26] 19:26–27; 20:2–9; 21:1, 20–23.

identification we uphold (*cf.* Introduction, 'Authorship'). Some find difficulty with the phrase *the disciple whom Jesus loved*, as it seems to reflect poorly on John, for apparent arrogance, and poorly on Jesus, for apparent favouritism. If, however, the disciple in question is John the son of Zebedee, whom Jesus had called from his fishing trade to be a witness and preacher of the gospel, then the description, though open to misunderstanding, surely testifies to the overwhelming nature of his experience of Christ's love. 'Christ loves *me!*' Paul speaks in very similar terms of the identical experience: 'the Son of God, who loved *me* and gave himself for *me!*' (Gal. 2:20, my emphasis). The love of Jesus Christ, in its sheer graciousness, necessarily imparts to its recipient a sense of being uniquely chosen and blessed by it. Rather as the reflection of the setting sun on the surface of the ocean appears to stretch a golden pathway to our feet alone, so the love of Christ as it beams into our lives confers at moments an overwhelming, personal sense of privilege. Alternatively, the title may simply be a nickname which arose from John's repeatedly testifying in his later years to the supreme experience of having been personally loved by Jesus.

Some comment about the physical arrangements for the meal are in order in explaining verses 23–30, and they can be reconstructed with some confidence. Like most westerners today, Jews in the first century generally ate seated at a table. For special meals, however, such as the Passover celebration, the Greek custom of reclining had been adopted. Thus a number of couches, probably three in a 'U' shape, would have been drawn around a low central table. It was the custom to lie on one's left side, head inwards, resting on the left elbow and eating with the right hand. The 'beloved disciple' must have been placed on Jesus' immediate right, and so to ask his question about the traitor would have needed simply to lean back, so that his head was on Jesus' breast (as described in verse 25). The Greek literally says, 'who was reclining on his bosom' (*cf.* 12:2).

John's *who is it*? provokes Jesus to identify the traitor by handing him a morsel from the dish (26). The gift of a titbit by the host at such a meal was a mark of special favour. Thus even as he unmasks the traitor Jesus reaches out to him in a final astonishing act of loving friendship and appeal. This gesture is further augmented if, as appears to have been the case (26), Judas was within arm's reach of Jesus through occupying the place on his other side, the host's left, the place of special honour. For one last, lingering moment Judas' destiny hangs in the balance as the love of God incarnate shines one more time into his benighted heart. But the moment is no sooner present than it passes, as Judas in a final act of defiance closes his heart against the light, and turns away into the darkness that has no end. Thus 'that final act of love becomes, with a terrible immediacy, the decisive moment of judgment . . . the final gesture of affection precipitates the final surrender of Judas to the power of darkness.'[27] *As soon as Judas took the bread, Satan entered into him* (27). Judas, having made his fateful choice, is directed by Jesus to act quickly. The night is coming, but Jesus is ready for the horror of great darkness which must engulf him so that Satan may be driven out and salvation won for the world. Judas went out *And it was night!* (30; *cf.* Lk. 22:53).

The other disciples do not grasp the meaning of Judas' departure, interpreting it as a treasurer's errand related to the feast arrangements, or a visit to the temple in keeping with the custom of special almsgiving during Passover evening (28–29). Jesus' reply to John had presumably been quietly spoken, and John is too astonished to react.

This paragraph is a powerful and disturbing reminder of the ambiguity of the life of the people of God in every age. Despite all the laudable and entirely appropriate attempts, particularly since the Reformation, to obtain a 'pure membership' for the church, it remains, as Calvin acknowledged in the sixteenth century, a 'mixed multitude'. Only Christ can truly unveil the heart, as he will do at the coming judgment day (*cf.* Mt. 24:30f.; Jn. 5:22; *etc.*). Then and only then will the true 'flock of the Lord' be assembled by the good shepherd. Until then the church is an irreducibly ambiguous company, at once both holy and profane, embracing the servants of Christ and the servants of Satan. This must not surprise us, however, or cause us to stumble (20). The presence of Judas among the visible company of the disciples throughout the course of Jesus' mission did not prevent the completion of the purpose of the Son, nor the coming of the Spirit, nor the witness of the apostles, nor the going of Jesus to the world through them. It need not, it must not, prevent it now.

The most disturbing element in this passage, however, is the awesome warning represented in the figure of Judas. There is, tragically, 'a road to hell at the very gates of heaven' in the sense that it is possible to resist even the prolonged, personal appeals of Jesus Christ and turn away at the last into the darkness. There are those whom even Jesus cannot, and will not, save. Not that his grace is insufficient for them. On the contrary, it truly is 'enough for all, enough for each, enough for evermore', as Charles Wesley eloquently declared. But they will not come to receive it. The corollary to the stress on the crucial importance of faith in this gospel is the seriousness of unbelief, the refusal of faith. Hell is no

[27] L. Newbigin, p. 173.

mere theoretical possibility. It is an awesome and fearful reality. To refuse the light means to choose the darkness where no light will ever shine again. Judas also eliminates the excuse often expressed or implied, that 'if only I had been there, when Jesus was on earth, seen his miracles, heard his teaching, and experienced his personal invitation, then of course I would have committed my life to him'. Judas was there, he saw, he heard, he experienced . . . and went out to hell. 'Put your trust in the light while you have it' (12:36).

Finally, this section demonstrates again the mastery of Jesus. Even amid the trauma of unmasking the traitor's scheming and the handiwork of Satan right there among his closest friends, he remains in control. There is a telling use of 'handing over' in these verses. Jesus 'hands over' the sop to Judas (26). Judas 'hands Jesus over' to the authorities (2, 21). Behind all, however, is the sovereign presence of the Father who has 'handed all things over to Jesus' (3). Nor is there any exception to that delegated lordship. Thus, as Judas leaves the meal in order to be about the business of his infernal father, he goes at the express command (27) of him whose Father's business is his food and life (4:34).

The encouragement is clear. If Jesus in his purpose used the dark forces of chaos convulsing within the cauldron, which was Jerusalem that Passover feast-time, he can still master and harness the darkness which daily threatens our personal lives. In handing all over to him, we need not exclude the darkness in our past or that which threatens us in the present and future. He is still the Lord of the night, who can make darkness the vehicle of his praise.

c. The farewell discourses (13:31 – 16:33)

(i) 'Let not your hearts be troubled' – discourse A (13:31 – 14:31)
(ii) 'So I send you' – discourse B (15:1 – 16:33)

The departure of Judas permits Jesus' final discourses. Within this block of teaching a break of some sort is indicated at the end of chapter 14, *Come now let us leave* (14:31). The material of chapters 15 – 16 would then perhaps have been shared during the progress through the city to the Garden of Gethsemane. More plausibly, the injunction to *let us leave* was not immediately acted upon until the teaching was completed and Jesus had offered his prayer (17). This latter view would accord with 18:1: 'Jesus left with his disciples and crossed the Kidron Valley.' Either way we should recognize a break at the end of 14 which is confirmed by the content, and so divide the material into two distinguishable parts.

A more general question concerns the essential focus of these chapters. What does Jesus have in view in his instruction of his disciples here? We have already indicated the emergence at this point of what could be referred to as a minor motif in the earlier music, the mission of the disciples. While it is stated only in a preliminary way at 13:20, and will not emerge fully until the second discourse in chapters 15 – 16, it is arguably the underlying theme throughout. Jesus is preparing the disciples for their post-Easter work. If this perspective is correct, then these discourses have an urgent relevance to a church facing the enormous challenge of world evangelization at a time of exploding population and diminishing resources. Viewing the discourses in this way also, one hopes, removes them from the rather esoteric and enclosed atmosphere in which they have been traditionally set, and allows us to bring them out into the marketplace where they and this whole gospel surely belong.

(i) 'Let not your hearts be troubled' – discourse A (13:31 – 14:31)

1. *The absence of Jesus* (13:31–38). Jesus' first words, *Now is the Son of Man glorified and God is glorified in him* (31), serve as a fitting title for the entire discourses, and indeed for the remainder of the gospel. That revealing of his glory has a clear focus, however – the hour of suffering. *Son of Man* echoes Daniel 7:13, but it is to be linked with the Servant who suffers.[28] *Now* (31) implies that with Judas' departure the trap is sprung; the sequence of the arrest, trial and crucifixion is already set in motion, a succession in relation to which Jesus must be submissive. But this very submission is the glorifying of the Father through him, and the completing of his work (17:4). 'For the glory of God is not the self-glorification of a supreme monad; it is the glory of perfect love forever poured out and forever received within the being of the triune God. It is the glory of Sonship.'[29]

The glory of the Son, and the Father through the Son, is so intimately one reality that it can be expressed the other way round, *God will glorify the Son in himself* (31). All this will happen 'immediately' in the events of the following hours. Possibly the 'immediately' can be interpreted in the sense of 'at one moment', *i.e.* at the same time. The glorification of the Son and the Father will be one indivisible act. The title of the Father here is 'God', but carries no implication of any subordination of being as far as

---

[28] *Cf.* 'the Son of Man must suffer': Mk. 8:31; Is. 49:7; 50:6f.; 52:13 – 53:12.

[29] L. Newbigin, p. 175.

Jesus is concerned. He is the one whose glorification *is* the glorification of God.

Jesus' endearing *my children*, or 'my dear (little) children',[30] is appropriate to the Passover meal setting, which was celebrated according to the law, *en famille*. Jesus' feelings of endearment towards the disciples are made more tangible as he recognizes that *I will be with you only a little longer* (33) and that they cannot, for the present, follow him. In this regard their case has some parallels to the Jews to whom Jesus had spoken in similar terms some months before (*cf.* 7:33–34; 8:21). It is in this context that Jesus shares the love commandment, *A new commandment I give to you: Love one another*, and adds the promise, *All men will know that you are my disciples, if you love one another* (34–35).

Here Jesus expresses *the meaning of love*. For a concept in such wide everyday use love is surprisingly poorly defined. In common usage the emotional aspect, 'feelings of love', is often paramount. Jesus' definition focuses rather on loving action. Love is defined by what he has been and would soon be to his disciples. 13:1 links the exposition of love 'to the full extent' to the foot-washing, which is an acted parable of his washing away of sin through his sacrifice. Love is defined by the cross. It is love of that calibre which his disciples are called upon to express towards each other.

This commandment is *new*, not because it is intrinsically different from the law of love of the Old Testament.[31] Nor is it new because of Jesus' redefining of 'neighbour' (Lk. 10:29–37), though that is certainly significant. The 'newness' lies rather in its being the law of the 'new covenant' which Jesus is to establish through his death, and which he has so recently proclaimed during the supper they have shared.[32] The new covenant brings with it the new life in the Holy Spirit which will as never before enable the fulfilling of the law.[33] It is 'new' also in the sheer depth and demand of the summons to love which Jesus issues. In the light of the cross all other descriptions and definitions of love pale into insignificance. Here indeed is love 'so amazing, so divine' (Isaac Watts). Yet according to Jesus this is the norm for Christian community.

We note also *the evangelistic power of love*. A loving community, says Jesus, is the visible authentication of the gospel. Love is the 'final apologetic' (Francis Schaeffer). Jesus places no limit on this demonstration; *all* will recognize and know it. Unlike other associ-

---

[30] *Cf.* 1 Jn. 2:1; 2:18; 2:28; *etc.*
[31] *Cf.* Lv. 19:18, 'love your neighbour as yourself'; Mt. 22:34–40; Mk. 12:28–31.
[32] *Cf.* Lk. 22:20; also Je. 31:31; Ezk. 34:25.
[33] Je. 31:33–34; Ezk. 36:26–27; *cf.* Rom. 5:5; Gal. 5:22.

ations which are based upon common interest or outlook, the church is to be marked by an inclusiveness which echoes the universal appeal of Jesus. It is designated as a community which welcomes all people, irrespective of background, age, gender, colour, moral history, social status, influence, intelligence, religious background or the lack of it. To love like Jesus is to love inclusively, indiscriminately and universally. When that kind of love flows within a congregation the world will take note that 'they have been with Jesus'. Nor need this standard daunt us. Tertullian reported in the late second century the comment of the pagans in his day: 'Behold, how these Christians love each other! How ready they are to die for each other!' Their mutual love was the magnet which drew the pagan multitudes to Christ. It has the potential to do so still.

Finally, there is here *the promise of love*. The immediate setting of the command is important; Jesus is about to leave the disciples. Here is the consolation for a community soon to be bereft of the tangible presence of its Lord – loving each other, in reflection of his love for them. 'No-one has ever seen God; but if we love one another, God lives in us and his love is made complete in us' (1 Jn. 4:12). In the caring and costly service of 'the brothers and sisters', we shall meet with Jesus himself (Mt. 25:31–45). Mother Teresa's prayer has direct application within every Christian community. 'Dearest Lord, may I see you today and every day in the person of your sick, and, whilst nursing them, minister unto you. Though you hide yourself behind the unattractive disguise of the irritable, the exacting, the unreasonable, may I still recognize you and say, "Jesus, my patient, how sweet it is to serve you." '[34]

Peter, however, has no ears for Jesus' sublime instruction. He is agitated by the talk of Jesus' departure (36). Jesus assures him that while he cannot follow immediately, he will later; a reference to his future martyrdom (21:18–19). Peter, vociferously loyal as ever, expresses his willingness to die for Jesus (37). Like the others around him, however, he has no appreciation of the dark and terrible forces abroad that night in Jerusalem. Before the cock crows (38), these forces will search him and his colleagues to the very core and leave Peter, the confident, self-reliant leader, as a broken, Christ-denying failure. Even then the sheep will not be snatched from the shepherd's grasp (10:28).

It is important before concluding this section to note the parallels, as well as the contrast, between Judas and Peter. Both had

[34] Mother Teresa, cited in M. Muggeridge, *Something Beautiful for God* (Collins, 1971), pp. 74f.

associated with Jesus across the previous years. Both had seen his signs and heard his truth. To both he gave his love and extended his appeal. In the final hours of Jesus' mission both abysmally failed him, and abandoned him in the hour of his greatest need. Both grieved Jesus' heart and added to his pain. The failure of both was spectacularly public. Both are known today around the world for the failures they perpetrated. One, however, was lost and the other saved. One repented, sought Christ's mercy, and went to heaven. One, overwhelmed with remorse, turned upon himself, took his own life, and went unforgiven to hell.

The seeds of the failure of both Peter and Judas lie embedded in each of our hearts. We know what it is both to deny Jesus and to betray him. We can only cast ourselves daily on his limitless mercy, knowing that he will not cast away even one of all who come to him, and that not one will be lost of all that the Father has given him (6:37, 39).

> because we are all
> betrayers, taking
> silver and eating
> body and blood and asking
> (guilty) is it I and hearing
> him say yes
> it would be simple for us all
> to rush out
> and hang ourselves
>
> but if we find grace
> to cry and wait
> after the voice of morning
> has crowed in our ears
> clearly enough
> to break our hearts
> he will be there
> to ask us each again
> do you love me.[35]

2. *The blessings of his 'absence'* (14:1–31). While there are obvious points of transition in this chapter (from verse 4 to 5; and 14 to 15) the material hangs together as a unified discourse around a specific theme. The theme is stated in the opening words, *Do not let your hearts be troubled* (1). We gather the exposition under two

[35] 'Judas, Peter' from *The Sighting* by Luci Shaw (Harold Shaw, 1981), p. 82.

heads: first, why the disciples (and we) become 'troubled'; and secondly, what brings peace to troubled hearts (27).

The disciples are experiencing perceptible anxiety. The reasons for it are to hand.[36] The most obvious is that Jesus has informed them he is about to leave them (13:33). Their whole world had been so wrapped up with Jesus over the last few years that the prospect of his departure must have been devastating. The image he uses for them is 'orphans' (18). Emotionally they can only contemplate the loss of Jesus as like a child's loss of its parents. He had asked them to invest their whole future in following him and they had made the commitment he demanded. If they thought of the future at all during these years it was in terms of sharing the glory of his coming reign (*cf.* Mt. 20:20–24). A future without Jesus comes as a shattering prospect, despite his repeated attempts to prepare them for such an eventuality. A further cause of anxiety was Jesus' foretelling Peter's denial (13:38). It is not difficult to imagine the others arguing that if Peter was not going to stand the coming test, what hope had they? In addition to these immediate threats were the indicators that they, the disciples, had some great task to fulfil once Jesus was gone. True, with Jesus around they had undertaken a mission tour with some success (Mk. 6:7–13), but such activity without Jesus to direct them was a very different prospect. It was all deeply troubling.

'Troubled hearts' expresses the mind-state of multitudes in the modern world. Paradoxically many of these troubled folk live within western society, which is in most respects sheltered from the starker deprivations, such as the chronic lack of food, shelter and health care which plague the millions in the third world. Plenty, however, does not equal peace of mind. Even the followers of Jesus are frequently plagued with anxiety.

Jesus addresses these 'troubled hearts' by urging them, first of all, to have faith (1). The answer to trouble is *trust*. The NIV, following earlier translations, uses *trust* here, which is defensible, though the Greek word is the basic verb for 'believing' (*pistueō*). While the manuscripts indicate some support for a reading such as 'You already believe in God, now have the same faith in me', a double imperative is probably correct: 'Have faith in God; have faith in me.' On any reading this reflects a high Christology. Jesus presents himself unambiguously as the object of faith. 'For John there is only one faith and that is in Jesus and God at the same time.'[37] Faith needs adequate grounding, however, if it is to experi-

---

[36] The word for 'troubled' in verse 1 is used of Jesus in 11:33; 12:27 and 13:32.

[37] R. Schnackenberg, 3, p. 57.

ence serenity and to overcome the 'troubled hearts' of the disciples. The effectiveness and strength of faith are bound up with the greatness and dependability of the God in whom the faith reposes. ' "Have faith in God" means "hold God's faithfulness" ' (Hudson Taylor).

Jesus accordingly relates the grounds for the disciples' faith by showing them, in a series of thrilling paragraphs, that his leaving them is *not* the unmitigated disaster they imagine. On the contrary, all manner of remarkable blessings will flow from it. Jesus will even be able to assert in conclusion that his going away is something they can *be glad* about (28; cf. 16:7, 'It is for your good that I am going away').

Jesus' departure will have three major benefits for the disciples.

1. His going away will secure their future destiny (2–6). Jesus will continue in the fullness of his life, but in a different place. He is returning to life, he tells them, *in my Father's house* (2). His going there will be by a specific route, through death and resurrection (10:17–18; 12:31–32). Thus his going to the Father is an act of power which will win eternal life for all who believe in him.[38] In the terms of his 'homely' (literally) metaphor, his going will prepare rooms for the disciples in God's eternal home, the transcendent dwelling of God depicted in Hebrews 12:22 as 'the heavenly Jerusalem, the city of the living God' (cf. Rev. 21 – 22).[39]

Jesus appeals to their knowledge of him. If there were no glorious dwelling for the children of God beyond the limits of this earthly life, Jesus, as the true Son who has come from the Father's bosom, would certainly have warned them. The hope of life beyond the grave is thereby rooted in the most certain of realities, the veracity and trustworthiness of Jesus Christ. Jesus is going away to make that ready. By implication, if they resist his departure the 'making ready' will not take place. The price of their refusal to be 'made orphans' now through the departure of Jesus is finding themselves homeless orphans on the other side of death. Besides which, Jesus will not forget them in his departing. Having prepared their rooms, he *will come back and take you to be with me that you also may be where I am* (3). Scholars have disputed what this 'coming back' refers to, whether his appearances after the resurrection, or the gift of the outpoured Spirit at Pentecost, or his repeated 'coming'

---

[38] 1:12f.; 3:14–16; 6:51–57.

[39] The word in Greek, *monai* (pl.), means literally dwelling-place(s). Since, however, the heavenly order is depicted here as 'my Father's house', it is natural to think of dwelling-places within a house as 'rooms'. 'Mansion' is an unfortunate mistranslation sparked by the Latin Vulgate rendering, *mansiones*. For today's urban dweller, 'In my Father's apartment block are many apartments' would be possible as a translation.

through the sacraments or other moments when faith's realities are especially vivid. The most obvious meaning is arguably the correct one. Jesus is referring to his glorious appearing at the end of the age, his 'coming back' at his *parousia*.

John's stress on the second coming of Christ is more muted than that of the other evangelists, who record many of Jesus' parables about the end, and also give the details of his great eschatological discourse (*cf.* Mk. 13:1–37; *etc.*). Jesus' glorious appearing is not ignored by John, however, as this verse makes clear (*cf.* also 5:25f., 28f.; 21:22f.). Though the centuries have stretched since this promise was made, its fulfilment is certain. The Lord is coming to take his people home to share his glory (17:24). History is not at the mercy of the whims or passions of politicians or tyrants. The reins are firmly in the hands of the Lord of history, and 'he has set a day when he will judge the world with justice' (Acts 17:31). That day was entered in the calendar of God when the world was made. It is drawing daily nearer.

It is noteworthy that Jesus gives no details concerning that future state. It is simply being where he is. That, however, is sufficient; 'Where Jesus is, 'tis heaven there.' This great blessing, the assurance of eternal life with Jesus in his heavenly home, is possible only because Jesus goes away from us through his cross, resurrection and ascension. If part of the reason for our 'troubled hearts' is the loss of dear ones through death, or our disillusionment with this present world, we are called to renew our trust in him and rediscover his gift of peace, in the confidence that he is coming as he promised and that he has prepared a place for all who love him, in the glory that will surely be.

The way to this future life is known, Jesus asserts (4). But Thomas, nothing if not honest, expresses his ignorance not just of the way but of the destination itself. Clearly, what Jesus has been speaking about has passed Thomas by. While we cannot be glad for the dullness of the disciples (would we have done better?), we can be thankful that their questions not infrequently draw out an important response from Jesus, albeit none quite as memorable as this one: *I am the way and the truth and the life* (6).

The stress falls on *the way*, since that is the issue in question. The way to heaven is Jesus himself. Faith in him shatters the barrier of sin and death, and blasts open the road to the eternal life of the kingdom of God. It is 'the road that leads to life' (Mt. 7:14).

He is also the truth[40] and the life.[41] The reality and truth of God are incarnated in Jesus Christ, who embodies the indestructible life of the ever-living God. This audacious claim carries a major

---

[40] *Cf.* 1:14; 1 Jn. 5:20.   [41] *Cf.* 1:4; 5:26; 11:25; 1 Jn. 5:20.

corollary, *no-one comes to the Father except through me* (6). The exclusivism of this statement must not be reduced. Peter makes exactly the same claim in Acts 4:12. 'Salvation is found in no-one else, for there is no other name under heaven given to men by which we must be saved.' At a time when religious pluralism and syncretism are widespread, such claims are never going to be popular. Nothing less, however, is the implication of Jesus' incarnation. If, in Jesus, God has come among us in person to reconcile his rebellious lost world, it follows necessarily that through him, and him alone, is the way to God. The exclusiveness of Christ's salvation is simply the uniqueness of his divine person.

To say that Jesus is the only way to God does not imply that every idea in non-Christian religion is devoid of value. Non-Christians may find that their conscience approves them, in terms of fulfilling this or that element of the law of God engraved upon their hearts, as Paul recognizes in Romans 2:14. In the same way non-Christians as religious seekers may at one point or another express a response which reflects a valid truth. Such factors, however, do not rescind the general biblical verdict that the non-Christian conscience also universally accuses, and so invariably needs Christ's atonement and forgiveness (Rom. 3:23), or that non-Christian religion is idolatrous at its heart and cannot offer salvation. Jesus alone is the way to God, but he is the way for all, and so whatever the religious background of an individual, or lack of religion, Jesus in his grace welcomes every one of them to the Father if they will come through him. For them too he is ready to prepare a place in the Father's house.

2. The second benefit for his disciples of Jesus' going away is that it will complete his revelation of the Father (7–11). He again calls for faith to still the troubled hearts of the disciples, a faith rooted in the revelation of the Father which he has shared with them. The identity of Jesus with the Father, and hence the validity of the revelation of the Father through him, will be significantly enhanced *from now on* (7). Jesus is once again expressing his need to 'go away'. Only thus can the world *learn that I love the Father and that I do exactly what my Father has commanded* (31). The revelation through Jesus is made possible by Jesus' total submission to the Father, and his unswerving obedience to his commands. That obedience will be made complete in his 'obedience unto death'. Thus it is the death of Jesus which will complete his revelation of the Father, and without it the world would not be able to say that it has truly known and seen God (7). Furthermore, the act of final obedience is also simultaneously an act of infinite love and holiness as Christ, the Sent One of the Father, bears the sins of his creatures. So, in a second sense, the revelation of the Father is completed in

Jesus' 'going away', since through it alone the wonder of the love of God, and the terror of the holiness of God, are made truly and fully known.

Philip this time expresses the groping faith of the disciples. If they could only truly know and see the Father, that would be all they need (8). His plea articulates the longing of the heart of humanity across all the ages to see and to know the living God. Moses had uttered it centuries before when he communed with God in the tent of meeting, 'Show me your glory' (Ex. 33:18). How discouraging for Jesus, however, to be faced in these final moments of his instruction with this particular request, and with its obvious ignorance of his true relationship to the Father! *Don't you know* ME (my emphasis), *Philip, even after I have been among you such a long time? . . . Don't you believe that I am in the Father, and that the Father is in me?* (9–10). This statement is 'a linguistic way of describing the complete unity between Jesus and the Father'.[42] It parallels 'I and the Father are one' (10:30), hence *anyone who has seen me has seen the Father* (9). The words and works of Jesus are the words and works of the Father in him. No other explanation of them is possible (10–11).

Here Jesus touches another great cause of 'troubled hearts', not merely among these first disciples, but among his followers over the ages. Life at times does not appear to make discernible sense; the vastness of the universe oppresses us, the seemingly impersonal cycle of nature evidences no master plan, and the story of humanity rolls on generation after generation with little apparent meaning at the heart of it all. In our personal lives unexpected happenings break in unbidden, sometimes cruelly, and we find ourselves lisping the verdict of Macbeth, 'Life is a tale told by an idiot, full of sound and fury, signifying nothing.' In such moods we cry out from our 'troubled hearts' for some word from beyond to reassure us that there is a meaning; that a heart of love still beats behind the cold indifference and arbitrariness of things.

That word is spoken to us here. In Jesus and his coming, in his death and his rising, God speaks his Word of peace. There *is* meaning. Life can make sense, and purpose can be reborn for us amid the years. In this man, and his life of lowly service unto death, God is made known, a God in whom we can truly believe and find peace. The answer to the anxiety of troubled hearts is assured knowledge, and assured knowledge comes through Jesus.

---

[42] R. Schnackenburg, 3, p. 69.

> Him will I find, though when in vain
>   I search the feast and mart,
> The fading flowers of liberty,
>   The painted masks of art,
>
> I only find him at the last
>   On one old hill where nod
> Golgotha's ghastly trinity –
>   Three persons and one God.
>
> G. K. *Chesterton*

3. A third benefit for Jesus' disciples is that his going away will equip them for living for him, and serving his mission in the world (12–26). At this point Jesus makes the first of his references to the Holy Spirit (15–17; 25–26).

Before commenting on the title he uses, we first underline the context. Jesus is about to depart to the Father by way of exaltation in death and resurrection. This act of exaltation will secure the ministry of the Holy Spirit (16:7, 'Unless I go away, the Counsellor will not come to you', *cf.* 7:37–39). The Spirit (as Jesus will later teach them, 20:22) is nothing less than the life-breath of the exalted Jesus, who makes the victory of Jesus available for the people of God in history. The title Jesus uses is in Greek, *paraklētos*, which (with the sole exception of 1 Jn. 2:1) occurs in its nominal form only in these chapters of John. Literally, a 'paraklete' is 'one called alongside (to help)'. It has a legal context outside the New Testament, and is used in that sense in 1 John 2:1. The meaning in these farewell discourses is arguably wider, as in the verbal form of *paraklētos* which occurs regularly throughout the New Testament, and is variously translated 'exhort', 'comfort', 'entreat' and 'encourage'.

The translators and commentators offer a range of equivalents including 'counsellor' (NIV), 'helper' (GNB), 'comforter' (AV) and 'advocate' (NEB). Perhaps the most important consideration is that expressed in verse 16: . . . *give you* ANOTHER (my emphasis) *Counsellor*. The Spirit will fulfil a role parallel to the role Jesus had fulfilled to this point; he is 'another Christ' (*alter Christus*: Luther). Such is the gift of the departed Jesus.

Like the other answers to 'troubled hearts', this blessing also is utterly dependent on the 'going away of Jesus'. This one gift encloses at least six more particular gifts which are mentioned in these verses.

First, the Spirit imparts power for the service of Jesus (12–14). The Spirit's enabling presence is put more specifically in a remarkable promise in verse 12: *greater things than these* you will do *because I am going to the Father.* Since Jesus' *things* included spectacular healing and nature miracles, even the raising of the dead, we find ourselves struggling to interpret this saying. As a matter of historical fact the apostles were to perform nothing more spectacular in their ministries than Jesus had done in his, and so *greater things* obviously cannot mean 'more spectacular miracles'. As D. A. Carson argues, the key probably lies in the link to the phrase *because I am going to the Father,* and the other reference to *greater things* in 5:20. This refers to the *greater things* which the Father will show the Son in the future, specifically judgment and resurrection (*cf.* 5:17, 24–26). The difference between Jesus and his disciples lies in the event which marks the boundary between the old and new aeons, the Easter triumph of Jesus. Because of that, the disciples will serve in the new time of the kingdom's presence.

This new thing is consequent upon the dawning of the kingdom, the era of salvation history in which the last judgment and the final resurrection are anticipated. It is the universal preaching of the gospel.[43] The 'greater works' therefore are the works of the greater mission in 'Jerusalem, Judea, Samaria and to the ends of the earth'. ' "Greater works" means more conversions. There is no greater work possible than the conversion of a soul.'[44] Such an interpretation is perfectly in keeping with the 'mission' perspective, which as we have already shown is the key to interpret this whole 'last discourses' section of the gospel. This interpretation does not imply that the church ought not to anticipate tangible demonstrations of the presence of the risen Lord in its midst. But it does not encourage unhealthy sensationalism, or unworthy arrogance on the part of the disciples. In the final analysis, the one who works in the church is its Head and Lord, and hence the powers of the kingdom are available only through believing prayer in Jesus' name (13–14). The outcome then will be the glory of the Father through the Son (13).

Secondly, another blessing of Jesus' gift is that the Spirit will unite the disciples to the risen Jesus in a new intimacy of communion (17–21). Here is Jesus' deepest reassurance to hearts troubled by his departure – he will not in fact leave them! Jesus himself will come to them through the Holy Spirit in an experience which a world confined within naturalistic categories can neither discern nor measure (17). They will not be bereft orphans: *I will come to you . . . you are in me, and I am in you* (18, 20).

[43] *Cf.* Mt. 28:18–20; Acts 1:8.
[44] J. C. Ryle, pp. 275f. *Cf.* Morris, *John,* p. 646: 'What Jesus means may be seen in the narratives of the Acts. There are a few miracles of healing but the emphasis is on the mighty works of conversion.'

215

Jesus speaks here of an intimacy which is without precedent or parallel. Even 'the disciple whom Jesus loved', leaning on his breast at the supper, could not make such a claim. The key to it is expressed in these terms, *because I live, you also will live* (19). Thus 'Jesus comes at Easter to be reunited with his disciples and to lift to a new plane his relationship with them, for which that in the ministry could be only a preparation.'[45]

A third gift is that the Spirit will also unite the disciples with the Father, who will make his home with them (23). The gulf separating Creator from creature, the Holy One from sinners, will be bridged. The fruit of the going away of Jesus will be the reconciling of those who believe with the living God, producing a life which fulfils the ancient divine purpose, 'I will dwell among [them] and be their God.'[46] Since the one whom Jesus sends is the indwelling Spirit (17), what Jesus is asserting is nothing less than that our poor and needy hearts will become the residence of the triune God, as all three persons of the Godhead make a home within us. It is difficult to do any justice in words to so immense a vision, or so rich a gifting.

A fourth blessing is that the Spirit will support them in their loving obedience to the teaching of Jesus (21–24). The new life of communion with the risen Lord will be expressed under moral conditions. Love for Christ implies obedience to him (23). Conversely, obedience is the evidence of love (15, 21). Thus the promise of the prophets concerning the new covenant is fulfilled. It is fulfilled as 'the Law' written on the heart is fulfilled through the indwelling Spirit.

We should note further that this loving response on the part of the disciples (15, 21, 23) is made possible because Jesus has made God known to them (9, 10). Here lies the answer to the bleak conclusion of Wittgenstein: 'You cannot love God, for you do not know him.' In Jesus the hidden God is made known, and we love him.

A fifth blessing is that the Spirit will teach them (26). He is the Spirit of truth (17). His truth is inward and spiritual, not received or understood by the world (17). He will teach *all things*, and *remind you of everything I have said to you* (26). This function was to become especially critical for succeeding generations of Christians. Paul testified to a parallel divine inspiration in 1 Corinthians 2:6f. The imparting to these first chosen witnesses of a special insight and recollection concerning the words and works of Jesus ensured their preservation for the church in every generation. The

[45] G. R. Beasley-Murray, pp. 258f.
[46] Ex. 19:4–6; 29:45–46; 33:14–17; Pss. 9:11; 68:16; 80:1; 132:14.

fruit of that ministry is the New Testament. 'The Spirit's ministry in this respect was not to bring qualitatively new revelation, but to complete, to fill out, the revelation brought by Jesus himself.'[47]

Sixthly, the Spirit will impart the gift of Jesus' own peace (27). While the link to the Spirit is not explicit, the proximity of the reference to the Spirit and the gift of peace makes it a natural linkage, and the later New Testament does not lack explicit support for it (Rom. 14:17; Gal. 5.22). Peace is a category rich in meaning (cf. comment on 20:19). It is a summing up (Hebrew, *shalom*) of the blessings of the messianic age. Jesus was to use it in their hearing again as he met them after the resurrection (20:19, 21). The peace he imparts to them as the fruit of his Spirit is a unique and supernatural reality, not *as* that of *the world* (27).

Few things are more sought after than peace. For some it amounts to no more than a longed-for release from the relentless pressures of business or home. In the first century the *pax Romana* was widely heralded, but it was a peace won and maintained by the brutal force of the sword. In that sense it typified the peace that the world gives. The human spirit, however, reaches beyond these lesser expressions for an inner tranquility of spirit, not abstracted from the world of responsibility and relationships, but nourished and expressed in the midst of it. Such is the peace Jesus offers: *MY* (my emphasis) *peace I give you*, in the very face of unspeakable suffering. It is a peace born from a living personal relationship with Jesus, and deepened through a growing surrender of life to his gracious rule. This the Holy Spirit makes available to the troubled hearts of the disciples, and to ours.

All of these remarkable gifts depend on the departure of Jesus. In the light of them we are summoned, like the disciples in the upper room, to trust in Jesus (1), to banish our anxiety and to face the challenge of God's call to us.

Before concluding the discourse Jesus has one further reason to offer the disciples why they should not be troubled. In the previous teaching he has concentrated wholly on the blessings which his going away will procure for them. In a sense he has appealed to their own self-interest. In a final comment he invites them to rise above what his departure is going to mean for them, to consider what it will mean *for him*. '*I am going away and I am coming back to you.*' *If you loved me, you would be glad that I am going to the Father, for the Father is greater than I* (28). This can of course simply mean that Jesus' presence with the Father is a further benefit to them because he will mediate in a more intimate way the Father's sovereign power. But it may also imply, as we believe, that their

[47] D. A. Carson, *John*, p. 505.

love for Jesus should allow them to be happy *for him* that he is going away, since that journey, albeit through the horrors of the cross, will take him again to the intimacy of the Father's bosom, and to the 'glory I had with you before the world began' (17:5). Let the disciples stop being preoccupied with their own loss, and in their love for Jesus think also of him and his coming joy (Heb. 12:2).

On *the Father is greater than I*, Barrett comments helpfully, 'The Father is the *fons divinitatis* in which the being of the Son has its source; the Father is God sending and commanding, the Son is God sent and obedient. John's thought here is focussed on the humiliation of the Son in his earthly life, a humiliation which now, in his death, reached both its climax and its end.'[48]

So Jesus concludes his first upper-room message. In the light of all that Jesus' 'going away' will accomplish they can trust him. It is 'for your good'. His time with them is almost finished. Satan is coming for his moment of apparent victory (30). He has no claim upon Jesus, however, and Jesus does not fear him. His grasp upon Jesus therefore will be only the grasp which is permitted for the world's redemption, and which the Father commands for his love's revealing. Even in the fire of hell he will be seen to be the Lord whose love for his own is matched only by his love for the Father.

(ii) 'So I send you' – discourse B (15:1 – 16:33)

Jesus' second upper-room discourse is the last major teaching section in the gospel. The opening paragraph has been particularly popular with expositors over the centuries due to its arresting imagery. This very fascination awakens the danger of detaching it from its larger context, a danger which arises for these discourses in their entirety. The context, the post-Easter mission of the disciples, gives an impressive unity to this whole body of 'upper-room' teaching. Discourse A, which is primarily concerned with allaying the disciples' fears, lays the foundation for their education in mission, the explicit centre in discourse B. Within discourse B Jesus does three things. First, he confronts the disciples (and ourselves) with the cruciality of mission, and some of the basic principles of its effective pursuance (15:1–17). Secondly, he warns about the cost of mission (15:18 – 16:4). Thirdly, he points to the resources available in the work of mission (16:5–33). This framework will not enclose all the strands in these chapters, but it does allow the major themes to be clearly expressed and creates a helpful unity overall.

---

[48] C. K. Barrett, p. 468.

1. *The cruciality of mission and principles of effective mission*
(15:1–17). The earliest indication of the coming 'disciple mission'
was noted at 13:20. Its full statement occurs in 17:18 and 20:21.
Its centrality for this discourse is signalled at 14:31. Dodd notes
that in normal Greek usage this phrase implied, 'Let us go to meet
the advancing enemy,'[49] a meaning exactly right for this setting.
Jesus has just asserted that 'the prince of this world is coming'.
They now go to engage him. It is a call to arms. 'The gracious
indwelling of God with his people is not an invitation to settle
down and forget the rest of the world: it is a summons to mission,
for the Lord who dwells with his people is the one who goes before
them in the pillar of fire and cloud.'[50]

The image of the vine serves the 'mission' theme in two important
ways. In the first place, it was the supreme symbol of Israel. A
great golden vine trailed over the temple porch, and the coinage
minted in Israel during the revolt against Rome (AD 68–70) also bore
a vine symbol. The Old Testament has many pertinent allusions.[51]
Possibly the most important in connection with Jesus' claim, *I am
the true vine* (1), is Psalm 80, which blends talk of Israel as 'the
vine out of Egypt' (Ps. 80:8) with 'the son of man you raised up
for yourself' (Ps. 80:17).

But the vine 'is burned with fire' (Ps. 80:16). Israel has failed
God in the long-term role she was called to fulfil, that of being 'a
light for the Gentiles' (Is. 49:6), to bring God's salvation 'to the
ends of the earth'. 'The election of Israel coincides with God's
promise of blessing for the nations' (H. H. Rowley). Israel, however, was more attracted by the gods of the surrounding nations
than by her potential for penetrating them as a missionary. Her
centuries-long declension from God's purpose now reaches its nadir
in the rejection and crucifying of the Messiah and the repudiation
of the kingship of God (19:15). But God's purpose, from which
Israel turns in final apostasy, does not fall to the ground. It is
grasped anew by the one who stands in the midst of Israel, and
among the disciples. In contrast to the vine which has destroyed
itself by disobedience, Jesus is 'the true vine'. He is the obedient
Son through whose sacrifice and consequent mission the age-old
purpose of Israel would find fulfilment, the nations would be
reached, and 'all the families of the earth shall bless themselves'
(Gn. 12:2).

The image of the vine has a second, less theological, pointer to
mission. The vine is an essentially utilitarian plant; it exists to bear

---

[49] C. H. Dodd, p. 409.   [50] L. Newbigin, p. 196.
[51] *Cf*. Ps. 80:8–16; Is. 5:1–7; 27:2f.; Je. 2:21; 12:10f., Ezk. 15:1–8; 17:1–6;
Ho. 10:1–2.

fruit. Temple eloquently portrays the fruit-bearing function of the vine. 'The vine lives to give its life-blood. Its flower is small, its fruit abundant, and when that fruit is mature and the vine has become, for a moment, glorious, the treasure of the grapes is torn down and the vine is cut right back to the stem.'[52] This function is reflected in Jesus' stress on fruit-bearing (explicitly in verses 2, 4–5, 8, 16). We should therefore beware of interpretations of this passage which concentrate solely on our inward relationship with the Lord. Its real thrust is the renewal of the mission of Israel through Jesus the Messiah and the disciple community. While more 'subjective' aspects are not entirely absent (cf. Jesus' references to 'love' and 'obedience' to his commands; 10, 12, 17), the primary focus remains bracingly objective and missionary. Jesus by his exaltation in death and resurrection will be removed tangibly from the world. The disciples are sent into the world, as was Jesus, to carry on the task in his 'absence'. That is the principle implication of Jesus' saying, *I am the vine; you are the branches* (5).

The purpose of this fruit-bearing function is stated – *this is to my Father's glory, that you bear much fruit* (8). This links with 13:31, the statement which is the 'text' of these entire discourses: 'Now is the Son of Man glorified and God is glorified in him.' The ultimate purpose of the coming of Jesus, *viz.* the glorifying of the Father (12:28; 17:4; *etc.*), is realized primarily through the effective mission of the disciple community. 'The fruitfulness of believers is part and parcel of the way the Son glorifies the Father.'[53] To seek the glory of God will therefore imply a commitment to mission, and, not least, world mission. As elsewhere in the New Testament, worship and evangelism become one.[54] Further, it is by involvement in mission and becoming 'fruit-bearers' that we show ourselves to be authentic disciples (8). 'True grace is never idle.'[55]

Having clarified the centrality of mission, Jesus identifies the secrets of effective mission.

'Pruning' by the Father (2) is the first secret. The ministry of the Father as the vine-dresser is a double one. 'The vine-dresser does two things to ensure that there will be as much fruit as possible – in the winter, he cuts off the dry and withered branches and in the spring he removes the rank and useless growths from the branches.'[56] The Greek actually plays on similar-sounding verbs for the two functions. Newbigin suggests that some branches he 'clears off', and some he 'cleans up' (p. 197).

The more drastic case is referred to again in verse 6: branches

---

[52] W. Temple, p. 243.   [53] D. A. Carson, *John*, p. 518.
[54] *Cf.* Jn. 12:28; Acts 17:16–17; Rom. 15:16.   [55] J. C. Ryle, p. 291.
[56] R. Schnackenberg, 3, p. 97.

which *do not remain in me* and end up in the fire. Jesus may have in mind the tragic case of Judas, who had appeared as a branch indistinguishable from the others, but the coming of the winter frosts of temptation exposed him as a withered and dead branch, fit only to be 'thrown away'. Within every disciple community there are probably those who at the last will be exposed as dead branches. Let each one make his or her 'calling and election sure' (2 Pet. 1:10).

The Father's other, positive function is to prune the branches to make them more fruitful (2). The following verse (3) refers to the cleansing, purging effect of Christ's word. That word now embedded in the corpus of Scripture is God's primary means of pruning disciples' lives. As that word works in us we become in a new way attractive and authentic in our Christian living and witness.

In his pruning the Father also uses hard circumstances and trials. None of these appear 'pleasant at the time, but painful. Later on, however, it produces a harvest' (Heb. 12:11). 'Pain produces' is one of the primary laws of spiritual growth. It is a commonplace both of horticulture and of Christian experience that the harder the pruning, the greater the fragrance and beauty which will later be released. Our heavenly Father is hungry for fruit from his vine, and in order to produce it will often in his pruning cut deeper than we should ever have chosen. At the harvest, however, both 'the sower and the reaper may be glad together'! (4:36).

The second secret of effective mission is to *remain in me*, the Son (4, 5). Jesus had earlier encouraged the disciples by speaking of the wonderful new relationship with him which will be theirs through the agency of the Holy Spirit after his exaltation (14:20). Here he teaches them that their relationship with him is also fundamental to fruit-bearing. Indeed, *no branch can bear fruit by itself* (4). Fruit-bearing for God is *not* a human possibility; it is Christ's work through us. The alternatives are starkly expressed: separate from Christ, 'no fruit'; united to Christ, *much fruit* (5). A continual dependence upon a living Saviour, 'communing' with him through the Holy Spirit, and submission to him in all things – these are the characteristics of a life in which God is glorified through the bearing of fruit to his praise.

Jesus makes clear, however, that this relationship is a moral one (*cf.* 10, *if you obey my commands, you will remain in my love*). Jesus here draws a parallel between our 'remaining' in him and his 'remaining in the Father', a relationship characterized in his case by obedience. 'Remaining' is conditional upon 'obeying'. 'Abiding (or remaining) in Christ' must not be reduced to a subjective, mystical, inner state. The mark of an abiding heart is not only, or even principally, a sense of inward serenity, but a 'conscience clear

221

before God and man' (Acts 24:16). It is allowing Jesus' words to remain in us (7).

This obedience is not, however, a grim, forbidding thing, *I have told you this so that my joy may be in you and that your joy may be complete* (11). To submit to Christ is no hardship. Rather is it the road to liberation. It therefore brings joy, the joy of Christ's presence welling up in our hearts (1 Pet. 1:8). The reference to joy in the context of the vine image is appropriate, for, as Newbigin observes, 'the "fruit of the vine" is celebrated in the Psalms as that which God has given "to gladden the heart of man".'[57] But again it is joy with a moral basis, the joy of submission and whole-hearted obedience. The connection with fruit-bearing is obvious, for the joy of the Lord in the lives of his people is supremely attractive to the non-Christian world.

In emphasing the missionary perspective of this section, however, we must not *over*-press this application. 'Fruit-bearing' is primarily here the winning of the lost, but it is not exclusively so. In Isaiah chapter 5 the same imagery is applied to social justice (Is. 5:7). Nor can we forget Paul's employment of it in Galatians 5:22: 'the fruit of the Spirit is love, joy, peace, patience, kindness, goodness, faithfulness, gentleness and self-control'. The fruit-bearing which glorifies the Father, and is the product of 'pruning' and 'remaining', is finally inclusive of all the works, graces and ministries of the living Lord in his people. Wherever the Son is seen the harvest has ripened and the Father is glorified.

The third secret of mission is praying in Jesus' name (7, 16). The range of the promise is remarkable: *whatever you wish* (7), *whatever you ask* (16). At first sight this seems a surprising relinquishment of responsibility on the part of the Lord of the mission. But there is a condition – *if you remain in me* (7). When we 'remain in Christ' we are in such harmony with God's purpose that the yearning of our hearts accords with his divine concerns and so prayer is answered 'according to his will' (1 Jn. 5:14).

Prayer is crucial to the effective mission of the people of God. Sadly, the truth of many churches is expressed in a penetrating sentence in James 4:2, 'You do not have, because you do not ask God.' Not that prayer is a talisman which in itself ensures success-ful, fruit-bearing mission. There is prayer and prayer. Jesus acknowledges elsewhere the possibility of 'vain repetition' (Mt. 6:7, AV). But where hearts are set to conform to his will, and open to share his yearning for the world, prayer's potential is limitless. In the work of mission, the church advances on its knees.

---

[57] L. Newbigin, p. 210.

A fourth secret is love for fellow disciples (9–10; 12–17).[58] A Christ-like love between Christians is a further fundamental of effective mission. We noted that 'only Christ can draw others to Christ', but Christ is revealed when his people love one another. The meaning of love is again spelled out. We are to love *as I have loved you*. The verb here is surprisingly in the aorist tense, implying a completed action. 'So imminently does the cross stand in view.'[59] His love is demonstrated in his laying *down his life for his friends* (13). Hence, by implication, 'we ought to lay down our lives for our brothers' (and sisters; 1 Jn. 3:16).

No greater dignity could be conferred upon us, or greater evidence of love shown us, than Christ's dying for us. Indeed, we are no longer servants but friends (15). The proof of this divine friendship is not only the cross on which he died, but the truth which he has revealed. *I have called you friends, for everything that I learned from my Father I have made known to you* (15). His truth shared is an evidence of his love given. Never were friends so generously provided for, or so signally honoured. 'There is nobody so rich, so strong, so independent, so well off, so thoroughly provided for, as the person of whom Christ says, "This is my friend." '[60] Nor is this remote from the work of mission, for when the dignity of our status as the friends of Jesus is imprinted on our hearts, we shall be more effective ambassadors for our Lord and Master. And what better inducement to share the gospel with others than the recognition that he offers them also the supreme honour of becoming the friends of Jesus (14).

Lest all this should create an undue self-importance, Jesus reminds the disciples of their election. *You did not choose me, but I chose you* (16). Their standing and relationship with him is a matter of grace. Therein, however, lies the ultimate encouragement in mission. We go, not because we are worthy, or equipped, or attractive, or skilled, or experienced, or in any way suitable and appropriate. We go because we have been summoned and sent. Since he has called us he will equip and enable us for our witness. As with Israel his choice is with a view to service. We are chosen to *go and bear fruit*.

Their being chosen is followed by their being 'set apart' (16). NIV omits this, seeing the verb for 'set apart' as simply a repetition of 'choose'. This is unfortunate as the verb is clearly distinct. It is used in verse 13 for Jesus' 'setting apart' his life for us. It has other New Testament usage in the context of people being set apart for special service within the church (Acts 13:46–47; 1 Tim. 1:12).

---

[58] *Cf.* 13:34f.; 17:20–23.   [59] D. A. Carson, *John*, p. 520.
[60] J. C. Ryle, p. 299.

Formal 'ordination' need not be exclusively in mind, although Jesus does appear to be thinking of a specific occasion when God's choice results in acknowledgment and submission. During times of testing which inevitably arise in the course of mission, and which Jesus warns about in the following paragraph, such 'ordination' moments have a ministry of reassurance.

The quality of the fruit should also be noted: *fruit that will last* (16). Such fruit honours God. It is a mark of a worldly church and of a worldly discipleship when we are content with short-lived 'fruit' that feeds the fallen appetite for praise, but effects no long-term changes. That there are those who respond with a sudden burst of enthusiasm and then die away, is, as Jesus himself acknowledges, a regrettable fact of human nature and missionary experience (Mt. 13:20–21; *cf.* 6:66). The fruit that honours God is the *fruit that will last*, and bring glory to the Father and the Son on the coming harvest day. For such fruit we need have no hesitation to pray (16).

2. *The opposition to mission* (15:18 – 16:4). Jesus now focuses on the context in which the disciples' mission must be conducted – the identical context to his own, *viz. the world*. In its rebellion against God, the world has rejected Jesus, and because their mission is the continuation of his, they can expect no different treatment. The context of mission is opposition. 'Mission sooner or later leads into passion . . . Every form of mission leads to some form of cross . . . the very shape of mission is cruciform. We can understand it only in terms of the Cross. . . .'[61]

Jesus says at least four things about this opposition to the disciples' mission.

Opposition is, first, *inevitable* (18–25). Jesus does not want disciples under false pretensions (4). As a teacher who is the embodiment of integrity he wants every disciple to be clear about the cost of bearing Jesus' name in a sinful world. The opposition has three sources.

One is the disciples' new nature (19). Christ died for the world and the Father still loves it, but it remains in a state of spiritual rebellion against him. If we were still of the world we would be 'loved' by it because the world, not surprisingly, loves its own kind (19). But we have been *chosen . . . out of the world* (19) and are not part of the opposition. We are from a different place and are going to a different place and so we are 'hated' rather than loved (19).

A second source of opposition is our association with Jesus (21).

[61] Douglas Webster, *Yes to Mission*, p. 101, cited in J. R. W. Stott, *Our Guilty Silence* (Hodder and Stoughton, 1967), p. 73.

As disciples we share his life. Hence the way the world treats Jesus will be the way it treats us. He cites again the principle stated in 13:16, *No servant is greater than his master....* Earlier it had meant being committed to humble service one of another. Here it means being ready to be persecuted. True, some did submit to Jesus' words, and we too will have some positive response (20), but in general the results will be no different. Being identified with Jesus makes opposition inevitable. 'God has called you to Christ's side, and the wind is now in Christ's face in this land; and since you are with him you cannot expect the sheltered or the sunny side of the hill.'[62] Jesus is implying that the opposition comes not because people do *not* recognize Christ in us but precisely because, intuitively, they do. The world still crucifies Jesus.

A third source of opposition is our exposure of evil. Jesus disclosed evil during his ministry by his words (22) and his works, including his miracles (24). He is the light of the world by whose coming the shameful deeds of darkness are exposed (3:19–20). As Christians we are called to be 'the light of the world' (Mt. 5:14–16). If we are living consistent lives our 'works' and 'words' will regularly contradict the lifestyles of those around us. By our code of practice in the workplace, by our attitudes to work, by our personal ethical standards, by our life-goals and values, we shall inevitably, without consciously setting out to do so, expose the unfruitful works of darkness (Eph. 5:11). Like our Master, the integrity of our speech, our unwillingness to spread slander, our words of kindness and forgiveness, will at times provoke opposition. Shakespeare's Iago says of Cassio, 'He hath a daily beauty in his life that makes me ugly.' It can be a short step from that to hatred.

The world's reaction to Jesus and his disciples is its judgment. In the coming of the light the darkness is opened to view. Here is disclosed the irrationality of evil, its foul perversity. The only perfect life of love ever lived ends on a gibbet. *They have no excuse* (22). In words of Ignatius of Antioch, writing a few decades after John, 'Christianity is not a matter of persuasiveness, but of true greatness when it is hated by the world.'

Secondly, Jesus teaches that opposition to the disciples' mission may be *terrible* (16:2). Since the treatment of Jesus is the standard for the treatment of his disciples the opposition may take the form of murder. The first-century Christians to whom John wrote had already experienced that. During the succeeding years of the Roman empire, men, women and even children would at different times be hounded, abused, beaten, tortured in the most appalling ways

[62] Samuel Rutherford, *The Loveliness of Christ* (Bagster, n.d.), p. 18.

225

and slaughtered by the thousand, at times with a refinement of cruelty which numbs the mind.

Martyrdom for Christ, however, is not confined to the first century. Indeed, by any estimate the supreme century of the martyrs for Jesus has been our own one. It is estimated that in the twentieth century to date somewhere in the region of 26 million Christians have lost their lives for Christ's sake, in places like China, the Soviet bloc, Cambodia, Mozambique, Angola, Ethiopia and Uganda.[63] Faced with Jesus' teaching and these contemporary realities, those who profess Christ's name in the comfortable West need to hear the words of Yugoslavian evangelical leader Peter Kusmic. 'So much popular Western evangelical religiosity is so shallow and selfish. It promises so much and demands so little. It offers success, personal happiness, peace of mind, material prosperity; but it hardly speaks of repentance, sacrifice, self-denial, holy lifestyle and willingness to die for Christ.'[64] Every reader of this commentary, along with its author, needs to face the question soberly – am I ready to die for Christ? It is not a theoretical question: Jesus has the clear right to ask it of us, and he gives no guarantee that he will not. Following Jesus is not a game.

> Hast thou no scar?
> No hidden scar on foot, or side or hand?
> I hear thee sung as mighty in the land,
> I hear them hail thy bright ascendant star,
> Hast thou no scar?
>
> Has thou no wound?
> Yet I was wounded by the archers, spent,
> Leaned me against a tree to die; and rent
> By ravening beasts that compassed Me, I swooned;
> Hast thou no wound?
>
> No wound? no scar?
> Yet, as the Master shall the servant be,
> And piercèd are the feet that follow Me;
> But thine are whole: can he have followed far
> Who has nor wound nor scar?
>
> *Amy Carmichael*

[63] 'The World of Figures', David B. Barrett and F. K. Jansen, paper presented at Lausanne II in Manila, July 1989, pp. 13–14. 'Martyrs in 20th century (1900–1990)' cited as 26,625,000.

[64] P. Kusmic, 'How to Teach the Truth of the Gospel', *Proclaim Christ Until He Comes* (Worldwide, 1990), p. 200.

Jesus teaches further that opposition to the disciples' mission may be *respectable* (16:2). He recognizes a variety of motives in those who will oppose the Christian mission. One is religion. Jesus is referring to official Jewish opposition in particular. Rabbinic citations from the first century show that his assessment was well founded; *cf.* 'everyone who pours out the blood of the godless is like one who offers a sacrifice.'[65] By the time John wrote, his readers, if they were Jews by upbringing, were faced with expulsion from the synagogue and possibly worse if they committed themselves to Jesus Christ. In our own time Muslim fundamentalists among others have authorized persecution of Christians, which is motivated by a concern for God's name. Sadly, in the centuries which followed the writing of this gospel, Christians, or at least those nominally identified with Christ, were to repay the persecution at the hands of the Jews with interest many times over.

The principle, however, needs to be recognized. Not all who oppose the missionary witnesses of Jesus are depraved, half-crazed persecutors brandishing machine guns. They may be outwardly fine people, upright, high-minded and with religious scruples, like a Jewish Pharisee in the first century named Saul from Tarsus. But they are nonetheless enemies of Christ until they, like Paul, find mercy (*cf.* 1 Tim. 1:13–16).

Finally, Jesus urges that opposition to the disciples' mission is nonetheless *endurable*. It is so for at least three reasons. The first is because God remains Lord in spite of it. That is the force of the citation of Scripture in verse 25. Centuries before, the Word of God had anticipated this very opposition. It is 'to fulfil what is written in their Law', *i.e.* the very Scriptures which the Jews revere and profess to follow prophesied their rejection.

Opposition is also endurable because in the midst of it we experience 'the fellowship of [Christ's] sufferings' (Phil. 3:10, *cf.* 19). 'The implacable hatred of the world for the friends of Jesus is the sign of the verity of that friendship.'[66] In our experience of persecution, however slight, we are assured of Christ's presence. The mission is *his* through us and hence to suffer for him is in the end to suffer with him. This is the clear implication of Jesus' words to Saul on the Damascus road (Acts 9:4), 'why do you persecute *me*?' (my italics). 'The persecution of Christians is not only patterned after the persecution of Jesus, but the persecution of Christians *is* the persecution of Jesus.'[67] Such has been the testimony of those who have suffered for Christ in every generation. Let Yosif Bondarenko speak for many. He was imprisoned by the Soviet

---

[65] Cited by G. R. Beasley-Murray, p. 278. [66] E. C. Hoskyns, p. 479.
[67] R. Brown, 2, p. 687.

authorities for nine years in Riga, Latvia, for preaching Christ. During a moment of deep personal crisis in his confinement cell, he recalls that 'suddenly I saw a light in the darkness of my cell, and in the light two hands reaching out to me; I saw they were the hands of Jesus.'

Again, opposition is endurable because our being opposed is a confirmation of our belonging to Christ (19). The attitude of the world to the Christian disciple is evidence that we have indeed been 'chosen out of the world' to belong to him. 'Blessed are you when people insult you, persecute you and falsely say all kinds of evil against you because of me. Rejoice and be glad, because great is your reward in heaven' (Mt. 5:11–12).

Moreover, we are able to endure because the Holy Spirit also testifies with us (26). Jesus will teach more fully about the resource of the Holy Spirit in the following paragraph. Here we note that *our* witness to Jesus in the world is not the primary one. The Spirit's witness precedes ours (26). Our witness to an individual is neither the first witness borne to them nor the most important. It is not 'all up to us'. This is not an argument for reneging on Christ's command to be his witnesses, *you also must testify* (27), but it is to recognize, particularly when we are being opposed, and when our witness seems dismissed out of hand, that God the Holy Spirit is the great senior partner in the work. Not only can he sustain us in face of the opposition, but he can work in the heart even of persecutors like Saul of Tarsus, and turn them to Christ. He can do it even if our witness, like that of Stephen, has apparently been fruitless and ineffectual (Acts 7:54–58; 22:20).

This leadership of the Spirit needs to be underlined. 'The Spirit is not the Church's auxiliary. The promise made here is not to a Church which is powerful and "successful" in a worldly sense. It is made to a Church which shares the tribulation and humiliation of Jesus, a tribulation which arises from faithfulness to the truth in a world which is dominated by the lie. The promise is that, exactly in this tribulation and humiliation, the mighty Spirit of God will bear his own witness to the crucified Jesus as Lord and Giver of life.'[68]

3. *The resources which God makes available for the work of mission* (16:5–33). In view of the enormous challenge identified in these last verses the disciples are again in urgent need of encouragement. Their deepest concern continues to be the prospect of Jesus' departure (5–6), re-awakened no doubt by his warnings about coming opposition from the world. Jesus therefore concludes his discourse with an exposition of the resources available to them in his service. We can broadly distinguish two aspects as far as

[68] L. Newbigin, p. 208.

resources are concerned, though the two are inseparable. They are the Spirit (5–15) and the Son (16–33).

First, *the gift of the Spirit* (16:5–15). The essence of the disciples' mission is to 'do the work of an evangelist', to proclaim the good news of Jesus to the world.[69] In this task the disciples will not be alone. The Paraclete, the Holy Spirit, will also be at work 'testifying' to Jesus (15:26–27). He will in fact be the real evangelist; he is 'God the Evangelist'.[70] Jesus now expounds the evangelistic ministry of the Spirit. It encloses three basic elements: preaching (5–7); counselling (8–11); and discipling (12–16).

Preaching (5–7). Jesus has chided the disciples for not asking him about his destination (5). In a sense they have already done so, of course (*cf.* 13:36), so we must presume either that the earlier query had been only cursory, or, more probably, that it is now obliterated from their minds due to their personal anxiety about Jesus being taken from them. Either way, they need to stop focusing on themselves and consider what Jesus' going away will mean for *him*. Immediately they do so they will find encouragement because his going away will permit the coming of the Holy Spirit (7).

Unless I go away, the Counsellor (the Holy Spirit) *will not come to you* (7) is a crucial saying for an understanding of the Spirit's work. Jesus is not implying that the two persons of the Godhead cannot be co-present. The triunity of God means that both (all three) persons are always co-present. The crucial phrase is *go away*. This is not so much a spatial movement as a spiritual exaltation. Jesus will now 'go away' through death and resurrection to the glory of the Father's presence! It is this going away which will make the ministry of the Spirit possible, and, in default of this going away, the Spirit's ministry is rendered impossible. The ministry of the Spirit is accordingly not a vague impartation of spiritual energy, but the specific ministry of proclaiming, and applying to the disciple community, the triumphant procession of Jesus through death and resurrection to the right hand of the Father. The ministry of the Spirit is the unleashing of the powers of the promised kingdom of God in the world. The effects of the kingdom's coming are clear in the Old Testament.[71] These realities will now be actualized through them in the world. It therefore is *for your good* that Jesus departs, since his departure will obtain these promised blessings.

Like John the Baptist 'who was sent . . . as a witness to testify concerning that light' (1:6), the Holy Spirit will testify to the good

[69] 13:20, 34f.; 15:1–16, 27; 17:18–20; 20:21–23.
[70] Title of book by D. Wells, *God the Evangelist* (Eerdmans, 1987).
[71] *Cf.* Is. 11:1–10; 32:14–18; 42:1–4; 44:1–5; Ezk. 11:17–20; 36:24–27; 37:1–14; Joel 2:28–32.

news of the death and resurrection of Jesus, proclaiming it like a preacher (14). Unlike John the Baptist, however, he will not only point to Jesus but will bring him to them (17–33). He will not only proclaim the coming of the kingdom but actually impart it. The Spirit's preaching will be incomparable, like that of Jesus, whose 'word was with power' (Lk. 4:32, AV).

Counselling (8–11). This 'evangelist' is unique. As we have noted, he imparts as well as proclaims. He does not remain in a pulpit or behind a podium, but comes down among the congregation. This 'coming down' is the Spirit's ministry in the world, *i.e.* in the hearts of the listening, and in this case, unbelieving, congregation (8f.). He is an evangelist who also does the counselling, by applying his message personally to his hearers. Specifically, the Spirit *will convict the world of guilt* (8). The verb literally means 'to show someone his sin and summon him to repentance'.[72] 'Expose' is probably the best single term. The force is caught in 3:20, 'Everyone who does evil hates the light, and will not come into the light for fear that his deeds will be *exposed*' (my emphasis).

This exposure will be with reference to three realities: sin, righteousness and judgment (8). In relation to *sin*, the Spirit will expose guilt, *because men do not believe in me* (9; *cf.* 1:11; 3:19; 15:22). The guilt which the Spirit exposes is that hidden guilt which we refuse to own up to, even to the point of crucifying God's Son rather than admitting it (*because* they *do not believe in me*). This 'exposing' ministry of the Spirit occurred classically at Pentecost. 'Jesus of Nazareth was a man accredited by God . . . as you your-selves know', and 'they were cut to the heart' (Acts 2:22, 37). The Holy Spirit, working through the preaching of Peter, brought to the surface their suppressed resistance to the light of the world, the rebellious refusal to trust in him as Saviour and Lord. Sin, at root, is a refusal of grace, the proud titanic assertion that we can atone for ourselves.

In relation to *righteousness* the Holy Spirit will expose the guilt of the human heart, *because I am going to the Father* (10). The death and resurrection of Jesus (by which he goes to the Father) vindicate Jesus as the Righteous One of God. The Jewish authorities claimed that executing Jesus would be a 'righteous' act. 'It is better for you that one man die for the people than that the whole nation perish' (11:50). It was 'better' since it preserved the nation, and with it the temple worship and the sacred law. It was therefore a 'righteous act', even 'offering a service to God' (2). But all the while, their hearts spoke another language.

The Holy Spirit will expose this suppressed guilt, as he did at

[72] *TDNT*, 2, pp. 473f.

Pentecost: 'you . . . put him to death . . . But God raised him from the dead,' and 'God has made this Jesus, whom you crucified, both Lord and Christ' (Acts 2:24, 36). 'They were cut to the heart' (Acts 2:37). Jesus' going to the Father, a journey proved by the resurrection, exposed their guilt in having him crucified. Thus their flimsy claim to 'righteousness' is torn aside, as are all standards of 'righteousness' which rationalize our guilty rebellion against God, and our refusal to acknowledge Jesus as the Righteous One, the embodiment of everlasting righteousness.

The Spirit exposes the guilt of the human heart in respect of *judgment* (11), *because the prince of this world now stands condemned*. The Jews submitted Jesus to the process of a legal tribunal and sought to pass judgment upon him. The Spirit in testifying to the gospel shows that the one judged on the cross was Satan, and with him all who are his children and slaves (8:42–47). The devil 'has no hold' on Jesus (14:30) and so was 'driven out' (12:31) by the perfect obedience of Jesus. He now *stands condemned*, anticipating his final 'driving out' at the last judgment (Rev. 20:10).

Thus at Pentecost they who accused (Acts 2:23, 36) now accuse themselves (Acts 2:37), and can only ask in despair, 'Brothers, what shall we do?' (37). The cross for them, as for the devil, was the decisive moment of judgment. They now have no standing with God and no means of atonement. They are under judgment and without hope. To them the Spirit brings the answer of the sheer grace of God, unearned and unsought, 'Repent and be baptised, . . . in the name of Jesus Christ' (Acts 2:38).

In these ways the Holy Spirit, like a personal counsellor, applies the good news of Jesus to the hearts of individuals. 'Once more we see that the Spirit is not the domesticated auxiliary of the Church, he is the powerful advocate who goes before the Church to bring the world under conviction.'[73]

These three ideas, sin, righteousness and judgment, belong to the common stock of ethical concepts which jostle in today's pluralistic society. In the prevailing relativistic atmosphere, ethical absolutes are dismissed. People claim the right to determine for themselves what will count as sin, what will be their standard of righteousness, and where judgment has, or has not, been properly expressed. Jesus, through the Holy Spirit's witness, challenges this ethical autonomy, uncovers the rebellion against God which underlies it, and confronts the world with the true character of sin, the true meaning of righteousness and the true place of judgment. Through the Spirit of God the human heart is summoned to repentance and then offered the salvation which is life indeed.

[73] L. Newbigin, p. 211.

Discipling (12–16). Finally, this evangelist is also a *discipler*, so that the 'follow-up' ministry is also engaged. The Holy Spirit as the *Spirit of truth* will *guide into all truth* (13). In essence this is a reportorial ministry: *he will speak only what he hears.* Jesus cannot say everything they need to hear at this point, since they are in no position to receive or grasp it. Later they will be, and the Spirit will share Jesus' words with them. This promise is made to the apostles as the assurance of a special future ministry of the Spirit, which will bring to completion the truth Jesus wants his disciples in every generation to know. Thus the Spirit will unfold *what is yet to come* (13), including 'the total revelatory and redemptive work of Jesus in his ministry, death and resurrection, sending of the Spirit of the Kingdom, and the consummation of life and judgment at the end.'[74] In view of subsequent claims to the Spirit's revelation through church tradition and the like it needs to be clearly recognized that this promise applies primarily and uniquely to the apostles. The 'you' of 14:26, as here at 16:13, refers to that special inspiration of the apostles which enabled the composition of the books of the New Testament, not least this Gospel of John.

The Holy Spirit's ministry as the teacher of his converts today consists essentially in leading them to understand and apply the normative truths of Scripture. Although this ministry is not innovative in the terms of his earlier enlightenment of the apostles, it is nonetheless a glorious and powerful 'discipling' function which *will bring glory to* Jesus by unveiling the greatness and fullness of his salvation (14). The Father has put everything at Jesus' disposal (5:19–20) and now the Spirit will share that fullness with his disciples (15).

The second resource which God provides for us is *the gift of the Son* (16:16–33). The work of the Spirit culminates in his glorifying Jesus through 'taking from what is mine and making it known to you' (14). In context this refers to the truth of Jesus which the Spirit will share with the disciples after his exaltation. But Jesus teaches that it has another and greater dimension, for the Spirit will share not only Christ's truth but Christ himself! *You will see me* (16). Jesus' absence will be only for *a little while.* He who is leaving will return! Of all the resources made available to the church in its mission none is comparable to this; Jesus himself is among us![75] The mission is his, not ours. We go forth not so much *for* him as *with* him; and that means joy.

---

[74] G. R. Beasley-Murray, p. 284.

[75] *Cf.* Acts 1:1, '. . . began to do and to teach'; Rom. 15:18 'what Christ has accomplished through me . . .'; supremely, Mt. 28:19–20, 'go . . . And surely I am with you.'

In this section we can distinguish three reasons for our joy, which are at the same time ways in which Jesus is our mission resource.

First, we have *Jesus' personal presence* (16–22). When a great leader passes from the human scene we are left with a store of memories and the treasured memorials of his or her life (such as desk, books, slippers, or handwriting), to be guarded and displayed, amid the pathos of the leader's absence. Jesus, the supreme leader, is different; he has not left us! Like the grieving of Mary and Martha, the disciples' sorrow would turn into joy, for Jesus would come back to them.

Interpreters divide over what he meant when referring to their seeing him (16). We can perhaps be forgiven our uncertainty since clearly the disciples were not a little confused! (17–19). Many, following Augustine and, later, Calvin, see the second *little while* (16) as a reference to the age of the church, the present period in redemptive history, and hence Jesus' statement, *then . . . you will see me*, refers to his visibility at his glorious return. Many more recent scholars prefer to interpret the saying as a promise of his return to the disciples after the resurrection. It is certainly notable that the *little while* in the former case (16a) was only a matter of hours, the time between his present speaking with them and their last sight of him in the Garden of Gethsemane. Hence the second *little while* is arguably also a short time, the two to three days until Easter Sunday evening and their 'seeing' him as the risen Lord.

Jesus captures the experience of the disciples in a vivid parable, which has Old Testament echoes – a woman in childbirth whose pain is transformed into joy at the coming forth of her child (21). The clearest Old Testament passage is Isaiah 26:16–21,[76] which combines a reference to 'a little while' with a clear anticipation of the resurrection of the dead. This transformation from pain into wondering joy is repeated daily around the world in every hospital delivery room, and every home where a baby is safely born. It is an elemental human joy which can be known fully only by those who have endured the pain and experienced the subsequent relief and exultation. This, says Jesus, is the condition of the disciple after the resurrection. 'In whom . . . believing, [you] rejoice with joy unspeakable and full of glory' (1 Pet. 1:8, AV).

Because the presence of Christ is rooted in the resurrection, an event which has happened in history and which therefore can never be undone, it is a joy *no-one will take away* from us (22). No power in heaven, earth, or hell can separate us from the love, and the presence, of the Risen One. 'You may take away from me my

[76] *Cf.* also Is. 21:2f.; 66:7–14; Je. 13:21; Mi. 4:9f.

life, but you can never take Christ from my heart.'[77]

This wonderful promise, 'I will see you,' is given to those to whom he was shortly to say, 'As the Father has sent me, I am sending you' (20:21). The enjoyment of his presence is bound up with mission in his name. At this point mission merges imperceptibly into celebration. Those who long for a deeper experience of the presence of Christ may find here the road to that blessing, a new commitment to serve the world in his name. He is the Lord of the mission and is to be found still at the frontiers where his people confront and minister to the wounds of the world.

Secondly, we have *Jesus' boundless provision* (23–28). Jesus mentions a further source of joy, answered prayer (24). Until this point the disciples have brought their requests directly to Jesus and have been encouraged by his prayers for them to the Father. With his 'going away' the entire terms of their relationship with the Father will be changed. By his death and rising he will remove the barrier of sin and establish a new relationship in which they will be able, with utter confidence, to address the Father directly through him (23). On the basis of Jesus' name, which means a trusting reliance on his sacrifice to cover their unworthiness, and a sincere commitment to seek only those things which would accord with his glory, they can be assured that *my Father will give you whatever you ask in my name* (23). Here is all that the disciples or ourselves can ever long for; enough for all and for ever.

To experience the meeting of our needs in answer to our prayers in Jesus' name is also a source of supreme joy, because it assures us that the Father loves us (27). Calvin aptly comments, 'we have the heart of God as soon as we place before him the name of his Son.'[78] It also proves that Jesus truly has prevailed in his death and resurrection, and that he is now the exalted Lord at the right hand of the Father.

It is to be greatly regretted that too often Christians confine prayer either to such vague generalities that it would be difficult to identify any specific answer on the Father's part, or to specific requests which are so self-centred that to tag 'Jesus' name' on to them shows a failure to understand what that sacred phrase implies. For our encouragement we note that this great promise was first made to a group of very ordinary and fallible disciples who were soon to desert their Master. Like them we may take this promise to ourselves, pray specifically to the Father in Jesus' name, and discover the joy that he has promised. Observe that the model of

[77] Testimony of a Korean martyr before his execution by the Communists.

[78] J. Calvin, 2, p. 130.

prayer which Jesus commends here is prayer to the Father through the Son. All Christian prayer should be offered through Jesus Christ. The addition of 'in Jesus' name' is not some pedantic formality. It witnesses to the only basis of all intercession, namely the earthly sacrifice and heavenly intercession of Jesus, by which alone to all eternity we may draw near to 'the throne of the heavenly grace'. Calvin even asserts that to bypass Christ in our prayers is a 'profanation of God's name'.[79]

Prayer directly to the Son is not excluded in the New Testament (cf. Cor. 12:8, where 'Lord' is, surely, the Lord Jesus Christ). It is, however, the exception. Like Paul, the early Christians customarily knelt 'before the Father, from whom his whole family in heaven and earth derives its name' (Eph. 3:14–15). We need to be sensitive to the dangers of an exclusive focus on Christ in worship and prayer which lacks the support of the Scriptures and which, not surprisingly, tends to imbalances in Christian experience.

Thirdly, we see *Jesus' triumphant position* (29–33). Jesus summarizes his message to his disciples in the last sentence (27–28): 'I came from the Father and entered the world; now I am leaving the world and going back to the Father.' There is an attractive simplicity and directness here to which the disciples respond with acclaim. *Now you are speaking clearly ... Now we can see that you know all things ... This makes us believe that you came from God* (29–30). Their enthusiasm is touching, but insecurely based. 'Like young recruits, they had yet to learn that it is one thing to know the soldier's drill and to wear the uniform, and quite another thing to be steadfast in battle.'[80] Jesus will not allow them the dangerous assumptions of self-confidence. *You believe at last!* (31) is probably sadly ironical. This 'faith' is shortly, like themselves, to be scattered to the four winds (32). Jesus' prediction of their coming defection echoes Zechariah 13:7 (cf. Mk. 14:50). The Scripture must be fulfilled.

All is not despair, however. His final note is exultant: *I have overcome ...* (33). It is so for two reasons. The first is that his Father is with him (32). Here is his supreme consolation, the secret, inner communion of the Godhead, refined through the experience of the incarnation, the unshakeable ground of his life and mission. It will not fail him through the dark waters which stretch ahead.

The second reason for his exultation is that he will triumph. The last word does not lie with the evil one who draws ever nearer, nor with the tragic, rebellious world in its flight into the darkness. It lies with the Father, and hence with the one who came as the Father's everlasting Son and Servant. Through his obedience unto

[79] J. Calvin, 2, p. 127.   [80] J. C. Ryle, p. 322.

death, death itself will fall defeated, and with it all the rebellious powers of darkness and sin. *But take heart! I have overcome the world!* (33).

'In the end *he* can say this word, and only he. The victory is wholly his. At the end the triumph song is not "We have overcome", but "Worthy is the Lamb, who was slain" (Rev. 5:12).'[81] And say it he does! 'I have conquered!' And in this triumph the disciples too will share, and so by grace may we. Their apostasy will be fearfully real, but it will not be the end of them. Their struggle in the mission of Jesus with the evil powers abroad in the world will be long and bloody, and bring most of them to a martyr's grave. *In this world you will have trouble* (33). Through it all, however, the victory will be theirs (and ours) in the gift of peace through our union with him who has for ever conquered in the battle (33). But before that final conflict is engaged one more ministry remains to be performed: the holy work of prayer.

3. Intercession: the prayer of consecration

We come now to one of the mountain peaks of revelation in this gospel. Temple describes it as 'perhaps the most sacred passage in the four gospels'.[82]

The common designation, 'The High Priestly Prayer', has a long history going back by way of the sixteenth-century Lutheran theologian, David Chytraeus, to Cyril of Alexandria in the early fifth century. While this title establishes a natural link to texts referring to our Lord's heavenly intercession (*cf.* Rom. 8:34; Heb. 7:25), it is important to keep clearly in view that this prayer is prayed on earth, not in heaven, and prayed at a specific juncture in Jesus' ministry. The alternative suggestion of Hoskyns, following Westcott, 'The Prayer of Consecration', reflects this historical setting and has much to commend it.

The larger question, however, is simply: why did Jesus pray at *this* point? And, why has the Holy Spirit seen fit to give us such a detailed account of the prayer? These questions are scarcely raised in most scholarly discussions of the chapter but they are surely crucial for interpretation.

Calvin addresses these issues. Noting the link between the prayer and the preceding discourses, he observes: 'Jesus here shows teachers an example, that they should not only occupy themselves in sowing the Word, but by mixing their prayers with it should implore God's help, that his blessing should make their work fruitful.'[83] All who are entrusted with the solemn responsibility of

[81] L. Newbigin, p. 222.   [82] Temple, p. 293.   [83] J. Calvin, 2, p. 134.

teaching God's Word, whether from pulpits or in Sunday School classes, study groups or theological colleges, or in more informal settings, need to identify with the model of Jesus and 'mix the teaching with our prayers'. Spiritually dead sermons, lessons, or lectures do not produce living students, or disciples. While prayer never can be measured by mere quantity, it is generally true of the western church today that there is simply not nearly enough prayer. The exposition of the Word of God and prayer belong together. It is in prayer, costly, sustained and prevailing, that the Word of God is released through teaching and preaching. Prayer is the price of power, and the church of Jesus Christ is not likely to recover its lost authority until this basic biblical truth is recovered.

We note also that the prayer is offered at *this* point, as Jesus approaches the cross. Jesus' commitment to his work of atonement is not automatic. The fact that he has come from the glory of the Father's presence for this very purpose (4), or that he has been determined upon this course right through his ministry to this point (*cf.* references to 'the hour'), does not imply that the conclusion is inevitable. Yesterday's consecrations will not serve for today's crises. The giving up of himself to death is a new and specific act of obedience on Jesus' part, and in a sense everything has still to be done as the 'hour' strikes. He must come afresh before the Father and deliberately present himself on the altar of sacrifice in a further, crucial act of self-abandonment to the Father's purpose. Repeated 'prayers of consecration' are necessary to any life in the will of God.

There is a further rationale for the prayer, however, which is the needs of the disciples – *for them I sanctify myself* (19). Hence we ask: what is the significance of the fact that Jesus, in sending the disciples out into the world in his name, not only instructs them concerning the mission, but prays for them in their mission (6–23), and in the course of the prayer offers himself in sacrifice? The answer lies in the amazing truth that the work of the disciple community in mission is taken up into the inner dialogue of the Godhead, and into vital association with the self-giving of the Son which lies as its heart. Thus the historic mission of the church in the world, encompassing both the immediate witness of the disciples (6–19) and the widening mission across all the ages to the present (20–26), is embraced by this prayer, and in it presented and offered to the Father. This is our ultimate resource for mission. The gifts we exercise, the prayers we offer, the proclamation we share, the acts of compassion and mercy we endeavour, all flow from this primal moment in the shadow of Calvary as Jesus in prayer presents the mission of the church to the Father.

Here also is supreme encouragement for the servants of Jesus.

237

Our work and witness, in all their variety, are already, in advance, gathered up, healed, renewed and perfected by being gathered into Jesus' holy response to the call of the Father. Thus the sin in our service – its unworthiness, its unbelief, its many disobediences, all its sordid self-promotion, its lethargy, cowardice and worldly compromise – is overcome. Mission becomes celebration, an act in which the sacrifice and exaltation of Jesus are proclaimed to the world, before *he* comes who perfects our mission even as he makes all things new.

To argue in this way is not to eliminate our human responsibility, but to recognize the true basis of our ministry, and to set it within the parameters of the ultimate purpose of God. So viewed, mission is a profoundly hopeful activity, despite the sombre fact of the world's rebellious unbelief, the staggering numbers still to be reached with the gospel, and the desperate needs among the nations which cry out for the compassionate service of the servants of Jesus. Jesus has prayed for us. All *those you have given me* (9) will come to him. The mission, like the sacrifice, will be complete.

The prayer also reminds us of our infinite value to God. That Father and Son are united in mutual concern for the good of the church underlines its significance to God. True, the mission is also and always for the glory of God himself (13:31; 17:1), but that glory does not exclude his church. It is deeply moving to realize that we who follow Christ in the twentieth century are personally prayed for in verses 20–23 among those *who will believe in me through their message*. In this sense the prayer is the forerunner of the continuing high-priestly ministry of Jesus in the heavens. He prayed for us, he prays for us. No greater encouragement is conceivable.

The best division of the prayer is the most obvious one. Jesus prays in turn for himself (1–5), for the disciples (6–19), and for all believers (20–26).

a. Jesus prays for himself (17:1–5)

The location of the prayer is not indicated. If, as we have suggested, the entire two discourses were delivered in the upper room, then a similar setting for the prayer seems in order. The first verse of chapter 18 gives the impression of a change of location at that point. A related question is the relationship between this prayer and the prayer of Jesus in Gethsemane which is recorded in the synoptics (Mk. 14:32–42 and parallels). There are clear overlaps. Both are focused around the impending sacrifice of Jesus, and both lead to moments of supreme self-consecration. In other respects, however, both mood and content diverge, and so they are best understood as complementing one another.

Jesus' first word is crucial – *Father*. Underlying the Greek, *patēr*, is the Aramaic word, *Abba* (*cf*. Rom. 8:15; Gal. 4:6). We have a record in the gospels of twenty-one prayers of Jesus. On every occasion he uses this characteristic word of address. (The one exception, significantly, is the cry of dereliction, Mt. 27:46.) There is no real precedent for the use of this word in addressing the Godhead, whether in Old Testament prayers, or in the extensive liturgies which have come down to us from first-century Judaism, or at Qumran. The reason is to hand – *Abba* means 'Daddy', or 'my own dear father'. It is the tiny child's word of address to its male parent. To Jesus' predecessors and contemporaries it was an overfamiliar and hence unseemly term to use in addressing the Almighty. But Jesus uses it constantly, a significant witness to his unique sense of intimacy with the Father, to which this gospel bears untiring testimony. It is in the supreme confidence expressed in this word that Jesus goes to the cross.

That the moment of crisis has at last arrived is not in question; 'the hour has come'.[84] The prospect of imminent death uncovers our deepest concerns. Jesus' death is unique, and yet at this level it is no different. As Jesus prays in the shadow of Calvary we learn what are *his* deepest concerns. In fact he has only one, and one that does not surprise us, the glory of his Father (1; *cf*. 12:28). The means to that is his own glorification, *Glorify your Son*, since it is in his exaltation and obedience unto death that the Father will be supremely honoured. In this the glory of God is distinguished from our human experiences of 'glorying'. The Son seeks the Father's glory; the Father seeks the Son's. The honouring of another rather than ourselves is true honour (12:43).

This first petition gathers up the whole prayer; the rest is commentary. It also links the prayer with the beginning of the discourses. 'Now is the Son of Man glorified and God is glorified in him' (13:31).

The glorifying of the Father is achieved through two closely related means. The first is *the impartation of life* (2). As we have noted, the mission of Jesus is the means to the glorifying of both Father and Son. The cross, however, is not a lonely 'play' in which the Father and Son indulge for purposes of mutual self-glorification, detached from the world within which the event takes place. The very action which glorifies Father and Son also brings life to lost sinners. In other words, the honour which seeks the honour of another is expressed not only in the relationship of Father to Son but in their unitedly seeking the good and honour of the creatures

---

[84] *Cf*. 2:4; 7:6, 8; 8:20; 12:23, 27f., 31f.; 13:1, 31.

of God which comprise the world. It is out of love for the world that the Father has sent the Son, and the Son now lays down his life (3:16; 1 Jn. 4:7–14).

Eternal life is of course, as elsewhere in John, the life from above, the life of the kingdom of God. Two particular aspects of this life are now shared. The first is its *source*; it is a gift from the Son (2). Before this gift can become available to us a prior gift is necessary, the 'granting' of universal authority to the Son by the Father. Christ's universal reign is sealed in his Easter victory (Rom. 1:4). That universal reign makes possible the universal mission of the disciples (Mt. 28:18), and as the fruit of that mission, the impartation of eternal life. As Lord of all, Christ has authority to give life to all. Due to human unbelief not all will receive this life. Those who do, know that its source lies not in themselves but in the action of God upon them. They are the gift of the Father to the Son (2). 'In the contrast between "all people" and "all those you have given him" is expressed the inevitable tragedy of the mercy of God – it is offered to all but received by the few, and these the elect.'[85]

Secondly, Jesus shares the *nature* of eternal life. It is life knowing the Father and the Son (3). Eternal life is in essence quality of life rather than quantity of life. True, it participates in the victory over the grave which the Son has won through his death and rising, and is therefore 'endless', but that is certainly not its most important feature. It is life 'knowing God'. 'Eternal life is not so much everlasting life as knowledge of the Everlasting One.'[86] We were made to experience this and in the absence of it the human spirit is for ever unsatisfied. Augustine expressed it memorably: 'You have made us for yourself and our hearts are restless till they rest in you.' This gift of the direct, personal knowledge of God is the promise of the new covenant.

> 'No longer will a man teach his neighbour,
>   or a man his brother, saying, "Know the LORD,"
> because they will all know me,
>   from the least of them to the greatest,'
>   declares the LORD (Je. 31:34).

This knowledge is of both Father and Son. Jesus is the point at which we come to know God, but, if one may so put it, Jesus is not all there is to know about God. God is Father, Son and Spirit, and though each person is truly and fully God and therefore infinite, there is nonetheless a richness to the Godhead which we acknowledge by confessing the three persons. 'Knowing God'

---

[85] E. C. Hoskyns, p. 498.   [86] D. A. Carson, *John*, p. 556.

means knowing all of the Godhead. For this we were made, and it is life indeed!

To speak of 'knowing God' as the supreme purpose of existence, as Jesus does here, does not imply a flight from the world into some supramaterial order. The God we know is Creator as well as Redeemer (*cf.* comment on 1:3). But the world in and of itself cannot satisfy us; that was never the intention. Beyond the world we seek the world's Lord, the ever-living God of glory, grace and majesty, Father, Son and Spirit. Eternity will bring the deepening of our knowledge through ever richer appreciation of him who is without end. To receive eternal life is not the end of our journey; in the deepest sense it is only the beginning.

The second expression of the glory of God is the *completion of work* (4). This reference to Jesus' work obviously includes the coming work of his cross and resurrection by which the glorifying of the Father is uniquely secured. The statement is also applicable to the disciples, sent into the world in mission. We too are to bring glory to the one who has called us, and in the same way, by doing his work in the world.

The text clarifies several aspects of Christian service. It first identifies our *supreme motivation*, the glorifying of God. 'It is for God above all things, and not for ourselves, that we were created' (Calvin). If our chief end is 'to glorify God and enjoy him for ever' then here is a means to that end, the service of his mission in the world. This truth also eliminates any polarizing of worship and witness. A worship which does not lead to witness is sterile, and less than truly glorifying to God. Witness is itself a form of worship, a genuine honouring of the Father and Son. Further, if the motive in mission is God's honour then mission undertaken to promote human organizations or to inflate human egos, whether covertly or overtly, stands self-condemned. We go for his glory.

Jesus refers to a glorifying of God *on earth*. Heaven will have its own means of adding to his praise, but it will not include our present missionary service. Only here have we opportunity for that particular form of our fulfilment. 'As long as it is day, we must do the work [of mission] of him who sent me. Night is coming, when no-one can work' (9:4).

This text also speaks of a *specific limitation* (4), *the work you gave me to do.* From several points of view there was limitation placed upon Jesus. Geographically his whole career was confined within the boundaries of central Palestine. He never saw Rome, or Athens, or Alexandria, to say nothing of the further flung lands of the globe. His ministry was circumscribed also in terms of his life experience. He never knew the intimacies of marriage, the struggles of parenthood, the challenges of middle age, or the limitations of

241

aging. Even within the sphere of his teaching and healing ministry, there were multitudes of his needy contemporaries in Palestine to whom he never ministered, whether in word or deed. Yet his ministry was perfect and whole, because he did, with complete and single-minded dedication, 'all that he was given to do'. So at the end he could truly say, 'I have finished the work'; or more profoundly in his final moments on the cross, 'It is finished.' A similar limitation rests upon every disciple. We are not called to reach the whole world or to minister to every need. There is a specific work for us to do, and in finding and doing that specific thing to the limits of our powers lies our fulfilment, and our peace.

Finally, this text speaks of *a necessary completion*. The honour of God is bound up not only with the enthusiastic commencement of a project but with the faithful completion of it. 'He that endures to the end will be saved' has its application to service as well as to salvation. Paul's testimony is to be coveted by every servant of Christ: 'I have finished the race' (2 Tim. 4:7). The prayer of Sir Walter Raleigh may fittingly focus this challenge:

> O Lord God, when you give your servants to endeavour any great matter, grant us also to know that it is not the beginning, but the continuing of the same to the end, until it be thoroughly finished, which yields the true glory; through him who for the finishing of your work, laid down his life, our redeemer, Jesus Christ.

For Jesus the finishing was to be infinitely costly, yet in that final carrying through of the Father's will there lay his own glory and the Father's through him, and, no less, our whole redemption.

This opening segment of the prayer concludes with a petition that the Father restore to the Son his pre-incarnate glory. As Haenchen points out, this implies that 'becoming flesh' entailed a forfeiture of glory on the part of Jesus (*cf.* Phil. 2:5–8).[87] The costliness of Jesus' mission reaches back into his pre-incarnate life.

In this final request, Jesus' vision sweeps on beyond the seething waters of his passion to embrace the bright shore which beckons him on the further side of the river. 'Who for the joy set before him endured the cross, scorning its shame ' (Heb. 12:1f.). Like a champion who shrugs off the vain efforts of his enemies to detain him as he moves upon his triumphant way, so Jesus marches into the dark valley of pain and humiliation with eyes upon the glory which the Father holds out to him beyond the sufferings of death.

[87] E. Haenchen, 2, p. 502.

b. Jesus prays for his disciples (17:6–19)

Jesus has prayed that the Father will glorify him as he finishes the work which has been given him to do. He then prays for the disciples. The implication is clear. The disciples are the tangible expression of the completion of his work. He has come to sanctify himself, but the end result of this is *that they too may be truly sanctified* (19). So the great historic redemptive purpose of God focuses in on that little company in the upper room in Jerusalem on Passover evening, as they are about to forsake and deny their Master and scatter like panicking sheep. Yet, as Jesus knows, and bears witness in this passage, they will not be lost but become the seed of the great world-wide harvest of the last day, the glorified church who behold his glory (24). 'The glorified Son of God has completed his work by bringing into concrete existence in the world the messianic congregation of the faithful disciples. Thus the work of Jesus is not defined as a general proclamation of the Fatherhood of God and the brotherhood of men, but rather as the creation of the Church, consisting of men and women of flesh and blood extracted from the world to which they had hitherto belonged, by the "power of God".'[88]

The prayer of Jesus for the disciples has two parts. In the first he redefines the disciples who are the *subjects* of his prayer (6–10); and, secondly, he prays several petitions on their behalf, the *concerns* of his prayer.

(i) The subjects of Jesus' prayer (17:6–10)

Verses 6, 9–10 tell us of their *owner*. The disciples had been the possession of the Father – *they were yours* (6), but have been given by the Father to the Son – *those whom you gave me* (6), *those you have given me* (9). In verse 10 the ownership is reciprocal between Father and Son: *All I have is yours, and all you have is mine*. A predestinarian element is present, as elsewhere in this gospel,[89] though one in which ultimately Father and Son share together (*cf.* comments on 1:1 and 6:37). We should note, however, that these same men are spoken of as 'knowing' (7) and 'believing' (8), though that does not eliminate the fact of their election, nor its mystery. The practical implication is significant – because they have been claimed by God they are utterly secure. This is very much to the point, since Jesus is about to unveil the powerful and malignant spiritual foe who seeks their harm.

Verses 7–8 describe their *knowledge*. *They know that everything you have given me comes from you* (7). Despite the many limi-

[88] E. C. Hoskyns, p. 499.   [89] *Cf.* 6:37; 12:37–40; 15:16.

243

tations of their understanding the disciples have grasped the fundamental truth that Jesus can be explained only in terms of the Father. *They knew with certainty that I came from you, and they believed that you sent me* (8). It is to be noted that their *certainty* about Jesus came through accepting his words (8). Other grounds, historical, philosophical or ethical, may be adduced for producing assured conviction about Jesus. The surest, and most common, is trusting his words, which brings its own authentication.

Verse 10 speaks of their *achievement*. *Glory has come to me through them*. There can be few more encouraging statements in the New Testament. If we recall the disciples' level of achievement to this point, it is a remarkable claim. Its full truth would be realized only after Pentecost and in the years beyond. Even then, however, the disciples were always less than perfect. Bringing glory to Christ as his disciples is rooted in our trust in him as Saviour, which vindicates his work and in that sense honours him. There is no suggestion here, however, that our glorifying him is confined to our trust. What a marvellous incentive to living for Christ this is, that he who has need of nothing may yet be glorified through our obedience and service.

(ii)   The concerns of Jesus' prayer (17:11–19)
Jesus' relationship to these men is about to change in a fundamental way. *I will remain in the world no longer, but they are still in the world* (11). The departure of Jesus is a crisis for the disciples, prompting Jesus' prayer. In this time of his 'absence' (covering both the days until Easter Sunday, and the much longer period afterwards when he will no longer be a tangible presence), Jesus prays four things for them.

1. Jesus prays that they may be *protected* (11–12, 15). This is necessary because they face two formidable foes. The first is the world, which 'has hated them' (*cf*. 15:18–25). This summarizes his teaching in the second discourse. The world's antagonism to Jesus and the disciples derives from its correct perception that they do not belong to the world and as a result pass judgment on it.

The second foe has also been hinted at previously, the devil (15). Jesus states his conquest of the devil at several points in these chapters, but he is never in danger of dismissing this opposition as merely nominal. The case of Judas (12), who had turned aside to do the will of the devil from within the intimate disciple company, was sobering evidence of the impressiveness of Satan's power. Judas is spoken of in a way that makes clear that Jesus has not been thwarted by this attack (12). Judas' defection was even foretold in the Scriptures centuries before. *Doomed to destruction* is, literally, 'son of perdition/destruction', which in the Greek may refer either to his character, or, as NIV takes it, his destiny. The case of Judas made it clear that the disciples were facing a genuine conflict. Peter, who learned from Jesus, was later to speak of the devil as a 'roaring lion' (1 Pet. 5:8). Paul would refer to 'spiritual agents from the very headquarters of evil' (Eph. 6:12, JBP).

The world and the devil are daunting enemies, and Jesus' concern about them in his prayer is a summons to vigilance and prayer for protection. D. A. Carson pointedly observes: 'The spiritual dimensions of this prayer of Jesus are consistent and overwhelming. By contrast we spend much more time today praying about our health, our projects, our decisions, our finances, our family, and even our games than we do praying about the danger of the evil one.'[90]

How then are the disciples to survive? By the power of God's name (11–12). God's name is basically his revealed character. In the Old Testament, God represents himself to the people of Israel under a variety of names, each of which teaches something important about who he is. Jesus has brought the disciples a whole new understanding of God. In a sense he has given God a new name. That revelation of God will now keep them. As they remain loyal to the truth Jesus has shared with them, and allow it to remain in their minds, shaping understanding and directing conduct, they will continue 'in his name' and be protected from all the attacks of world and devil (11). 'The name of the LORD is a strong tower; the righteous run to it and are safe' (Pr. 18:10).

2. Jesus prays that they may be *united* (11). The result of the disciples remaining 'in the name' is their experiencing the unity which Jesus prays for them. In a moment he will petition for their unity in the context of their witness; here the context is spiritual assaults upon them. Their unity will itself be a victory over the devil, since part of his strategy will be to attack it. It will also be part of their armoury against him, since their fellowship will be an expression of the *power of* God's *name* which protects them. This unity will be patterned after the unity of the Father and Son (11). It is therefore a vastly richer reality than social camaraderie, as we shall note more fully below.

3. Jesus prays that they may be *delighted* (13). Despite the formidable foes which will confront them, the disciple community can experience the very joy of Christ, and Jesus prays that they will. It is surely remarkable that he can refer to his own 'joy' when he knows that the most appalling suffering is about to engulf him. Nor is it a passing or spasmodic joy to which he refers. It is the *full measure* of his joy (13). Neither the hostility from without nor

[90] D. A. Carson, *Discourse*, p. 191, = *Jesus*, pp. 188f.

the apostasy from within has quenched the joy of Jesus, nor need it do so in the case of the disciples.

Joy is a mark of the kingdom in Old Testament prophecy (*cf.* Is 35:1; 55:11–12). In contrast to the time of John the Baptist, the time of Jesus was a time for celebration (Mk. 2:19). True, the bridegroom would be taken away, but only for a 'little while' (16:16). He will soon be back with them and the brief pains of childbirth will give place to the joy of the kingdom in their midst.

4. Jesus prays that they may be *dedicated* (17–19). Although the world is a threatening place for the disciples, Jesus does not want them removed from it (15). A major reason why they are to remain in the world is because he has a purpose for them there (18). 'They are not to inhabit a ghetto, they are to go forth on a mission.'[91] *As you sent me into the world, I have sent them into the world* (18). The full terms of this commission would await the resurrection and the out-breathing of the Spirit (20:20–22), and our exploration of this remarkable statement will accordingly be deferred until that point in the text.

The importance of the mission of the disciples (and through them of the whole church) cannot be overstated. Jesus is to depart from the world; the disciples are to go into the world. This does not mean, as might appear at a superficial level, that they are to replace Jesus as the light to the nations. The parallel drawn in verse 18 is crucial. The entire mission of Jesus in the world has in reality been the mission of the Father in and through him, the Sender in the Sent. The mission of the disciples, sent into the world by the Son, is likewise not theirs but *his through them*. The mission of the church is nothing other than the continuation of the mission of its Lord. Equally, however, the demand will be real. Being sent meant for Jesus his utter dedication to the claim and call of the Father. The disciples' commission can mean nothing less. Thus Jesus' prayer is, finally, *Sanctify them by the truth*.

'Sanctify', like 'holy', comes from a Hebrew root meaning 'separate'. Earlier, Jesus had prayed to him who is the 'holy Father'. It is the Father's holiness which is the basis of the Son's mission. That holiness, in its separation from sin and its dedication to the way of righteousness, Jesus now desires in the disciples. The mission is one of light confronting darkness. Its instruments hence must be the sons of light who do not walk in darkness (8:12). They are to be 'set apart for the gospel of God' (Rom. 1:1).

The means of their sanctification, no less than the means of their protection, is the Word of God (17). Jesus has conveyed that Word to them. He himself is the incarnate Word of God (1:14). He will

[91] L. Newbigin, p. 231.

send his Spirit to enable the further expression of that Word in them and others. The reality which will make their consecration effective is, however, the consecration of Jesus himself. *For them I sanctify myself, that they too may be truly sanctified* (19). Thus the work of Christ, which will be 'finished' in its atoning virtue in the moment of his death, will be 'finished' in a further sense only when the mission of the disciples is fulfilled. 'He died for all, that those who live should no longer live for themselves but for him who died for them and was raised again' (2 Cor. 5:15). Living no longer for themselves means, among other things, living as those available for the service of the gospel. To be a disciple is to be a missionary.

c. Jesus prays for all Christians (17:20–26)

I pray also for those who will believe in me through their message (20). This final section of Jesus' prayer is a deeply moving one because it brings Jesus into direct relationship with us. There are hints elsewhere of Jesus' recognition that further generations of believers would arise and express allegiance to him.[92] Nowhere in the New Testament, however, is that larger company (including the readers of this exposition!) so clearly in Jesus' direct vision as here. Jesus is poised between the conclusion of his earthly task and the glory awaiting him at the Father's side. Like a mountaineer gazing out from an eminence across the expanding vista as range succeeds range into the distant horizon, so Jesus gazes out across the rolling centuries. He beholds and embraces the harvest of the ages, the church of the Redeemer, gathered from every nation, people, language and tribe. He is praying for us.

He prays three things.

1. He prays that the church may be *united*. *That all of them may be one* (21); *May they be brought to complete unity* (23). This unity for which Jesus prays is amplified in the surrounding phrases.

It is first a *supernatural* unity, defined by and included in the unity of the Father and the Son: *cf. as we are one* (21–22). The life we share as Christians is therefore nothing less than a participation in the life of the Godhead! 'It is a unity which not merely reflects but actually participates in the unity of God – the unity of love and obedience which binds the Son to the Father.'[93] Earlier, Jesus had explained that new life in terms of the ministry of the Holy Spirit (3:1f.), the life of the kingdom of God, by which we are 'born anew' into the family of God (1:12). Accordingly it is a unity which is brought about, not by the efforts of human ingenuity, but by Jesus giving us the glory that the Father had given to him (22).

---

[92] 10:16; Mt. 24:14; Lk. 13:29.   [93] L. Newbigin, p. 234.

Glory, in this context, has a meaning similar to that in verses 4–5, the glory of the revelation of the Father through the Son, completed by the cross and resurrection. Paul's perspective is identical in Ephesians 4:1: 'keep the unity of the Spirit . . .'. Our part is not to create this. Patently we cannot. Our responsibility lies in maintaining and expressing it.

Secondly, the unity of the church is a *tangible* one, which will cause the world to believe (21) that Jesus was sent by the Father and that the Father loves the church. This unity will make a definite impact on the world. Just as Jesus disclosed the unseen God to the world by becoming flesh (1:14), so the church will be a visible revelation of the unseen Father and his love. Thus, while the unity Jesus prays for us is not organizationally produced, it is equally not historically invisible. The world needs to see our unity.

Thirdly, the unity of the church is *evangelical*. It is a unity which is derived from the witness of the church, and which produces faith on the part of at least some of those who encounter it, *so that the world may believe that you have sent me . . .* (21, 23). It finds expression in the context of making known the message which elicits faith, *those who will believe in me through their message* (20). 'This is not simply a "unity of love". It is a unity predicated on adherence to the revelation the Father mediated to the first disciples through his Son, the revelation they accepted (verses 6, 8) and then passed on.'[94]

The challenge of Jesus' prayer is inescapable. He envisages and petitions his Father for a unity among his followers which, grounded in a relationship with the Father through Son and Spirit, is sufficiently visible to promote a positive response to the church in its mission.

We can apply this challenge to the local congregation. Here is where the world most immediately encounters the church. There, relationships are to be such that the watching world will come to recognize not only that Jesus is the true revelation of God, but also that *you . . . have loved them even as you have loved me*. Our churches are to be 'love centres' where relationships between members are a persuasive reflection of the mutually supportive, utterly loyal and eternally accepting love of the Father and the Son. This is true whether the relationships are of men with women, young with mature, laity with clergy, new members with long-standing members, rich with poor, cultured with unsophisticated, socially upper with socially lower, leadership with membership, new converts with established Christians, racially other with racially traditional, and whatever other polarities the church embraces.

[94] D. A. Carson, *John*, p. 568.

Beyond the local church, also, the challenge is unavoidable. Unity at the expense of truth is not supported by this passage. The mediaeval church is witness to a 'unity' which certainly did not cause the world to 'believe'; quite the reverse. Its was a unity, as the sixteenth-century reformers had painfully to make clear, maintained at the expense of the truth of the gospel revealed by Jesus. That unity had to be sacrificed, at least in the short term, to recover the gospel. It is impossible to believe, however, that the present fragmentation of the Protestant churches (on a recent computation the global denominational total was over twenty-two thousand!) is tolerable in the light of Jesus' prayer. Where the Holy Spirit has created the common life of the body of Christ among us, and agreement on the fundamentals of the revelation given through Jesus is present, it is unthinkable to pursue the mission of Jesus in isolation from, and even in competition with, those who are as truly the beloved objects of Jesus' prayer as we are.

There is encouragement as well as challenge, however, in Jesus prayer, on two accounts. First, the unity Jesus prayed for is a reality which God himself gives. We do not have to create anything. Our challenge is to give authentic expression to that which God has already worked in our midst. The churches are already one in God. We need to allow that supernatural unity to find expression both in the local church and between the churches.

We can also draw encouragement from the fact that Jesus prays for the unity, and Jesus' prayer prevails. If our prayers in Jesus' name are assured of an answer,[95] how much more Jesus' prayer in Jesus' name! He cannot be denied, nor will he be. Despite all the contrary indications, the church is one, and will be one, in the glory of the consummation. This assurance does not absolve us from working for the expression of that unity in the present, but it does deliver us from an unbelieving despair. Jesus has prevailed. All Christians, and all churches, will one day love one another as the Father loves the Son and the Son loves the Father.

2. Jesus prays that the world may be *persuaded*. There is some disagreement as to whether the *hina* ('in order that' or 'so that' in verses 22 and 23) expresses purpose (*i.e.*, 'May they be one "with a view to" the world coming to believe'; unity as the precondition of faith), or, more probably, whether it expresses consequence (*i.e.*, the unity will in fact result in the world's coming to believe).

Even on the second alternative the importance of the 'coming to believe' is evident. Jesus desires that the world may be persuaded; he longs that it may come to him. We have already witnessed this

---

[95] 14:13–14; 15:16; 16:24.

yearning during his public ministry.[96] It is a yearning which is not contradicted by his conviction that only those whom the Father has given him will in fact respond. The heart of Jesus is as wide and broad as the heart of the God who so loved the world as to send his only Son. The same love underlies his refusal to pray that the disciples may be taken out of the world (15), but rather accepts that they will be left there, in order to fulfil the mission to the whole world. He prays that the world may believe, and the means of answering his prayer is the mission of his people.

This mission has two hands. The 'first hand' is that of proclamation, the communicating to the world of the revelation of the Father in the Son, climaxed by his self-sacrifice for the world's sin. This revelation (6) is commonly expressed in words (8), and must be shared in words so that the world may believe that the mission of Jesus is authentically the mission of the Father in him, and hence that he is the Saviour and Lord of sinners.

But the mission has a 'second hand'. It is visible as well as verbal, relational as well as audible. The content of this 'second hand' is clearly stated in verse 23: *May they be brought to complete unity to let the world know that you . . . have loved them even as you have loved me.* Well may Brown exclaim that 'the standard of comparison is breathtaking'.[97] Indeed it is! The Father's love for his Son in all its richness is persuasively reproduced in the mutual relationships of the Christian congregation! Nothing less than that is Jesus' prayer.

This 'second hand' represents a dimension in evangelism which is commonly ignored or underestimated, and yet which is central to Jesus' evangelistic strategy for his church (*cf.* 13:34–35). The local church is the obvious point of application. A group of Christians who are so knit together in the love of God that others can say of them, 'Look how they love each other,' is a church where the gospel will be 'the power of God for . . . salvation' (Rom. 1:16). Evangelism is a community act. It is the proclamation of the church's relationships as well as its convictions. The preacher is only the spokesperson of the community. The gospel proclaimed from the pulpit is either confirmed, and hence immeasurably enhanced, or it is contradicted, and hence immeasurably weakened, by the quality of the relationships in the pews. In this sense *every* Christian *is* a witness. Every time we gather together we either strengthen or weaken the evangelistic appeal of our church by the quality of our relationships with our fellow church members.

The biggest barriers to effective evangelism according to the

---

[96] 6:37; 7:37; 12:44; *cf.* Mt. 9:36; 11:28; Lk. 19:41.
[97] R. Brown, 2, p. 772.

prayer of Jesus are not so much outdated methods, or inadequate presentations of the gospel, as realities like gossip, insensitivity, negative criticism, jealousy, backbiting, an unforgiving spirit, a 'root of bitterness', failure to appreciate others, self-preoccupation, greed, selfishness and every other form of lovelessness. These are the squalid enemies of effective evangelism which render the gospel fruitless and send countless thousands into eternity without a Saviour. 'The glorious gospel of the blessed God', which is committed to our trust, is being openly contradicted and veiled by the sinful relationships within the community which is commissioned to communicate it. We need look no further to understand why the church's impact on the community is frequently so minimal in spite of the greatness of our message. We are fighting with only one hand!

Roger Fredrikson, in his commentary on John, recounts a deeply moving moment when a church he was pastoring shared a public service of reconciliation with another congregation more than twenty years after an angry division. 'As we sang, "Great is Thy Faithfulness" many people embraced in the crowded sanctuary and their tears of gratitude and joy were mingled. The next day on the street people stopped some of us saying they had heard the "good news". The message we proclaimed had become . . . credible.'[98]

3. Jesus prays that his mission may be *completed* (24–26). The conclusion of the prayer returns to the themes of its beginning, in particular to the glory which Jesus prayed might be revealed in him and hence offered to the Father (1, 5). Jesus prays that those the Father has given him *may be with me where I am, and to see my glory* (24). The reference appears to reach beyond the glory immediately disclosed in the cross to the revelation of the glory of Christ at his parousia. Here is the 'finishing of the work the Father has given him to do', the presentation of all those whom the Father has given him, from all the ages and from around the globe, before 'him who sits upon the throne' (Rev. 5:13).

'With me' is the language of love. The beloved longs for the lover's presence. So Jesus, in these final moments, as the last grains of sand trickle through the hour glass before his rendezvous with darkness, gazes across the rolling aeons of the future and anticipates the embrace of his beloved bride in the glory that is to be.

'We have seen his glory,' was John's testimony as he contemplated Jesus' earthly ministry, a glory that has been unveiled as the story has unfolded. Shortly we shall gaze upon the 'glory' of his awful sacrifice and triumphant resurrection, and over the centuries the Spirit will glorify him as he takes what is Christ's and makes

[98] R. Fredrikson, p. 259.

it known to his disciples (16:14). But beyond all these 'glories' is the sure promise of a further unveiling, as at his coming the glory which Christ had with the Father is laid open to our eyes. Until that day of glory we walk by faith, not sight. The church must travel on her pilgrim way, the *ecclesia militans*, in a world that 'does not know' the Father, but sustained on her journey by the revelation of Jesus given and renewed (26), by the love of the Father embracing and supporting us and, above all, by the presence of Jesus in our midst and within our hearts (26).

4. Consecration (18:1 – 19:42)

a. The arrest (18:1–11)

In the circumstances leading to the apprehension of Jesus, it has already become clear that the whole scenario was anticipated, even planned, by him. There is a strange sense of inevitability about his arrest and conviction. Jesus has come from the Father into the world. He goes from the world to the Father. His mission will not have a happy and triumphant conclusion in the eyes of the world. Its wicked rebellion against the claim of God will reach its awful climax in the murder of the Son of God. Only in this way, however, can the darkness be overcome, and the Father's love for the world truly disclosed.

The account of the arrest is narrated in a simple and direct paragraph. After the conclusion of his teaching and his prayer Jesus leads the disciples from the house of the last supper out into the Jerusalem night. If the traditional sites are to be relied upon they faced a journey of about a mile, first northwards and then east past the great looming shadow of the temple. As they passed along the streets they would have glimpsed, through lighted windows, groups of pilgrims celebrating the feast, just as they had done a few minutes before. Jerusalem was teeming with visitors, and it would have been a relief to find themselves at last at the city gate and able to move out into the fresher air beyond. Their track led first downwards and then across the low valley of the Kidron stream, rising gently upwards as they ascended the lower slopes of the Mount of Olives. A short climb would have brought them to their destination, an olive grove which was part of the garden area of the city.

Passover law forbade a journey of any length on that evening, but this was permissible. Besides, it was a familiar spot (2). Jesus clearly had a rich benefactor who made his garden available on such occasions. More importantly, on this particular night it was where Judas would know where to find him. Having sent Judas on his foul errand (13:2), Jesus had deliberately sprung the trap and was now offering himself as the bait in a setting ideal for his capture, in the darkness of night with no thronging crowds to rise in his support.

The synoptic writers fill in other details here – Jesus' renewed sense of heaviness, the exhortation to the disciples to pray, and then Jesus' own lonely vigil through the long hours of the night as he agonized over his terrible obedience and found at length angelic strengthening (Mk. 14:32–42; Lk. 22:39–46).

At last through the darkness came the noise of tramping feet as a throng approached with lights and commotion (3). Judas is there at their head. The Jewish temple police are prominent since they must make the arrest, but a Roman force has also been provided (3). Normally garrisoned at Caesarea on the coast, the Roman troops were brought up to the capital at feast times and stationed (where Jesus would meet them during his examination) in the fortress of Antonia to the north-west of the temple complex. The word translated *detachment* (3) could mean a force of a thousand. Such is unlikely here, but it was probably a considerable number. Jesus' popularity with the crowds was known and the Palm Sunday demonstration would not have gone unnoticed by the Romans.

Significantly, it is Jesus who takes the initiative. John summarizes the whole event, and indeed the whole passion story: *Jesus, knowing all that was going to happen to him, went out* (4). The reference to 'going out' may imply that the grove was walled and Jesus emerged alone at the doorway. *Who is it you want?* (4). John omits Judas' kiss. It is unnecessary to his account. Jesus' *I am* (5, *egō eimi*) contains the by now familiar ambiguity. It could be no more than an identification for purposes of arrest. But the reader is being invited to appreciate a deeper meaning, the sacred name for God in the LXX, with clear overtones of Exodus 3:14 and Isaiah 40–55.

The effect of his words is striking. *They drew back and fell to the ground* (6). 'We are the world to whom our God comes forth in the person of Jesus the Nazarene saying, "Who is it you want?" The world is groping after its true leader: he offers himself, and the world, after yielding for a moment to the impact of his divinity, arrests him and crucifies him.'[99] Whether something of Jesus' divine majesty breaks in upon them for a moment, as Temple suggests, or they experience a sudden wave of terror as they are faced with actually laying hands on one whose supernatural powers were already legend, we are not told. Either way there is a perceptible loss of control on the authorities' part. Jesus, however, relieves the

[99] W. Temple, p. 321.

tension of the moment by re-identifying himself and then request-
ing an assurance of safe passage for the disciples (8), in fulfilment
of the word Jesus had spoken (9; 6:39) some months before.
Interestingly Jesus' words are cited in a way identical to the Old
Testament quotations studded through the gospel.

No doubt immensely relieved at being able to take Jesus without
a struggle, the authorities are apparently happy enough to accept
his terms. There is a moment of minor scuffle. Peter has probably
newly awakened. Overwhelmed with a sense of needing to do his
loyal duty by Jesus, and showing no small degree of courage in
view of the considerable armed presence, he swings the sword he
has brought along and catches the high priest's servant on the side
of the head, taking off his right ear (10). The Greek word used by
John, and Mark, could imply that it was only the lobe of the ear
that was cut off and not the whole organ. The fact that it was on
the right side is an interesting eye-witness detail which Luke also
notes (Lk. 22:50). 'The blow was as clumsy as Peter's courage was
great; the tactic was as pointless as Peter's misunderstanding was
total.'[100] Jesus staunches the bleeding with a touch (Lk. 22:51) and
is led away into the darkness, to drink the cup the Father has filled
and placed in his hands (11).

Several things stand out in this account.

(i)   The regal poise of Jesus (18:1–7)
Throughout the whole episode he occupies the centre of the stage
and directs the events. The soldiers by contrast are background
figures. The key statement is at verse 4: *Jesus, knowing all that was
going to happen . . . went out.* Similarly, this happened *so that the
words he had spoken would be fulfilled* (9). The sense of Jesus'
control is especially prominent in his *I am*. Significantly, in the
Jewish trial before the Sanhedrin, which John does not detail, it is
this phrase, unpacked in terms of the Son of Man of Daniel 7,
which triggers the frenzied response of the court and the unanimous
capital charge of blasphemy (Mk. 14:62f.). On the utterance of
these words the temple snatch-team fall backwards, by their posture
expressing the overwhelming nature of the revelation of divine
majesty.[101] Thus the forces of evil in that sinister confederacy –
personal treason in the person of Judas, corrupt religion expressed
by the temple police, political ruthlessness embodied in the Roman
soldiery, and behind all, the malignant form of the prince of this
world – all fall back before this meek monarch who offers himself
up to their will.

[100] D. A. Carson, *John*, p. 579.
[101] *Cf.* Ezk. 1:25–28; Dn. 10:4f.; Acts 9:4f.; Rev. 1:13f.

The relevance of this to our world needs no elaboration, for these same forces and many another are still abroad. The hour of darkness lingers, but its mastering is proclaimed here. What is described in these chapters is not simply one more skirmish in the unending conflict between light and darkness, good and evil, so that Jesus' victory, though impressive in its way, gives no guarantee that next time, or some time in the future, the roles may reverse and the outcome be different. John's point in writing his gospel is to share the great and glorious good news that this is the decisive conflict, the critical encounter, the outcome of which determines the whole war for ever. That and nothing less is the significance of Jesus' poise and mastery.

> O love of God! O sin of man!
>   In this dread act your strength is tried,
> And victory remains with love,
>   For he, our Lord, is crucified.

> *F. W. Faber*

This truth is as applicable to our personal world as to the larger universe. No matter what dark threat hangs over us, it is less than him who fought and mastered it in his Easter victory. For 'the devils we meet were all foredamned in the Satan Christ ruined. The devil is in the end a bull in a net, a wild beast kicking himself to death.'[102]

(ii) The caring heart of Jesus

As he faces the ultimate challenge of his life it is moving to observe Jesus' deep concern for the disciples. The scene is set for this in 13:1f.: 'Jesus knew that the time had come for him to leave this world and go to the Father. Having loved his own ... he now showed them the full extent of his love.' That same caring heart beats here as Jesus requires that the disciples be freed: *let these men go* (8). He draws the full enmity of the enemy to himself in order to deflect it from them, and this in the context of his *knowing all that was going to happen to him* (4).

That caring heart is our security. Because of it he will not lose one of those the Father has given (9). The good shepherd has committed himself to his sheep. When the wolf comes he will remain and defend the flock he loves. Whatever the wolf may represent in our lives today – guilt and shame from past failures, the accusing voices of criticism, sudden paralysing feelings of inadequacy as they come snapping and snarling at our heels, the good shepherd is there to meet them and to issue his word of command, 'Let my disciple go!'

[102] P. T. Forsyth, p. 7.

The action of Jesus in drawing the enmity upon himself for the freeing of the disciples is, more generally, a depiction of his whole work of atonement. He takes our place, absorbing our guilt and all its implications, that we might go free.

> Bearing shame and scoffing rude,
> In my place condemned he stood.
>
> *Philipp Bliss*

(iii) The awesome submission of Jesus

Nothing shines clearer in this account than the fact that Jesus goes willingly to his arrest. He who might have summoned twelve legions of angels, whose regal majesty could send his enemies reeling to the ground, accepts his arrest, trial and death in willing submission. His words to Peter unveil his heart: *Shall I not drink the cup the Father has given me?* (11). This saying picks up the language of his prayer in the garden as the other evangelists record it: '*Abba*, Father, . . . everything is possible for you. Take this cup from me. Yet not what I will, but what you will' (Mk. 14:36). What does the cup signify? For one steeped in the Old Testament prophets as Jesus was it can have only one meaning. The cup is the symbol of the judgment of God; it is the cup of the wrath of God against human sin.[103] 'In the strange mercy of God the cup of his righteous wrath is given into the hands, not of his enemies, but of his beloved Son. And he will drink it, down to the dregs until the moment comes when "I thirst" gives place to "It is finished".'[104]

b. The Jewish trial and Peter's denials – the hour of darkness (18:12–27)

This central section of the chapter represents one of the saddest, darkest sections in the whole of Scripture, if we except the ultimate darkness of the cross. Even here, however, stars also shine in the night sky.

Jesus, now in the hands of the Jewish authorities, is taken, bound, to Annas (13). Since the official high priest at this point was Caiaphas (11:49), the interposition of Annas calls for some explanation. Annas was a former high priest, from AD 6–15, who had been deposed by Pilate's predecessor, to the chagrin of the Jews for whom the high priesthood was traditionally a lifetime appointment. In the intervening years, no fewer than four of Annas' sons held the office, and Caiaphas, the current official appointee, was a son-in-law. Significantly, Acts 4:6 refers to 'the high priest's family', and actually identifies Annas as the high priest, though Caiaphas

---

[103] Cf. Is. 51:17–22; Je. 25:15–28; Zc. 12:2.   [104] L. Newbigin, p. 240.

is mentioned immediately after him. Luke's reference to 'the high priesthood of Annas and Caiaphas' gets it about right (Lk. 3:2). In every sense Annas was the power behind the throne and so claims 'first go' at Jesus.

Jesus is at this point 'helping the police with their enquiries'.[105] Annas attempts to draw Jesus into an incriminating admission which can be used to gain the Sanhedrin's support for the death penalty when it meets a few hours later.

Three other general comments are in order.

1. John does not give any detail of the trial before the Sanhedrin, although Jesus' appearance before them, and their verdict, were critical for the pursuance of the case against Jesus with the Roman authorities. The reason for John's omission is probably that he has already reported a Sanhedrin meeting which agreed upon a capital sentence (11:45–53) and explained at length Jewish rejection of Jesus. In reporting Jesus' trial he concentrates on the other element, the arraignment before the Roman procurator.

2. This preliminary hearing before first Annas, and then Caiaphas, is conducted immediately following Jesus' arrest by the temple police, which means in the early hours of the morning. If that conveys a sense of haste we are getting the picture accurately. Because of the proximity of the Passover Sabbath, and the week of the feast of unleavened bread which followed, it would not be possible to crucify an offender during that entire period as it would infringe the holiness of these days. Frank Morison, in his intriguing bestseller, *Who Moved the Stone?*, suggests that the authorities had probably decided against taking Jesus before the feast days, and that it was Judas' unexpected appearance, with the offer to lead them to Jesus in a highly opportune circumstance for arrest, that sent them scurrying to get their act together on the Thursday evening. If Jesus' execution was to be carried through they had to have him tried and formally condemned by the Sanhedrin early on the Friday, then get Pilate's confirmation by mid to late morning, so that he could be on the cross by midday, and dead and off the cross again before sundown inaugurated the Sabbath. It could be done, but it would be very tight.

3. The proceedings before Annas are interrupted to take in events in the courtyard outside. John thereby captures something of the atmosphere of that 'night of darkness' as the travesty enacted within Annas' house is replicated in the tragedy of Peter's denials outside it. Peter had followed behind the soldiers as they brought Jesus in, accompanied by *another disciple* (15), who clearly has ready access to the high priest's courtyard. The identity of this disciple is not

---

[105] L. Newbigin, p. 242.

divulged by John. Many have seen here a reference to the author of the gospel. The denial story has certain eye-witness details which would confirm that. On the other hand, the idea of a humble fisherman's son from Galilee having this kind of familiarity with the centres of power in Jerusalem raises problems. William Barclay mentions as a possibility a legend which identifies a house in Jerusalem as having once belonged to Zebedee, John's father. If so, it was arguably a 'branch office' for his Galilean fishing business, with the high priest as one of his clients. The salt-fish trade from Galilee was certainly important in Jerusalem at the time, and so this reconstruction, with its explanation of John's familiarity with the high priest's staff, is not impossible, though necessarily tentative.[106]

Peter is vouched for and allowed to enter the courtyard, where the girl who is monitoring the door challenges him: [Surely] *You are not one of this man's disciples, are you?* (17). The question calls for a negative answer. Peter, caught completely off guard, provides it. He denies his association with Jesus (17).

Meanwhile, Jesus' interrogation is proceeding inside the house. The essence of the Jewish legal process was the sworn testimony of witnesses. 'On their testimony everything depended. If two witnesses agreed in essentials, then the accused was doomed, no matter what he might say in his defence.'[107] Strict legal process therefore called for the interrogation of the witnesses rather than of the accused. Witnesses indeed should have figured in the arrest in the garden; but this is no time for the finer points of process.

Annas focuses on Jesus' *disciples and his teaching* (19). These represented the two areas where he attempts to incriminate Jesus. The *disciples* probably alludes to the 'false prophet' figure of Deuteronomy 13:1–10, who would perform 'miraculous signs and wonders' and 'lead astray' the people from the worship of the God of Israel. Conviction of such activity carried the death penalty. Congruent with an attempt to get this charge to stick, Annas' questions about his *teaching* would probably have covered his claim to be divine. Jesus disavows any secret, heretical teaching of his disciples. All he has said to them is in fullest accord with what he has said in his public teaching (20). If there is heresy alleged, let the witnesses be produced and interrogated (21).

Jesus' refusal to be cowed in the slightest by Annas provokes an angry reaction from one of his officials, who slaps Jesus across the face (22), a painful foretaste of the much greater physical abuse

---

[106] W. Barclay, 2, p. 229.

[107] K. Bornhauser, *The Death and Resurrection of Jesus Christ*, tr. A. Rumpus (C. L. Press), p. 98.

which was to come. Jesus, however, will not withdraw. '*If I said something wrong, . . . testify as to what is wrong. But if I spoke the truth, why did you strike me?*' (23). Jesus refuses to be manipulated into any false admissions, and demands that the due process of justice involving the calling and interrogation of witnesses be followed. 'In other words, Jesus is calling for a just trial.'[108] Annas, outmanoeuvred by Jesus' implacable integrity, can get no further and sends him on to his son-in-law (24) and thereafter to the Sanhedrin.

Once more the scene moves outside. The reference to the fire (18:25) is an interesting eye-witness detail supporting the fact that it was night. 'Jerusalem, a half-mile above sea-level, can be cold on spring nights.'[109] Peter has now moved into the courtyard shadows and joins others there awaiting further developments within. His fraternizing with the enemy is his downfall, as he is again challenged concerning his association with Jesus (25). He is considerably more vulnerable now. What if they recognized him as the one who had struck out in the garden? Peter retreats again and for a second time denies Jesus. A third time Peter is challenged, on this occasion with added threat as the interrogator is a known relative of the man Peter had wounded an hour or two before. *Didn't I see you with him?* (26). 'Not me.' *At that moment a cock began to crow* (27). Once again Jesus' foreknowledge is vindicated (13:38). So as Jesus testifies faithfully Peter denies pathetically. 'John has constructed a dramatic contrast wherein Jesus stands up to his questioners and denies nothing, while Peter cowers before his questioners and denies everything.'[110] With the cock crow Peter's wretched apostasy is suddenly exposed to him, and 'he went outside and wept bitterly' (Lk. 22:62). The hour of darkness!

We can identify several ingredients in the darkness of that night in Jerusalem. The first was the *rejection of God* on the part of Annas. In this scene Annas represents Judaism, the faith of God's people reaching all the way back to Abraham. The Jews had experienced many notable blessings throughout their history: wonderful victories at the Red Sea and in the conquest of Caanan; great leaders like Moses, Samuel and David; prophetic voices such as Elijah, Amos, Isaiah, or Jeremiah. They had received the supreme gift of a covenant relationship with God, his written law and the promise of the Messiah and the kingdom. All that tradition is gathered up in the person of the high priest, who now stands in the presence of the Messiah whom God has finally sent. Instead of falling before him in adoring acknowledgment, however, we find Annas in this

[108] G. R. Beasley-Murray, p. 325.   [109] R. Brown, 2, p. 825.
[110] R. Brown, 2, p. 842.

passage using every trick in the book to have him condemned to death. A profound pathos hangs over the interview, the pathos of Israel, the people who have rejected their God. While no modern nation is identically a theocracy like Israel, there are many peoples in today's world who, in the last decades, have expressed a not dissimilar rejection of the values and convictions of their founding fathers. Nor does Annas lack followers at the personal level.

A second 'darkness' that night in Jerusalem was the *denial of God* on the part of Peter. Peter was the designated leader of Jesus' new kingdom community. He had witnessed Jesus' miracles. He had seen Jesus' glory on the Mount of Transfiguration, five thousand fed, the lame leap, the blind see, the paralysed carry their beds home, even the dead raised. He had heard Jesus' teaching, including his solemn warnings of the impending crisis, not least for Peter himself (Lk. 22:31f.). Three times, however, publicly and emphatically, he had said it – 'I am not with Jesus, I do not know this man.' In the moment when Jesus had needed him most, Peter had turned his back on him and walked away. That darkness also lingers. How many Christians live with a continual sense of failure because of their inability, or unwillingness, to stand clearly for Christ in their public lives! Like Peter, we find ourselves drawn step by step into ever deeper compromise until existence is a continuous denial, and worship with God's people on a Sunday, instead of renewing and invigorating us, serves only to underline the hypocrisy of our lives.

There is a third darkness, however, more terrible in its way than the others, the *apparent weakness of God* – the darkness, not of our failure of God, but of God's seeming failure of us. Here is God's very Son, the creating and upholding Word of life, an apparently helpless pawn in the hands of his enemies, tossed from one to another like a shuttlecock, by men who appear able to bend the processes of justice at will, and to plot the most unjust sentence in the history of jurisprudence. The one who in the garden sent his assailants reeling back with his majestic 'I am' now succumbs, like any other prisoner, to his interrogators and torturers in a scene replicated daily (and documented graphically in the files of Amnesty International) in any of a hundred countries around the world. In Jesus' pilgrimage to Calvary we encounter not just the triumph, but also what Paul perceptively called 'the weakness of God' (1 Cor. 1:25). We can all identify with that 'weakness'. The God who apparently was not there when we needed him, the prayers that have gone unanswered, the disappointments that have shattered our dreams, the tragedies that have befallen us, the problems that prayer, pleading and praising, and every other prescribed panacea, seem unable to remove or even alleviate. God's 'weakness' also appears in the wider world in the atrocities that are daily 'permitted' around the globe, and in the spectacle of the needy millions, the starving, the refugees, the abused, the diseased. God, if he really owns this globe, is it seems, at best weak and limited, and clearly not up to the demands of ruling his world.

There are positive elements also in this passage, shining like stars in the darkness. We can identify three.

1. *God's presence.* At verse 14, in introducing Caiaphas, John reminds his readers that he *was the one who had advised the Jews that it would be good if one man died for the people* (11:50). Immediately a shaft of light is thrown across the whole landscape. What Caiaphas expounded as a principle of cynical expediency, God is using in his purpose. Peter was to tell them weeks later, 'you, with the help of wicked men, put [Jesus] to death' (Acts 2:23), but 'This man was handed over to you by God's set purpose and foreknowledge'.

God is no stranger to the darkness.

> If I say, 'Surely the darkness will hide me
> and the light become night around me,'
> even the darkness will not be dark to you;
> the night will shine like the day,
> for darkness is as light to you (Ps. 139:11–12).

So as Jesus stands before the flawed high priest of his nation he vindicates in a wonderful way his title as the true High Priest of the people of God. He is one who is not 'unable to sympathise with our weaknesses' because 'he himself is subject to weakness'; 'tempted in every way, just as we are', and so 'is able' ... 'to help us in our time of need' (see Heb. 4:15–16; 5:2; 2:18). Nothing, literally nothing, separates from him.

2. *God's plans.* If we look again at Peter we can discern another star. On the surface his threefold denial appears as an unmitigated disaster. Amid his bitter tears his whole life seemed to have collapsed about him; hope was extinguished, the lights had all gone out and darkness reigned. But Luke 22:31 gives another perspective. 'Satan has asked to sift you as wheat. But I have prayed for you, Simon, ... And when you have turned back, strengthen your brothers.' Even this disastrous failure was not outside God's plans for Peter. He is not abandoned. Rather, is it a moment of 'turning back', of conversion.

Peter's supreme characteristic, and also his supreme point of vulnerability, was his self-confidence: 'Even if all fall away on account of you, I never will ... Even if I have to die with you ...' (Mt. 26:33, 35). He rebukes Jesus when he speaks of his cross. 'Never, Lord! ... This shall never happen to you!' (Mt. 16:22).

261

Then comes this terrible, humiliating failure. It was no surprise to Jesus because he knew what was in Peter (2:24). In his denial Peter is being brought face to face with himself, his inner evil, and his moral helplessness. In that discovery, however, there is hope. So, when Jesus confronts him with it later, Peter no longer trusts in what *he* knows, but falls back upon what Jesus knows (21:15–18). The cross which brings Peter to an end of himself is the cross that raises him up to God and his purpose. In that moment of self-disillusionment, Simon, the inadequate man of sand, becomes Peter, the rock who is strong and dependable precisely because he has learned to depend utterly on Christ. So in our lives, 'His love is strong enough to resist pity until shame and penitence have done their gracious work' (P. T. Forsyth). For us, as for Peter, failure need not be final.

> Is my gloom, after all,
> Shade of his hand, outstretched caressingly?
>
> *Francis Thompson*

3. *God's prisoner.* The supreme star shining on in the darkness of that night is Jesus himself. He stands within the darkness and takes its terror into his own heart, but he remains standing; it does not engulf him. So in the midst of the darkness he bears his witness, *if I spoke the truth* ... (23). He is 'the faithful witness' (Rev. 1:5) who embodies the truth of God in the midst of the shadows of falsehood which encircle him. 'The light shines in the darkness, but the darkness has not overcome it' (1:5 mg.). 'One person speaking the truth has more power than a whole city living in falsehood' (Solzhenitszyn).

In this faithful witness Jesus has blazed a trail for countless thousands of his disciples across the centuries. Like Luther at Worms in 1521 ('Here I stand, I can do no other, so help me God'); or like Dietrich Bonhoeffer before the Nazis in 1944; or as Archbishop Jalani Luwum before his Ugandan accusers in 1977; or like the countless unnamed martyrs for Jesus through the last decades in Red China and Eastern Europe, Africa, South America and Asia, the light still shines in the darkness.

What is true in the world, however, is true also for us personally. The darkness may encompass us, dreams remain unfulfilled, sorrow or tragedy strike, prayers fall back unanswered, weaknesses linger, but the light of God's truth still shines in the darkness, until the day breaks and the shadows for evermore will flee away.

c.   *The Roman trial before Pilate (18:28 – 19:16)*

The appearance of Jesus before the Jewish supreme court, which

John omits, belongs at this point.[111] The next event recorded by John is therefore the trial before the Roman procurator, Pontius Pilate. The effect of his detailed account of the Roman proceedings, with its vivid images, gripping dialogue and heightening tension, is to provide a strongly legal atmosphere to the account of Jesus' death. We are therefore faced with the paradoxical fact that the one perfect life our planet has witnessed, universally recognized as the epitome of goodness, love, kindness, purity and integrity, reached its conclusion in a court facing capital charges. He who lived as the Holy One dies as the condemned one. He who breathed as the guiltless expires as the guilty. Yet, strange as it may seem, this very fact is fundamental to God's purpose in the death of Jesus, as we will shortly discover.

The hearing before Pilate divides naturally into two parts, corresponding to the chapter division.

(i) Verses 18:28–40 embrace the lodging of charges and Pilate's initial interrogation, leading up to his conclusion that Jesus is not guilty as charged, and his fateful attempt to achieve Jesus' release by offering him as the Passover amnesty prisoner.

(ii) Verses 19:1–16 cover Pilate's increasingly futile attempts to escape the noose which the Jewish authorities have tied for him, until he is eventually forced to bow to their desire and hand Jesus over for execution.

(i)   18:28–40

Verse 28 begins *Then*, encompassing the Sanhedrin appearance (see Mt. 26:57–27:1; Mk. 14:53–65). There, when Jesus had refused to answer questions or defend himself, the witnesses having signally failed to bring damning testimony, the high priest put Jesus under oath and demanded to know whether he believed himself to be the Messiah. The procedure was, like much of the Jewish proceedings in this case, strictly illegal. But it had the hoped-for result from the standpoint of Annas and Caiaphas. Jesus' response is not only to affirm his messianic title, but to take the 'I am' upon his lips and claim to be the heavenly Son of Man of Daniel 7, who shares the glory of the Ancient of Days and exercises the divine judgment at the end of history (Mk. 14:62; *cf.* Mt. 26:64). The Sanhedrin immediately explodes in revulsion, united in horror at this blasphemous claim. The verdict is a foregone conclusion. So he is brought forthwith to Pilate to have the governor confirm their verdict and authorize the immediate implementation of the execution.

The scene is now the governor's house in Jerusalem, usually

---

[111] *Cf.* Mt. 26:57 – 27:1; Mk. 14:53–65; Lk. 22:66–71.

identified as the Herodian palace on the West Hill, dominating the city. It is still early in the morning, which probably would not have inconvenienced Pilate. Social historians report that the day began early in the Empire. (The Emperor Vespasian made such an early start that he commonly had his day's work completed by noon.)

There is a profound irony in verse 28, which is certainly not lost on John as he recounts the story. In order to remain ritually clean, the Jewish leaders will not enter Pilate's house to speak with him. Entering a Gentile home would have meant defilement and would have barred them from participation in the Passover celebrations. Thus they seek cleansing before God while plotting and scheming the destruction of God's beloved Son. 'In their zeal to eat the Passover lamb they unwittingly help to fulfil its significance through demanding the death of the Lamb of God, at the same time shutting themselves out from its saving efficacy.'[112]

A similar tragedy is re-enacted whenever people depend upon fulfilment of ritual observances to alleviate their consciences before God. That the rituals of non-Christian religions cannot cleanse the heart is already clear to the readers of this gospel; Jesus alone is the way to God. Empty ritual, however, can arise also in the context of the Christian faith. Receiving baptism (by whatever mode), taking communion (in whatever church), attending worship (with whatever regularity), offering prayers (of whatever length), giving money (of whatever amount), in themselves, do not, have not, will not, and cannot save us from our sins and their inevitable judgment. 'Religion' cannot achieve redemption; ceremonies cannot save. Witness these accusers of Jesus.

Pilate, however, appears willing to accommodate their scruples and so to *come out* of his palace to meet them. The effect is to lend to the proceedings a certain bizarre rhythm as Pilate comes out to meet the leaders and then periodically retires back indoors with Jesus to question him. We can perhaps picture the Jewish delegation at the top of the steps leading to the entrance door of the palace, Jesus standing suitably bound and secured nearby, a noisy, expectant crowd gathered in the courtyard below, and Pilate emerging through the door to exchange with them, flanked no doubt by officials and soldiery.

Pilate begins the formal proceedings by enquiring about the charge. *What charges are you bringing against this man?* (29). The reply, *If he were not a criminal, . . . we would not have handed him over to you* (30), is a surly, even disrespectful response, not particularly designed to get Pilate on their side, and, moreover, not

[112] G. R. Beasley-Murray, p. 325.

really making any point at all. It may reflect a certain unreadiness for his question and leads one to surmise that they had already had conversation with Pilate concerning Jesus and secured what they thought was his approval for Jesus' execution without the need for a fresh examination. Pilate, however, will do it his way and arrive at his own judgment, hence his formal question. If this reconstruction is correct it would accord perfectly with what we learn from Roman sources of Pilate's general attitude to the Jews. Appointed in AD 26, he showed unrelieved contempt for the Jewish people. When the mood seized him he was liable to order brutal acts of suppression, and predictably his proconsulate was a difficult one. He was eventually recalled to Rome by the Emperor Tiberius in AD 35.

Take him yourselves and judge him by your own law (31). It is possible that Pilate doubted whether they would have had time to hold a meeting of the Sanhedrin by this hour in the morning. More probably Pilate is deliberately rubbing their noses in the dirt by this comment, since he and they knew that the Jewish leadership wanted Jesus dead and that they needed Pilate's approval for the death penalty. Pilate is therefore taking the opportunity to remind them yet again of their subjugation to Rome which had deprived them of the right to execute.

Some scholars have questioned whether this restriction was in fact the case at this point in time, but the evidence from independent Roman records appears roundly in support. It was no small issue. 'The capital power was the most jealously guarded of all the attributes of government.'[113] In the provinces Rome kept it to herself. This did not apparently exclude the Romans from being prepared to turn a blind eye on occasion to a spontaneous act of mob execution such as Stephen suffered (Acts 7:54ff.), or as Jesus was threatened with on more than one occasion (8:59; 10:31); but a full legal execution was another thing, and they retained the right to it.

This in turn makes clear that the authorities were intent not just on Jesus' death but on having him formally executed, *i.e.* crucified. The reason is not hard to find. Sympathy for him and his claims was widespread. They therefore had to move carefully. Indeed, during the whole procedure they give the appearance of men looking over their shoulders much of the time. There would be no surer way to dampen any backlash provoked by his execution than by having him crucified by the Roman overlords. Crucifixion was proscribed in the law as a sign of God's curse (Dt. 21:23), hence a 'crucified Messiah' was about as likely as a square circle. It was a

---

[113] A. N. Sherwin-White, *Roman Society and Roman Law in the New Testament* (Oxford, 1963), pp. 24–47.

moral and spiritual impossibility, the more so when it expressed submission to the Gentile power.

The request for the death sentence (31) requires Pilate to conduct his own examination of the prisoner, since the matter is now in his hands. He takes Jesus into the palace to question him (33). His lead question, *Are you the King of the Jews?*, implies that fuller details of the Jewish leaders' accusations had been expressed than John has recorded. It is to be noted, however, that the claim to be a king was not the issue which enraged and united the Sanhedrin. Their concern had been religious, a charge of blasphemy. They are well aware, however, that this religious issue would cut no ice with Pilate. People claiming to be gods were commonplace in the Empire. Their case would have then become simply a matter of their (Jewish) superstitions and he would have dismissed it. So they change tack and refashion the case in political terms, a format which Pilate was bound to take seriously. Jesus, they allege, had been claiming to be 'King of the Jews', *i.e.* he was a political revolutionary guilty of inciting rebellion against Rome. Pilate certainly knew the type. He had recently secured a notable example, one Barabbas. The *you* in Pilate's question is emphatic, expressing some surprise (33). From Pilate's knowledge of the species he was aware immediately that Jesus did not fit the stereotype picture of the revolutionary, a breed all too familiar in the twentieth century.

Jesus is not in the least degree intimidated by this personal representative of the Roman Emperor and attempts to personalize the conversation, reaching out to Pilate as a man needing to find the grace of God. *Is that your own idea . . .?* (34). Pilate replies contemptuously, *Am I a Jew? . . . It was your people . . . who handed you over to me. What is it you have done?* (35). Pilate is concerned to find out if there is any criminal activity involved from Rome's viewpoint. Jesus concedes that he is head of a kingdom, but not one which Rome need fear as a political rival. If it were he would be supported at that very moment by the military action of his 'servants'. Some see here a possible reference to angelic servants 'from another place', *i.e.* from the heavenly realm from which Jesus himself had come (*cf.* Mt. 26:53).

Jesus' disassociating the origin of his kingdom from 'this world' should not be taken as implying that the kingdom of Christ has no political concerns, or that its righteousness is not to be applied in the political arena. Even a cursory reading of the Sermon on the Mount would eliminate that error. Jesus' point here is that his authority is not derived from, nor dependent upon, political agency.

Pilate is both relieved, and provoked. *You are a king, then!* (37). Jesus does not back away from the title. *You are right.* Having just explained the nature of his kingship negatively (*i.e.* what it is not), he turns to explain it positively. It is a kingship defined by his mission *to testify to the truth*; his kingdom is a kingdom of truth.[114] Truth here has a meaning close to 'reality'. In a world subject to unreality and illusion, Jesus offers the reality of a personal relationship with 'the only true God' (17:3), a life in the truth which sets free (8:32). Jesus offers that to Pilate. He, the imprisoned, offers his judge true freedom.

For a moment Pilate appears fascinated and held, as he faces the issues of his personal destiny. *What is truth?* (38). Is this cynical dismissal? So, famously, thought Francis Bacon: ' "What is truth?" asked jesting Pilate, and would not stay for an answer.' But perhaps it was asked wistfully also, from a lifetime's struggle as a professional politician, steeped in the daily compromises, the prudential balancing of forces, the application of ruthless power, that half-light world of greys and polka dots where people grope wearily for truth and the soul shrivels and dies. Did Pilate, as his destiny for a fleeting second hung in the balances, catch a glimpse in Jesus of a truer, purer, brighter world? We cannot be sure. What is certain is that if the moment came it also passed. The forgiving moment slipped by as Pilate turned on his heel to report his decision to the Jewish leaders.

As he makes his way back to them and the waiting crowd, he determines on a daring and politically astute manoeuvre. He reports his conclusion. *I find no basis for a charge against him.* That could have ended it all, and should have done so. Pilate would have been an unpopular, but nonetheless just, governor. He cannot leave it there, however. So he plays his further card. According to custom a prisoner was released by the governor at Passover. He will offer to release Jesus, their 'king' (39). Three advantages might have accrued to Pilate by this ploy. First, he would be tacitly admitting that Jesus is a criminal, which would please his accusers. Secondly, he would thereby allow the people to speak because 'he perceived it was out of envy that the priests had offered him up' (Mt. 27:18). Thirdly, he would clear his own conscience since in his heart he knows that Jesus is no criminal.

In all this, Pilate, not for the first time in his political career, sadly miscalculated. If this is his winning card, then Pilate's opponents have their ace. The crowd are ready. This is not the Palm Sunday pilgrim company which had greeted Jesus with hosannas a few days before. This is more recognizably the urban mob, laced no doubt with the flunkeys of the high priest, the revolutionary sympathizers who hated Rome, and among whom Barabbas the mobster was a popular hero. This crowd wants no part in any

[114] *Cf.* 1:14; 8:36; 14:6.

'kingdom of truth' that will not pit itself against the spears and swords of the hated Roman occupiers; no part with a king who would rebuke their sins and expose their hearts' rebellion against the living God before they could truly express his rule in their society. So they scream their rejection. 'No, not him! Give us Barabbas!' In a moment Pilate's clever plan shatters before his eyes. The governor is hoist by his own petard. 'Having failed to acknowledge the truth he is in the power of the lie.'[115] Though Pilate will make token attempts to wriggle free, in fact he has lost, trapped in the coils of his own presumed wisdom. Jesus is doomed.

If this gripping account teaches *the emptiness of mere religion* (*cf*. 28) it speaks also of *the wonder of God's salvation*. The authorities are determined that Jesus should die by crucifixion, *i.e.* under the curse of God, and they will have their way. In the wonder of God's grace, however, their wish coincides precisely with our need. We all live under a curse, 'the curse of the law' as Paul calls it in Galatians 3:10: 'All who rely on observing the law are under a curse.' Then, citing Deuteronomy 27:26, 'Cursed is everyone who does not continue to do everything written in the Book of the Law.' To break the law, or whatever our moral standard be, is to fall under its curse, the curse of guilt in the presence of God, a curse we all experience daily. We desperately need some means whereby that curse is lifted from us. We need a Saviour who will bear the curse for us. That is precisely who Jesus is, as this passage clearly shows. By dying 'on a tree' (Dt. 21:23) he has 'become a curse for us' (Gal. 3:13). The judgment of God against our law-breaking was taken by him on the cross. A crucified Messiah, a Messiah under curse, is the only Messiah who can meet our need and reconcile us to the Father. Let Luther state it:

> Our merciful Father, seeing us to be oppressed and overwhelmed with the curse of the law, and to be so holden down by the same that we could never be delivered by our own power, sent his only Son into the world and laid upon him all the sins of all men, saying: be thou Peter that denier; Paul that persecutor, blasphemer and cruel oppressor; David that adulterer; that sinner which did eat the apple in Paradise; that thief which hanged upon the cross; and briefly, be thou the person which hath committed the sins of all men; see therefore that thou pay and satisfy for them.[116]

And he has 'satisfied for them', out of his eternal love, for our eternal salvation.

[115] L. Newbigin, p. 247.
[116] M. Luther, *The Epistle to the Galatians* (Jas. Clarke, 1953), p. 97.

Finally, this section underlines *the urgency of decision*. The choice that faced the mob in Jerusalem is still before our world. Whom will we follow? Whom will we make our king? Barabbas continues to represent an alluring alternative, the fulfilling of this-worldly ambitions and dreams, the gratification of human lusts and hungers, the nationalist dream, the political kingdom. Jesus still stands before us also, offering his way of truth, a knowledge of the Father which, beginning in the valley of confession and repentance, leads forward along the pathway of daily surrender to him as Lord. Though on the surface less attractive, however, that choice frees those who make it to serve him in the world. It carries them at the last beyond the passing shadows of the earthly into the enduring order of the kingdom which will have no end. Who is our king, Jesus or Barabbas? The world still chooses. So must we all.

This arresting account of the trial of Jesus is probably an opportune moment to address the accusation of anti-Semitism which has been levelled periodically at the fourth gospel. It is not difficult to see why this charge has arisen, as the gospel portrays in stark terms the heightening conflict between Jesus and 'the Jews',[117] climaxing in his accusation at their instigation (18:31f.; 19:7–16). Upon examination, however, the anti-Semitism appears shakily founded. Apart from the not insignificant fact that John himself is a Jew, among the over seventy occurrences of 'the Jews' are occasions when it is used in a quite neutral sense, as when explaining a ritual to non-Palestinian readers (*e.g.* 2:6), as well as occasions when it has clearly positive content, as in 4:22, 'salvation is from the Jews', or 4:9 where Jesus himself is identified as a Jew. Crucially, the opposition is regularly referred to as the Jewish leaders, especially in Jerusalem, rather than the people as a whole.[118] J. A. T. Robinson's conclusion may be cited: 'Writing as a Jew for other Jews he is concerned to present the condemnation of Jesus, the *true* king of Israel, as the great betrayal of the nation by its own leadership.'[119] We should further note that John omits the Sanhedrin trial (Mk. 14:53–65) and also the cry of the mob recorded in Matthew 27:25, 'Let his blood be on us and on our children!'

In addition there can be no doubting the role of Pilate in the execution of Jesus as we have seen. The fact that Jesus' crucifixion hung finally on his verdict means that any attempt to lay sole responsibility for the death of Jesus on the Jews as a whole, or even the Jewish leadership in particular, cannot be meshed with

[117] 5:16f.; 7:1; 8:40f., 59; 9:22; 10:31.
[118] *Cf.* 1:19; 7:32; 9:22; 11:45–53; 12:42; 19:6, 15.
[119] J. A. T. Robinson in *The Priority of John*, ed. J. F. Coakley (SCM, 1985), pp. 273f.

John's presentation of the facts. One of John's concerns in compiling his gospel is, as we saw in the introduction, to appeal to his fellow Jews at a time when to embrace Christianity meant rejection by Israel. John shows that the same implications faced Jesus as a witness to the truth. As he was vindicated in resurrection, however, so too would believers from among Israel be vindicated as they embraced him who is at once both 'King of the Jews' and 'Saviour of the world'.

(ii)   19:1–16

Pilate's attempt to free Jesus having rebounded on him, he does not immediately surrender Jesus to their will. He tries a different tack – having him flogged, presumably in the hope that this lesser punishment will mollify his accusers (1; cf. Lk. 23:16).

Some uncertainty exists about what exactly this punishment was. The Romans had three levels of flogging: the *fustigatio*, a lighter beating for lesser offences; the *flogellatio*, a brutal flogging for more serious crimes; and the *verberatio*, the most terrible of all, which was administered as part of the preliminary to crucifixion. The *verberatio* has been described as follows: 'the victim was stripped, bound to a post or pillar, and beaten by a number of torturers until the latter grew tired and the flesh of the victim hung in bleeding shreds. In the provinces such as Judea this was the task of soldiers. In the case of slaves or criminals such as Jesus, scourges or whips were used, the leather thongs often fitted with a spike or several pieces of bone or lead joined to form a chain. It is not surprising to hear that prisoners not infrequently collapsed and died under this procedure.'[120] That Jesus received this fearful examination as the prelude to the crucifixion is certain, and it may have been what was administered by Pilate at this point. The cruel streak in the man is certainly borne out by Roman records. Some scholars believe that Jesus may have received the 'lighter' *fustigatio* at this point, as Pilate's attempt at appeasement; and then the *verberatio*, in addition, before his execution.

The physical beating is followed by a further refinement of cruelty (2–3) as Jesus becomes for a time the plaything of the Roman soldiery, a large crowd in all likelihood. Their natural contempt and hatred for the Jews knew few bounds and now here was the Jewish 'king' delivered into their hands. What an opportunity to vent their pent-up anger and frustration with these uncivilized, fanatical people!

A king, eh? Then a king he will be! So Jesus is arraigned for his

---

[120] J. Blinzler, *Der Prozess Jesu Regensburg* (Verlag Pustet, 1969), pp. 321f., cited in G. R. Beasley-Murray, pp. 336f.

'coronation'. A king needs a crown; thorns will do nicely. Not the innocuous imitation laurel wreath beloved by pious art, but great jagged spikes from the date palm, up to twelve inches in length, meshed together and then rammed agonizingly on to Jesus' head. An old purple sheet is found for a cloak and probably a box or bench for a throne. Matthew and Mark mention a staff pushed into his hands as a sceptre. Let the coronation proceed! Let the sport begin! So they come forward in turn in mocking homage: 'Hail, O King of the Jews', in deliberate parody of obeisance to the Emperor, 'Ave, Caesar!', and then the spit, the slap, the punch. Matthew and Mark speak of them taking the staff and striking Jesus on the head with it 'again and again' (Mt. 27:30).

When they had taken their fill they send Jesus back to Pilate and the crowd, the latter waiting no doubt in considerable impatience for the end of the trial and Pilate's formal verdict. Pilate has Jesus brought out again before them and reaffirms his inability to find any crime deserving of death. *Here is the man!* (5). If Pilate hoped to elicit pity for Jesus as he presents this bleeding, beaten figure to them with his grotesque headdress and the pathetic insignia of his kingship draped about him, he is again to be surprised. The mob's blood-lust is up. *Crucify! Crucify!* (6).

Outflanked once more, and by now becoming infuriated by his increasing helplessness, Pilate attempts to shrug off responsibility. *You take him and crucify him. As for me, I find no basis for a charge against him* (6). The Jewish leaders, however, are not bothered by that responsibility being passed to them. In their darkened hearts this *is* a just sentence. *We have a law . . . because he claimed to be the Son of God* (7). Thus the real basis of their accusation is laid bare. The 'law' is probably Leviticus 24:16, 'Anyone who blasphemes the name of the LORD must be put to death' (*cf.* Jn. 10:30f.). Deuteronomy 13:1–6 may also be in the background (*cf.* comments on 18:19).

This exposure of the theological roots of the Jewish enmity troubles Pilate (8) – the Greek can be rendered 'was very much afraid' – and he once more takes Jesus inside the palace for questioning (9). Already impressed by Jesus, and no doubt himself a superstitious pagan, this reference to Jesus' divine claims is alarming. He was probably also affected by a message from his wife warning him to have nothing to do with Jesus, 'that innocent man', as she had had a nightmare about him (Mt. 27:19).

Where do you come from? Pilate asks. 'Are you from earth or heaven?' Is this some other-worldly visitor he has on his hands who will perhaps return to haunt Pilate with his strange powers? Jesus does not make it easy for Pilate. Just as previously with his Jewish interrogators, he refuses to reply (Mk. 14:60–61). Pilate's

271

fear quickly turns to exasperation and annoyance. *Don't you realise I have power either to free you or to crucify you?* (10). Pilate is supremely aware of wielding the authority of the most powerful man on earth, Tiberias Caesar in Rome. Jesus, however, is conscious of an authority infinitely greater than any wielded by Pilate, or Caesar, or Caiaphas, or the Jewish mob; an authority in whose hands these human forces are but reeds in the wind. His 'hour' has come, hence he is now 'given up' by the Father to Pilate's will. Pilate's mastery is purely a 'gift' from above (11). As to human responsibility, that lies the more with Caiaphas and his cronies, who had been exposed to the light of God's Word and risen up in evil confederacy to extinguish it (11).

The drama moves swiftly to its inevitable conclusion. Pilate, following this further questioning, is even more concerned to free a man who he is now convinced is innocent, but he is beaten into submission as the Jewish leaders play their trump card. *If you let this man go, you are no friend of Caesar . . .* (12). The phrase 'friend of Caesar' may possibly be an allusion to an honorific imperial title awarded by the Emperor to senators and selected individuals. Roman sources inform us that Pilate had gained Tiberias' favour and become a 'Friend of Caesar' through the good graces of one Sejanus, a highly placed imperial official. Some months before the crucifixion, during a palace purge in Rome, Sejanus had been removed and executed, along with many of his supporters. Pilate was therefore conceivably in a highly precarious position at this point due to his known connections to Sejanus. His life may even have been in some danger when Jesus appeared before him. In these circumstances a show of disloyalty, by failing to deal firmly with a revolutionary leader implicitly challenging the rule of Caesar, might be the final nail in Pilate's coffin. A whisper in the right ears in Rome, and Pilate was a dead man.

We cannot be certain of this background, nor of the precise order of the various events. What is clear is Pilate's extreme discomfort the moment these accusations were expressed. *When Pilate heard this* (13), his recalcitrance evaporates and he proceeds with notable haste to his pronouncement of verdict. So *the judge's seat*, the official symbol of the Roman judiciary, is brought out on to the terrace outside Pilate's residence. Pilate takes his seat as the official representative of the Roman power. The crowd hushes for the verdict. Matthew adds the vivid detail of Pilate calling for water and washing his hands before the crowd in protestation that he is innocent of responsibility for Jesus' death. Then in a further gesture of defiance, and in expression no doubt of his contempt for the whole proceedings, Pilate utters as his verdict, not a pronouncement of sentence, but a proclamation of sovereignty, *Here is your king!*

(14), a truth far deeper than Pilate could know. Immediately there is an explosion of anger: *Take him away! . . . Crucify him! Your king? . . . We have no king but Caesar*, answer the chief priests (15).

This retort is a fateful utterance on the part of these official representatives of the Jewish theocracy, for it represents nothing less than the rending of the sacred covenant with God. Nothing was more fundamental to that covenant than the kingship of God, over the world in general, but in a special way over his chosen people, Israel. It was a conviction that no invading power could weaken or eradicate, whether Persian, Ptolemaic, Syrian, Greek or Roman. 'O LORD, our God, other lords besides you have ruled over us, but your name alone do we honour' (Is. 26:13). Secure in that conviction, they waited patiently through the long centuries for the appearing of his Messiah to vindicate Israel's faith and establish his rule visibly and powerfully over the whole world. But now, in a terrible moment of apostasy, that sacred tryst is violated, and the holy place is desecrated as the centuries of anticipation are cast aside: *We have no king but Caesar.* 'It is nothing less than the abandonment of the Messianic hope of Israel.'[121] From that moment the church comes to replace Israel at the centre of God's purposes in history, and will continue to do so to the end.

With this fateful sentence the verdict is sealed, Pilate has lost, the trial is over, and Jesus will die. So *Pilate handed* Jesus *over to them*, for the *verberatio* (had it not already been administered), and the cross.

In the account of Jesus' trial possibly the key statement is that made by Pilate when presenting Jesus, *Here is the man!*, or in the traditional AV translation, *Behold the man!* (5). Two aspects of Jesus the Man are to be noted.

1. *Jesus is a real man.* In these closing scenes of Jesus' life the claim of 1:14, 'the Word became flesh', is supremely vindicated. He was truly 'made like his brothers [and sisters]' (Heb. 2:17), and in particular in this passage, our companion in the experience of suffering.

The presence of God in our suffering is one of the supreme distinctives of the Christian faith. Beside this, other world religions fall largely silent. The Qur'an's contribution to our response to suffering is expressed in this insight: 'Every misfortune that befalls you is ordained.'[122] Buddhism's limitation is reflected in the following paragraph by a leading modern Buddhist scholar. 'I saw a report a while ago of a tragic accident, that in which a woman lost her

---

[121] G. R. Beasley-Murray, p. 343.
[122] *The Koran* (Penguin, 1956), 57.21, p. 383.

son. Weeping beside his body, the mother kept saying, "I could bear anything else, but this boy was my only hope in life!" Faced by the cold fact of death, there was nowhere she could turn in her sorrow. We cannot help but sympathize with her, but there is little we can say in consolation. All we can do is wait for time to veil her grief in the mist of resignation.'[123] By contrast, as this section eloquently shows, in Jesus we have a God who enters into our sufferings and shares them with us.

We can distinguish three strands in the suffering of Jesus in this passage.

First, it was *physical* suffering. It is usual to play down this aspect due to an unbalanced over-emphasis upon it in some Roman Catholic devotion. The New Testament records certainly do not major there. Equally, neither do they minimize the physical sufferings, as this section makes clear. That is crucial for ministry in Christ's name in a hurting world, where the hurt is often physical in nature. He 'suffered in his body' (1 Pet. 4:1). Compare the testimony of the Christian paraplegic, Joni Eareckson Tada. 'I discovered that the Lord Jesus Christ could indeed empathise with my situation. On the cross for those agonising horrible hours, waiting for death, he was immobilised, helpless, paralysed. Jesus did know what it was like not to be able to move – not to be able to scratch your nose, shift your weight, wipe your eyes. He was paralysed on the cross – Christ knew exactly how I felt!'[124]

Secondly, it was *relational* suffering. Jesus not only suffered appalling physical pain, but, as this passage makes clear, he suffered it at the hand of others. To put the matter starkly, Jesus was abused! Unhealthy imagination about all that Jesus was subjected to at the hands of the Roman garrison is not appropriate (1–3), but it certainly was not nice.

Today spousal and sexual abuse have been brought out of the closet and we have to come to terms with the grim statistics of the numbers of women and children who are the daily victims of physical and sexual abuse in our societies. Inevitably, these often tragic victims will include a significant number of the readers of this commentary. In addition to the need to get help from available agencies, this passage assures us of the support and understanding of a Saviour who has been there. His body was violated. He is the God of the abused.

Thirdly, it was *emotional* suffering. Pilate's presentation of Jesus was designed to appeal to the pity of the crowd (5). But his

---

[123] Takashi Hirose, *Lectures on Shin Buddhism* (Higashi Honganji, 1980), p. 71.
[124] Joni Eareckson Tada, *Joni* (Pickering and Inglis, 1976), p. 107.

appearance went beyond the pitiful to the ridiculous, that broken figure with his tattered robe and the weird, spiky headdress protruding grotesquely from his head. 'More like a clown than a King.'[125]

That touches us deeply, for there is almost nothing we dread more than being thought ridiculous. Most people in fact are much more ready to be thought bad than silly; nothing so readily penetrates the armour of our self-esteem than mocking laughter. Yet it was with precisely that ringing in his ears from the soldiers' ridicule that Jesus appeared for the further mockery of the crowd. 'I am a worm and not a man, scorned by men and despised by the people' (Ps. 22:6); 'he was despised, and we esteemed him not' (Is. 53:3). When such moments sweep paralysingly across our hearts and we collapse inwardly in a hidden torment of shame and confusion, or when the tapes of yesterday's humiliations and shames begin to whir in our minds, there is a 'fellowship of his sufferings' which is wonderfully releasing and reassuring. He is indeed our 'fellow sufferer'. He knows and he can share.

Jesus comes to our side, however, not only to sympathize with us. He is also our inspiration and example as we confront our pains. The writer to the Hebrews draws this out. 'Consider him who endured such opposition from sinful men, so that you will not grow weary and lose heart' (12:3).

2. *Jesus is a representative man.* If the first application was in terms of incarnation, God with us, the second is in terms of redemption, God for us. We note in particular that the death of Jesus was a judicial death, the conclusion of a legal process in which charges were formulated and presented, and judgment passed. This fact is not incidental, as Calvin noted centuries ago when he argued that it is 'part of our redemption' that Jesus was 'arraigned before the judgment seat as a criminal, accused and condemned by the mouth of a judge to die.'[126]

In exploring this truth we note that the charges against Jesus were twofold; that of *blasphemy*, brought by the Jewish authorities (Mk. 14:60–64), and *treason*, the issue in the Roman trial before Pilate (12). Jesus died as a blasphemer and traitor. But precisely these two perversions are at the heart of all human sinning. Genesis 3 unveils it clearly. Sin is *blasphemy*: 'you will be like God' (3:5). 'The essence of sin lies in man's pretension to be God.'[127] But further, sin is *treason*, an act of rebellion against God's rightful

---

[125] G. R. Beasley-Murray, p. 337.

[126] J. Calvin, *Institutes of the Christian Religion*, II. vi. 5.

[127] R. Niebuhr, *Nature and Destiny of Man*, vol. 1: *Human Nature* (Nisbet, 1941), p. 148.

rule. 'Of the tree of the knowledge of good and evil you shall not eat . . . she took of its fruit and ate; and she also gave some to her husband, and he ate' (Gn. 2:17; 3:6, RSV). 'As a race we are not even stray sheep, or wandering prodigals merely; we are rebels, taken with the weapons in our hands.'[128]

Precisely the charges we face at the judgment seat of God therefore are the charges Jesus faced at the judgment seat of Caiaphas and Pilate. The trial of Jesus accordingly assumes a new dimension of meaning. Pilate and Caiaphas disappear from view and Jesus stands instead before the judgment seat of God. He comes to that judgment as our representative, to face our charges and to stand in our place, the 'second Adam' come to face the accusations which stand against the first Adam and his seed. This identification is perhaps hinted at in the question of Pilate to Jesus. 'What is it you have done?' (18:35) echoes the question to Adam and Eve in the Garden of Eden after their sin (Gn. 3:13). More clearly it goes towards explaining the otherwise astonishing silence of Jesus before his accusers (Mk. 14:60–61; verse 9). Like the sheep that was dumb before her shearers, so Jesus takes the place of those whose 'mouth is stopped' (see Rom. 3:19, RSV) before the throne of God. He took our place, he was condemned for us! He is our representative man. He died, 'the righteous for the unrighteous', that he might 'bring you to God' (1 Pet. 3:18).

But because he took our place at the judgment, and faced our charges, and bore our judgment, we can go free.

> O Christ, what burdens bowed thy head!
>   Our load was laid on thee.
> Thou stood'st in the sinner's stead,
>   Didst bear all ill for me.
> A victim led, thy blood was shed;
>   Now there's no load for me!

Anon.

'Therefore, there is now no condemnation for those who are in Christ Jesus' (Rom. 8:1).

d. The crucifixion – the death of Jesus (19:16b–30)

The trial of Jesus would have formally concluded with Pilate pronouncing the formula '*Ibis ad crucem*' ('You will go to the cross'). Jesus would then immediately fall into the custody of the 'execution squad' comprising four Roman soldiers. The condemned man was

[128] P. T. Forsyth, *Positive Preaching and the Modern Mind* (Grand Rapids, 1964), p. 38.

forced to carry, not the entire cross, but the horizontal crosspiece (*patibulum*). It is likely, since crucifixions were relatively common, that the upright posts were permanently in place at the execution site beside the main highway just outside the city. As Jesus sets off on that last terrible journey, carrying the wooden beam, we witness a re-enactment of the scene on Mount Moriah (the very hill on which the city of Jerusalem stood) when another son carried the wood for an altar on which he was to be secured as the victim (Gn. 22).

The Romans, never blind to the deterrent value of punishment, usually prescribed a circuitous route to the execution site, with a placard announcing the crime carried in front. It is likely that the need for haste on the authorities' part to ensure death before sundown may have dispensed with that in Jesus' case. Certainly the journey was profoundly draining following upon the wretched *verberatio*, and the synoptics tell of Jesus collapsing under the beam and requiring assistance to reach the site (Mt. 27:32). The place of execution was named Golgotha, 'The Place of the Skull', probably a small hill at the entrance to the city. *Here they crucified him* (18).

The victim was laid out on the crosspiece and fixed to it by iron nails driven through the top of the wrists; the crosspiece was then raised on a ladder or pulley and nailed or bound to the upright, and the feet, placed one over the other, nailed below. The victim was then left to die. It could take days; a long, slow agonizing descent into hell, ended finally by suffocation as the victim, unable any longer to relieve the constriction of the chest, mercifully expired. Invented by the Persians, developed by the Carthaginians, perfected by the Romans, such was crucifixion. Josephus refers to it as 'the most wretched of deaths'. Cicero called it 'a most cruel and terrible penalty . . . incapable of description by any word, for there is none fit to describe it'. So terrible was crucifixion that no Roman was permitted to undergo it, however heinous his crime.

Jesus is not alone as he hangs there; there are 'two others' crucified with him, possibly henchmen of Barabbas, one on either side.

John adds three further cameos. First, there is the matter of the inscription over Jesus' head, the one carried in front of him on his journey through the city (19–22). It read JESUS OF NAZARETH, THE KING OF THE JEWS in the three great tongues of the day, Aramaic, (the local dialect of Hebrew); Latin and Greek. The title incensed the Jewish leaders and they remonstrated with Pilate (21). But vacillating Pilate is for once implacable. It is a final gesture of contempt. If this is their king, what does it say of them as a nation? Perhaps in addition it expresses Pilate's dim yet authentic

277

recognition that in some sense Jesus *is* a king. 'He refuses to change the truth into a lie.'[129]

Secondly, there is the matter of dividing up Jesus' clothes (23–24). According to custom the victim was stripped naked for crucifixion and his clothes became the perquisites of the execution squad. General agreement sees the items in Jesus' case consisting of an outer garment or robe, a head-covering or scarf, a belt, and sandals, leaving the fifth, a seamless undergarment, to be gambled for. Some have noted that the high priest's robe was similarly seamless. John's point of significance is that this fulfils the Scripture, in Psalm 22:18.

Thirdly, John records the presence of loyal supporters. It seems a long time since we have been in touch with Jesus' disciples, so utterly have the last hours been dominated by the enemies of the Master. Now they reappear, principally a company of women, whose commitment to Jesus was so deep that they were 'last at the cross and first at the tomb'. The only male disciple mentioned is *the disciple whom* Jesus *loved*, John, as we believe.

The personal detailing of the women in the other gospels may imply an identification of *his mother's sister, Mary* (25), with Salome (Mk. 15:40), 'the mother of Zebedee's sons' (Mt. 27:56). If this is so then James and John were, like John the Baptist, Jesus' cousins, and that helps give meaning to Jesus' action (26–27). In his concern for his mother he puts her in the care, not of his natural brothers who at this point do not believe, but of the other side of the family, in the person of his cousin John, where she would find a believing and supportive relationship.

Through all of this Jesus struggles on in agony, and darkness falls over the whole land 'from the sixth hour until the ninth hour' (Mt. 27:45; Mk. 15:33).

Amid the unfolding horror we do not lose sight of the ultimate perspective, which is victory, not defeat. Jesus has consistently struck this note; his death will be a 'lifting up' on the cross, an act of elevation as well as of identification; his crucifixion is his coronation; his cross, his throne.[130] The Palm Sunday pilgrims had set the scene for the events of the following weekend: 'see, your king is coming' (12:15). So the words of Pilate's verdict interpret the crucifixion as John depicts it: 'Here is your king' (14). It is therefore nothing but the simple truth that is placarded over his head as he hangs there: JESUS . . . THE KING.

Several aspects of his kingship are particularly reflected in this section.

---

[129] G. R. Beasley-Murray, p. 347.   [130] *Cf.* 3:14; 8:28; 12:28–30.

(i) He is a hidden king (19:18)

The claims for his reign are, on the surface, the most blatant fraud. Never was one less kingly, or possessed of so little evidence to support his claim, than Jesus at this moment. One need but compare, even in the most superficial way, the account of the splendours of Solomon's kingdom in 1 Kings 7–10 with the opening verses of John 19 to sense the outrageous absurdity of it. The Roman soldiers as they bow in mock obeisance epitomize the audacity of the claim, yet for the evangelist, they in fact speak truth: 'Hail, King of the Jews: Yes, indeed, all hail, King Jesus! But reason alone cannot arrive at this verdict on the crucified. From the rational standpoint, Jesus' story is one of tragic failure. It can see no God in the cross. Only through the revealing Spirit can the victory of the cross be recognized. Luther understood this when he argued: 'In Christ crucified is the true theology and knowledge of God ... as long as a man does not know Christ he does not know the true God, the God hidden in sufferings.'[131]

This hiddenness needs to be acknowledged. There are times when we are called to believe, not 'because of', but 'in spite of'. At this point the 'health and wealth' gospels of our day stand exposed in their hollowness. To follow Jesus Christ is to take up a cross, and that means there may be moments when life's circumstances contradict our claims as surely as they did for Jesus at Calvary.

(ii) He is a universal king (19:20)

The languages in which Jesus' kingship was proclaimed embrace three great sectors of human experience which help unpack the full terms of his title.

It was written in *Greek*, the language associated historically with the development of culture, the pursuit of beauty of form and thought. The church at times has turned a jaundiced eye upon all things artistic and creative. But the world of culture is a world Christ claims no less than any other. Human creativity is the gift of him who made all things. If creative gifts and instincts are brought to his feet he will ennoble and enrich them, and make them still the vehicle of his praise.

It was written in *Latin*, the language of government, law and institutions. Too often the church appears marginalized, unwilling to get involved in the messy, sometimes evil, world of business, politics and power. But Christ claims that world too as his own, and he is able, through lives surrendered to his lordship, to bring the salt and light of his kingdom to the arenas of public life.

[131] M. Luther, cited in J. Atkinson, *Martin Luther and the Birth of Protestantism* (Marshall, 1968), p. 159.

It was written in *Hebrew*, the language of religion. Religion is once again a relatively respectable component in the popular quest for meaning. But the world of religion is today a chaotic pantheon of spiritual ideas, of gurus, mediums, shamans, and mythologies. Christ claims this world as his own. He alone is the truth; he calls us to acknowledge him and then to seek in his name to summon the lost millions who follow the empty gods of other religious visions to bow the knee before this king who is 'exalted' on a cross.

Jesus still seeks today the realization of his claim, 'I, when I am lifted up from the earth, will draw all men to myself' (12:30).

(iii)   He is a personal king (19:25–27)

The great problem with the human saviours who, over the centuries, have dreamed their great dreams and flung their empires around the world, is that in the process they lose sight of the individual. Our little personal universe of hope and pain, struggle and achievement, pales into insignificance beside the great all-inclusive plan; the individual becomes expendable. But this king who reigns from a cross on Golgotha is different. Here is a king whose embrace is as wide as the world, the one to whom 'all authority in heaven and on earth has been given' (Mt. 28:18) and yet who can simultaneously embrace each of us in a personal, loving commitment which is the dance of our hearts. It is perfectly illustrated in this paragraph, for, as Jesus hangs there with the burden of a world's redemption upon his shoulders, he finds time to express his personal loving concern for his mother and one of his special friends.

> Lord of the brooding blue
> Of pleasant summer skies,
> Lord of each little bird that through
> The clear air flies,
> *'Tis wonderful to me*
> *That I am loved by Thee.*
>
> Lord of the blinding heat,
> Of mighty wind and rain,
> The city's crowded street,
> Desert and peopled plain,
> *'Tis wonderful to me*
> *That I am loved by Thee.*
>
> Lord of night's jewelled roof,
> Day's various tapestry,
> Lord of the warp and woof
> Of all that yet shall be,

'Tis wonderful to me
That I am loved by Thee.

Lord of my merry cheers,
My grey that turns to gold,
And my most private tears
And comforts mainfold,
'Tis wonderful to me
That I am loved by Thee.

Amy Carmichael

So we come at last to the supreme moment of all history, the death of Jesus.

John gives his presentation a context: Jesus, *knowing* . . . (28). Amid the unimaginable horror of the physical and mental torture, Jesus retains control; he is conscious that this agony is fulfilling the Father's plan and bringing it to triumphant conclusion. The Greek for *completed* is the identical verb rendered *finished* in verse 30.

He speaks a further time: *I am thirsty*; at the natural level a wholly comprehensible cry in view of the dehydration which was a prominent feature in the torture of crucifixion. But John sees deeper than the natural. Jesus here fulfils the Scripture, and, John implies, to some degree deliberately. Already so many details of the Old Testament depictions of the divine sufferer have been fulfilled; Jesus seeks one more, that in Psalm 69:3, 21, 'my throat is parched . . . and gave me vinegar for my thirst' (*cf.* also Ps. 22:12–18). So the one who offered living water, which would mean never thirsting again, the one who cried on the last day of the feast, 'If anyone is thirsty, let him come to me and drink', *he* now cries, *I am thirsty*. The soldiers respond with a momentary show of pity, and Jesus is offered a sponge on a hyssop branch, soaked in the cheap vinegar wine the soldiers had brought along to refresh themselves through their vigil.

While the other evangelists detail further words of Jesus in these final moments as he travels ever further into the valley of the shadow (*cf.* Mk. 14:33–37; Lk. 23:46), John relates a final, triumphant cry which gathers up Jesus' entire ministry: 'It is accomplished!' (*finished* is a rather weak rendering which misses the thrust of John's presentation). The Greek word is that used in 17:4. The task is therefore now complete; Jesus has been 'obedient unto death'; the Father has been glorified. The actual dying is described in terms of the action of Jesus: 'no-one takes it [my life] from me, but I lay it down of my own accord' (10:18). So *he bowed his head and gave up his spirit* (30).

281

Thus Jesus dies: he who was from all eternity, dies; the eternal Word through whom all things were made, including life itself, dies; he who raised the dead, who at the tomb of Lazarus plundered its dread abode, himself dies.

> 'Tis mystery all! The immortal dies:
> Who can explore his strange design?
> *Charles Wesley*

What does it mean for us? All of eternity will be needed to answer that. For Christ's love unto death is the wonder of the ages, the theme of heaven's adoring millions, the supreme mystery committed to the church on earth. We can explore only a little of it in the light of Jesus' triumphant cry, 'It is accomplished!'

What was *finished* at the cross? For Jesus, at least three things.

1. *His response to his Father's will* was completed. Again and again this gospel witnesses Jesus' unparalleled consciousness of oneness with the Father. But alongside that he expresses an unparalleled sense of obligation to the Father. He who can say, 'I and the Father are one', says also, 'My food is to do the will of him who sent me and to finish his work' (4–34). With his death his obedience was completed. His passion to do his Father's will, and thereby to bring glory to him, here reaches its triumphant conclusion as he gives up his life at the Father's command. In doing so he becomes the great model for all who would live the life God purposed for us, a life of complete obedience.

2. *His revealing of the Father's heart* was completed. It is striking in chapter 17 that his recommitment to the finishing of the work his Father had given him (4) is followed immediately by his affirmation, 'I have revealed you to those whom you gave me' (6). This echoes 1:18: 'no-one has ever seen God . . . the One and Only, who is at the Father's side, has made him known.' The work of making the Father known finds its completion in the cross.

There we see, as nowhere else, how *holy* is the heart of God. That God should purpose this terrible deed as the means of dealing with the sin of the world tells us, as nothing else ever could, that these sins matter terribly to God. All our human efforts to please him fall short, all our best moments are vitiated by sin. Jesus' death shows us that in ourselves we are utterly lost. 'He who can be saved only in the person of another is clearly in himself a lost man.'[132] There is nothing in all our human endeavours and in all the human story that God can find fully acceptable or concerning which he can say, 'That has no need of redemption.' We see there how awful, how implacable, is the divine resistance and antipathy

---

[132] K. Barth, *Church Dogmatics* (T. and T. Clark, 1956), IV (1), p. 413.

to sin and evil; we see there how holy God is.

But in that same deed of wonder we see how *loving* God is. That he should 'give his only Son' for us, going to the depths of the hell of Golgotha in order to snatch us back from everlasting shame and judgment, is the supreme wonder of the ages. It is the proof, which nothing else could ever give, of how loving God is. He has indeed 'opened his heart to us' at the cross (Luther). At Calvary we hear not simply 'Behold the man'! and 'Behold your king!' but also 'Behold your God!'

3. *His redeeming of his Father's world* was completed. Not that all the world will respond, but the grace that can save and redeem the whole world was there expressed. John has a particular perspective on Christ's death and how it achieved redemption. It is the category of Passover sacrifice. It is not an accident that 'the hour' of Jesus' death falls during a Passover feast, or more specifically that it is following the Passover meal with the disciples that Jesus went out to arrest, trial, and execution. The Passover ritual, rooted back in the deliverance from Egypt, called for each worshipper to bring a lamb 'without blemish' or broken bones, and present it to the priest to be slain and for its blood to be dashed against the base of the altar. This recalled the slaughter of the Passover lambs in Egypt and the smearing of their blood with the hyssop plant on the lintels of their houses, by which the people's escape from judgment and their liberation from bondage were won. So Jesus comes, as God's own Lamb, without blemish or broken bone (33) in the perfection of his obedience, and there at Calvary, in the presence of the hyssop plant (29), he offers freely the one 'full, perfect and sufficient sacrifice, oblation and satisfaction for the sins of the world'. As he cries, 'It is finished,' and gives himself up for death, the knife falls, and all the sacrifices of the ages are gathered up and rendered obsolete for ever. Because he has died, the Lamb of God who takes away the sin of the world, for all who have come and trusted in the virtue of that sacrifice there is 'no longer any sacrifice for sin' (Heb. 10:18).

The Christian is called to affirm the completeness and sufficiency of that sacrifice by trusting in it constantly and by exhibiting the peace and confidence which are the fruit of such a trust. Our often strained and frenetic forms of Christian life are witness to how much we need to affirm again with Jesus, 'It is accomplished!' *It is finished*!

e. *The burial of Jesus (19:31–42)*

We return to the Jewish leaders; peace of mind still eludes them, and once again it is their religious scruples which are the problem.

283

True, Jesus is dead, but even then he may spoil the performance of their religious duties if he remains on the cross into the Sabbath. It is sobering to remind ourselves again that those chiefly responsible for the death of Jesus were profoundly religious men. As Niebuhr observed, 'religion is not, as is frequently supposed, a fundamentally virtuous human quest for God; it is rather the final battle ground in the struggle between God and human self-esteem.'[133] The Sabbath which would begin on the Friday sundown was a 'special' one, falling as it did during the Passover feast. They accordingly ask Pilate to have the *crurifragium* applied to Jesus and his fellow victims. This consisted in hastening the death of the crucified by smashing their legs with an iron mallet. As a result it was no longer possible to push up with the legs for air, and the victim quickly expired.

The soldiers begin with the two 'robbers' on Jesus' either hand. Finding Jesus already dead, they desist with the hammer, with the result that his bones remain unbroken. Instead, presumably lest there be any lingering uncertainty, in an act of savage violence one of the soldiers launches his spear into Jesus' side. In a world where gratuitous violence is depressingly common we note that Christian faith is no stranger to it.

The result of this spear thrust is surprising; instead of a gush of blood, which would have been expected, there emerges an efflux of *blood and water* (34). This is vouched for as an eye-witness detail (35); the man who was there and saw it with his own eyes stands behind the gospel record. It seems most straightforward to understand this as another oblique reference to the evangelist himself who has already been identified as present at the cross (26).

Medical opinion has long wrestled with this interesting phenomenon. A common view is that the spear penetrated the heart of Jesus, not unlikely if, as other crucifixions appear to indicate, the cross was not particularly high off the ground. This would explain the flow of blood. The clear fluid which John identifies as water is less easy to explain. In cases of heart failure, however, due to traumatic shock, fluid gathers in the pericardial sac, with the result that John witnessed. Certainty here is not attainable, but it is nonetheless a possible indicator that the cause of Jesus' death was mental and spiritual suffering rather than the physical effects of the beating and crucifixion. In this sense Jesus died *because of* the cross, but not *of* the cross.

John, however, has another, clearer, point to make from the flow of water, as we will see in a moment. For John these two actions of the soldiers (negatively, their not applying the *crurifragium* to

[133] R. Niebuhr, *op. cit.*, p. 213.

Jesus, and positively, their thrusting him through with a spear) both impressively fulfil Scripture. The former is probably for John a reaffirmation of Jesus as the Passover Lamb of God, in terms of Exodus 12:46: 'Do not break any of the bones.' Some scholars, however, prefer to see this as a reference to the 'righteous man' in Psalm 34:20: 'Not one of them [his bones] is broken.' The latter action of the soldiers fulfils Zechariah 12:10, a particularly apt passage speaking of the piercing of God's shepherd, producing mourning among the nations: *they will look on the one they have pierced* (37).

At this point a new and important character enters the story, Joseph from Arimathea (38). He is mentioned in all the gospels at this point. A prominent member of the Sanhedrin, he was rich, and (most important) a secret disciple of Jesus. Presumably he was among the leaders who 'believed in him. But because of the Pharisees they would not confess their faith for fear' (12:42). Whatever his former reservations, the crucifixion brings him to new commitment. With considerable daring he goes to Pilate and requests that Jesus' body, now the property of Rome, be released to him for burial. This was contrary to practice. In the case of criminals the remains normally ended up in a special criminals' burial plot outside the city. Pilate is prepared to make exception, a further expression of his truculence towards the chief-priestly clique.

Joseph is joined by Nicodemus, whose credentials have been more clearly established by this point (3:1f.; 7:50f.). One wonders where these two were when the Sanhedrin voted for Jesus' death. It remains possible, since their sympathies with Jesus were probably known, that they were not informed of the hurriedly arranged meeting since only a majority vote was required.

If Joseph supplied the tomb for Jesus, Nicodemus supplies the embalming spices (39). Myrrh and aloes were used for embalming among the Egyptians about this time. It recalls the wise men's gift to the baby Jesus years before (Mt. 2:11); the mixture of spices also echoes Psalm 45:8. The body was wrapped in a number of cloths generously laced with the spices (40). The body was then carried to a nearby garden where there was a convenient tomb. Although it is not stated to be Joseph's own family grave, that appears a highly likely inference. Since he was wealthy, it would have consisted of a cave hewn out of rock, with shelves in the side walls to accommodate the corpses. This one is unused. Jesus' body is laid there, in some haste as the Sabbath will commence with sundown (42). Though John does not make the point, we can add without any sense of inappropriateness that this was to fulfil the scripture, 'He was assigned a grave with the wicked, and with the rich in his death' (Is. 53:9). So concludes John's account of this

285

traumatic day that has changed for ever the history of the world.

In considering the application of this passage we are struck by the contrast between the outward realities and their inner significance. On the surface lies a great contradiction; Jesus dies, and what is more, is laid in a tomb. He therefore belongs unmistakably to the company of the dead. In recording this John no doubt has an eye to the docetists in his day who denied the true humanity of Jesus, and the genuineness of his death. These theological errors arose from their dualistic philosophical world-view, which identified matter with evil and spirit with good. This framework, the assumption of much of the then current philosophy, could not accommodate the idea of incarnation. For God to unite himself with matter was philosophically impossible. That he should actually experience death was simply unthinkable. Accordingly they argued that Jesus did not truly die on the cross, but was still alive when he was taken down from it. The same error was to resurface in Islam centuries later and remains a part of Islamic criticism of Christianity to this day. There is not a single shred of evidence in its support. The records, like John's here, could not be more graphic in their accounts of the reality of Jesus' death, a fact ratified by the Romans (cf. Mk. 15:44) who were rather expert at recognizing the symptoms of death.

Further, a Jesus who, according to this theory had simply swooned from the effects of his wounds and subsequently appeared to his disciples on the Sunday as 'risen', would never have begun to convince them, not simply that he was returned from death, but that in him death itself had been overcome. In other words the theory, apart from its other inadequacies, leaves wholly without explanation the radiant conviction of early Christianity, and the proven willingness of these early disciples, because of their persuasion that Christ had conquered death, to forfeit their lives for his sake. The theory is undermined by all the relevant historical data and it is high time it was exposed for the nonsense it is.

In truth, Jesus died and was laid away in a tomb. The contradiction of his claim to be Son of God was total. He enters into the full reality of death, not merely walking with us right up to the door only to pull back at the final second, leaving us to walk the dark valley on our own. He comes all the way with us right into the grey, after-death world of funeral parlours and the making of arrangements for the disposing of the body, the world of strained faces, hushed voices and tear-stained eyes. He takes his place within the world of the receding past where death's destructive power is so real and irreversible; dead . . . buried . . . gone.

But in the midst of all that, the claim asserts itself; he is the king, even here. *These things happened so that the scripture would be fulfilled* (24, 28, 36), right down to the incidental details of the crucifixion, such as the fact, seemingly wholly accidental, that there was no *crurifragium* performed (*cf.* 36), or the fact, seemingly the arbitrary result of a soldier's spontaneous violence, that his side was pierced by a spear thrust (*cf.* 37). Yet both were known of in advance.

It is worth noting just how far in advance these prophecies we are talking about were uttered. Zechariah's prophetic ministry was around 500 BC. David, the author of the Psalm, lived and reigned around 1000 BC. The exodus was some 1300 years before Christ. Together this amounts to an impressive indicator of the sovereignty of God and his Christ in face of the contradiction represented by Jesus' death and burial.

Another, more incidental, detail is the amount of spices applied to Jesus' body. The weight is recorded by John, and it is significant. Seventy-five pounds (thirty-four kilos) was far more than normally used. The only occasion when such amounts were used was specifically at the burial of kings.

The involvement of Nicodemus and Joseph is another crucial pointer to the continuing rule of Jesus. We noted John's witnessing the efflux of blood and water from Jesus side. In reporting it he comments that he does so *so that you also may believe* (35). What does John have in mind? Why does the flow of water from Jesus' side lead to faith? The answer is to hand in the earlier chapters of the gospel. Water has repeatedly appeared as a symbol of the gift of the Holy Spirit, the new life of the promised kingdom of God brought by the Messiah. So Nicodemus is told in chapter 3 of the birth by water and Spirit, or, as we saw (*cf.* 3:5), water which is the symbol of the Spirit. In the fourth chapter the woman of Samaria is offered 'living water'. The connection is most plainly made in chapter 7 on the final day of the feast of tabernacles, when Jesus invited all to come to him that they might experience from him the rivers of living water: 'by this he meant the Spirit, whom those who believed in him were later to receive. . . . the Spirit had not be given, since Jesus had not yet been glorified' (7:39). 'The water had to be mingled with Jesus' blood before the Spirit could give his testimony.'[134] But now this has happened, and so the Spirit can come. Thus to John's amazement the Spirit is symbolically released from the crucified body of Jesus, indicating that by his death the kingdom has come which all may enter through faith in him. Thus, even though dead, he imparts the Spirit who is the power of his kingly reign.

No clearer witness to his continuing triumph is conceivable. It

[134] R. Brown, 2, p. 950.

is no accident that his death has the effect of moving Joseph and Nicodemus to abandon their secret discipleship as they unite boldly to identify with Jesus and share together in work in his service. In other words, right there at the cross the nucleus of the new community is already forming, and the mission of the church under the leadership of the risen Jesus is already foreshadowed. Thus the flow of blood and water is a further 'sign' for John, anticipating the 'sign' of the community of the risen one among whom he bears his witness and through whom the light of his gospel beams into every generation.

This last point focuses the challenge of the passage. As the death of Jesus drove Nicodemus and Joseph into open identification with him, so he calls his people, on the basis of his death for them, to receive the gift of his powerful Spirit and to be his bold and unashamed witnesses in the world.

C.   The ministry of the risen king
John 20:1 – 21:25

20:1–31

1.   The appearing king

1.   The empty tomb (20:1–9)

Like his fellow evangelists John begins his account of the resurrection with the discovery of the empty tomb. Also in common with them Mary Magdalene features prominently. The Sabbath imposed a limitation on travel and Jesus' bereaved and shattered followers would have spent the day in mourning. Jewish custom dictated a responsibility to mourn at the tomb during the first three days (*cf.* on 11:17) as the soul of the deceased was thought to be still present. Accordingly, the *first day of the week*, Sunday by our reckoning, brings the friends of Jesus to the tomb to fulfil that sacred duty. The other gospels have Mary in the company of other women for this early visit. John certainly does not deny that, indeed there is the hint of others in Mary's statement in verse 2, *we don't know*. John concentrates on Mary.

The visit is made very early indeed; 'before dawn' would set it between 3 and 6 a.m. Archaeological excavation affords us a distinct impression of the kind of tomb used for Jesus. As well as being quarried out of rock, expensive tombs like Joseph's would have been sealed with a disc-like stone which was rolled down a sloping groove across the door. Thus, while relatively easy to close, it would require several strong men to open it.

On arrival, to her astonishment, Mary finds that the stone has been rolled back. Alarmed at the possible implications, she decides to get help. It is a significant indicator of the strength of Peter's personality that she goes to him despite the disgrace of his public denials of Jesus. John ('the disciple Jesus loved') is with Peter, as again in chapter 21. Mary's message indicates her fears that the grave has been plundered, whether by the authorities (perhaps as

289

a further expression of malignity) or by grave robbers. The latter were not unknown, which explains the habit of sealing graves. A decree of the Emperor Claudius has been uncovered at Nazareth, dated some years later, prescribing execution for those removing bodies from graves.

Peter and John, sharing Mary's alarm, head for the tomb at top speed (3–4). John, by all accounts a significantly younger man, wins the race. Their response is in character. John is more restrained and reflective. He contents himself with peering inside and noting the discarded grave wrappings. Peter, coming up behind him, rushes straight inside (6).

The evangelist gives some time to describing the grave clothes; clearly they were important for him (6–7). Indeed John's 'believing' in verse 8 (presumably believing that Jesus was raised from the dead) is related to his 'seeing' the graveclothes. In general the scene is orderly and calm, lacking evidence of the violence and disturbance which intervention by the authorities, or grave robbers, would have involved. More significant is the way the linen cloths are lying. The head turban is *folded up by itself, separate from the linen* (7). The verb for *folded up* can be translated 'twirled'. What John appears to have seen was the clothes which had been wrapped around Jesus' body lying as if still enfolding it, with the spices adhering to them, and the head turban a little distance away. They appear undisturbed, as though Jesus' body had simply passed through them, 'in much the same way that he later appeared in a locked room'.[1] John Stott uses a vivid image to suggest that what they saw was 'like a discarded chrysalis from which the butterfly has emerged'.[2] Unlike Lazarus, who was merely restored to physical life after death and so had to be freed from the grave clothes (11:44), Jesus left them behind him as he moved to a new order of existence.

The evidence of the scene in the grave brings John to faith in Jesus' resurrection (8). That is viewed, however, as inferior to a faith based on the witness of God's Word. *They still did not understand from Scripture that Jesus had to rise from the dead* (9). No doubt John is thinking of passages such as Psalm 16:9–11, as well as the whole Old Testament witness to the triumph of the Messiah and the eternity of his reign.

2. Mary (20:10–18)

The scene then shifts back to Mary, alone by the tomb after the

[1] D. A. Carson, *John*, p. 637.
[2] J. R. W. Stott, *Basic Christianity*, (IVP, ²1971), p. 54.

others have left. She is weeping (11). The loss of the body is the final indignity, the last straw; even her mourning for Jesus is violated. It is not hard to imagine the enormous emotional strain which the last few days had placed on Mary, not least the anguish of having looked on at Calvary. Her tears were more than understandable.

Deciding to look once more into the tomb she sees two angelic figures, *seated where Jesus' body had been, one at the head and the other at the foot* (12) 'The place of Jesus' death was between two thieves, the place of his burial was between two angels.'[3] They ask her about her tears. *Woman, why are you crying?* (13). From the perspective of heaven nothing is more incongruous than tears at the empty tomb of Jesus. If there is one place in space and one moment in time when tears are least appropriate, it is at the empty tomb of Jesus on Easter morning! Mary repeats her concern at the disappearance of *my Lord*. It is significant that the devotion of her heart prevents her referring to a 'body'. He is still 'her Lord'.

Before Mary has time to reflect on the significance of these heavenly visitors she becomes aware of another presence behind her. A man is standing (14). It is Jesus, but unrecognized. Mary would hardly have expected to see Jesus alive at that moment, but her initial failure to identify him accords with the records of the resurrection appearances generally (*cf.* 21:4; Lk. 24:16). This failure to recognize the risen Jesus immediately is not surprising. Jesus has not just been resuscitated, like Lazarus. He has passed through death and is now part of a new order in the glory of the Father's presence. The form in which he appeared among the disciples was 'no more necessarily connected with his glorified person than the robes which he wore'.[4] Accordingly, his appearing 'different' in some indefinable sense is entirely as might have been expected.

Mary, at any rate, does not recognize him, but, perhaps sensing an authority in his demeanor, she takes him to be the person responsible for the garden within which the tomb is set. Again there is a question concerning her distress. *Woman, . . . why are you crying?* (15). 'She is not yet conscious of the unsuitability of her tears.'[5] Jesus adds a further question: *Who is it you are looking for?* There is perhaps an implied challenge in his words. Mary's problem, in common with all the disciples, was that she did not hold a large enough view of Jesus; she is searching for a corpse

---

[3] W. Temple, p. 361.
[4] E. F. Westcott, *The Gospel of the Resurrection* (Macmillan, 1906), p. 95.
[5] E. C. Hoskyns, p. 542.

instead of seeking a victorious Lord; though it is fair to ask, would
we have acted differently?

Still under the assumption that he is the gardener, Mary asks if
he is responsible for the disappearance of Jesus from the tomb (15).
In the profoundest sense he certainly was! Mary's promise to *get*
the body from wherever the gardener may have taken it (though
Mary refers to *him*) may simply imply the language of devotion,
or that 'she was a woman of some wealth and standing'.[6]

Then comes the moment of recognition, and it is beautifully told.
Jesus said to her, 'Mary' (16). One word which remade her world
and transformed her life for ever after, and the word was her own
name! This is a memorable confirmation of the personal nature of
our Lord's dealings with his people. Mary responds in ecstatic joy,
Rabboni! ('My own dear teacher!'). 'The Good Shepherd calls his
own sheep by name and they recognise his voice.'[7] Well may Dodd
comment on the scene: 'There is something indefinably first-hand
about it ... there is nothing quite like it in the gospels. Is there
anything quite like it in all of ancient literature?'[8] Falling before
Jesus, Mary clasps his feet in a rapture of delirious happiness and
awe. Jesus gently, but firmly, disengages himself. *Do not hold on
to me* (better than the AV 'Touch me not'), *for I have not yet
returned to the Father* (17).

There are two ways these words can be interpreted. Either Jesus
is saying, 'The time of my final return to the Father (after which
you will not see me again) has not yet come; this will not be my
only appearance to you and the others, so you don't need to cling
on to me as though you will never see me again.' Alternatively,
Jesus is trying to help Mary understand that from now on, although
the resurrection appearances are a special exception, Jesus is not to
be known by means of touch, as had been the case. The resurrection, and the ascension which is its inner meaning, imply a new
kind of relationship with Jesus, to be shared with all disciples in
every age and place, that of faith-union through the Holy Spirit
sent by the ascending Lord (*cf.* 14:18–26).

Mary is further commissioned to take the glad news of his rising
to the other disciples (17). *Instead* may imply a concern that she
should not go on and on clinging to Jesus and enjoying the blessing
of it when there was a group of broken men and women no great
distance away who had as much need and right as she to know of
his rising. If that is implicit, the application to the church is a direct
one. Tragically, over the centuries the Christian community has

---

[6] D. A. Carson, *John*, p. 641.   [7] C. K. Barrett, p. 564.

[8] C. H. Dodd, *The Historical Tradition in the Fourth Gospel* (Cambridge, 1965), p. 148.

shown a far greater interest in sitting at Jesus' feet, holding on to him amid the comfort of his presence, than in going out into the world to share the good news of the risen Lord with broken, needy hearts who have as valid a claim to know of him as we.

The terms of the message to the disciples are arresting (17). It is a word of victory. Jesus has conquered death. The king lives and continues in his reign. The initiative has been wrenched from the hands of Caiaphas and Pilate. Ascension, the assumption of authority at the Father's right hand, is now his. Let them rejoice!

It is also a message concerning amazing privilege: *my Father and your Father, ... to my God and your God* (17). Whereas Jesus' relationship to the Father had been a 'holy ground' that the disciples might not tread upon or even approach, his death and rising, which ascension will ratify, open a new relationship with the Holy One. He is now also *their* 'holy Father' (*cf.* 17:11). Although the relationship between Jesus and the Father would remain for ever unique, in a new sense that special communion between the living God and a man in the flesh, previously the sole preserve of Jesus, is thrown open also to them.

Like a good missionary, Mary acts on the Lord's command and tells the good news to the disciples – a message illuminated by her own radiant testimony, *I have seen the Lord!* (18).

Three comments appear in order concerning John's presentation of the resurrection.

1. The resurrection is *historical*. John shares the event in precisely the same terms as his earlier descriptions of the ministry of Jesus. In chapter 19 we have 'carrying ... drinking ... breaking ... wrapping'; in chapter 20 we have 'running ... speaking ... weeping ... embracing'. Familiar characters reappear, such as John, Peter and Mary Magdalene. The crucifixion takes place on 'the day of Preparation' (19:14); the resurrection is set *on the first day of the week* (20:1). The resurrection emphatically is *not* another example of the religious 'myth', a genre which consists essentially in offering 'clues to the potentialities of human life.'[9] Rather was it, John tells us, a happening in space and time; the space was the tomb of Joseph of Arimathea, the time was 'the first day of the week' following passover in the year AD 33.

> Make no mistake: if He rose at all
> it was as His body;
> if the cells' dissolution did not reverse, the molecules
> reknit, the amino acids rekindle,
> the Church will fall.

[9] Joseph Campbell, *The Power of Myth* (Doubleday, 1988), p. 5.

Let us not mock God with metaphor,
analogy, sidestepping, transcendence;
making of the event a parable, a sign painted in the
  faded credulity of earlier ages:
let us walk through the door.

The stone is rolled back, not papier-mâché,
not a stone in a story,
but the vast rock of materiality that in the slow
  grinding of time will eclipse for each of us
the wide light of day.

John Updike[10]

There are in addition numerous incidental historical pointers. The fact that the women were the first to discover the empty tomb is certainly authentic, as this alone would have discredited the story with the Jewish public (in Jesus' society, sadly, women were not even thought fit witnesses in court).

Another historical pointer is the reference to the race to the tomb, a feature which contributes nothing to the main storyline but is simply there for the most obvious reason – it happened. In addition, we have already noted Dodd's comment on the appearance to Mary. It really does bear all the marks of authenticity.

Besides that, the larger realities stand out clear. The tomb was empty. Today this is widely conceded. The subsequent highly successful witness by the apostles to the truth of the resurrection simply would not have been possible had Jesus' body remained in the grave. 'Without having a reliable testimony to the emptiness of Jesus' tomb the early Christian community could not have survived in Jerusalem.'[11]

But if the tomb was empty, how is that fact to be accounted for? The claim that the disciples were responsible for the removal of the body, as well as being in clear contradiction to the records, is simply impossible to believe in the light of their subsequent behaviour, the radiance and sincerity of their faith, and the impressive fact that to a man they suffered excruciatingly for their claims about Jesus. The alternative explanation, that the authorities were responsible, runs aground on the fact that during the subsequent embarrassingly successful apostolic mission, the Jewish leaders would have given anything to have been able to produce the evidence that Jesus was dead and gone. Their silence is eloquent; they did not produce the evidence because it was not available to them.

[10] From 'Seven Stanzas at Easter'.
[11] W. Pannenberg, 'Did Jesus really rise from the dead?' in *New Testament Issues*, ed. R. Batey (Harper, 1970), p. 113.

Thus since alternative explanations of the empty tomb are inadequate we are brought back to the one which the available sources unanimously affirm: 'On the third day he rose again from the dead.'

Further, there is the fact of the appearance of Jesus to Mary and later to all the apostles. These experiences simply refuse to be expunged from the records. 'It is virtually impossible to dispute that at the historical roots of Christianity lie experiences of the first Christians who understood them as appearances of Jesus, raised by God from the dead.'[12] If hallucination will not fit the evidence, and it will not,[13] we are brought once more to the same historical conclusion.

Furthermore, there is the fact of the preservation of these accounts. Their existence two thousand years after these happenings is due to the church, which emerged like a phoenix from the ashes of his shattering death to become a living, world-wide community whose expanding mission led John to write his gospel, and whose vitality of faith has preserved his record to the present day to be read, studied, and treasured by countless millions in every corner of the globe. 'The existence of the Church; the existence of the New Testament: these incomparable phenomena are left without adequate or convincing explanation if the resurrection of Jesus be denied.'[14]

In a sense we are in a position not altogether dissimilar to John's as he stood in the empty tomb and saw the grave-clothes. We, like John, without the benefit of a visual meeting with the risen Jesus, may nonetheless be assured that Jesus was truly raised, on the basis of the available historical evidence. *He saw* the tomb and the grave clothes *and believed* (8); and so may we! Faith based upon historical probabilities, rather like the faith based on miracles met earlier in the gospel (*cf.* 4:48f.), needs to grow beyond that to a full commitment related to all of God's revelation in his Word and Son, as John himself concedes (9). But, like a miracle, it can be a starting point.

2. The resurrection is *personal* in its implication. The thrust of John's presentation of Easter is the life-transforming appearance of Jesus to Mary beside the tomb. As in the case of Mary, Christ's rising is intended to generate a personal discovery of Jesus which will produce a like transformation of life.

Mary was weeping at the time, a burdened woman. This was primarily due to being bereaved of one she loved dearly. She may

[12] J. D. G. Dunn, *The Evidence for Jesus* (Westminster, 1985), pp. 66f.

[13] W. Craig, *The Son Rises* (Moody, 1981), ch. 4, especially. pp. 119ff.; J. P. Moreland, *Scaling the Secular City* (Baker, 1987), pp. 176f.

[14] James Denney, *Jesus and the Gospel* (Hodder, 1909), p. 112.

also conceivably have harboured a lingering sense of betrayal. Somehow the hopes which Jesus had built within her had not been realized. In addition we can also probably identify a strand of fear. Luke 8:2 reports that Mary was a woman 'from whom seven demons had come out'. With Jesus gone, what assurance was there of her being able to keep these devils at bay in the future?

But Christ was there for her, and his coming was the banishing of her sadness, betrayal and fear. The whole point of the resurrection at this level is that we can meet Jesus today – true, not precisely in Mary's tangible terms, but through the Spirit and by faith. And the encounter can be no less life-changing. Triumphant over death, he is alive for ever and hence our contemporary. He still comes to transform broken, sorrowing and fearful lives with the sheer uninhibited gladness of discovering him, alive and with us.

> Now is the shining fabric of our day
> Torn open, flung apart, rent wide by love.
> Never again the tight, enclosing sky,
> The blue bowl or the star-illumined tent.
> We are laid open to infinity
> For Easter love has burst His tomb and ours.
> Now nothing shelters us from God's desire –
> Not flesh, not sky, not stars, not even sin.
> Now glory waits so He can enter in.
> Now does the dance begin.
>
> *Elizabeth Rooney*[15]

3. The resurrection is *universal*. The account ends with Mary sent to share the good news with others. Here John anticipates the missionary commission of the risen Lord and this inescapable implication of Easter faith in every generation. For '*I have seen the Lord!*' must lead to 'Go and make disciples of all nations' (Mt. 28:19). The resurrection is the vindication of the life and death of Jesus as the one in whom God, in person, entered our world that salvation might be won for every tribe and people and nation. Easter is gospel, and it belongs to the world!

3. The apostles (20:19–23)

The resurrection has personal implications, but that does not exhaust its significance. Jesus' vision is not of a multitude of inspired individuals each acting independently out of his or her personal encounter with the risen One. The fruit of his exaltation

---

[15] 'Opening', from *A Widening Light: Poems of the Incarnation*, edited by Luci Shaw (Harold Shaw, 1984), p. 117.

is a community, bound together by their common participation in the Spirit, sent forth to gather his 'other sheep' from every corner of the world. Accordingly, in the final two chapters of the gospel, which are concerned with expounding the post-resurrection ministry of Jesus, the appearances which have individual significance (to Mary, 20:10–18; Thomas, 20:24–29; and Peter, 21:15–17) are balanced by those which have reference to the wider mission of the community.[16] An encounter with the living Christ is where faith is born; the church of the living Christ is where faith grows and matures. A mature Christian experience will develop from loving Christ in and of himself in an immediate one-to-one relationship, to loving him (no less personally or deeply) in the fellowship of his own.

The setting is Jerusalem on the evening of Easter day in a room which may well have been where the last supper was held just three days before (*cf*. Acts 1:13; 12:12). While John may have 'believed' (8), and Mary may have testified to her meeting with the risen Jesus (18), the reality of the resurrection has still to emerge among the disciple group with any degree of conviction; hence the locked doors and the continuing fear for their skins (19). Suddenly the Easter glory breaks upon them – Jesus is there visibly in their midst!

He stills their inevitable anxiety and confusion with a familiar word of greeting, 'Shalom', *Peace be with you!* (19). *Shalom*, the familiar Hebrew greeting, is a considerably richer notion than mere absence of stress, which tends to be our understanding of 'peace' today. In its Old Testament context, *shalom* basically means 'well-being' in its fullest sense. It gathers up all the blessings of the kingdom of God; *shalom* is life at its best under the gracious hand of God. Jesus' use of it on that Easter evening therefore represented the first truly authentic bestowal of *shalom* in the history of the world! Precisely because he has brought the kingdom of God into realization by his death and rising, now and only now is *shalom* a realizable blessing. 'Thus his "Shalom!" on Easter evening is the complement of his "It is finished!" on the cross, for the peace of reconciliation and life from God is now imparted. "Shalom!" accordingly is supremely the Easter greeting. Not surprisingly it is included, along with "grace", in the greeting of every epistle of Paul in the NT.'[17]

Jesus further reassures the disciples that it is truly himself they are encountering, no ghost or phantom: *he showed them his hands and side*. How important for our needy, hurting generation, that Jesus is recognized by his scars! The effect is predictable, but no

---

[16] 20:19–23; 21:1–14, 18–25.   [17] G. R. Beasley-Murray, p. 379.

less moving: *The disciples were overjoyed when they saw the Lord* (20). 'Joy is the basic mood of Easter.'[18]

Jesus, however, has come not merely to assure them of his conquest of death and the triumph of his kingdom. He has come also to instruct and prepare them for what lies ahead. The mission about which he had taught them in the upper room is now imminent and he sets them apart for it in a solemn moment of commissioning. *As the Father has sent me, I am sending you* (21). Echoing words uttered in his prayer before his passion (17:18), it is the form in which the 'Great Commission' appears in this gospel.

Several of the fundamentals of the church's mission in every generation are expressed here.

1. The *importance of mission*. The key to the statement is the parallel it draws between the sending of Jesus into the world by the Father and the sending of the apostolic community into the world by the risen Son. If the parallel holds good, then mission must have the same importance for the community as it had for Jesus. In the latter case, as we have seen, the significance could not be greater. In the Gospel of John, Jesus defines himself as the 'sent one';[19] and correspondingly the Father is defined as 'the Sender'.[20] Thus the Godhead is defined in terms of mission. Mission reaches back into the eternal relations of the Trinity in the dynamic interrelationship of Sender and Sent.

The challenge is evident. As Jesus is defined by the mission of the Father, so the church is defined by its mission to the world.

The same conclusion is arrived at by another route when we recognize that if God is in this sense a missionary God, the summons to be like him assumes a precise focus. The degree to which individuals and churches are committed to mission, both locally and throughout the world, will be a measure of how God-like (or how godly) they are.

2. This commission of Jesus helps us understand *the character of mission*. The tenses of the two verbs in the sentence are different. The second verb is present: *I am sending you*; but the first is a perfect, which implies a past action continuing in the present: *the Father has sent me*. What Jesus has in mind therefore is not a double mission, first Jesus' mission and then afterwards our mission. Rather it is one single action, the great movement of the missionary heart of God sending forth his Son into the world,

---

[18] J. Blank, *Krisis* (Freiburg: Lambertus, 1964), p. 178; cited in G. R. Beasley-Murray, p. 379.

[19] 5:36; 7:29; 8:42; 10:36; 13:20; 20:21.

[20] 3:17; 4:34; 5:23; 6:44; 7:18; 8:29; 10:42; 12:44f.; 13:16; 14:24; 15:21; 17:8.

initially through the incarnation, subsequently through his church. The one mission of God has two phases: the first, that of the Son in his incarnate life; the second, that of the Son in his risen life through his people.[21] 'The apostles were commissioned to carry on Christ's work, and not to begin a new one.'[22] He is in our midst as we go forth for him to the world!

This understanding of the missionary task carries implications. It touches the issue of *authority* in our service. Because Jesus' mission continues through ours, our mission partakes of his divine authority. We can compare the classical form of the commission: 'all authority . . . has been given to me. Therefore go . . . and I am with you' (Mt. 28:18–20). The presence of the exalted Lord is the authorization of our mission. This is what 'apostle' means – one whom Jesus sends and accompanies. In this sense the church in every age is an apostolic community and every Christian witness, sent and authorized by the risen and reigning one, belongs to the apostolate of the Lord. Behind this Christian reality lies a Jewish model, the *šālîah* or messenger. In Hebrew culture the *šālîah* embodied the dignity and authority of the one in whose name he had come: 'one who is sent is as the one who sends him.'[23] To slight a *šālîah* was therefore to slight his master; correspondingly, to respect the *šālîah* by obeying the message he brought was to respect his master. As the 'sent ones' of Jesus we speak with his authority.

In practice, the exercise of that authority is bound up with our mirroring the mission of Jesus at another point, *viz.* obedience. Jesus exercised the authority of his Father because he was utterly obedient to the will of his Father (*cf.* comment on 8:12f.). 'The transaction [of the *šālîah*] could not be properly concluded without a resolute subordination of the will of the representative to that of the one who commissioned him.'[24] Our wielding his authority is related to our accepting a similar subordination. Here is the paradox of Christian ministry: we find freedom insofar as we permit his enslavement of us; we bring life to others to the degree to which we give up our own; we have authority and power in the measure to which we are willing to become helpless. Positively, however, this opens up unimaginable possibilities, as verse 23 indicates.

This statement, about loosing and retaining sins, has been appealed to in terms of the authorization of a magisterial office in the church with the direct authority to forgive or retain sins. That implication appears unjustified when the context is taken seriously. The 'loosing' and 'binding' are the effect of the preaching of the

[21] *Cf.* Acts 1:1; Rom. 15:8; and Mt. 28:20.   [22] E. F. Westcott, p. 294.
[23] *TDNT*, I, art. *apostolos*, p. 415.   [24] *TDNT*, I, pp. 413ff.

gospel in the world, when we go forth in the name and with the authority of the risen Lord. As when he was on earth, so now, the coming of the light of God's Word draws some to the light for salvation and confirms some in the darkness for damnation (3:19–21; 9:39). 'There is no doubt from the context that the reference is to forgiving sins, or withholding forgiveness. But though this sounds stern and harsh, *it is simply the result of the preaching of the gospel*, which either brings people to repent as they hear of the ready and costly forgiveness of God, or leaves them unresponsive to the offer of forgiveness which is the gospel, and so they are left in their sins.'[25]

3. One other aspect of the character of mission is to the point; the *cost of it*. For the risen one who sends us is identified not by his kingly glory, but by the marks of his cross and passion (20). To be sent by such a Master in his mission must have had the most sobering effect on the apostles. *As the Father has sent me* had meant for Jesus costly self-sacrifice to the point of the hell of Calvary; it could not henceforth mean less in principle for them. 'Whoever serves me must follow me' (12:26).

4. Finally, lest these terms of the mission be thought too overwhelming, Jesus also points to *the resources of mission*. The first has already been stressed; Jesus himself. He will continue to be the leader of the disciple community. As before, so now, they will go out under his leadership and with the inspiration of his living presence. In particular we note, as we did above, the recurrence of this commission formula in the consecration prayer of Jesus (17:18). Here is our all-embracing and all-sufficient resource, that our mission is undergirded by the praying presence of Jesus!

The other major resource is shared in verse 22: *With that he breathed on them and said, 'Receive the Holy Spirit.'*

Considerable debate has swirled around the interpretation of this statement. In particular, how does it relate to the coming of the Spirit some fifty days later as described in Acts 2? The notion that this is actually John's account of Pentecost, and in his mind replaces the subsequent coming of the Spirit (a view much in favour with critical scholarship), requires a qualifying of John's historical reliability which is unwarranted. Accepting the historicity of both Acts and John, and hence the apparent double gifting of the Spirit, some interpret in terms of a relative difference between the two enduements of the Spirit. Thus Calvin distinguishes between 'sprinkling' with the Spirit (here), and 'saturation' with the Spirit at Pentecost.[26] Westcott sees the power of new life imparted in

[25] J. Marsh, pp. 641f.
[26] J. Calvin, 2, p. 205.

John and the power for ministry in Acts.[27] Bruce inverts Westcott's distinction.[28]

It seems preferable to recognize that the true coming of the outpoured Spirit took place at Pentecost. Apart from other considerations it would appear that it was only after the Acts 2 experience that any marked change came over the behaviour of the apostles and the kingdom's arrival became apparent.

The 'expiration' of the Spirit described here in John can then be viewed as symbolic, and hence essentially didactic. Jesus here is teaching the apostles who the Spirit is. Lest a 'symbolic' interpretation be thought to reduce this incident to an insignificant affair, let it be noted that until they understood who the Spirit was they were in no position to receive his outpouring. The coming of the Spirit at Pentecost was in a deep sense dependent upon this action on the evening of Easter. Who is the Spirit? He is the life-breath of the exalted Jesus! Jesus the risen one breathed on them and said, *Receive the Holy Spirit.* 'The Holy Spirit is Christ himself in the power of his resurrection ... the outstretched arm of the Exalted One.'[29]

This understanding of the relationship between Jesus and the Spirit is precisely the one expressed by Peter at Pentecost. When the bewildered crowds demand to know the meaning of the phenomena, Peter's answer is: 'this Jesus ... Exalted to the right hand of God, he has ... poured out what you now see and hear' (Acts 2:33). No purer expression of this Johannine incident and its meaning is conceivable.

Thus Christianity at its outset was saved from the danger of becoming a religion focused essentially on supernatural phenomena, 'signs and wonders' as such. Instead, from its earliest moments, it was the religion of Jesus of Nazareth, the glorified Servant and Messiah of God, exalted at God's right hand, and hence the ruler of the universe. He manifested his rule when he so willed by 'signs and wonders', but also and more generally, by all the other works of his people in the world. The Spirit is the 'Spirit of Jesus'. Thus the phenomena of Acts are understood, as are the signs in John, as *semeia*, 'signs' of the person and reign of Jesus the exalted Son and Servant, the Word made flesh. The key to that crucial identification is this moment on Easter evening. But if this perspective is valid, what a resource this represents for the apostolic task! Nothing less than the power which brought Jesus through death and resurrection to the right hand of the Father is the power which is made available to the church in its mission (so Paul in Eph. 1:18).

[27] E. F. Westcott, p. 245.   [28] F. F. Bruce, p. 392.
[29] K. Barth, *Church Dogmatics*, IV (2), pp. 322f.

4. Thomas (20:24–31)

The first appearance of the risen Lord in this gospel was to an individual, Mary Magdalene. The second was to a group of disciples. This third appearance combines both. It takes place within a group but with specific focus on an individual, Thomas.

Thomas was not with the others when Jesus appeared (24). That may have been wholly circumstantial, but there is a hint in the story that his absence and his attitude were linked. It is difficult, perhaps unwise, to weave full-blown character types out of the meagre information the gospels give us about the men and women who followed Jesus. Thomas is a case in point. He has appeared twice before in the gospel, first at 11:16 expressing a resigned but impressive loyalty; he is willing to go to Jerusalem and die with Jesus. In 14:5 he is the spokesperson for those who have not grasped even the basic content of Jesus' 'going away to the Father'. Not too much to build upon. Perhaps we can tentatively conjecture a loyal but somewhat unimaginative person who will act only on what he is sure of. No bad quality in itself, but those of this temperament can carry this instinct to its limits and so may miss out on many of the positive and hopeful things in life. If this description fits Thomas with any degree of accuracy then his absence after the cross is perhaps explicable. The death of Jesus was such an overwhelming reality that he must get alone to try and come to terms with it. So when Jesus comes to the disciples on the Easter evening, Thomas is not there.

The exuberant testimony of the others, no doubt in echo of Mary's earlier words, *We have seen the Lord* (*cf.* 18), apparently does nothing to persuade him. He lays down his conditions for believing: *Unless I see the nail marks in his hands . . . and put my hand into his side, I will not believe it.* The negative in the final phrase is emphatic, possibly 'I'll never believe it'.[30] As a result the character of Thomas has been for ever typecast, 'doubting Thomas'.

A week later, on the first commemoration of the resurrection, the disciples are again together with Thomas now present, when suddenly and wonderfully, it happens again; Jesus appears among them (26)! Again the '*Shalom*' is pronounced, appropriately so, as we saw above. Peace in all its dimensions is theirs beyond the experience of any others before them. Jesus then turns to Thomas, *Put your finger here . . . Reach out your hand . . . Stop doubting and believe* (27), or perhaps, 'Stop being unbelieving and show yourself a believer.'[31] These words focus the failure of Thomas. He had received the apostolic witness which is the basis for faith

---

[30] R. Brown, 2, p. 1025.   [31] G. R. Beasley-Murray, p. 385.

(30–31), but had failed to trust it.

Here are two wonders for Thomas. The first is that Jesus is truly raised from the dead and now meets him. But secondly, Thomas' stated conditions for faith are explicitly met in language which proved that Jesus had clearly 'overheard' his earlier stipulations. The 'other world' of the Spirit is not beyond earshot.

Whether Thomas actually acted on Jesus' invitation is not stated. The assumption must be that he did not, and for the best of reasons, he had no need. Besides which the awe he now directs towards the person of Jesus would surely have inhibited so crass an action.

Abasing himself in Jesus' presence he utters his great confession, *My Lord and my God!* (28). 'For him, the doubting one, the final consequence of Jesus' resurrection was laid bare in the encounter with the risen one: Jesus is of divine essence, in him God himself comes to him.'[32] Jesus receives Thomas' worship without demur, in contrast to the reluctance of his later followers when similarly addressed.[33] It is his right.

Thus the gospel comes full circle. John began in his opening words with a confession of the deity of Christ: 'In the beginning was the Word . . . and the Word was God' (*cf.* comments on 1:1). Now that original confession of the Godhead of the pre-incarnate Lord is echoed by a mortal sinner, *My Lord and my God!* In a profound sense this concludes John's account.

Jesus speaks a further word of beatitude: *blessed are those who have not seen and yet have believed* (29). In recording these further words of Jesus, John clearly has an eye for his readers, whether in the first or twentieth century, who 'see him no more', and are assured therefore that their position is not inferior to that of Thomas. Indeed, in Jesus' mind it is in some respects a better position, since to them is extended this special blessedness: 'though you have not seen him, you love him' (1 Pet. 1:8).

John appropriately rounds off this concluding section with a statement of the purpose of his writing (30–31). Chapter 21 was quite possibly composed later, though added to the gospel before it began to be circulated (see comment below, 21:1f.). This is not to imply that the last chapter is less inspired or less authoritative and important. Its special contribution lies in relating the revelation of chapters 1 through 20 to the ongoing life of the church.

In his statement of purpose (30–31) John tells us that in composing his gospel he has selected from the *many other miraculous signs* which Jesus performed *in the presence of his disciples* those that will help his readers *believe that Jesus is the Christ* (Messiah), *the Son of God, and that by believing you may have life in his name*

[32] R. Schnackenburg, 3, p. 333.   [33] Acts 3:12; 10:26; 14:14f.

303

(31). D. A. Carson remarks that 'to expound in detail each word and phrase (of verse 31) would be to expound the book'.[34]

'Believe' has two different, and both well supported, grammatical forms in the manuscripts (*cf.* comments in the Introduction under 'Purpose'). The first alternative is the present subjunctive, with the force 'go on believing', *i.e.* John's purpose in writing is to encourage Christians to hold to and grow in the faith. The second is the aorist subjunctive, carrying the force of 'believe decisively'; John's purpose is to awaken his readers to faith in Jesus. By the former, John's purpose would be a discipling one; by the latter, an evangelistic one. On balance the case for the latter appears stronger. If, however, we affirm an evangelistic purpose as primary (and the impact of this gospel in evangelistic contexts needs no documentation), there appears no reason why John should not also have consciously intended that Christian readers would be taught and encouraged to grow through what the wrote (which has also been signally achieved through the study and exposition of this gospel over the centuries).

We thank God for the witness of John by which we have been entrusted, through the Holy Spirit, with this great gospel, by means of which those in darkness can be brought into the glorious light and liberty of Jesus Christ, and those already walking in the light can have the road of discipleship significantly illuminated to enable them to walk more confidently and fruitfully.

The key theme in this closing section of chapter 20, as in a sense throughout the gospel, is the nature of faith. In particular four aspects of faith are focused.

1. We are taught here about faith's *agony*. The experience of Thomas makes the point that faith is not always, perhaps not even typically, a straightforward affair. 'Lord, I believe; help thou mine unbelief' (Mk. 9:24, AV) is a heart-cry that arises across the ages. As Thomas models it here, faith is a battle with unbelief, at times agonizing.

Several of the common ingredients of doubt are illustrated in Thomas' case. One was *disposition*. Thomas' personality was very likely part of his problem, if our earlier characterization is correct. A gloomy, pessimistic person frequently struggles to make the great positive affirmations at the heart of the faith. Such folks feel that the gospel is almost 'too good to be true'; that somehow the story cannot end happily. A risen Lord is therefore not altogether credible. This attitude is often fed by a scrupulous conscientiousness expressed in the feeling that even if a 'happy ever after' ending may be true for others, *we* don't deserve it, and so it can't be true for us.

---

[34] D. A. Carson, *John*, p. 661.

Another ingredient here was *isolation*. Thomas cut himself off from the disciple community, possibly to try to work through his problems on his own, or perhaps because he no longer felt able to identify with what they represented. For whatever reason, he missed the coming of the Lord and so was penalized for his absence by a week of agonizing struggle. Christ has promised to be with his people when even two or three gather in his name (Mt. 18:20). We are always more likely to find him in the company of the faithful than in a lonely vigil. As Ryle points out, this underlines 'how much Christians may lose by not regularly attending gatherings of God's people . . . The very sermon that we needlessly miss may contain the message our souls need. The very assembly for praise and prayer from which we stayed away may be the very gathering that would have cheered, established, and uplifted our hearts'.[35]

A third ingredient was *contradiction*. The sheer stark reality of the cross overwhelmed Thomas. At this point nothing had comparable significance, whether the exuberant testimony of his fellow disciples, or the clear and repeated teaching of the Scriptures or of Jesus himself. Often the root of doubt lies precisely here. Some specific happening has broken into our world, seeming to contradict all else we have known or previously believed, and as we remember and repeatedly ponder this happening it blots out all other realities, including the Word and promise of God.

It is to the great encouragement of those who experience such agony of faith that Jesus does not dismiss Thomas. Indeed, this further appearance would seem to be essentially for his benefit. Doubt is not sin. Further, Jesus so clearly knows exactly what has been passing through Thomas' mind. He knows our doubts in all their detail and circumstance.

But Thomas does not entirely escape censure. There is at least a mild rebuke in Jesus' words, 'Stop being a doubter and show yourself a believer.' There *were* grounds for faith all around Thomas if he only had eyes for them. Jesus calls us to battle through our doubts to a renewed confidence in him. As a supreme incentive to that it is Thomas, the man who struggled to believe, who is enabled to utter the sublime confession which is the copestone of this gospel, *My Lord and my God!*

2. This incident illustrates, secondly, the *assurance* of faith. Thomas came through his doubts into clear and firm conviction. Not only did he participate in the events of the following years in Jerusalem as the church was born and grew[36] but, according to fairly reliable tradition, he also took the gospel eastwards as far as

[35] J. C. Ryle, pp. 380f.   [36] Acts 2:14; 5:12; 6:2f.; 8:1; 15:2f.

India and laid down his life there for Christ. Thomas therefore is not simply the representative of the doubter, but of the doubter become firm believer! The resurrection was what made the difference; it was clearly sufficiently real and verifiable to lay Thomas' doubts to rest. Indeed, apart from it, the subsequent life and career of Thomas are simply inexplicable.

It is of course tempting to urge that it was different for Thomas, since he had the privilege of actually seeing the risen Lord, a difference which Jesus himself acknowledges (29). Without questioning the validity of Jesus' distinction, however, at another level the bases of Thomas' faith remain available to us today. They are twofold.

The first is *eye-witness testimony*. Thomas had been there with Jesus and seen the whole drama unfold before his eyes. But that 'first-hand' engagement with the ministry of Jesus at the historical level is also possible for us. John's whole point in writing his gospel, as he tells us in verses 30–31 (*cf*. 19:35; 21:24), is to provide a record of the signs Jesus performed, including the supreme sign of his death and resurrection, so that we may come to faith. In this John stands with the other evangelists. We are able today, with a degree of conviction at the historical level not available to many of our forefathers, to confirm the fundamental reliability of the New Testament records as the compositions of those who were, as Luke calls them, 'eye-witnesses . . . of the word' (Lk. 1:2).

We *can* take the view, if we choose, that these early writers were deluded; we *can* choose, if we will, to disagree with their interpretation of the events that took place before their eyes (though on both these points there are very cogent arguments in support of their reliability). What we are *not* at liberty to do is to dismiss their accounts as mere myths and legends largely detached from the historical realities lying behind them. The gospels *are* first-century writings composed within a few years of the events described, by people who had been there when it all happened. Let Peter once again take the role of spokesperson for the apostles: 'We did not follow cleverly invented stories when we told you about the power and coming of our Lord Jesus, but we were eye-witnesses . . .' (2 Pet. 1:16). Jesus tells us that he sent the Holy Spirit precisely for the purpose of ensuring that just such a reliable record was written.[37]

The second basis of Thomas' faith was *first-hand experience*. He met Jesus personally. Clearly there is a significant difference between the kind of meeting described in this section and our experience of Christ today, but it is nonetheless the claim of the

[37] 14:26; 16:12f; 1 Cor 12:6–16; Heb. 2:3f

Christian centuries that we *can* still meet Jesus. This is not emotion, but logic, since if he rose, as the evidence overwhelmingly indicates, then he is the conqueror of death and therefore alive continually; and if alive continually, then alive today as our contemporary. It is a plain fact of present history that all round the world millions daily fall at his feet and whisper, *My Lord and my God!* Hence the general bases of Thomas' faith are available to us. We too can experience the assurance of faith.

3. This passage witnesses, thirdly, to the *glory of faith*. We have already noted that Thomas' heartfelt confession, *My Lord and my God!* (28), sets in place the final stone in the great arch of truth which this gospel represents. Here lies faith's special blessedness, that mortal and sinning creatures can glorify the living God by placing their adoring trust in his eternal Son and call him *Lord and God*.

The two terms of the confession are virtually equivalent. *Lord* carried definite overtones of deity for the first-century Jew. It was with this word that the Septuagint commonly rendered the holy name of the creator and covenant partner of Israel. Thus 'Thomas makes clear that one may address Jesus in the same language in which Israel addressed Yahweh . . . Nothing more profound could be said about Jesus.'[38]

It is not beside the point that when John wrote his gospel the province he resided in was a centre for emperor-worship. It is likely that John and his readers were familiar with processions of devotees through the streets of Ephesus chanting their slogan, 'Caesar is Lord, Caesar is God!' Over against that deluded paganism Thomas articulates the cry which arises in the heart of every true Christian, 'Jesus is Lord, Jesus is God!' Such is the glory of faith. And the challenge is ours today to make the same fearless witness in face of the 'lords many and gods many' of our generation. For Caesar-worship is not dead – the false deities are still chanted in our streets, the gods of state and nation, and all the other traditional religions or their amalgam, of New Age and satanism, and selfism in its multiple forms. In face of these false claimants we exalt in our worship the one who alone is worthy, 'our Lord, our God' – Jesus Christ!

That confession is made in the midst of a world that denies Christ's claim. In the light of Jesus' distinction in verse 29, we can dare to assert that there is a special glory brought to the Lord, a special vindication of his name in the heavenly places, when we, amid this broken order and in face of the assaults and contradictions of the world, the flesh and the devil, affirm in faith his utter

[38] R. Brown, 2, pp. 1047f.

trustworthiness and rest our whole selves upon his everlasting grace. It is a ministry of worship which will not be available hereafter when faith has given place to sight. May we experience its blessedness now while we may!

4. Finally, there is here the *invitation* to faith. John's purpose is clear and the challenge is insistent as he reaches his conclusion. In the light of his presentation of Jesus through the gospel, the 'signs' of his life and ministry, his teaching and claims, his death and resurrection, where do we stand? John invites us to respond by 'believing'; that is, by committing ourselves personally to Jesus Christ as our Lord and God, trusting his death as that of God's sacrificial Lamb to atone for our sins, and following him in the way of discipleship as our Way, Truth and Life. The result, John assures us in closing, will be *life in his name*, the eternal life of God's kingdom, which in the end is Jesus Christ himself.

21:1–25

2. The beginning of the mission

1. Fishing with Jesus (21:1–14)

Chapter 20 appears to conclude John's account of Jesus, with the confession of Thomas and the declaration of the evangelist's purpose (20:30–31). Many scholars accordingly see this twenty-first chapter as a kind of addendum composed at a later point, possibly even by another hand. It needs to be said, however, that the manuscript evidence uniformly supports the unity of the twenty-one chapters. If this chapter *was* added later, it was soon enough afterwards to preclude the publication of the gospel without it. Besides, the content of chapter 21, as we will see in a moment, is perfectly congruent with the earlier chapters and represents a fitting epilogue to all that has been described in chapters 1–20.

For one thing, this chapter serves the important task of recounting the rehabilitation of Peter. It also supplies important information about Peter's later ministry and that of John, especially valuable if Peter had died by the time the gospel began to circulate. It also develops Jesus' teaching about the disciples' mission, a basic theme of the closing chapters. In this connection Hoskyns helpfully comments that 'a Christian gospel ends properly, not with the appearance of the Risen Lord to his disciples, and their belief in him, but with a confident statement that his mission to the world, undertaken at his command and under his authority, will be the means by which many are saved.'[1]

The setting of this further appearance is the *Sea of Tiberias*, better known as the Sea of Galilee. This location has led to the disciples coming under suspicion. Why were they back here in their old haunts, and about their old business, when Jesus had died and risen and had sent them on their new task, 'beginning in Jerusalem'? Accordingly this whole expedition is commonly interpreted as

[1] E. C. Hoskyns, p. 656.

expressing the disciples' disobedience and apostasy. As G. R. Beasley-Murray trenchantly observes, 'Never has a fishing trip been so severely judged!'[2]

In defence of the disciples, however, it needs to be noted that the synoptic writers record a message from Jesus telling the apostles to return to Galilee 'where you will see me' (Mt. 28:7; Mk. 16:7). It has also to be said that in terms of their psychological and emotional well-being a fishing expedition back in the old familiar surroundings of the Sea of Galilee was therapeutically ideal. The last few days had been an emotional roller-coaster. In a matter of a week they had been lifted up to the giddy heights of Palm Sunday, sent spiralling down into the utter depths of despair on Good Friday, and then been swept up again to the heavens by the glory of the resurrection. A good night's fishing was probably just what a doctor would have ordered. Besides, 'Even though Jesus be crucified and risen from the dead, the disciples must still eat!'[3]

Seven disciples are involved (2), notably all from the Galilee region, unless we except the two *other disciples*; but they could well have been Andrew and Philip, in which case the group comprised 'the Galilee Seven' within the apostolic twelve. It is noteworthy that Thomas is no longer inclined to forsake the fellowship of the others – wisely, as events proved.

Peter is as ever the initiator (3). Night was a favoured time for fishing the Sea of Galilee, but the trip proved fruitless. As they return to shore in the dim early morning light a stranger hails them from the shore (4f.). It is Jesus, but again he is not recognized (*cf.* comment on 20:15). His challenge is colloquial; we could render it, 'Hey, lads . . . haven't caught any fish, have you? . . . Try there on the right side of you and you'll catch some!' (5–6).

Experienced fishermen are not noted for their ready appreciation of the advice of strangers, particularly one still on land, but there is something about Jesus' tone which inspires confidence. They do as he bids them, and at once make an astonishing haul (6).

Peter and John react rather as they did in the previous chapter to the news of the emptiness of Jesus' tomb. For John there is a moment of revelation: *It is the Lord!* (*cf.* 'he saw and believed', 20:8). For Peter there is a summons to action: *As soon as he heard him say 'It is the Lord,' he wrapped his outer garment around him . . . and jumped into the water* (7). (*Cf.* 'then Simon Peter, . . . arrived and went [straight] into the tomb', 20:6.) Peter's girding himself probably implies that he was lightly clad for his work and simply tucked the garment up around him so as not to impede his swim ashore. There may also be just a hint of the proprieties of

[2] G. R. Beasley-Murray, p. 399.   [3] *Ibid.*

worship which both Old and New Testaments mention (Ex. 20:26; 1 Cor. 11:2f.). Peter is about to meet his 'Lord and God'; he will be suitably clad.

Coming ashore they discover that Jesus has provided for them. A cooked breakfast awaits them on the beach; exactly right after a long, fruitless night on the Sea (9). Graciously Jesus invites them to contribute from 'their' catch (10) which they have struggled to land and bring ashore, with notable assistance in the final stage from Peter (11). The catch is counted (how could fishermen have resisted the temptation! 153 whoppers!) and the net has been able to hold them all.

Jesus invites them to breakfast as a sense of holy wonder falls upon them. 'In awestruck silence they eat. They dare not ask, "who are you?" for the answer could only be "I AM". So they eat what the Lord gives them and the sharing of the meal is the unveiling of his presence.'[4]

The account of this *third time Jesus appeared to the disciples after he was raised from the dead* (14) is replete with symbolic inference. Jesus himself earlier declared fishing to be a basic symbol for his service (*cf.* Mk. 1:16–17, 'Come, follow me, . . . and I will make you fishers of men'; Lk. 5:10, 'Don't be afraid; from now on you will catch men'). The reference in Luke 5 is particularly notable since it follows a miraculous catch of fish, again at Jesus' instigation (Lk. 5:1–11), following which 'they . . . left everything and followed him' (Lk. 5:11).

Due to the obvious points of similarity between the two miracles, some scholars have seen a single incident underlying the two accounts and suggest that John has simply reworked an earlier story to serve his purpose of anticipating the post-resurrection mission of the disciples.

Apart from the basic questions this would raise about John's historical reliability, the differences between the two stories are considerable.[5] The earlier incident, however, *is* important background for interpreting and applying the present passage, for it makes clear that in the minds of Jesus and the disciples, 'fishing' was a symbol for their mission. With Jesus now raised from the dead and his ascension impending (20:17), the hour of that mission is at hand (17:18; 20:21). This incident therefore becomes a parable of their impending work, and ours. Actually, the very geographical setting would in itself have stirred the memories of that initial calling, for the miracle is set possibly on the very stretch of shore

---

[4] L. Newbigin, p. 277.
[5] D. A. Carson, *John*, pp. 670f; also I. H. Marshall, *The Gospel of Luke* (Paternoster, 1978), pp. 199f.

beside which Jesus had walked when first they fell under his spell.

Two features are worthy of note.

1. First, Jesus illustrates *the secret of effective mission*. There is a stark contrast between the results when the disciples went out on their own initiative, and *caught nothing* (3), and when they fished at the direction of Jesus and the boat was *full of large fish* (11); 'apart from me you can do nothing' (15:5).

This story has much to say to current practice in evangelism. The church in the western world has never had such an array of helps, resources and methodologies as at present. The psychological and sociological sciences, as well as the fruits of the technological and communications revolution, have been plundered for secrets of successful mission. Sadly, although much time and money are often spent acquiring these tools or attending the inevitable conferences and seminars where they are unveiled, the long-term results are commonly meagre. One recent responsible survey of the evangelical churches in a major Canadian city showed that, after the dust has settled on the often frenetic struggle to employ 'successful' strategies of evangelism, these congregations reach on average only 1.9 genuine outsiders for Christ per year![6]

Interestingly, by contrast, the churches of the Third World are, by and large, uninformed concerning these new discoveries and 'success' methodologies. In their poverty and weakness they have to rely on prayer for the power of God and the simple direct sharing of the gospel. The results are often remarkable. Christianity in some Third World areas appears to be growing almost out of control. Obviously there are massive generalizations involved in these observations (though they are made from first-hand experience on several continents). The trouble with the 'know-how' of the western churches is not the knowledge in itself, in most cases, but the insidious temptation *to trust in it*. It is there that the breakdown occurs, and where this story speaks so relevantly. There was nothing wrong with the disciples' fishing 'know-how'; it simply did not bring them any fish when they relied upon it. When they followed Jesus and relied on him, to some extent in defiance of the instincts of their experience, the harvest was overwhelming.

In this context prayer is a reliable barometer. The level of our prayer ministry will be the level of our dependence on the Lord. Not surprisingly, prayer is generally at a low ebb in many North American, and western churches, whereas it is the very life-breath of many churches in the underdeveloped world. 'This kind is not cast out except by prayer'; the secret of effective mission lies on the other side of a discovery of our own utter impotence to produce

---

[6] R. W. Bibby, *Fragmented Gods* (Irwin, 1987), pp. 29f.

'fruit that will remain' no matter how learned or technically equipped we are. What we can do without Jesus is not 'a little'; we can do *nothing* (3; *cf.* 15:5). It is by dying to our reliance on ourselves and our abilities that we discover resurrection life and the harvest of the kingdom.

2. This passage also speaks concerning *the scope of mission* work. The catch was an astonishing one, far beyond any expectations that the disciples might have had. The impressiveness of the catch is clearly stressed in the story: *they were unable to haul the net in because of the large number of fish* (6); the net was *full of fish* (8); *It was full of large fish, 153, but even with so many the net was not torn* (11).

The disciples' missionary expectation, now that Jesus was demonstrated to be the promised Messiah of Israel, was still centred in Israel. Acts 1:6 gives a pertinent indication of their mind-set: 'Lord, are you at this time going to restore the kingdom to Israel' (Acts 1:6). Jesus may be hailed as the Saviour of the world in Samaria (4:42), and have 'other sheep' among the nations (10:16), but the disciples retain an Israel-centred vision. It may indeed have been part of Jesus' purpose in directing them away from Jerusalem to Galilee to try and open them to the larger dimensions of his mission, for Jerusalem with all its profound nationalistic associations was less fertile ground for such thinking than Galilee with its window to the larger world to the north, west and east.

The scope of the mission may perhaps also be indicated by the number of the fish caught, though this is disputed. John may simply tell us the number of fish because to a fisherman the size of the catch was important; a not unimpressive eye-witness detail. The most celebrated attempt to interpret the 153 symbolically was by Jerome, who cited authorities to the effect that there are 153 species of fish in the sea. Hence the catch is representative of the mission to all the nations. Difficulties have emerged in confirming this number, however, among the authorities cited by Jerome, and the number of species alleged is of course quite arbitrary in the light of today's knowledge of marine life. Other ingenious interpretations are on offer, for which any of the major commentaries may be consulted. Sufficient to say that none has to date enjoyed major support. The application can be made, however, without discovering any arcane significance in 153 – the catch is vast, though even then (unlike the incident in Lk. 5 when the disciples were called), the net does not break. The mission will involve a great harvest among the nations, though one that will never be too great to accommodate.

The scope of the apostolic mission is something we can appreciate today as could almost no other generation before us; in our era

Christianity has become truly a faith for all the nations. 'It is only rarely that it is possible in the history of the Church, or in the history of the world, to speak of anything as being unmistakably new. But in the twentieth century one phenomenon has come into view which is incontestably new – for the first time there is in the world a universal religion, and that the Christian religion.'[7]

Today a massive vindication of the claims of Jesus Christ is taking place before our eyes, for whenever he is freed from the grave-clothes of western cultural perspectives and allowed to stand in his own authentic reality within the biblical witness to him, Jesus Christ exercises an incomparable attraction. 'There is no need of the human heart which Jesus Christ cannot meet ... that is why the Christian faith belongs to east and west, and why no greater than Jesus will ever come ... no one else is required.'[8] The fields can rarely have been whiter. The world waits to hear of, and respond to, its redeemer.

The passage also vividly illustrates our communion with Jesus. The invitation to share a meal has larger significance in the east than a simple social pleasure. It implies an invitation to fellowship, to the communion of hearts. Jesus had promised his disciples that after the 'little while' he was taken from them he would come back to be with them (16:16–21). This new relationship, they are learning, cannot be in the same tangible terms as before. But it is nonetheless real and satisfying; indeed it is part of the 'better' thing that the Holy Spirit will bring at his coming (16:7). Jesus himself will come and make his home among them (14:23); they are not to be abandoned like orphans (14:18).

This passage illuminates this new relationship which is still available. It is based on his initiative, as we noted (12). It is a practical relationship, expressed amid the everyday, concrete realities of hard work, professional skills, the search for food and the preparing of meals. Jesus' provision for them is thoroughly practical also. Just as in the upper room he took a basin and towel and ministered to their practical needs, so by the lake-shore his provision is similarly down-to-earth. 'My God will meet all your needs according to his glorious riches in Christ Jesus' (Phil. 4:19).

To speak of Jesus' provision, however, inevitably links this celebration meal with the one they had shared only a few days before in the upper room (cf. Mt. 26:26–29). There Jesus had taken bread and a cup, as now he took bread and fish, and distributed it to them. That meal, he taught them, expressed the sacrifice of his

---

[7] S. Neill, *A History of Christian Missions*, p. 559.

[8] E. Norman, cited in A Webster, *Christ is Enough* (Epworth, 1963), p. 7.

body and blood on the cross. What they had dimly understood then, they now saw with new clarity. Jesus' provision had been supremely the giving of himself for them on the cross, to cleanse away their sins and to nourish them with the new life of the kingdom of God. Jesus still invites his disciples to eat with him (Rev. 3:20; also 1 Cor. 11:23–26).

> Come and dine! the Master calleth, come and dine!
> You may feast at Jesus' table all the time.
> He who fed the multitude,
> Turned the water into wine,
> Says to hungry, thirsting sinners,
> Come and dine!

Anon.

The graciousness of that communion with Jesus is also indicated. These are ordinary men whom Jesus invited to his table of fellowship that day; public failures like Peter, known doubters like Thomas, loyal and faithful souls like Nathanael, men of irascible temperament like the sons of Zebedee, and two others who do not even rate having their names mentioned, 'background' folks like the *two other disciples*. To that deeply human company Jesus opens the riches of his friendship – also, therefore, to us.

The meal shared together had another dimension, for the communion celebration is also a symbol of the glory of the coming kingdom, the marriage supper of the Lamb (Rev. 19:9), when people will come 'from the east and west and north and south, and will take their places at the feast in the kingdom of God' (Lk. 13:20). To respond to his invitation now is to secure our participation in the celebration then; that day when, as Maclaren beautifully puts it, 'in the morning light we shall see Him standing on the steadfast shore. The "Pilot of the Galilean Lake"; who will guide our frail boat through the wild surf that marks the breaking of the sea of life on the shore of eternity; and when the sun rises over the Eastern hills we shall land on the solid beach, bringing our "few small fishes" with us, which He will accept. And there we shall rest, nor need to ask who is He that serves us, for we shall know that "It is the Lord!".'[9]

2. Following Jesus (21:15–25)

We come to the final paragraph of the gospel. Appropriately it stakes out the path for those who, having become convinced that Jesus is indeed 'the Christ, the Son of God', now wish to commit

[9] A. Maclaren, 3, pp. 357f.

themselves to 'believe' in him (20:31). Jesus takes us back to an image of the Christian life which surfaced in the very first chapter where Andrew and an unnamed disciple of John the Baptist are directed to Jesus by John, and so 'they followed [him]' (1:37). Later Jesus finds Philip and says to him, 'Follow me' (1:43).

Now, as the gospel closes, Jesus instructs the leader of the new disciple community, *Follow me!* (19) ... *You must follow me!* (22). The words echo the terms in which Peter himself had been called by Jesus at the first: 'Come, follow me, ... and I will make you fishers of men' (Mk. 1:17), and the setting, as we have suggested, may indeed have been the same stretch of shore.

So, as Jesus brings the disciples back to where it all began, seeing it now through eyes which have been opened by the experience of the years with Jesus and above all by his death and resurrection, he calls them to reaffirm that first commitment, and then go on with him in the power of the coming gift of the Holy Spirit for the remainder of their earthly pilgrimage.

Five things are implied in following Jesus then and today.

a. A barrier to be removed (21:15–17)

The breakfast on the beach leads to a confrontation with Peter, though one to which the others are apparently party. The public nature of the conversation is important, for part of what Jesus is doing here is to reinstate Peter after the public disgrace of his denials. *Simon son of John, do you truly love me more than these?* (15). Note that Jesus does not address him as Peter, the rock, for he had failed to live up to that name. Jesus is facing Peter with his own limitations so that he might entrust himself in a new way to Christ's leadership. Simon on his own will always be Simon. He has no capacity to rise beyond that. But Simon trusting in Jesus is Peter-the-rock, from whose witness and leadership the church will receive its earliest foundation.

The question has been raised: what does *more than these* refer to? Almost certainly Jesus is noting the other disciples gathered around. Peter's boast had been, 'Even if all fall away on account of you, I never will' (Mt. 26:33). In replying now, however, he significantly makes no reference to what he can or cannot do; he is thrown back on Christ and Christ's knowledge of him, *Yes, Lord, ... you know that I love you* (15). The question is asked twice more: *do you truly love me?* (16), *do you love me?* (17). Each time Jesus commissions Peter with respect to ministry in the church.

The word used for 'love', both in Jesus' questions, and in Peter's answers, switches between *agapaō* and *phileō*. This accounts for the distinction in the NIV translation between *truly love* (rendering *agapaō*), and *love* (rendering *phileō*). Attempts to identify subtle distinctions between the two verbs fail to carry conviction. John has a habit through his gospel of using pairs of terms interchangeably, and, for example, in this very passage he has two different Greek words for *take care of* and *feed* (16–17), for *lambs* and *sheep* (15–16), and for *know* (17), both of which NIV, in common with other versions, renders *know*. The *lambs/sheep* distinction may have some significance, but it is difficult to see what points can be made from the others. Classical studies have shown that the two Greek verbs for *love* were used fairly interchangeably in most contexts. The likelihood that no major distinctions are intended is rendered the more credible by the lack of a clear consensus among those who want to make a distinction. It is probably therefore wiser to see this as a Johannine stylistic feature rather than as the basis of a major exegetical truth.

The true significance of the incident lies in Peter's being confronted with the last occasion on which he had warmed himself at a charcoal fire (9; *cf.* 18:18), and being called to undo his denials with these three public reaffirmations of his love and loyalty to Jesus. Until that has been done Peter is not ready to be a follower of Jesus; the barrier of failure and sin has not been removed.

Behind the specifics of Peter's situation lies a principle of universal application. Before Jesus can be followed and served, the sin in our lives has to be addressed. Jesus is insistent on this, even to the point of Peter's being hurt (17), and probably also embarrassed on account of the public forum of Jesus' insistence on full repentance. 'Without holiness no-one will see the Lord' (Heb. 12:14).

Peter did not forget this principle when he proclaimed the gospel to others. 'What shall we do?' . . . 'Repent and be baptised, every one of you, . . . for the forgiveness of your sins' (Acts 2:37–38). A relationship with Jesus begins when, in his presence, we face up to all that grieves and contradicts God's holy will in our lives, whatever this may cost us.

This principle applies in a special way at the beginning of Christian life; but it is continually applicable. As Peter discovered, and as Paul was to find later (*cf.* 1 Tim. 1:12–16), no matter how desperate our failure, or how deep-seated our shame, he can forgive and renew us and then use us in his service. Failure is never final with God. 'You ask me what forgiveness means; it is the wonder of being trusted again by God in the place where I disgraced him' (Rita Snowden).

b. A responsibility to be accepted

The experience of being forgiven clears the way for serving Jesus. Peter restored is Peter recommissioned. Jesus' concern here is not just for Peter's welfare and self-confidence; he is also genuinely concerned for his fledgling church. So Peter is directed to his work: *Feed my lambs, Take care of my sheep, Feed my sheep* (15–17). Following Jesus and loving Jesus mean accepting responsibility for Jesus' people, a truth which is in need of rehabilitation at the present time. Commitment to Christ involves commitment to the church of Christ. Jesus Christ is not a 'single' person in the sense that he comes to us without other attachment. He is a 'married' person; he comes to us with a bride, whom he loves and for whom he sacrificed himself (Eph. 5:25). To be in relationship to Christ while ignoring or even despising his bride is no more acceptable than such behaviour would be in human contexts when relating to a married friend; far less so, because the relationship with Jesus has infinitely greater dimensions. Genuine New Testament conversion means not only turning to and accepting Christ. It also means turning to and accepting his bride, the church. Jesus' love for his church remains undiminished even though the church be torn, ill-clad, dirty in places, and generally malnourished and diseased. The church is still his bride, the people for whom he died, and who are therefore the burden of his concern. So he speaks his word today to those who will hear it: *Feed my lambs, Take care of my sheep, Feed my sheep.*

c. A cross to be carried

Peter, having accepted his commission, is immediately confronted with its cost (18–19) as Jesus prophetically prepares him for his eventual martyrdom. He will serve into old age and in the end die with hands outstretched, a euphemism for crucifixion. The details are not known with certainty, but there is fairly reliable tradition that Peter followed his Lord in the form of his death, probably in Rome under the Emperor Nero in the early sixties of the first century. This literal 'carrying' of the cross would be preceded by an experience in which Peter's self-will would be thwarted as he is led where he does not want to go (18).

This principle applies all the way along the path 'following Jesus'. The road of discipleship is the road of the cross, as Jesus had earlier made clear. 'The man who hates [*i.e.* views as secondary] his life in this world will keep it for eternal life. Whoever serves me must follow me' (12:25–26; Mk. 8:34–35). The Christian life is in this sense a 'continual mortification' (Calvin), in which, daily and in a

318

thousand ways, we die to self-will and do the will of the Lord. 'Not I, but Christ' (see Gal. 2:20) is the essence of the Christian walk. This is negative in form, inevitably so because our hearts are naturally inclined to rebellion. But, in experience, it is the most positive of lifestyles, for death *for* Christ is the door to living *with* Christ. As with Jesus, crucifixion leads to resurrection, death to life. Peter, and we with him, by dying bring glory to God (19).

d. A partnership to be maintained

Having received the Lord's recommission and an insight into his own future, Peter, seeing *the disciple whom Jesus loved* close behind, asks concerning *his* future ministry, *Lord, what about him?* (21). Jesus rebukes Peter over this. *What is that to you?* (22) really means 'Mind your own business!' Peter, having got 'in the know' about his own future, now wants to use the privileged position he has obtained with the Lord to find out about others.

It is so very human, but, as Jesus indicates, also so very wrong. The personal relationship between the Lord and individual Christians, including issues like the future form and sphere of their service, the degree of their obedience, or the quality of their contribution, is 'holy ground', sacred to the individuals concerned. We may not walk there unless with express invitation or clear obligation, and even then only with the greatest sensitivity and reserve. The ministries of Peter and John would be different. Peter would be the shepherd, John the seer; Peter the preacher, John the penman; Peter the foundational witness, John the faithful writer; Peter would die in the agony and passion of martyrdom, John would live on to great age and pass away in quiet serenity.

Peter is faced here, as we all are, with the fact of partnership in following Jesus. There are many others on the road with us, as truly Christ's, as surely commissioned, as deeply loved, as greatly valued. Their calling and gifts may be different; their instincts, and even their convictions in certain matters, may not coincide with our own; but we can thank God for them and at times be inspired and challenged by their example. In the end, however, our focus must remain on Jesus himself. 'Keep following me.' Jesus alone is our Master; to him we belong, to him we must give account; we are to live 'looking unto Jesus' (Heb. 12:2, AV).

e. A destination to be attained

In these concluding verses of the gospel, Jesus articulates the full terms of the Christian's hope for the future by referring to his 'return' (22–23). One of the marked features of the teaching of

319

Jesus as John records it is the stress upon the presence of the kingdom of God in the here and now. *Now*, by faith in Jesus Christ, we enter the kingdom, *now* we receive eternal life, *now* we escape from the world, *now* we pass from darkness into light. The eschatology is realized in the present. But that does not exhaust the Christian's hope. 'A time is coming . . . when the dead will hear the voice of the Son of God . . . a time is coming when all who are in their graves will hear his voice and come out' (5:25, 28–29); 'I will come back and take you to be with me' (14:3). In harmony with the other New Testament writers, John reflects the conviction that Jesus will return in tangible majesty at the end of this age, to complete his work, to judge all people and to inaugurate the everlasting age of glory. The King is coming, and that crowning encounter is the ultimate destination of the Christian disciple and the pilgrim people of God.

Jesus' comment on John's future provoked controversy *among the brothers*, as reflected in verse 23. John is careful to underline that Jesus spoke hypothetically only to deflect Peter's mistaken inquisitiveness. The Lord did not commit himself categorically to return within the lifetime of John.

The trustworthiness of the evangelist's witness is then affirmed (24). Who are the *we* who pronounce this accreditation? Conceivably this is a testimonial by the elders of the church in Ephesus where John was resident. Alternatively, and perhaps preferably, it is an editorial *we* on the part of the author himself, rather as he had expressed himself at the beginning of the gospel: 'we have seen his glory'. If so, it forms a fitting conclusion.

The glory of Jesus Christ, which has been unveiled chapter by chapter through the gospel, finally points us forward to our ultimate destination, when he returns and the glories discerned by faith will be replaced by the glories opened to sight. Until then we 'follow him'.

The earliest reference to this image in the gospel beautifully blends these two perspectives. Like the disciples (1:37), we follow him until that moment, whether before or after our earthly death, when he will 'turn round' and look at us, and we will see him face to face. We will ask him where he is staying, and he will take us there, in fulfilment of his great prayer, 'I want those you have given me to be with me where I am, and to see my glory' (17:24).

But that will not be the end of our journey. For, as John's last words underline, there is no limit to the greatness of Jesus Christ. He has done *many other things as well* (25), not only during these few brief years among us, but as the pre-incarnate Word through whom all things were made (1:3), as the upholding Word who sustains the life of the universe (1:3), and as the everlasting centre of all the redeeming purposes of God. He is literally infinite, and hence no conceivable library in earth or heaven can adequately or fully 'tell the story' of Jesus Christ (25). So in eternity our exploration will go on in ways at present beyond our imagining as we discover more and yet more of 'the unsearchable riches' of Christ.

> The stars shine over the earth,
> The stars shine over the sea,
> The stars look up to the Mighty God,
> The stars look down on me;
> The stars will live for a million years,
> For a million years and a day!
> But Christ and I shall live and love
> When the stars have passed away.

Anon.

But although no book can ever tell it all, we thank God for the book that John wrote, more than nineteen hundred years ago, which we can take in our hands today. By reading it we begin to see 'the glory of the One and Only, who came from the Father' (1:14).

STUDY GUIDE

The aim of this study guide is to help you get to the heart of what the author has written and to challenge you to apply what you learn to your own life. The questions have been designed for use by individuals or by small groups of Christians meeting, perhaps for an hour or two each week, to study, discuss and pray together.

The guide provides material for each of the sections in the book. When used by a group with limited time, the leader should decide beforehand which questions are most appropriate for the group to discuss during the meeting, and which should perhaps be left for group members to work through by themselves or in smaller groups during the week.

In order to be able to contribute fully and learn from the group meetings, each member of the group needs to read through the section or sections under discussion, together with the passages in the gospel to which they refer.

It's important not to let these studies become merely academic exercises. Guard against this by making time to think through and discuss how what you discover *works out in practice* for you. Make sure you begin and end each study by focusing on God in praise and prayer. Ask the Holy Spirit to speak to you through your discussion together.

Introduction

1. Authorship

1 Does it matter who actually wrote John's gospel? Why (p. 15)?
2 What grounds are there for saying that the apostle John was the author (p. 16)?
3 Is John 'the disciple whom Jesus loved' (pp. 16f.)?
4 What 'two major problems' were associated with the early church's acceptance of John's gospel? How do these help us to assess its authenticity (p. 18)?

2. John and the synoptics

1 What general common ground can you pick out between John's gospel and the others (pp. 19f.)?
2 In thinking about the differences, how may we account for John's omission of significant incidents such as the transfiguration (pp. 20f.)?
3 What differences are there between a biography and a 'gospel' (p. 21)?
4 Why does Jesus' teaching style in John's gospel differ so markedly from that in the synoptics (pp. 21f.)?
5 What major differences in historical detail and chronology between John and the synoptics have been identified? Is it important to try and explain them? How may this be done (pp. 22f.)?

'. . . the real test of understanding is not an ability
to use theological ideas and titles but action based
upon the truths professed.' (p. 23)

---

3. Purpose and date

1 Why did John write his gospel (p. 24)?
2 What clues are there about *when* it was written (p. 25)?

4. John and Jesus

1 How is John's gospel 'of particular help in undergirding the confession of One who is both true God and true man' (p. 26)?

The Gospel of John

'Matthew and Luke take us to the cradle and the manger, Mark to the prophecies of old, but John takes us back into the mists of eternity.' (Alexander Maclaren, quoted on p. 29)

---

1 What does the opening paragraph of the gospel achieve (pp. 29f.)?

A. The ministry of the pre-incarnate king (1:1–18)

1. Jesus Christ and the eternal God (1:1–2)

1 What would John's first readers have understood by his use of the Greek word *logos*? (pp. 31f.). How does John's understanding of this word depart from that of the Greek philosophers (p. 31)?
2 What three things does John tell us about Jesus as the Word of God in these opening verses (pp. 32f.)?
3 Why is the fact that 'God is always Jesus-like' important for the way we read the Old Testament (p. 33)? Is this how you approach it?
4 In the phrase 'the Word was God' in verse 1, 'God' does not have a definite article in the original Greek text. To what controversial claims has this led? How may they be answered (p. 34)?

5   In what ways are you tempted to 'compromise the uniqueness of the revelation of Jesus Christ' (p. 35)? How can we avoid this without being bigoted?

'If Jesus Christ shares the nature of God, we are called to worship him without cessation, obey him without hesitation, love him without reservation and serve him without interruption. To him be all glory for ever.' (p. 36)

---

2.   Jesus Christ and the created universe (1:3–5)

1   In describing the Word as the origin of creation, why does John stress so strongly that 'without him nothing was made that has been made' (p. 37)?
2   Why is the truth that the universe is 'fundamentally distinct' from God such a crucial one today (p. 38)?
3   What is the significance of John's reference to 'light' (pp. 39f.)?
4   Are there ways in which your thinking about evil tends to 'undermine Christ's universal creative sovereignty ...' (p. 40)?
5   In what way is John's prologue a 'green' statement (p. 41)?

'A lack of concern for our natural environment is a sign of a limited view of Christ ...' (p. 41)

---

3.   Jesus Christ and redemptive history (1:6–18)

1.   *The preparation in Israel (1:6–13)*

1   In what ways was John the Baptist a 'model' of Christian witness (p. 42)?

2   What does John mean by 'world' (p. 43)? What does he tell us about it?
3   What does John's use of the phrase 'believe in' reveal about his understanding of the nature of faith (p. 44)?
4   What three points does the author make about John's description of salvation in verses 12–13 (pp. 44f.)? What do these mean to you?

2.   *The coming of Jesus (1:14)*

1   Why is John's use of the word 'flesh' (*sarx*) so 'startling' (p. 46)?
2   How does the incarnation 'directly address our need for salvation (p. 47)?
3   What other areas does the author draw on as implications of the incarnation (pp. 47f.)?
4   What events does John's language in verse 14b reflect (p. 48)? What is the significance of this?

4.   *The church's witness (1:16–18)*

1   What does John say that the coming of Christ has meant for the church (p. 49)?
2   '. . . the coming of God in his grace in Christ supersedes the grace of the "old covenant" revelation' (p. 49). The author goes on to say that 'this of course does not imply that the Old Testament revelation is set aside . . .' Why not?

'It is as if God has reached into his very being and plucked out his own heart in sending Christ to us.' (p. 50)

B. The ministry of the incarnate king (1:19 – 19:42)

1. The inauguration (1:19–51)

1. *The beginning of the ministry (1:19–51)*

a. *The witness of John (1:19–34)*

1 Why did the religious leaders of the day feel threatened by John the Baptist's ministry (p. 51)?
2 John applies four titles to Jesus in this section: Messiah, Lamb of God, Baptizer with the Spirit, Son of God. What does the title 'Messiah' mean? What does it imply about Jesus (pp. 52f.)?
3 What is significant about the fact that John the Baptist saw the dove *remain* on Jesus (p. 52)?
4 What does the title 'Lamb of God' mean (p. 53)? The author comments that 'Few aspects of the gospel need greater, or more frequent, reaffirmation than this one.' To what is he referring? Is he right?
5 What is the significance of describing Jesus as the 'Baptizer with the Spirit' (p. 54)?

b. *The call of the first disciples*

1 What difference is there between Jesus and traditional Jewish rabbis in the way they attracted disciples (p. 56)?
2 What 'goes a long way to explaining why [John the Baptist] made such an impact' (p. 57)? In what way might this apply to you?
3 What 'fundamental requisites' for becoming a disciple of Jesus does John mention here (p. 57)? Have you fulfilled them?
4 What 'lesson for over-zealous Christian witnesses for whom the only valid response to the gospel is one made immediately upon hearing it presented' is there here (p. 58)?
5 In what ways are you like Andrew (p. 58)?
6 What is the 'secret of the extraordinary spread of Christianity in the early centuries' (p. 58)? How do you react to this challenge?

7 'It is striking how regularly Jesus approached people from the perspective of their potential' (p. 59). Why is this so important?
8 What is significant about Jesus' description of himself as 'Son of Man' (p. 61)?

2. The procession (2:1 – 12:19)

1 Why does John call the miracles of Jesus 'signs' (p. 62)?
2 What distinction is there between John's view of the miracles and that of the synoptic writers (p. 62)?

1. The first sign – Cana (2:1–11)

1 In what way is Mary's request a 'helpful model of intercessory prayer' (p. 63)?

'Prayer without a willingness to obey is little better than faith without a willingness to work.' (p. 64)

---

2 Why is Jesus' response to his mother surprising (p. 64)?
3 Why is it wrong to use this incident to justify the consumption of alcohol by Christians today (pp. 64f.)?
4 How does this sign demonstrate the superiority of Christianity to other religious systems (p. 65)?
5 On miracles generally, how does the opening of the gospel help us to accept the possibility of their having taken place (p. 66)?

2. The cleansing of the temple (2:12–25)

1 How does this section 'link naturally' with what has gone before (p. 67)?
2 Given the differences between John and the synoptic writers at this point, what are the possible solutions to the apparent contradictions (pp. 67f.)? Which do you find most persuasive? Why?
3 What motivates Jesus to do what he does (p. 69)? In what ways is 'Jesus' entire ministry . . . encapsulated in this incident' (p. 71)? To what extent do you share his concerns?

4 What does Jesus mean by his statement in verse 19: 'Destroy this temple, and I will raise it again in three days' (p. 69)?

5 'The gospel material does not lend support to violent, revolutionary action . . .' (p. 72). Do you agree? Why? What role *do* Christians have in tackling wrongs in society?

3. Conversation with Nicodemus (3:1–21)

1 What was unique about Jesus' understanding of the kingdom of God (p. 75)?

2 Why would what Jesus says about entry into the kingdom of God come as such a surprise to Nicodemus (p. 75)?

3 What does Jesus mean by being 'born of water and the Spirit' (p. 76)?

4 'The dialogue with Nicodemus is a crucial section of the whole Bible . . .' (p. 79). Why?

'Becoming a Christian is always a miracle . . . Salvation is of God, and no advance in Christian evangelistic methodology will ever eliminate or replace this.' (p. 79)

---

4. John the Baptist and Jesus (3:22–36)

1 How does John the Baptist defuse the potential rivalry between himself and Jesus (pp. 80f.)? What relevance does this have for you?

2 How do these verses 'expound more fully' the pre-eminence of Christ (p. 81)?

3 'The wrath of God is a difficult notion to hold together with the love of God . . .' (p. 82). How do you hold these two ideas together?

5. Mission to Samaria (4:1–42)

1 What contrasts can you find between Nicodemus and the woman of Samaria (p. 83)? What do these tell you about Jesus?

2 Why was it so surprising that Jesus should talk to this woman (p. 83)? Are there any prejudices which govern the sort of people with whom you share the gospel?

3 What underlies Jesus' request that she should fetch her husband (p. 85)? Why is this so important?
4 What can we learn about how to share our faith from Jesus' example here (pp. 85f.)?

'Our failures in evangelism are so often failures in love. Nothing is so guaranteed to draw others to share our "living water" than an awareness that we genuinely care about them.' (p. 86)

---

5 What basic realities of his and their mission does Jesus share with his disciples (pp. 86f.)?
6 What is so significant about the fact that the Samaritans call Jesus 'Saviour of the world' (p. 87)?
7 What does this chapter teach about worship and hindrances to it (p. 88)? Which apply particularly to you?

6. The second sign – healing the official's son (4:43–54)

1 What is faith and why is it so important (p. 92)?
2 What is wrong with 'a "faith" based merely on miracles and signs' (p. 92)?
3 'Faith is a living thing which grows and develops' (p. 92). Does yours? How?
4 What does this passage teach about prayer (p. 93)?

7. The third sign – healing the lame man (5:1–15)

1 Why is Jesus' question, 'Do you want to get well?', such a penetrating one (p. 95)? Are there ways in which you need to face up to the same question?
2 Why were the Pharisees so vehemently opposed to what Jesus had done (p. 95)?
3 Given the importance for Jesus of his relationship with his Father, why is the 'Father' image 'suffering a degree of eclipse in much contemporary Christian consciousness' (pp. 96f.)?

8. Sabbath controversies and testimonies (5:16–47)

a. Sabbath controversies (5:16–30)

1 What does Jesus mean by claiming 'equality with God' (p. 98)? Why is this so important?
2 What amazing claims does Jesus make in this section (pp. 98f.)?
3 'Those claiming to have chosen . . . to call him Lord and God must face the question: What difference is this making in my life' (p. 100)? How do you answer this question?

b. Testimonies concerning the Son (5:31–47)

1 By what three channels does the Father authorize the Son (pp. 100f.)?
2 What was the 'fundamental failure' of the Jewish leaders (p. 102)? To what did this lead?

9. The fourth sign – feeding the five thousand (6:1–15)

1 Why is the reference in verse 4 to the Passover 'critical for the interpretation of this section' (p. 103)?
2 What significance is there for us in Jesus' command to preserve the leftovers (p. 104)?
3 What is significant about the sequel to the miracle (p. 105)?
4 In what way does this story express 'the ministry challenge facing the disciples of Christ in our generation' (pp. 105f.)? How do you face this challenge?

'People wish to remain quiet, in the peaceful little Church under the high Gothic arches; they would brood about God and be preoccupied with the needs of their own souls. They do not want to be shocked by the bewildering idea that there are still many hundreds of millions of people who have never heard the gospel.' (J. H. Bavinck, quoted on p. 106)

---

5 What does this story teach us about God's attitude to our inadequate resources (p. 106)?
6 'The key, beyond our believing in God's ability and will to use us, lies in . . .' what (p. 107)? How does this apply to you?

10. The fifth sign – walking on the water (6:16–24)

1 How appropriate is the picture of the church as a boat, in your experience (p. 107)?
2 What does this incident tell us about Jesus' attitude to his church (p. 108)?
3 What comfort is there for us here (p. 109)?

11. Discourse on the bread of life (6:25–71)

a. The congregation who do not believe (6:26–29)

1 What is the basic error of the Galileans (p. 110)? To what extent is this an error that you share in too?

b. The preacher who calls for faith (6:30–35)

1 In what way does the saying 'I am the bread of life' enshrine 'the essence of Jesus' message' (p. 111)?

c. The congregation who do believe (6:36–58)

1 What three things does Jesus tell us about those who respond to his invitation (pp. 111f.)?
2 In verses 53ff., is Jesus referring to the sacrament of the Lord's Supper? (p. 113). What else might he have in mind?

d. The cost of discipleship (6:60–71)

1 Why do so many find Jesus' teaching hard? (pp. 114f.).
2 'Jesus is not overwhelmed by the loss of commitment on the part of many who had professed some allegiance to him' (p. 114). Why not? What can we learn from this?
3 What is the cost of following Jesus (p. 115)?

12. The feast of tabernacles I (7:1–52)

Prelude (7:1–13)

1 Why is a hunger for spectacular signs 'the enemy of real faith' (p. 117)?
2 What significance is there in the fact that these discourses take place during the feast of tabernacles (p. 117)?

Discourse 1 (7:14–39)

1 Why does Jesus' teaching 'amaze' his listeners (p. 118)?
2 How is Jesus able to vindicate his claim that there is 'nothing false' about him (p. 118)?
3 How does Jesus justify his apparent breaking of the law (p. 119)?
4 Why do Jesus' claims incense the authorities (p. 119)?
5 What difference in interpretation arises from the alternative punctuations in verses 37–38 (p. 120)? Why is it important?

Postcript (7:40–52)

1 What light does Jesus throw here on the ministry of the Holy Spirit (p. 122)?

'The heart to which the Spirit is largely given is not the heart that hungers for personal manifestations of power or Holy Ghost ego trips, but the one which yearns and thirsts and pleads for the glorifying of our Lord Jesus Christ.' (p. 123)

---

13. Excursus – the woman taken in adultery (7:53 – 8:11)

1 Are we justified in including this passage in John's gospel (p. 124)? Why?
2 In what way was the trap set for Jesus a clever one (p. 124)?

3　What does this incident have to say to 'a world living in the aftermath of the sexual revolution' (p. 126)?

14.　The feast of tabernacles II – discourse 2 (8:12–59)

a.　Two kinds of teacher (8:12–30)

1　What Old Testament echoes are awakened by Jesus' claim to be 'the light of the world' (p. 127)?
2　Why are the Pharisees critical of this claim (pp. 127f.)? How does Jesus answer them?
3　'We can draw these threads together in the assertion that Jesus' authority lies in . . .' what (p. 129)?
4　How does Jesus characterize his opponents (pp. 129f.)?
5　Might we be able one day to harmonize all the great world religions (p. 130)? On what basis does Christianity claim unique precedence?
6　How can teachers teach with real authority (p. 131)?

b.　Truths for disciples – discourse 2 (8:31–47)

1　What is 'the mark of the true disciple' mentioned here (p. 132)? What does it mean?
2　Why does this group so vehemently deny that they are in bondage (p. 132)?
3　What do these verses reveal about human nature (p. 133)?
4　Why is a purely political solution to humanity's problems no good (p. 133)? Is there then a place for Christians in politics?

'*Earnest protestation and practice of religion on the one hand, and the plotting of murder and the embracing of lies on the other, are not incompatible.*' (p. 133)

5　How may the freedom offered by Christ be characterized (p. 134)?

> *'Our freedom is not the freedom to do as we
> want, but the freedom from being controlled by
> our fallen natures to do as God wants.' (p. 134)*

c. Greater than Abraham – discourse 2 (8:48–59)

1 'There is almost nothing we will cling to with greater vehemence than . . .' what (p. 135)? In what ways is this true in your experience?
2 What does Jesus mean by saying that 'if anyone keeps my word, he will never see death' (verse 51; p. 135)?
3 The author quotes Raymond Brown: 'No clearer implication of divinity is found in the gospel tradition' (p. 136). To what is he referring? Why is this so?

15. The sixth sign – healing the blind man (9:1–41)

1 'This chapter is the most unified of the gospel' (pp. 136f.). Why?
2 What wrong ideas do people have about the relationship between suffering and sin (p. 137)? What is the right perspective?
3 'The existence of human suffering and blindness is a call to work, not simply to reflect' (p. 138). How does this apply to you?
4 In what ways had Jesus infringed the Sabbath tradition (p. 139)?
5 The God of the Pharisees 'was petrified in the past' (p. 140). Why? Is yours?
6 What was wrong with the Pharisees' attitude to God's law (p. 141)? In what ways are you like them?
7 How may the apparent contradiction between 9:39 and 3:17 be resolved (p. 143)?
8 In what ways is this incident 'an important illustration for John of the meaning of faith' (pp. 143f.)?
9 In what ways have you experienced 'the division which the coming of Christ produces' (p. 144)?

16.   *The feast of tabernacles III (10:1–21)*

1   What are the links between this passage and chapter 9 (p. 145)?

a.   *Discourse 3 (10:1–5)*

1   Can you identify the five aspects which show Jesus to be a 'true' shepherd (pp. 146f.)? What are the contrasts with the false shepherds?

b.   *Discourse 3 (10:7–18)*

1   What benefits does Jesus bring to the flock he shepherds (pp. 147f.)? How do these things apply to us?
2   What 'unique feature' of John's picture of the shepherd shows how these blessings are won (pp. 147f.)? How does this apply to Christian leadership today?
3   What does Jesus mean by 'other sheep' in verse 16 (p. 149)?
4   What is 'remarkable' about verse 17 (p. 150)?

c.   *The sequel (10:19–21)*

1   In what way do the authorities 'come close to the unforgivable sin' (p. 150)? How is this relevant for you and your friends/family?

17.   *The feast of dedication (10:22–42)*

1   What did this feast celebrate (p. 151)? Why is this significant?

a.   *Messiah (10:24–33)*

1   Why does Jesus refuse 'to state categorically that he is the Messiah in the course of a public proclamation . . .' (p. 152)?
2   What privileges does Jesus mention for those who believe in him (p. 153)? How are these relevant for you?

'The enemies of their soul may be strong and mighty, but their Saviour is mightier; and none shall pluck them out of their Saviour's hands.'
(J. C. Ryle, quoted on p. 153)

3 If belief depends on the 'call of the Son and the gifting of the Father' (p. 154), why are those who do not believe still held responsible for their unbelief?

b. Son of God (10:31–39)

1 Why did the Jews accuse Jesus of blasphemy (p. 155)? How does Jesus seek to correct their understanding of God?
2 What is 'noteworthy' about the reference to being 'set apart' in verse 36 (pp. 155f.)?

c. 10:40–42

1 What lessons does the impact of John the Baptist's ministry have for you (p. 156)?

18. The seventh sign – the raising of Lazarus (11:1–57)

a. The sickness and death of Lazarus at Bethany (11:1–16)

1 What is the attitude of Jesus to sickness here (p. 158)?
2 'What is true here at the level of physical illness can be extended to all the trials we face as Christian disciples' (p. 158). In what way? What trials are you facing? How does Jesus' attitude help?
3 What does this incident teach us about God's delays (pp. 159f.)?

On the death of Lazarus: *'The pain and anguish of the family are still of less worth than the nourishing of the faith of both the family and the attendant disciples.' (p. 161)*

b. The meetings with Martha and Mary and Jesus' grief (11:17–37)

1 Why does Jesus wait until Lazarus has been in the tomb for four days (pp. 161f.)?
2 What do these verses reveal about Martha and Mary (pp. 163f.)?
3 In what way is Jesus' statement, 'I am the resurrection and the life', a 'culmination of the unfolding revelation in the preceding chapters' (pp. 163f.)?
4 Can you identify the different ways in which Jesus reacts to the death of Lazarus (pp. 164f.)? What causes these reactions?
5 What 'limits to the possibilities and power of Jesus Christ' (p. 166) have you set in your life?

c. The raising of Lazarus from the dead (11:38–44)

1 'These verses teach a number of lessons about prayer' (p. 167). What lessons?
2 Why has this miracle 'provoked considerable controversy' (p. 168)? What do you make of it?
3 What does this whole incident tell us about the love of God (p. 169)?

'Despite the massive propaganda to the contrary, our Lord's purpose for us is not to make us happy, but to make us holy.' (p. 169)

4 How does the raising of Lazarus give us hope for the 'long-forgotten dead' (p. 171)?
5 Martha's statement, 'I know he will rise again in the resurrection at the last day,' is all very well, but how does Jesus take it further (p. 171)?
6 How do you face the prospect of your own death and that of those close to you?

d. The Sanhedrin's decision to have Jesus killed (11:45–57)

1 What do we know about the Sanhedrin (p. 172)? Why were they so alarmed at reports of the raising of Lazarus?
2 What examples can you think of where the *status quo* is maintained at the expense of integrity?

19. Anointing at Bethany (12:1–11)

1 Why is Mary's action so strange (pp. 175f.)? In what way does it represent 'a model for service of Jesus in every generation' (p. 178)?
2 Why does Judas react as he does (p. 176)?
3 What 'extremes are to be avoided' in interpreting Jesus' comment that 'You will always have the poor among you' (p. 177)?
4 How does the chief priests' attitude to Lazarus illustrate 'the uncontrollable reality of sin' (p. 178)? Can you think of examples of this pattern in your own experience?

'Within the wonder of God's condescension to us in Jesus Christ is his ability – the Almighty who has need of nothing ... to allow us to minister to him in ways which bring delight to his heart and further his cause in the world.' (p. 178)

---

5 'It is possible to become so circumspect and balanced in our Christian profession that we lose touch with the extravagance of a heart like Mary's' (p. 179). How extravagant are you? Why?

STUDY GUIDE

20. The triumphal entry (12:12–19)

1 What is the significance of palm branches here (p. 180)?
2 Why does Jesus choose to come into Jerusalem on a donkey (p. 181)?
3 In what ways is the triumphal entry 'an exposition of the nature of Jesus' kingship' (p. 181)? Is this how you think of him?

3. The coronation (12:20 – 19:42)

1. Anticipation (12:20–50)

1 Why is this 'one of the profoundest and most demanding sections of the entire gospel' (p. 184)?
2 What attracted non-Jews to first-century Judaism (p. 184)?
3 In the light of this section, how would you answer someone who claimed that Christianity is simply about the moral teaching and ethics of Jesus (p. 185)?
4 What is 'the deepest truth of the Christian gospel' (p. 186)? Who are the modern equivalents of the 'Jews' and 'Greeks'? Why do they reject the gospel?
5 In what ways do our 'modern-day expressions of Christian faith and worship' (p. 186) tend to be immature? To what extent is this true of you?
6 'Fruitfulness is costly' (p. 187). In what ways have you found this principle to be true in your experience?
7 Why does Jesus face death 'with extreme agitation and revulsion' (p. 188)?

'Death proclaims that there is nothing in our lives which is finally fit to endure to eternity.' (p. 188)

---

8 In verses 30–32, what four things is the death of Jesus said to achieve (p. 190)?
9 Why would the Jews have found it so difficult to accept what Jesus was saying (p. 191)?
10 What are some of the benefits and drawbacks of 'sermons on hell' (p. 192)? Has the balance gone too far in the wrong direction?

11 How do you respond to the idea that 'Jesus has been rejected because God has so willed it' (p. 193)? What room does this leave for human responsibility?

12 What in your spiritual life suffers because of a preference for praise from men rather than praise from God (p. 194)?

13 'Preaching is more than delivering a message from God ...' (p. 195). What more to it is there? Why?

2. Instruction (13:1 – 16:33)

1 How does John signal the beginning of a new section at this point?

a. The foot-washing (13:1–17)

1 How does the foot-washing illuminate the meaning of the death of Jesus (pp. 196f.)?

2 In what way does the example of Judas Iscariot serve as 'the solemnest of warnings' (p. 197)?

3 What does it take on our part to be washed by Christ (p. 198)?

4 What 'secret of communion' does Jesus share with his disciples here (pp. 198f.)?

5 'One of the primary expressions of our submission to Jesus as our "Lord" is our willingness to allow him to be our "Teacher" ' (p. 199). How does Jesus teach you?

b. The coming of the night – Judas (13:18–30)

1 How does Jesus react to Judas' apostasy (p. 200)? How do you (or would you) react to such betrayal?

'The confession "Jesus is Lord" must not lead to a triumphalistic detachment from the world but rather to an appalled dismay that his lordship is contested, and a commitment to mission to the world in the name of its Lord.' (pp. 200f.)

341

STUDY GUIDE

2 Why is verse 20 a 'key statement for the interpretation of the entire block of teaching which will follow (chapters 13–16)' (p. 201)?
3 What is the relationship between the mission of the Son and the mission of his disciples (p. 201)?
4 In what way is this paragraph 'a powerful and disturbing reminder of the ambiguity of the life of the people of God in every age (p. 203)?
5 'There are those whom even Jesus cannot, and will not, save' (pp. 203f.). Why?

'[Jesus] is still the Lord of the night, who can make darkness the vehicle of his praise.' (p. 204)

---

c. The farewell discourses (13:31 – 16:33)

1 What is the 'essential focus' (p. 205) of these chapters?

(a) The absence of Jesus (13:31–38)
1 What do you understand by the word 'glory'? How can Jesus say that these events glorify him (pp. 205f.)?
2 What does Jesus mean by 'love' (p. 206)? In what ways is this different from what we tend to think?
3 Why does Jesus describe this as a 'new' commandment (p. 206)?

'Unlike other associations which are based on common interest or outlook, the church is to be marked by an inclusiveness which echoes the universal appeal of Jesus.' (p. 207)

---

4 What examples can you think of where the 'evangelistic power of love' (pp. 206f.) has been displayed?

(b) The blessings of his 'absence' (14:1–31)
1 Why are the disciples so anxious (p. 209)?
2 How does Jesus deal with their anxiety (pp. 209f.)?

342

3 In what ways is the departure of Jesus of benefit to the disciples (p. 210)?
4 Why is Jesus the only way to God (pp. 211f.)? Does this mean that other religions are of no value?
5 How does Jesus' going away 'complete his revelation of the Father' (p. 212)?
6 Why does Jesus call the Holy Spirit the 'Counsellor' (p. 214)? What does this mean?
7 The gift of the Holy Spirit 'encloses at least six more particular gifts which are mentioned in these verses' (p. 214). Can you identify these? What is your experience of them?
8 What 'three things' (p. 218) does Jesus do in the second part of his upper-room discourse?

(c) The cruciality of mission and principles of effective mission (15:1–17)

'The gracious indwelling of God with his people is not an invitation to settle down and forget the rest of the world: it is a summons to mission, for the Lord who dwells with his people is the one who goes before them in the pillar of fire and cloud.' (L. Newbigin, quoted on p. 219)

---

1 How does the image of the vine serve the 'mission' theme (p. 219)?
2 Why should we 'beware of interpretations of this passage which concentrate solely on our inward relationship with the Lord' (p. 220)?
3 What secrets of effective mission does Jesus share with his disciples here (p. 220)?
4 How does God 'prune' you (pp. 220f.)?

'Fruit-bearing for God is not a human possibility; it is Christ's work through us.' (p. 221)

---

5 What does 'remaining' or 'abiding' in Christ mean (pp. 221f.)?
6 Apart from 'winning the lost' (p. 222), in what other ways do we bear fruit?
7 'Prayer is crucial to the effective mission of the people of God' (p. 222). Why?

'In the work of mission, the church advances on its knees.' (p. 222)

---

8 In what way is Jesus' statement that 'You did not choose me, but I chose you' (verse 16) the 'ultimate encouragement in mission' (p. 223)?

(d)   The opposition to mission (15:18 – 16:4)
1 Why is opposition 'inevitable' (p. 224)? Where does it come from?
2 What opposition do you face because of your obedience to Jesus? Are *you* ready to die for Christ (pp. 225f.)?

'Following Jesus is not a game.' (p. 226)

---

3 What examples of 'respectable' opposition can you think of (p. 227)?
4 How can opposition be endured (pp. 227f.)?

(e)   The resources which God makes available for the work of mission (16:5–33)
1 'Unless I go away, the Counsellor [Holy Spirit] will not come' (verse 7). Why not?
2 'The ministry of the Spirit is . . . not a vague impartation of spiritual energy, but . ' what (p. 229)? Be as specific as you can.
3 How does the Holy Spirit 'counsel' people (pp. 230f.)? What experience have you had of these different aspects?
4 How does the Holy Spirit exercise his teaching ministry today (p. 232)?

5 What does Jesus mean by the disciples seeing him in verse 16 (p. 233)?
6 How may we find 'a deeper experience of the presence of Christ' (p. 234)?
7 What is the link between prayer and joy (pp. 234)?
8 What does it mean to pray 'in Jesus' name' (pp. 234f.)?
9 What are the 'dangers of an exclusive focus on Christ in worship and prayer . . .' (p. 235)?
10 How is Jesus able to be exultant in the face of what is about to happen (pp. 235f.)? What can you learn from this?

3. Intercession: the prayer of consecration (17:1–26)

1 What significance is there in the fact that Jesus' prayer is recorded at this point (p. 236)?
2 What is your experience of the link between prayer and power (p. 237)?

'Yesterday's consecrations will not serve for today's crises.' (p. 237)

---

3 What is the link between what Jesus prays for himself and what he prays for his disciples (p. 237)?

a. Jesus prays for himself (17:1–5)

1 What is the relationship between this prayer and the prayer of Jesus in Gethsemane recorded in the other gospels (p. 238f.)?
2 How is the Father glorified (p. 239)?
3 Why is it inadequate to describe eternal life simply as living for ever (pp. 240f.)?
4 How does the text clarify 'several aspects of Christian service' (p. 241)?

'The honour of God is bound up not only with
the enthusiastic commencement of a project but
with the faithful completion of it.' (p. 242)

b. Jesus prays for his disciples (17:6–19)

1 How do you react to the idea that you are 'the tangible
expression of the completion of [Jesus'] work' (p. 243)?
2 How do we know that, as disciples, we are 'utterly secure'
(p. 243)?
3 Where does the disciples' certainty about Jesus come from
(p. 244)? How does this apply to you?

'He [Jesus] who has need of nothing may yet
be glorified through our obedience and service.'
(p. 244).

4 In the light of his departure, what does Jesus pray for his
disciples (pp. 244f.)? How does this differ from what you pray
for yourself? Why?

'To be a disciple is to be a missionary.' (p. 247)

c. Jesus prays for all Christians (17:20–26)

1 He prays that the church may be united. When Jesus prays for
unity, what does he mean (pp. 247f.)? How does this differ
from your experience of 'church unity'? Why?
2 He prays that the world may be persuaded. What are the 'two
hands' of mission in Jesus' prayer (p. 250)? Which do you tend
to under-emphasize? Why?

'A group of Christians who are so knit together in the love of God that others can say of them, "Look how they love each other," is a church where the gospel will be "the power of God for . . . salvation" ' (p. 250).

3 He prays that his mission may be completed. What do you think of as the 'biggest barriers to effective evangelism' (pp. 250f.)? What does Jesus say they are?

4. Consecration (18:1 – 19:42)

a. The arrest (18:1–11)

1 What is significant about the fact that Jesus takes the initiative here (p. 253)?
2 What does the 'wolf' (p. 255) represent in your life? How does what Jesus says here help?
3 'Nothing shines clearer in this account than . . .' what (p. 256)? Why is this so?

b. The Jewish trial and Peter's denials – the hour of darkness (18:12–27)

1 How does Annas seek to incriminate Jesus (p. 258)?
2 What 'ingredients in the darkness of that night' (pp. 259f.) can you identify?
3 What examples of 'the apparent weakness of God' (pp. 260f.) can you think of? How do you cope with them?
4 What 'positive elements' can you discover in this passage (pp. 261f.)?
5 What was 'Peter's supreme characteristic, and also his supreme point of vulnerability' (p. 261)? What can you learn from his example?

'The darkness may encompass us, dreams remain
unfulfilled, sorrow or tragedy strike, prayers fall
back unanswered, weaknesses linger, but the light
of God's truth still shines in the darkness ...'.
(p. 262)

c. The Roman trial before Pilate (18:28 – 19:16)

(i) 18:28–40

1 What 'tragedy is re-enacted whenever people depend upon fulfilment of ritual observances to alleviate their consciences before God' (p. 264)?
2 Why were the authorities intent on Jesus' formal execution rather than simply his death (p. 265)?
3 What does Jesus mean by saying that his kingdom is 'not of this world' (verse 36; p. 266)? Does this mean that Christians should avoid politics? Why?
4 'The choice that faced the mob in Jerusalem is still before our world' (pp. 268f.). What choice? Which have you chosen?
5 Why is John accused of anti-Semitism in his gospel (p. 269)? Is this charge justified?

(ii) 19:1–16

1 What did it mean to be a 'friend of Caesar' (p. 272)?
2 What has happened to Judaism as a result of the chief priests' declaration, 'We have no king but Caesar' (verse 15; p. 273)?
3 Why is the fact that Jesus was really human so important (pp. 273f.)?

'The presence of God in our suffering is one of
the supreme distinctives of the Christian faith.'
(p. 273)

4 What 'three strands in the suffering of Jesus' (pp. 274f.) are there in this passage?

d. The crucifixion – the death of Jesus (19:16b–30)

1 What aspects of Jesus' kingship are emphasized in this section (pp. 278f.)?
2 What are 'the "health and wealth" gospels of our day'? Why are they so inadequate (p. 279)?
3 What is 'the great problem with the human saviours' (p. 280)? How does Jesus avoid it?
4 What does Jesus mean by saying 'It is finished!' (verse 30; pp. 282f.)? What was finished?
5 What is John's 'particular perspective on Christ's death and how it achieved redemption' (p. 283)?

'Our often strained and frenetic forms of Christ-ian life are witness to how much we need to affirm again with Jesus, "It is accomplished!" "It is finished!"' (p. 283)

---

e. The burial of Jesus (19:31–42)

1 What impact does the statement that 'those chiefly responsible for the death of Jesus were profoundly religious men' (p. 284) have on you?
2 What significance is there in the reference to 'blood and water' in verse 34 (pp. 284f.)?
3 Why is it so important for John that Jesus 'belongs unmistakably to the company of the dead' (p. 286)?
4 In what way is Jesus revealed as king, even in death (pp. 286f.)?

C.   The ministry of the risen king (20:1 – 21:25)

1.   The appearing king (20:1–31)

1.   *The empty tomb (20:1–9)*

1 Why are the grave clothes so important to John (p. 290)?
2 What was the difference between the resurrection of Jesus and that of, for example, Lazarus (p. 290)?

2.   *Mary (20:10–18)*

'From the perspective of heaven, nothing is more incongruous than tears at the empty tomb of Jesus.' (p. 291)

---

1 Why does Mary at first fail to recognize Jesus (p. 291)?
2 Why does Jesus tell Mary not to hold on to him (p. 292)?

'Tragically, over the centuries the Christian community has shown a far greater interest in sitting at Jesus' feet, holding on to him amid the comfort of his presence, than in going out into the world to share the good news of the risen Lord with broken, needy hearts who have as valid a claim to know of him as we.' (pp. 292f.)

---

3 How does John demonstrate that the resurrection was historical (pp. 293f.)?
4 To what extent is the resurrection 'personal' for you (pp. 295f.)?

3. The apostles (20:19–23)

1 'Jesus' vision is not of a multitude of inspired individuals each acting independently out of his or her personal encounter with the "risen one" ' (p. 297). What is it then?
2 What does Jesus' greeting of 'Peace be with you' (verse 19) mean (p. 297)?

'How important for our needy, hurting generation, that Jesus is recognized by his scars!' (p. 279)

---

3 Why should mission have the same importance for us as it did for Jesus (p. 298)? Does it for you?
4 Why is it misleading to think of *first* Jesus' mission and *then* that of the church (pp. 298f.)?
5 How has Jesus' statement in verse 23 about forgiving or not forgiving people's sins been misinterpreted (pp. 299f.)? What does it really mean?
6 Despite the events of verse 22, why does it seem 'preferable to recognize that the true coming of the outpoured Spirit took place at Pentecost' (p. 301)? What then is the significance of this verse?
7 To what extent is your Christianity 'a religion focused essentially on supernatural phenomena' (p. 301)? How can this be avoided?

4. Thomas (20:24–31)

1 Where does Thomas' failure lie (pp. 302f.)?
2 In what ways do you find faith to be 'a battle with unbelief, at times agonizing' (p. 304)?

'We are always more likely to find [Christ] in the company of the faithful than in a lonely vigil.' (p. 305)

351

3 In what sense are the bases of Thomas' faith available to us today (pp. 306f.)?
4 What ways can you think of in which 'Caesar-worship is not dead' (p. 307)? How should the Christian respond to it?
5 What does it mean truly to *'believe'* (p. 308)?

2. The beginning of the mission (21:1–25)

1. Fishing with Jesus (21:1–14)

1 Why is chapter 21 so important (p. 309)?
2 What 'symbolic inference' (p. 311) can you find in this incident?
3 How does Jesus illustrate the secret of effective mission (p. 312)?
4 What does this passage teach about the scope of mission (p. 313)?
5 'The passage also vividly illustrates our communion with Jesus' (p. 314). How?

2. Following Jesus (21:15–25)

1 What 'principle of universal application' (p. 317) lies behind the specifics of Peter's situation? How does this apply to you?
2 'Following Jesus and loving Jesus mean accepting responsibility for Jesus' people ...' (p. 318). In what ways does this truth 'need rehabilitation at the present time'?
3 What costs of following Jesus do you face (p. 318)?
4 What does Peter do which is 'so very human, but ... also so very wrong' (p. 319)? In what ways do you do the same?
5 What is your ultimate destination (pp. 319f.)? How do you know?